The Four Gospels

Commentary on the Holy Scriptures
of the New Testament
Volume I

Archbishop Averky (Taushev)

Translated from the Russian
by Nicholas Kotar

HOLY TRINITY SEMINARY PRESS
Holy Trinity Monastery
Jordanville, New York

Printed with the blessing of His Eminence,
Metropolitan Hilarion First Hierarch
of the Russian Orthodox Church Outside of Russia

The Four Gospels
© 2015 Holy Trinity Monastery

HOLY TRINITY
SEMINARY PRESS

An imprint of

HOLY TRINITY PUBLICATIONS
Holy Trinity Monastery
Jordanville, New York 13361-0036
www.holytrinitypublications.com

Second Printing 2018 Revised

ISBN: 978-1-942699-00-2 (hardback)
ISBN: 978-1-942699-05-7 (ePub)
ISBN: 978-1-942699-06-4 (Mobipocket)

Library of Congress Control Number 2015933220

Scripture passages taken from the New King James Version.
Copyright © 1982 by Thomas Nelson, Inc. Used by permission.

 CONTENTS

5. The Third Passover of the Lord Jesus Christ's Public Ministry **103**

 # PREFACE

It should be self-evident that I have used first and foremost all of the exegetical works of the Holy Fathers, especially St John Chrysostom and Blessed Theophylact of Bulgaria, as well as the interpretations of Scripture (based on patristic sources) provided in the *Holy Trinity Periodical*, published before the Revolution in Russia and "The Patristic Exegesis of the Gospel of Matthew," which was published by the journal *Eternal Things*, edited by Bishop Methodius these past few years in Paris, in three volumes.

Without aiming for any particular scholarly goals, I intended to give readers and those who study the New Testament a key to understanding and interpreting the Scriptures according to the teachings of the Orthodox Church. Such a handbook, considering the general scarcity of books and publications of this nature, could at least partially replace all the previous Russian prerevolutionary textbooks and guides. I beg the reader to be lenient in assessing my work since I never had the opportunity to wholeheartedly give myself to it, as such a lofty subject would require, working on it only sporadically. But even for such an opportunity I thank God, hoping that my work will not be without usefulness, and I ask every reader to pray for me.

—Archbishop Averky

Editor's Note: This text emerged from lecture notes. The translator and editors did not always have access to the same editions of the Russian language books used by the author. Furthermore, not all of these works exist in English translation, and where they do it is not always possible to cite a corresponding reference. Additionally, the author followed a Russian cultural and intellectual practice in which it is not considered essential to give all details of the source material but simply an indication of its origins.

Therefore the bibliography and endnotes at the end of this English edition are listed to facilitate the reader's understanding or indicate as closely as possible a source for further reading and study.

 Introduction

What Is the New Testament?

The New Testament is the collection of holy books that comprise the part of the Holy Bible that appeared in the world after the birth of Christ. These books were written by the disciples and apostles of the Lord Jesus Christ, inspired by the Holy Spirit.

The Purpose for Writing the Books of the New Testament and Their Content

The books of the New Testament were written by the holy apostles with the intention of describing the salvation of mankind, accomplished by the incarnate Son of God—our Lord Jesus Christ. In keeping with this great purpose, they tell us of incredible events—the Incarnation of the Son of God, His earthly life, His teachings, the miracles He performed, His redeeming suffering and death on the cross, His all-glorious resurrection from death and ascension into heaven, the first period of the spread of Christ's faith through the holy apostles. They also explain the teaching of Christ in its multifaceted application to life, and they further warn us of the final days of the world and mankind.

The Numeration, Names, and Order of the Books of the New Testament

There are twenty-seven books in the New Testament. Their names and order are as follows (note: this order follows the Russian synodal translation):

1. The Holy Gospel according to Matthew
2. The Holy Gospel according to Mark
3. The Holy Gospel according to Luke
4. The Holy Gospel according to John
5. The Acts of the Apostles
6. The General Epistle of the Holy Apostle James
7. The First General Epistle of the Holy Apostle Peter
8. The Second General Epistle of the Holy Apostle Peter

9. The First General Epistle of the Holy Apostle John the Theologian
10. The Second General Epistle of the Holy Apostle John the Theologian
11. The Third General Epistle of the Holy Apostle John the Theologian
12. The General Epistle of the Holy Apostle Jude
13. St Paul's Epistle to the Romans
14. St Paul's First Epistle to the Corinthians
15. St Paul's Second Epistle to the Corinthians
16. St Paul's Epistle to the Galatians
17. St Paul's Epistle to the Ephesians
18. St Paul's Epistle to the Philippians
19. St Paul's Epistle to the Colossians
20. St Paul's First Epistle to the Thessalonians
21. St Paul's Second Epistle to the Thessalonians
22. St Paul's First Epistle to Timothy
23. St Paul's Second Epistle to Timothy
24. St Paul's Epistle to Titus
25. St Paul's Epistle to Philemon
26. St Paul's Epistle to the Hebrews
27. The Book of Revelation (the Apocalypse) of St John the Theologian

THE DIVISION OF THE BOOKS OF THE NEW TESTAMENT

All the books of the New Testament together are usually simply called the "New Testament," as if in opposition to the Old Testament, because these books comprise the new commandments and new promises of God to men. They are in fact a new "covenant," or union of God with mankind, established on the Blood of the only mediator between God and man—Jesus Christ, Who came into the world and suffered for our sake (Luke 22:20; 1 Tim 2:5; Heb 9:14–15).

The books of the New Testament are divided into the "Gospel" and the "Epistle."[1] The first four books are the "Tetraevangelium," or just the "Gospels," because they contain the "good news" (the word "Gospel" in the original Greek means "good news") of the coming into the world of the divine Redeemer promised by God to our forefathers, and of His great work of the salvation of mankind.

All the other books of the New Testament are often combined and called the "Epistles" (in Russian, at least) because they contain the works referring to the Acts of the Apostles and their instructions, given to the first Christians.

THE DIVISION OF THE BOOKS OF THE NEW TESTAMENT ACCORDING TO THEIR CONTENT

According to their content, the books of the New Testament are usually divided into the following four sections:

1. The books of the New Law, in which we can include the Gospels, since they comprise the very essence of the law of God's new covenant with mankind, for they show us the salvific events of Jesus Christ's life and His divine teaching.

2. One historical book, the Book of Acts, since it tells of the history of the founding and initial growth of the Church of Christ on earth through the preaching of the apostles.

3. Books of instruction, which refer to the seven general Epistles (previously listed) and to the fourteen Epistles of St Paul, since they contain the teachings of the apostles, or rather their interpretation of the teachings of Christ, as applicable to various situations in life.

4. One prophetic book, the Book of Revelation, since it contains prophesies on the future of the Church of Christ, mankind, and the world, expressed in mystical visions and images.

A HISTORY OF THE CANON OF NEW TESTAMENT SCRIPTURES

The holy books of the New Testament are all canonical. They received their canonical status immediately after they were written because all Christians were aware of the writers, and they were considered authoritative. It is interesting to note in this context the words of the Apostle Peter in his Second Epistle (2 Pet 3:16), where he mentions his familiarity with "all the epistles" of the Apostle Paul. Also, having written his Epistle to the Colossians, the Apostle Paul gives an instruction that it be read out loud to the church in Laodicea (Col 4:16). We have many proofs that from the very beginning the Church has always considered the books of the New Testament to be canonical. If there were some doubts concerning certain individual books (a fact often cited by the so-called negative critics), it is still true that these doubts were limited to individual people and were never shared by the whole Church.

Already in the writings of the Apostolic Fathers we find quotations from almost all the books of the New Testament, and some of these books are directly and clearly indicated as books having indubitable apostolic provenance. Thus, for example, several citations from the New Testament canon are found in the Epistle of St Barnabas, the fellow traveler of the Apostle Paul; in the Epistles to the Corinthians of St Clement of Rome; and in the seven Epistles of St Ignatius the God-bearer, Bishop of Antioch and disciple of the holy Apostle and Evangelist John the Theologian, where it is evident that all four Gospels were well known to him. The disciples of St John the Theologian, St Polycarp of Smyrna in his Epistle to the Philippians, and St Papias of Hierapolis in his books (which only exist as fragments in the *Ecclesiastical History* of Eusebius) also cited the New Testament.

All these Apostolic Fathers lived during the second half of the first century and the beginning of the second.

A great number of references to the New Testament are found in the Fathers of the next generation after the Apostolic Fathers—the Apologists, who lived primarily in the second century. Thus, for example, St Justin Martyr the Philosopher, in his apologetic work *Dialogue with Trypho the Jew*, and in other writings, cites the Gospels no less than 127 times. St Irenaeus of Lyons, in his monumental five-volume work *Against Heresies*, witnesses to the canonicity of all four Gospels and cites them innumerable times. Tatian, in his *Oration Against Heresies*, revealing the foolishness of paganism, proved the divine origin of Holy Scriptures, using direct quotations from the Gospels; he was also the first person to try to write a synthesis of the four Gospels, which was known as the "Diatessaron." Clement of Alexandria, the famous teacher and head of the Alexandrian School, cites the New Testament many times in all of his extant works (such as the *Pedagogue* and the *Stromata*), showing by his usage that he had no doubts about their authenticity. The pagan philosopher Athenagoras, who began to read the New Testament with the intention of writing against Christianity, instead became a brilliant Christian apologist. His apology directly quotes several long passages from the Gospels, qualifying them with the phrase, "thus saith the Scriptures." St Theophilus of Antioch, in his *Three Books to Autolicus*, has many direct quotes from the Gospels, while, according to Blessed Jerome, he also wrote a synthesis of the Gospels and called it "Commentaries on the Gospel."

That most learned Christian orator Origen, who lived during the late second and early third centuries, was an incredibly prolific writer who used a staggering number of references to the New Testament canon. He also gives an indubitable witness to the fact that the four Gospels, as well as the Book of Acts, the Revelation, and the fourteen Epistles of the Apostle Paul were of apostolic and divine origins, accepted as such by the universal Church.

Also incredibly valuable is the witness of those "outside"—heretics and pagans. In the writings of the heresiarchs Basilides, Carpocrates, Valentinus, Ptolemy, Heraclion, and Marcion, we find many places that prove they were well acquainted with the New Testament canon. All of them lived in the second century. Especially important to note in this context is the work called *The True Word* by the pagan philosopher and self-proclaimed enemy of Christ, Celsus, in which all the material he uses to attack Christianity is taken directly from our four Gospels; in fact, he sometimes quotes passages from them verbatim.

It is true, however, that not all the ancient canonical lists of the books of the New Testament included all twenty-seven books that are now accepted by the whole Church. The so-called Muratorian Canon, dated to the second half of the second century and found in the nineteenth century by Ludovico Antonio Muratori, lists (in Latin) only the four Gospels, the books of Acts, thirteen Epistles of St Paul (excluding the Epistle to the Hebrews), the Epistle of Jude, and the Epistles and Revelation of St John the Theologian. However, there is no reason to consider this "canon" an official Church document. In the same second century appeared the *Peshitta*, a Syriac translation of the New Testament. It includes as canonical the Epistle to the Hebrews and the Epistle of James, but it omits the Epistle of Jude, the Second Epistle of St Peter, the Second and Third Epistles of St John, and the Book of Revelation.

All of these omissions could be the result of purely private reasons, and the same can be said of the doubts of individual writers concerning the authenticity of this or that book. These doubts do not present a serious problem because they are often no more than private opinions, not free from serious bias. Thus, for example, we know that the founder of Protestantism, Martin Luther, tried to cast doubt on the authenticity of the Epistle of James since it definitively underlines the insufficiency of faith alone without deeds for salvation (Jas 2:26—"faith without works is dead"), while a key tenet of the Protestant faith is the exact opposite—that a person is justified by faith alone without good deeds. Of course, all other such private opinions that attempt to bring our canon into disrepute are inevitably biased.

As for the whole Church, from the very beginning it has always accepted all of the canonical books of the New Testament, a fact witnessed to in A.D. 360 at the local Laodicean Council, which decreed (Canon 60) that all twenty-seven books of the current canon are canonical books of the New Testament. This decree was then further confirmed triumphantly, receiving an ecumenical character at the Sixth Ecumenical Council.

THE LANGUAGE OF THE NEW TESTAMENT BOOKS AND THEIR TEXTUAL HISTORY

All the books of the New Testament were written in Greek, but not in Classical Greek. Rather, they were written in a local Alexandrian dialect of the Greek language, so-called Koine Greek, which was the universally spoken (or at least universally understood) cultural language of not only the eastern but also the western halves of the Roman Empire at that time. This was the language of all the educated people of the time. The apostles chose this language for that reason, so that the New Testament books would be understandable and accessible for all educated citizens of the Roman Empire.

They were written either by the hand of the author (Gal 6:22) or by scribes to whom the authors dictated (Rom 16:22), on Egyptian papyrus with ink and stylus (3 John 13). Parchment was used much more rarely since it was prepared from the skins of animals and was thus very costly to make.

It is characteristic that only capital (uncial) letters of the Greek alphabet were used, there were no punctuation marks, and no spaces separating words. Small (miniscule) letters only began to be used in the ninth century, as were spaces between words. Punctuation marks were only introduced after the invention of the printing press in the sixteenth century by Aldus Manutius. Today's division into chapters was only introduced in the West in the thirteenth century by Cardinal Hugo de Santo Carlo, while division into verses was introduced by the typographer Robert Stephanus (Estienne) of Paris in the sixteenth century.

Through its learned bishops and priests, the Church has always tried to protect the text of the holy books from any corruption, which is always possible, especially before the invention of the printing press when books were copied by hand. There is evidence to suggest that corrupted texts were corrected by such learned Christian teachers as Origen, Hesychius of Egypt, and Lucian of Antioch. After the invention of the printing press, extra care was taken to make sure that the books of the New Testament would be printed only from the best ancient manuscripts. In the first quarter of the sixteenth century, two printed Greek New Testaments appeared almost simultaneously—the so-called Complutensian Polyglot in Spain and Erasmus's edition, printed in Basel. It is also very important to take note of the work of Constantine Tischendorff in the nineteenth century, who helped uncover more than nine hundred manuscripts of the New Testament.

Both of these well-intentioned critical editions, as well as the untiring vigilance of the Church, which is guided by the Holy Spirit that lives within it, give us more than enough reasons to be sure that we have, in our time, the pure, uncorrupted Greek text of the New Testament.

WHEN THE NEW TESTAMENT WAS WRITTEN

It is impossible to exactly determine the date of the writing of each book with perfect accuracy, but it is completely without doubt that all of them were written in the second half of the first century. This is clearly seen even in the fact that several writers of the second century—such as Justin Martyr, Celsus, and especially St Ignatius the God-bearer in his Epistles (dated to ca. A.D. 107)—cite the New Testament many times and quote it verbatim.

The first New Testament books to be written were doubtless the Epistles of the apostles, which were written in response to the necessity of confirming the faith of the newly established Christian communities. But soon, of course, there appeared a need for a systematic treatment of the earthly life of the Lord Jesus Christ and His teaching. No matter how much the negative criticism of the nineteenth century has tried to bring into doubt the historical authenticity and accuracy of our Gospels and other New Testament books, dating them to a much later time (F. C. Baur and his school, for example), recent discoveries in the field of patristic literature witness clearly to the fact that the entire New Testament was written in the first century.[2]

In the beginning of our Gospel lectionary, in a special preface to each of the four Gospels, it is written (based on the witness of the Church historian Eusebius and the famous interpreter of the Scriptures, Theophylact, Archbishop of Bulgaria) that the Gospel of Matthew was written eight years after the ascension of Christ; the Gospel of Mark, ten years; the Gospel of Luke, fifteen years; and the Gospel of John in the thirty-second year after the ascension. In any case, there is a whole list of reasons why we can safely determine that the Gospel according to Matthew was written before all the rest, no earlier than A.D. 50–60. The Gospels of Mark and Luke were written a little bit later, but certainly not before the destruction of Jerusalem in A.D. 70, while St John wrote his Gospel last, at the end of the first century, already as an old man (some people cite the year A.D. 96). He wrote the Apocalypse a few years earlier. The Acts of the Apostles were written soon after the Gospel according to Luke, since (as we see in its prologue) it was written as a continuation of the Gospel.

WHY ARE THERE EXACTLY FOUR GOSPELS?

All four Gospels tell of the life and teaching of Christ the Saviour, His miracles, His passion on the cross, His death and burial, and His glorious resurrection from the dead and ascension into heaven. All four together fill in each other's gaps and help explain difficult moments for interpretation. In fact, they are one whole book that has no contradictions or lack of agreement in the most essential and important elements—in the teaching on salvation, which was accomplished by the incarnate Son of God, wholly God and wholly man. Early Christian writers compared the four Gospels to the river that flowed out of Eden for the watering of the garden planted by God, which divided into four rivers that flowed through the area around the garden, making the land full of all manner of precious fruit. An even more typical symbol for the four Gospels is the mystical chariot that the Prophet Ezekiel saw at the river Chebar (Ezek 1:1–28) and which was made of four beings that looked like the faces of a man, a lion, an ox, and an eagle. These beings, taken separately, became the emblems of the evangelists. Beginning in the fifth century, Christian iconography represented Matthew with a man or angel, St Mark with a lion, St Luke with an ox, and St John with an eagle. St Matthew was given the symbol of a man because his Gospel especially accents Christ's human lineage from David and Abraham. St Mark received the symbol of the lion because he especially underlines Christ's kingly power. St Luke is given the ox (a sacrificial animal) because he speaks of Christ most of all as the Great High Priest who brought Himself as a sacrifice for the sins of the whole world. St John is associated with the eagle because his thoughts are especially exalted and his language is very majestic like the eagle that flies high above the earth, "above the clouds of human weakness," as St Augustine said.

Besides the four canonical Gospels, the first century after Christ saw many (more than fifty) other writings that called themselves "gospels" and claimed apostolic provenance. The Church, however, very quickly rejected them, relegating them to the list of the so-called apocrypha. Even St Irenaeus of Lyons, the disciple of St Polycarp of Smyrna (who in his own turn was the disciple of St John the Theologian), wrote in his *Against Heresies* that there are only four Gospels, and that there can be neither fewer nor more than four since there are "four directions in the world" and "four winds in the universe."[3]

St John Chrysostom brilliantly writes on this question of why the Church accepted four Gospels, not just one:

> Can one Evangelist write everything? Of course, he could have, but consider this: Four Evangelists wrote at different times, in different places, without talking or agreeing with each other about the contents. And yet, they wrote their Gospels in such a way that it seems they uttered their words with one mouth. This is a great proof of their truth.[4]

St John also brilliantly counters the objection that in some elements the Gospels even seem to contradict each other:

> If they were exactly in agreement with each other in every element (concerning times, places, exact words), then the enemies of Christ would never believe that they had written the Gospels without coming together and agreeing on the contents in advance. Such a prior agreement may have been seen in a pejorative light. But since there are insignificant differences among them, it removes any doubt about their authenticity, and speaks authoritatively in favor of the writers.[5]

Blessed Theophylact of Bulgaria argues in a similar vein:

> Do not tell me that they are not in agreement at all points. Rather, go and look at the moment where they do not agree. Did a single one of them say that Christ was not born? Did one of them say that Christ resurrected, while another said that He did not? God forbid! In the most important and essential they are all in agreement. Otherwise, people may have thought that they wrote the four Gospels while meeting together and counseling each other on the writing. But in reality, what one missed, another included, and so it only seems that sometimes they contradict each other.[6]

From these words, it is clear that the few insignificant differences in the telling of the four Evangelists do not speak against the genuineness of the Gospels, and instead clearly witness to it.

The Meaning of Such Phrases as: "The Gospel According to Matthew"

The word "Gospel," as we have already seen, means "good news" in the original Greek, which is why the Slavonic Gospels are usually titled, for example, "The Good News according to Matthew." It must be said, however, that this expression "according to" is relative. All four Gospels are the good news of our Lord Jesus Christ—He Himself gives us, through the four Evangelists, the joyful news of our salvation. The Evangelists are only mediators in the transmission of this good news. This is why the English "according to" is more proper.

THE INTERRELATION OF THE FOUR GOSPELS ACCORDING TO THEIR CONTENT

When considering all four Gospels, the content of the first three (Matthew, Mark, and Luke) coincides at many points, both in the sequence of events and the manner of telling. The fourth Gospel of John in this sense stands alone, being significantly different from the first three both in the events related and the style of writing.

Thus, the first three Gospels are generally called the Synoptics, from the Greek word "synopsis," which means "summary in the same fashion" (the same as the Latin *conspectus*). But while the first three Gospels are similar to each other both in form and content, which can be easily expressed in parallel tables, they do have their particularities. So, if we use 100 percent to mean "the entire content of all four Gospels," then Matthew's Gospel corresponds to all other Evangelists 58 percent of the time, while 42 percent of his content is unique. Mark's content agrees with the others 93 percent of the time, while 7 percent is unique to his Gospel. Luke has 41 percent corresponding, 59 percent unique. John, however, has only 8 percent correspondence with the other Evangelists; 92 percent of his Gospel is different from the rest. The corresponding material in all four is generally found in the words of Christ the Saviour; the differences are generally in the narrative sections. When Matthew and Luke literally agree with each other, Mark always agrees with them. There are many more areas of consonance between Luke and Mark than between Luke and Matthew. When Mark has additional material, it generally corresponds to unique material in Luke as well, which is not the case with the unique elements found in the Gospel according to Matthew. Finally, in those cases when Mark is silent, Luke often differs in his account from Matthew.

The Synoptic Gospels almost exclusively tell of the Lord Jesus Christ's preaching in Galilee, while St John speaks almost exclusively about Judea. The Synoptics for the most part write about Christ's miracles, parables, and external events in the life of the Lord, while St John discourses on the deep inner meaning of these events through the words of the Lord on the most exalted subjects of the faith.

Despite these differences between the Gospels, they have absolutely no internal contradictions. Attentive reading will reward one with clear marks of agreement between the Synoptics and St John. Thus, St John speaks little about Christ's Galilean mission, but he doubtless knows of His long sojourns in Galilee; the Synoptics write nothing about the early activity of the Lord in Judea and Jerusalem proper, but there are plenty of internal suggestions of this early preaching. Thus, according to their witness, the Lord had friends, disciples, and followers in Jerusalem, such as the owner of the house where the Mystical Supper was performed, and Joseph of Arimathea. Especially important in this sense are the words written by the Synoptics: "O Jerusalem, Jerusalem.... How often I wanted to gather your children together" (Matt 23:37), words that clearly express Christ's frequent trips to Jerusalem. It is true that the Synoptics do not write of the miracle of Lazarus's resurrection, but Luke knows his sisters in Bethany well, and the clearly described character of each of them (expressed in very few words) fully corresponds to their characterization as given by St John.

The main difference between the Synoptics and St John is in the manner of relating Christ's preaching. In the Synoptics, Christ speaks very simply, in a manner easy to understand, in a populist vein. In St John, Christ speaks about profound and mystical things, often difficult to understand, almost as if they were not intended for the crowd, but rather for a limited circle of listeners. But that is, in fact, the case. The Synoptics relate Christ's preaching to the Galileans, who were simple and ignorant people. St John, in contrast, relates the words of the Lord directed at the Judeans, the scribes, and Pharisees, people who knew the Law of Moses well, and were (by the standards of that time) quite well educated. In addition, St John, as we see later, has a special goal—to reveal as completely as possible the teaching of Jesus Christ as the Son of God, and this theme, of course, is much more difficult to understand than the simple and accessible parables of the Synoptics. But even here there is not a great divergence between the Synoptics and St John. If the Synoptics show a more human side of Christ, while John stresses the divine aspects, this does not mean that the Synoptics do not describe a divine Christ or that John does not show Christ's human side. The "Son of Man" of the Synoptic Gospels is also the Son of God, to Whom is given all authority, both in heaven and on earth. In the same way, the Son of God in John is also truly man, Who accepts the invitation to the wedding feast, Who has a friendly conversation with Martha and Mary, and Who weeps over the tomb of His friend Lazarus.

Not in the least contradicting each other, the Synoptics and St John complement each other and only in their wholeness do they give the most beautiful and complete image of Christ, how He is understood and preached by His holy Church.

Characteristics and Particularities of Each of the Four Gospels

The Orthodox teaching on the divine inspiration of the books of Sacred Scripture has always maintained that the Holy Spirit, while inspiring the holy writers and conveying certain thoughts and words to them, at the same time does not constrain their own mind and character. The inspiration of the Holy Spirit never suppresses the spirit of man, rather only purifies and raises it above its normal limits. Thus, while together they constitute one whole in their transmission of divine truth, separately the four Gospels have their differences that depend on personal qualities of each Evangelist's character, differences in the manner of writing, style, and phraseology. They also differ as a result of the various circumstances of their writing and the goal with which each of them undertook the writing of his particular Gospel.

Thus, to better understand and interpret the Gospels, we must become more intimately familiar with the personalities, characters, and life of each of the four Evangelists, as well as the circumstances leading to the writing of each Gospel.

The Gospel According to Matthew

The writer of the first Gospel was St Matthew, also called Levi, son of Alphaeus, one of the twelve apostles of Christ. Before he was called to be an apostle, he was a publican, that is, a tax collector, and for this reason was justly despised by his fellow Jews, who generally despised and hated the publicans because they were the servants of Gentiles who had enslaved their nation. The publicans oppressed their own people through heavy taxation, and were not above taking even more money than necessary for the sake of personal gain.

St Matthew himself mentions his calling to apostleship in the ninth chapter, ninth verse of his Gospel, calling himself "Matthew," while Mark and Luke, when describing the same event, call him "Levi." It was customary for the Jews to have several names, and so there is no reason to think that these are two different people, especially considering that all three Synoptics describe the subsequent invitation of the Lord and His disciples to the house of Matthew in exactly the same terms. Also, in the list of twelve apostles, both Mark and Luke already call the reformed publican "Matthew."

Touched to the depth of his soul by the mercy of the Lord, Who did not reject him despite the general hatred directed at him by the Jews and especially the spiritual leaders of the Jews, the scribes, and the Pharisees, Matthew accepted the teachings of Christ with his whole heart. He especially understood their superiority to the traditions and opinions of the Pharisees, who bore the stamp of external righteousness, self-satisfaction, and disdain for sinners. This is why he alone recounts in such detail the scathing, accusatory speech of the Lord against the scribes and the Pharisees, whom He calls "hypocrites" (Matt 23). For the same reason, it would be correct to assume that he especially took to heart the work of the redemption of his own Jewish nation, which was at that time so deeply imbued with the understandings and opinions of the Pharisees, and so his Gospel was written first and foremost for the Jews. There are reasons to believe that it was written originally in Aramaic and only a little later was translated into Greek by an unknown translator, perhaps by Matthew himself. This is witnessed by St Papius of Hierapolis: "Matthew wrote down the preaching of the Lord in the Hebrew tongue, and each reader translated it as well as he was able.[7] It is possible that Matthew himself later translated his Gospel into Greek, in order to make it accessible to a wider circle of readers. In any case, the Church accepted as canonical only the Greek text of the Gospel according to Matthew since the Aramaic text was very soon corrupted by certain Judaizing heretics.

Having written his Gospel for the Jews, St Matthew intended first of all to prove to the Jews that Jesus Christ is that Messiah of Whom the Old Testament prophets spoke, that He is the "fulfillment of the Law and the Prophets,"[8] and that the Old Testament revelation, obscured by the scribes and the Pharisees, can only be fully understood and explained in Christianity. Thus, St Matthew begins his

Gospel with the genealogy of Jesus Christ, desiring to show the Jews Jesus's descent from David and Abraham, and he cites the Old Testament numerous times in order to prove the fulfillment of its prophecies. There are no fewer than sixty-six such citations, and in forty-three of these, the citation is written down verbatim. The text itself witnesses to the fact that St Matthew's intended audience was Jewish—when he mentions some specific Jewish ritual, he never finds it necessary to describe it in detail, as if it were already fully understood by his readers; this also can be said of the use, without explanation, of certain Aramaic words that were commonly used in Palestine. In contrast, the other Evangelists take special care to describe these same rituals in detail (Matt 15:1–3; Mark 7:3–4; 10:46).

The Church historian Eusebius has St Matthew writing the Gospel eight years after the ascension of Christ, but St Irenaeus of Lyons believed that St Matthew wrote his Gospel "when Peter and Paul were both preaching the good news in Rome,"[9] that is, ca. A.D. 60.

Having written his Gospel for his countrymen the Jews, St Matthew continued to preach to them in Palestine for a long time, but later traveled to other countries and died a martyr's death in Ethiopia.

The Gospel according to Matthew has twenty-eight chapters or 116 lectionary readings. It begins with the genealogy of Christ from Abraham and ends with the parting instruction of Christ to the disciples before His ascension. Since St Matthew primarily writes about Jesus Christ's human origins, he is associated with the Evangelical symbol of the man.

The Contents of the Gospel According to Matthew by Chapter
   Chapter 1. The genealogy of Jesus Christ. The Nativity of Christ.
   Chapter 2. The adoration of the Magi. The flight of the Holy Family into Egypt. The killing of the innocent children. The return of the Holy Family from Egypt and their settling in Nazareth.
   Chapter 3. The preaching of John the Baptist. The baptism of the Lord Jesus Christ.
   Chapter 4. Christ is tempted by the devil. The beginning of the Galilean mission. The calling of the first apostles. Christ's preaching and healing of the sick.
   Chapter 5. The Sermon on the Mount. The Beatitudes, the apostles as the salt of the earth and the light of the world: "I have come not to destroy the law, but to fulfill it." The new understanding of the commandments: "thou shalt not murder," "thou shalt not commit adultery," the teaching on divorce, on oaths, and love for one's enemies.
   Chapter 6. Continuation of the Sermon on the Mount: The teaching on mercy, on prayer: "Our Father"; on fasting; on collecting treasures in heaven, not on earth; on the impossibility of serving both God and mammon; on laying

aside cares for the body and its needs; on seeking the kingdom of God and its righteousness.

Chapter 7. Continuation of the Sermon on the Mount: On not judging one's neighbors; on not casting pearls before swine; on constancy in prayer; on the narrow and wide gates; on false prophets; on the need to do good; the parable of the house built on stone and the house built on sand.

Chapter 8. The healing of the leper. The healing of the servant of the centurion of Capernaum. The healing of Peter's mother-in-law and many possessed and diseased: "The Son of Man has nowhere to lay His head"; "Leave the dead to bury their dead." The calming of the storm at sea. The healing of two possessed in the country of the Gergesenes and the destruction of the herd of swine.

Chapter 9. The healing of the paralytic. The calling of the publican Matthew: "I came not to call the righteous, but sinners to repentance." On the fasting of Christ's disciples. The raising of the daughter of a certain ruler and the healing of the woman with an issue of blood. The healing of two blind men and the dumb man who was possessed by a demon: "The harvest truly is plentiful, but the laborers are few" (Matt 9:37)."

Chapter 10. The calling of the twelve apostles and their preaching. The prophecy of their future persecutions by many. The meaning of confessing Christ before men and the danger of denying Him. On the necessity of complete love for the Lord, even greater than love for one's family and even for one's self.

Chapter 11. The delegation from John the Baptist and Christ's witness about John. Woe to Chorazin, Bethsaida, and Capernaum. The Lord calls to Himself all those who are weary and heavy laden.

Chapter 12. The disciples tear off the heads of wheat on a Sabbath. The healing of the man with a withered arm. The fulfillment of Isaiah's prophecy about Christ. The healing of the possessed man and the accusation that Christ is casting out demons by the power of Beelzebub. Jesus denounces the Pharisees for their unforgivable sin of blasphemy against the Holy Spirit. The Pharisees seek a sign from Christ. The parable of the unclean spirit that went out of a man and then came back. "Who are My mother and My brothers?"

Chapter 13. The parable of the sower. Why does Christ the Saviour speak in parables? The explanation of the parable of the sower. The parable of the wheat and the tares. The parable of the mustard seed, of the yeast; explanation of the parable of the wheat and the tares. The parable of the treasure hidden in the field, of the pearl beyond price, and the net cast into the sea. "No prophet is without honor."

Chapter 14. The beheading of John the Baptist. The feeding of the five thousand. The walking on water. The healing of the sick through merely touching Jesus's garments.

Chapter 15. Christ's accusation of the Pharisees, that they prefer their own traditions to the word of God. On the impure heart as the source of impurity in man. The healing of the possessed daughter of the Canaanite woman. The healing of many diseased, and the feeding of the four thousand.

Chapter 16. The sign of Jonah the Prophet. The warning against the leaven of the Pharisees and the Sadducees. The Apostle Peter confessed Christ as the Son of the Living God on behalf of all the apostles. The prophecy of Jesus about His imminent suffering and the rebuking of Peter. The teaching on self-denial, taking up one's cross and following after Christ.

Chapter 17. The transfiguration of Christ. The healing of the possessed youth. The miraculous payment of the temple tax.

Chapter 18. On the necessity for being as children to enter the kingdom of heaven. On temptations. The parable of the lost sheep. On accusing a fallen brother and on the highest authority of the Church. On forgiveness of offences. The parable of the unmerciful debtor.

Chapter 19. The teaching on the reprehensibility of divorce and on virginity. The blessing of the children. Of the rich youth and on riches as a hindrance to the inheritance of eternal life.

Chapter 20. The parable of the workers hired for the care of the vineyard. Jesus's prophecy of His own death and resurrection. The request of the mother of the sons of Zebedee and the Lord's instruction to His disciples on humility. The healing of the two blind men of Jericho.

Chapter 21. The entry of the Lord into Jerusalem and the expulsion of the sellers from the temple. The withered fig tree and the power of faith. The high priests question Christ's authority. The parable of the two sons. On the stone, which became the head of the corner.

Chapter 22. The parable of the bridal feast of the king's son. On taxes to Caesar. The conversation with the Sadducees on the resurrection from the dead. On the two major commandments—love for God and love for one's neighbor and on the divine Sonship of Christ.

Chapter 23. The Lord accuses the scribes and Pharisees. Prophecy of God's wrath regarding Jerusalem.

Chapter 24. Prophecy of the destruction of the Jerusalem temple, wars, persecution of His followers, the end of the world, and the Second Coming.

Chapter 25. The parable of the ten virgins. The parable of the talents. The Last Judgment.

Chapter 26. The council of the high priests and scribes on putting Jesus to death. Christ is anointed in Bethany. The betrayal of Judas. The Mystical Supper. The prophecy of Peter's denial. The prayer in the garden of Gethsemane. The Lord is taken by the servants of the high priest. Judgment before Caiaphas. The denial of Peter.

Chapter 27. Judgment before Pilate. The remorse of Judas and his death. The people ask for the release of Barabbas instead of Christ. The mockery of the soldiers. The crucifixion. Taunting of the Crucified One. Darkness over all the land. The death of the Lord. His burial and the sealing of the tomb.

Chapter 28. The myrrh-bearing women come to the tomb. The earthquake and the coming down of the angel who threw aside the stone from the tomb. The good news of the angel to the women of the resurrection of Christ. The guards are bribed to lie about the resurrection. The appearance of the Lord to the eleven in Galilee and His final words on the preaching of the Gospel to all nations.

The Gospel According to Mark

The second Gospel was written by Mark, who also had the name John. He was by birth a Jew, but was not one of the Twelve. Therefore, he could not have been such a constant follower and disciple of Christ, as was St Matthew. He wrote this holy Gospel from the words and under the guidance of the Apostle Peter. He himself, apparently, was a witness only of the last days of the earthly life of the Lord. This Gospel is the only one that speaks of a certain young man who, when Christ was taken by the soldiers in the garden of Gethsemane, went after Him, "having a linen cloth thrown around his naked body. And they laid hold of him, and he left the linen cloth and fled from them naked" (Mark 14:51–52). Ancient tradition identifies this young man with the author of the second Gospel, St Mark himself. His mother Mary is mentioned in the Book of Acts (12:12), as one of the women who was most dedicated to the faith of Christ. In her home in Jerusalem, faithful gathered for prayer. St Mark later participated in the first missionary journey of the Apostle Paul together with Barnabas, whose nephew he was on his mother's side (Col 4:10).

As we know from the Book of Acts, after their arrival in Perga, Mark separated from Paul's company and returned to Jerusalem (Acts 13:13). For this reason, St Paul did not want to take Mark with him on his second missionary journey, but since Barnabas did not want to be separated from Mark, they had a falling out, "so sharp that they parted from one another" (Acts 15:39), Barnabas going to Cyprus with Mark, and Paul continuing his journey with Silas. This momentary coolness, apparently, did not last long, since we find Mark later on together with Paul in Rome, from where Paul wrote his Epistle to the Colossians, whom St Paul greets on behalf of Mark as well, warning them of his possible arrival (Col 4:10). Later, St Mark traveled and worked with the Apostle Peter, a fact attested to especially by tradition and the words of the Apostle Peter himself in his First General Epistle, where he writes: "She who is in Babylon, elect together with you, greets you; and so does Mark my son" (1 Pet 5:13). Before his death, Paul once again called Mark to himself (2 Tim 4:6), writing to Timothy: "Get Mark and bring him with you, for he is useful to me for ministry" (2 Tim 4:11). According to tradition, the Apostle Peter made Mark the first bishop of the Alexandrian Church, and St Mark ended his life as a martyr in Alexandria.

According to the witness of St Papius of Hierapolis, as well as St Justin the Philosopher and St Irenaeus of Lyons, St Mark wrote his Gospel from the words of the holy Apostle Peter. St Justin calls it literally "the memoirs of Peter."[10] Clement of Alexandria says that the Gospel according to Mark is in effect the written down oral preaching of St Peter, which St Mark wrote due to requests of Christians living in Rome. This is also witnessed by many other Church writers, and even the content of the Gospel of Mark clearly shows that it was written specifically for Gentile Christians. There is very little written about the relationship of Christ's teaching to the Old Testament, and very few citations are given from Old Testament books. In addition, Mark uses occasional Latin words, such as *speculator* (6:27; executioner), "centurion" (15:39, 44, 45), "quadrans" (12:42). Even the Sermon on the Mount, which explains the supremacy of the New Testament law over the old, is completely left out.

Most of Mark's attention is directed to giving the reader a clear record of the miracles of Christ, underlining thus the royal majesty and omnipotence of the Lord. In his Gospel, Jesus is not the Son of David, as in Matthew, but the Son of God, the Lord and Master, the King of the universe (compare his first verse with the first verse of Matthew). Thus, Mark's emblem is the lion, the king of beasts, the symbol of power and strength.

In general, the content of the Gospel according to Mark is very close to the narration in Matthew, but it is shorter and more concise. It only has sixteen chapters, or seventy-one lectionary readings. It begins with the appearance of John the Baptist, and it ends with Christ sending the apostles to preach to the world after His ascension.

The Church historian Eusebius dates the writing of the Gospel according to Mark to the tenth year after the ascension of the Lord.

The Content of the Gospel According to Mark by Chapter

Chapter 1. The preaching of St John the Baptist. The baptism of Christ. The temptation in the wilderness. The beginning of Christ's Galilean mission. The calling of the first apostles. Preaching and miracles in Capernaum. The healing of the lepers.

Chapter 2. The healing of the paralyzed man who was lowered into the house through the roof. The calling of Levi. On the fasting of the disciples of Christ. Plucking the heads of grain on a Sabbath.

Chapter 3. Healing the man with the withered arm on a Sabbath. The Pharisees conspire to kill Jesus. The great multitudes following the Lord, and the miracles of healing. Calling the Twelve. The Lord is accused that He casts out demons with the power of Beelzebub, and the unforgivable sin of blasphemy against the Holy Spirit. "Who are My Mother and brothers?"

Chapter 4. The Parable of the sower. The parable of the mustard seed. Calming the storm at sea.

Chapter 5. Casting out the legion of demons from the possessed man in the country of the Gadarenes and the destruction of the herd of swine. The raising of Jairus's daughter and the healing of the woman with an issue of blood.

Chapter 6. "A prophet has no honor except in his own country ...." Sending the Twelve to preach. The beheading of John the Baptist. The miraculous feeding of the five thousand. Walking on water. Miraculous healing merely by touching the hem of Christ's garments.

Chapter 7. The Pharisees accuse the disciples of the Lord of disregarding the traditions of the elders. It is not proper to disregard the word of God in favor of the tradition of the elders. Not that which goes into a man, but that which comes out of his impure heart, defiles him. Healing the possessed daughter of the Syro-Phoenician woman. Healing the deaf and dumb man.

Chapter 8. Miraculous feeding of the four thousand. The Pharisees seek a sign from Jesus. Warning about the leaven of the Pharisees and Herod. Healing the blind man in Bethsaida. Peter, on behalf of all the apostles, confesses Jesus Christ as the Son of God. The Lord foretells His death and resurrection, and rebukes Peter. Teaching on self-denial, taking up one's cross and following Christ.

Chapter 9. The transfiguration of the Lord. Healing the dumb youth who was possessed. Another prophecy of Jesus's death and resurrection. The apostles argue about who is greatest and the Lord's teaching on humility. On the man who cast out demons through Christ's name. On temptations. On salt and mutual peace.

Chapter 10. On the impossibility of divorce. Blessing the children. On how difficult it is for a rich man to enter the kingdom of God. On the reward received by those who have abandoned everything for the sake of the Lord. A new prophecy of the Lord's suffering, death, and resurrection. The request for primacy by the sons of Zebedee, and the Lord's teaching about the necessity of humility. Healing blind Bartimaeus.

Chapter 11. The Lord's entry into Jerusalem. Cursing the fruitless fig tree. The chief priests ask Jesus about His authority.

Chapter 12. The parable of the wicked vinedressers. On paying taxes to Caesar. Answering the Sadducees on the resurrection of the dead. On the two main commandments—love for God and love for one's neighbor, and on the divine Sonship of Christ. Warning against the scribes. The widow's mite.

Chapter 13. Prophecy of the destruction of the temple and Jerusalem, on the last days, on the end of the world, and on the Second Coming of Christ.

Chapter 14. Jesus is anointed in Bethany. The betrayal of Judas. The Mystical Supper. Prophecy of Peter's denial. The prayer in the garden of Gethsemane. The Lord is taken by servants of the high priest. The flight of the disciples. Judgment before the high priests. The denial of Peter.

Chapter 15. Judgment before Pilate. The release of Barabbas and the condemnation of Christ. Scourging the Lord and the mockery of the soldiers. The crucifixion, death, and burial.

Chapter 16. The myrrh-bearing women come to the tomb and hear the good news from the youth in white clothes of the resurrection of Christ. The appearance of the risen Lord to Mary Magdalene, to the two disciples on the way, and to the assembled eleven. Christ's instruction about preaching the Gospel to all nations. The ascension of the Lord to heaven and the beginning of the preaching to the world by the disciples.

The Gospel According to Luke

It is not exactly clear who St Luke was by heritage. Eusebius of Caesaria said that he came from Antioch, and thus it is generally accepted that St Luke was a pagan by birth and a Jewish proselyte, that is, a Gentile who had accepted Judaism. He was a doctor by profession, which is evident from the Epistle to the Colossians (4:14), and tradition adds that he was also a painter. From the fact that only Christ's direction to the seventy disciples is included in this Gospel, written down with great detail, one can make the conclusion that Luke was one of the seventy disciples sent by Christ to preach. The unusual vividness of his account of Christ appearing to the two disciples on the road to Emmaus (note that only one disciple, Cleopas, is explicitly named), as well as an ancient tradition, attest to the fact that he was one of these two disciples who were deemed worthy to be visited by the risen Christ (Luke 24:13–33). Then, in the Book of Acts, it is evident that beginning with the second missionary journey of St Paul, Luke becomes his constant companion and inseparable fellow laborer. He was with the Apostle Paul during his first imprisonment, when Paul wrote the Epistles to the Colossians and Philippians, and his second imprisonment, when he wrote his Second Epistle to Timothy and which ended with his martyr's death. There are also reports that after the death of the Apostle Paul, St Luke preached and died a martyr's death in Achaia (Greece). His relics were moved to Constantinople during the reign of Emperor Constantius, together with the relics of the Apostle Andrew.

As is seen from the prologue to the third Gospel, St Luke wrote it in answer to the request of a certain nobleman, the "most excellent Theophilus," for whom he later wrote the Book of Acts, which is in effect a continuation of the Gospel's narrative (Luke 1:1–4; Acts 1:1–2). In addition, he not only used eyewitness accounts of the Lord's mission, but also some already existing written accounts of the life and teachings of Christ. According to Luke's own words, these oral and written reports were researched by him in great detail, and thus his Gospel is remarkable for its exactness in the determination of the times and places of various events, as well as a strict chronological order, something not necessarily evident in the previous Gospels.

The "most excellent Theophilus," for whom the third Gospel was written, was doubtless not a resident of Palestine and had not been in Jerusalem. Otherwise, St Luke would not have had to give him various geographical explanations such as the fact that the Mount of Olives is near Jerusalem, a Sabbath journey's distance, and so forth (Luke 1:26; 4:31; 24:13; Acts 1:12). Yet he was acquainted with Syracuse, Rhegium, and Puteoli in Italy, the Appii Forum and Three Inns in Rome, all of which are mentioned in Acts but not described in any detail. However, according to Clement of Alexandria, Theophilus was not a Roman, as one would perhaps think, but an Antiochian, a rich and well-known man who confessed the Christian faith, and his home was a church for local Antiochene Christians.

The Gospel according to Luke is heavily influenced by the Apostle Paul, St Luke's fellow traveler and laborer. As the apostle to the nations, St Paul tried more than anything else to reveal that great Truth: that the Messiah, Christ, came into the world not only for the Jews, but for the Gentiles also, and He is the Saviour of the whole world, and of all the people in it. In keeping with this major theme, which is developed clearly throughout the entire third Gospel, the genealogy of Christ leads all the way back to the ancestor of all mankind, Adam, and even to God Himself, in order to underline His significance for the entire race of mankind (Luke 3:23–38). Such scriptural events as the visit of the Prophet Elijah to the Sareptan widow, the healing of Naaman by the Prophet Elisha (Luke 4:26–27), the parable of the prodigal son (Luke 15:11–32), and the publican and the Pharisee (Luke 18:10–14) are intimately connected with St Paul's fully developed teaching on the salvation not only of the Jews but of the Gentiles as well, and of the justification of men before God not on the basis of the works of the Law, but by divine grace, given in abundance, only thanks to God's infinite compassion and His love for mankind. No one has described the love of God toward repentant sinners as vividly as did St Luke, who has a whole series of parables and events dedicated to this theme. It is enough to remember, in addition to the aforementioned parables of the prodigal son and the publican and the Pharisee, the parable of the lost sheep, the lost drachma, the merciful Samaritan, the repentance of the chief publican Zacchaeus (Luke 15:1–10; 19:1–10), and other places, as well as his remarkable words about the fact that there is joy in the ranks of the angels whenever a single sinner repents, and this joy is greater than the joy they have for the ninety-nine righteous ones who do not require repentance (see Luke 15:7, 10).

Seeing in all these facts the indubitable influence of St Paul on the author of the third Gospel, one can consider Origen to be right when he said that the Gospel according to Luke was approved by the Apostle Paul.

The time and place of the writing of this Gospel can be determined by considering that it was written before the Acts (Acts 1:1). The Book of Acts finished with the description of the two-year residence of St Paul in Rome (Acts 28:30). This occurred in A.D. 62 and 63. Consequently, the Gospel could not have been written after these years, and it was most likely written in Rome, even though Eusebius considers that it was written much earlier, fifteen years after the ascension of Christ.

Since St Luke speaks of the Lord Jesus Christ most of all as the Great High Priest, Who brought Himself as a sacrifice of atonement for the sins of all mankind, his emblem is the ox, because it was the animal most often used for temple sacrifices.

The Gospel according to Luke has twenty-four chapters, or 114 lectionary readings. It begins with the appearance of the angel to the priest Zacharias, the father of John the Baptist, and finishes with the account of the ascension of the Lord Jesus Christ to heaven.

The Content of the Gospel According to Luke by Chapter

Chapter 1. Prologue addressed to Theophilus. The appearance of the angel who tells Zacharias of the birth of his son John. The Annunciation. The Virgin Mary visits Elizabeth. The birth of John the Baptist.

Chapter 2. The birth of Christ, the appearance of the angel to the shepherds in Bethlehem and their adoration of the divine newborn. The circumcision of Christ. The meeting of the Lord. The youth Jesus in the Jerusalem temple in conversation with the elders.

Chapter 3. The preaching of John the Baptist. The baptism of Christ. The genealogy of the Lord Jesus Christ.

Chapter 4. The temptation by the devil. The Lord's Galilean sermon, in the Nazarene synagogue. The healing of the possessed in the Capernaum synagogue. The healing of Simon's mother-in-law and many other sick and possessed people. Preaching in Galilee's synagogues.

Chapter 5. The miraculous catching of fish in the lake of Gennesaret and the calling of the apostles. The healing of the leper. The healing of the paralytic who was brought in his bed and lowered through the roof. The calling of the publican Levi. On the fasting of the disciples of the Lord: the parables of the old garment and the new wine.

Chapter 6. Plucking the heads of grain on a Sabbath. Healing the man with the withered arm on a Sabbath. The calling of the twelve apostles. The Lord's sermon on the Beatitudes and the woes. On love toward enemies. On not judging others. On the necessity of doing good deeds.

Chapter 7. The healing of the Capernaum centurion's servant. The raising of the son of the widow of Nain. John the Baptist's disciples visit Christ, and the Lord's witness of John the Baptist. The Lord is anointed by the sinful woman.

Chapter 8. The preaching of the Lord Jesus Christ in the cities and country together with the Twelve and the women who supported Him financially. The parable of the sower. The candle on the candle stand. "Who are My mother and brothers?" The calming of the storm at sea. The casting out of the legion of demons and the destruction of the herd of swine. The raising of Jairus's daughter and the healing of the woman with an issue of blood.

Chapter 9. The twelve apostles are sent to preach. Herod wonders about the person of Jesus Christ. The miraculous feeding of the five thousand. Peter confesses Jesus Christ. The Lord's prophecy about His own death and resurrection. His teaching on self-denial and the need to take up one's cross. The transfiguration of the Lord. The healing of the possessed youth. The apostles dispute about primacy and the Lord's teaching about humility. Of the man who cast out demons in Christ's name. How the Lord was not received in the Samaritan village. On following Christ.

Chapter 10. The seventy are sent out to preach. They return with joy that the demons submitted to them. The Lord instructs them that they should rejoice rather that their names are written in heaven. Jesus praises His heavenly Father for the fact that He concealed these things from the wise and revealed them to babes. The merciful Samaritan. The Lord visits Martha and Mary.

Chapter 11. "Our Father," and the teaching on constancy in prayer. The Jews slander the Lord, as though He were casting out demons by the power of Beelzebub. The parable of the unclean spirit and the swept and cleaned house. "Blessed are they that hear the word of God and keep it!" The sign of Jonah the Prophet. The light of the body is the eye. Denouncing the Pharisees.

Chapter 12. Christ's warning of the leaven of the Pharisees. On the confession of Jesus Christ before men and fearlessness before temptations. On the unforgivable sin of blasphemy against the Holy Spirit. Christ's warning to avoid love of money and the parable of the rich man and an abundant harvest. On not laying upon oneself too many earthly cares, and of seeking the kingdom of God. On almsgiving. On constant vigilance in expectation of the Second Coming of Christ and the parable of the wise steward. Division in the world because of Christ the Saviour and preparation for the judgment of God.

Chapter 13. "If you will not repent, you will all perish likewise." The parable of the fruitless fig tree. The healing, on a Sabbath, of the woman bent over. The parable of the mustard seed and the leaven. "Are there few who are saved?" "One must enter by the narrow gates." The Lord's answer to Herod. The Lord rebukes Jerusalem.

Chapter 14. Healing on a Sabbath. Rebuking those who seek to be first. On inviting the beggars to the feast. Parable of those called to the bridal feast. The teaching on self-denial, taking up one's cross and following Christ.

Chapter 15. The parable of the lost sheep and the lost drachma. The parable of the prodigal son.

Chapter 16. The parable of the unjust steward. On divorce. The parable of the rich man and Lazarus.

Chapter 17. On temptations, forgiveness of one's brother, on the power of faith, on fulfilling all that is commanded. The healing of the ten lepers. "The Kingdom of God is within you." On the Second Coming of Christ.

Chapter 18. Parable of the unjust judge. Parable of the publican and the Pharisee. The blessing of the children. On the difficulty for those who have riches to enter the kingdom of God. The reward for those who have abandoned everything for the sake of Christ. Christ foretells of His sufferings, death, and resurrection. Healing the blind man from Jericho.

Chapter 19. The repentance of the chief publican Zacchaeus. The parable of the ten pounds. The entry of the Lord into Jerusalem. Casting out the sellers from the temple.

Chapter 20. The high priests and elders ask Jesus about His authority. The parable of the wicked vinedressers. On paying taxes to Caesar. The answer to the Sadducees regarding the resurrection from the dead. On the divine Sonship of Christ. Warning against the scribes.

Chapter 21. The widow's two mites. Prophecy of Jerusalem's destruction, of the end of the world, and of the Second Coming of Christ. Call to vigilance.

Chapter 22. The betrayal of Judas. The Mystical Supper. Prophecy of Peter's denial. On the two swords. The prayer in the garden of Gethsemane. The Lord is taken by the guard. The denial of Peter. Judgment before the Sanhedrin.

Chapter 23. Judgment before Pilate. The Lord before Herod. Pilate tries to release Jesus. The people demand His condemnation. The release of Barabbas and the conviction of Christ. The crying of the women and the Lord's words to them. The crucifixion of Christ. The repentance of the wise thief. The Lord's death and burial. The women from Galilee prepare ointments.

Chapter 24. The angels appear to the myrrh-bearing women. Peter at the tomb. The appearance of the Lord to the two disciples on the road to Emmaus. The Lord appears to the eleven disciples and teaches them. The ascension of the Lord.

The Gospel According to John

The fourth Gospel was written by the beloved disciple of Christ, St John the Theologian. St John was the son of the Galilean fisherman Zebedee (Matt 4:21) and Salome (Matt 27:56; Mark 15:40). Zebedee was apparently well-off, because he was able to hire workers (Mark 1:20), and it seems he was also an important member of Jewish society because his son John was personally acquainted with the high priest (John 18:15). His mother, Salome, is mentioned among the women who supported Christ with their property. She traveled with Christ throughout Galilee, followed Him to Jerusalem to the last Passover, and was involved in acquiring the ointments for anointing His Body, together with the other myrrh-bearing women (Mark 15:40–41; 16:1). Tradition considers her to be the daughter of Joseph the Betrothed.

John was first a disciple of John the Baptist. Having heard his witness of Christ as the Lamb of God Who takes upon Himself the sins of the world, he immediately, with Andrew, followed after Christ (John 1:37, 40). However, John only became a constant disciple of Christ a little later, after the miraculous gathering of fish in the lake of Gennesaret, when the Lord Himself called him together with his brother James (Luke 5:10). Together with Peter and his brother James, John was counted worthy of a special closeness to the Lord, being near Him in the most important and triumphant moments of His earthly life. Thus, he was present at the resurrection of Jairus's daughter (Mark 5:37), he saw the Lord's transfiguration on the mountain (Matt 17:1), he heard His sermon on the signs of the Second Coming (Mark 13:3), and he was a witness of the prayer in the garden of Gethsemane (Matt 26:37). At the Mystical Supper, John was so close to the Lord that, according to his own words, he "was leaning on Jesus' bosom." Because of his humility, he never calls himself by his proper name, but in his Gospel he calls himself "one of His disciples, whom Jesus loved" (John 13:23). This love of the Lord to John was shown especially in the moment when the Lord, hanging on the cross, entrusted His all-pure Mother to John, saying to him, "'Behold your mother'" (John 19:27).

Full of fiery love for the Lord, John was full of indignation toward anyone who was antagonistic to Christ or who kept his distance from Him. This is why he forbade the person who did not walk with Christ from casting out demons by the name of Christ (Mark 9:38) and asked the Lord to allow him to call down fire from heaven on the inhabitants of a certain Samaritan village, because they did not accept Him when He was traveling to Jerusalem through Samaria (Luke 9:54). For this reason, both John and his brother James received the nickname "Boanerges" from Christ, which means "sons of thunder." Feeling the Lord's love for him, while not yet being illumined by the grace of the Holy Spirit, he boldly asked the closest places near Christ for himself and his brother in the coming kingdom, but he is answered with a prophecy about the cup of suffering both of them will have to endure (Matt 20:20).

After the ascension of Christ, we often see St John together with the Apostle Peter (Acts 3:1; 4:13; 8:14). Together with Peter, he is considered a pillar of the Church and he resided in Jerusalem (Gal 2:9). From the time of Jerusalem's destruction, the place of St John's residence and work became Ephesus in Asia Minor. During the reign of the Emperor Domitian (or, according to some traditions, Nero or Trajan, which is not likely), he was exiled to the island of Patmos, where he wrote the Book of Revelation (1:9–19). When he returned from his exile, he wrote his Gospel in Ephesus, and died a natural death (the only one among the apostles). There is a tradition that his death was very mysterious, but he was very old in any case—105 according to some reports and 120 according to others—during Trajan's reign.

As tradition tells us, the fourth Gospel was written by John after a request either by Ephesian Christians or the bishops of Asia Minor. They brought him the first three Gospels and asked him to supplement them with the words of the Lord that he had heard directly from His lips. St John confirmed the truth of all that was written in the Synoptics, but found that much information needed to be added, especially concerning the divinity of the Lord Jesus Christ, so that people after the passage of time would not begin to think of Him only as the "Son of Man." This was made all the more pressing by the appearance of heresies that denied the divinity of Christ—the Ebionites, the heresy of Cerinthus, and Gnostics. According to St Irenaeus of Lyons, as well as other ancient Fathers and writers of the Church, St John wrote his Gospel because of the local bishops' worries regarding the appearance of these heresies.

The purpose of writing the fourth Gospel was a desire to supplement the accounts of the first three Evangelists. The content of the Gospel itself witnesses to this. While the first three Evangelists often tell of the same historical events and bring the same words of the Lord (which is why their Gospels are known as the "Synoptic Gospels"), the Gospel according to John is quite different from them in content, containing events and words of the Lord that are never even mentioned in the first three Gospels.

The one unique characteristic of the Gospel according to John is vividly expressed by the name that was given to it in ancient times. In contrast to the first three Gospels, it was widely known as the "Spiritual Gospel" (*pneumatikon* in Greek). While the first three Gospels concerned themselves with the events of the Lord's earthly life, the fourth begins with a theological explanation of Christ's divinity, and later contains a whole series of the most exalted speeches of the Lord, in which His divinity and the deep mysteries of faith are uncovered, such as the conversation with Nicodemus on being born again in water and the spirit and on the mystery of redemption; the conversation with the Samaritan woman on living water and worship given to God in spirit and truth; the conversation about the bread that came down from heaven and the mystery of the Eucharist; the conversation about the Good Shepherd; and especially the wonderful final conversation with the disciples at the Mystical Supper with the incredible "high priestly prayer" of the Lord. Here we also find a whole series of personal witnesses of the Lord about Himself as the Son of God. For this teaching on God the Word and for the revelation of all these profound and exalted truths and mysteries of our faith, St John received the honored title "the Theologian."

He was a pure-hearted virgin, giving himself with his whole soul to the Lord, and beloved by Him for this reason with a special love. St John deeply understood the most exalted mystery of Christian love and no one has so fully, deeply, and convincingly written on the two chief commandments of the Law of God—love for God and love for one's neighbor—as he did in his Gospel and especially his three General Epistles. This is why he is also known as the "Apostle of Love."

An important particularity of John's Gospel is his focus on the events and words of the Lord's mission in Judea, while the Synoptics mostly focus on His time in Galilee. Thanks to this fact, we can accurately count the length of the Lord's preaching and also the precise length of His earthly life. While He preached for the most part in Galilee, the Lord traveled to Jerusalem, that is, to Judea, on all the major feasts of the Jewish calendar. The events and conversations in St John's Gospel are by and large taken from these journeys. As we see from the Gospel itself, Christ traveled to Jerusalem for the Passover three times, and was crucified before the fourth Passover of His preaching in the world. From this it follows that Christ preached for roughly three and a half years, and was about thirty-three and a half when He was crucified (He began his mission, as St Luke tells us in 3:23, when He was thirty years old).

The Gospel according to John contains twenty-one chapters, or sixty-seven lectionary readings. It begins with the theological prologue on "the Word," which was "in the beginning," and finishes with the appearance of the risen Lord to the disciples assembled near Lake Gennesaret, the reinstatement of the Apostle Peter to the dignity of apostleship and the words of the author that "his witness is true," and that if everything that Jesus did were written down in detail, then the world itself would not be able to the contain the number of written books.

The Content of the Gospel According to John by Chapter

Chapter 1. The teaching on God the Word. John the Baptist witnesses to Jesus Christ. Two disciples of John follow Christ. The first disciples come to Christ—Andrew, Simon Peter, Philip, and Nathaniel. The Lord's conversation with Nathaniel.

Chapter 2. The first miracle in Cana of Galilee. The expulsion of the merchants from the temple. The Lord's prophecy of the destruction of the temple of His Body and His resurrection from the dead on the third day. Miracles done by the Lord in Jerusalem and those who believed in Him.

Chapter 3. The Lord's conversation with the Jewish leader Nicodemus. A new witness by St John the Baptist regarding Jesus Christ.

Chapter 4. The Lord Jesus Christ's conversation with the Samaritan woman at Jacob's well. The faith of the Samaritans. The Lord returns to Galilee. Healing the son of the nobleman in Capernaum.

Chapter 5. Healing the paralyzed man near the pool of Siloam on a Sabbath. The Lord Jesus Christ witnesses to Himself as the Son of God who has the power to raise the dead, and tells of His relationship with God the Father.

Chapter 6. The miraculous feeding of the five thousand. Walking on water. Conversation about the bread that came down from heaven that gives life to the world. On the necessity of partaking of the Body and Blood of Christ in order to inherit eternal life. Peter confesses Jesus Christ as the Son of the Living God. The Lord prophesies that He will be betrayed.

Chapter 7. Jesus Christ rejects the request of the brothers. Jesus Christ teaches the Jews in the temple on the feast. His teaching on the Holy Spirit as the living water. The Jews argue concerning Him.

Chapter 8. The Lord forgives the woman who was taken in the act of adultery. The conversation of the Lord with the Jews about Himself as the Light of the World and as the One Who Is. The Lord accuses those who do not believe in Him of desiring to fulfill the will of their father, the devil.

Chapter 9. Healing the man blind from birth.

Chapter 10. The Lord speaks of Himself as the Good Shepherd. Jesus Christ in the Temple of Jerusalem for the feast of dedication. His conversation about His oneness with God the Father. The Jews try to stone Him.

Chapter 11. The raising of Lazarus. The chief priests and Pharisees decide to put the Lord to death.

Chapter 12. Mary anoints the Lord in Bethany. The entry of the Lord into Jerusalem. The Greeks want to see Jesus. Jesus's prayer to the Father, that He would glorify Him. The Lord tells the people to walk in the light, while the light is among them. The Jews' lack of faith in accordance with Isaiah's prophecy.

Chapter 13. The Mystical Supper. The washing of the feet. The Lord warns of Judas's betrayal. The beginning of the Lord's final conversation with the disciples: His teaching on mutual love. He prophesies Peter's denial.

Chapter 14. The continuation of the final conversation: on there being many mansions in the house of the Father. Christ is the Way, the Truth, and the Life. On the power of faith. The promise of the Holy Spirit's descent.

Chapter 15. The continuation of the final conversation: the Lord's teaching of Himself as the Vine. Mutual love. Prophesies of future persecution.

Chapter 16. Continuation of the final conversation: a new promise that He would send the Paraclete-Holy Spirit.

Chapter 17. The high-priestly prayer of the Lord regarding His disciples and all the faithful.

Chapter 18. The Lord is taken in the garden of Gethsemane. Judgment before Annas. Peter's denial. At Caiaphas's. Judgment before Pilate.

Chapter 19. The Lord is scourged. Pilate questions the Lord. The crucifixion. The soldiers cast lots over Christ's garments. Jesus commits His Mother to John. The death and burial of the Lord.

Chapter 20. Mary Magdalene at the tomb where the stone has been cast aside. Peter and the other disciple find the tomb empty with the linen sheets still lying inside. The risen Lord appears to Mary Magdalene. The risen Lord appears to the assembled disciples. Thomas doubts, and Christ's second appearance to the assembled disciples, together with Thomas. The purpose of writing the fourth Gospel.

Chapter 21. The Lord appears to the disciples at the Sea of Tiberias, His threefold questioning of Peter: "Do you love me?" and His command to feed His sheep. Prophesy of Peter's death as a martyr. Peter asks about John. Affirmation of the truth of the Gospel.

GENERAL SUMMARY OF ALL FOUR GOSPELS WITH EXPLANATIONS OF IMPORTANT PASSAGES

As we have already said, not all the Evangelists write of the life of Jesus Christ with the same amount of detail. Some have details that others lack. Some speak with more depth and detail about events that others mention only in a few words, as if in passing. Even in the chronology one can see some variations, in some cases even seeming inconsistencies or contradictions, which the "negative critics" especially love to find and point out.

This is why, even in the earliest times of Christianity, attempts were made to synthesize the four Gospels into one text, that is, to give a summary of all the materials contained in the four Gospels in exact chronological order, in order to determine the exact order of the events described in the Gospels, as if it were in fact one book.

The first such attempt that we know of was undertaken in the middle of the second century A.D. by the apologist Tatian, the disciple of St Justin the Philosopher, who wrote a summary of all four Gospels that was widely known as the Diatessaron. The second such work was attempted, according to Blessed Jerome, by Theophilus, Bishop of Antioch, who lived in the second half of the second century. He also wrote *A Commentary on the Gospel*, an exegetical work.

Such attempts to synthesize the events of the four Gospels into one account continued later, even in our time. Currently, we know of the work of Boris I. Gladkov, who wrote *An Interpretation of the Gospels*. The best such work is that of St Theophan the Recluse, called *The Gospel History of God the Word, Incarnate for Our Salvation, in Chronological Order Taken from the Words of the Holy Evangelists*.

The importance of such works is that they give us a complete, whole picture of the entirety of the earthly life of our Lord and Saviour.

My own work is based on these aforementioned texts. I have tried, as much as possible, to establish a proper chronology of Christ's life, stopping to consider differences in the accounts of each of the four Evangelists and to explain important passages in agreement with the authoritative exegesis of the Holy Fathers of the Church.

The entire Gospel narrative can be naturally divided into three parts: the coming into the world of the Lord Jesus Christ, the preaching of the Lord Jesus Christ, and the last days of the earthly life of the Lord Jesus Christ.

 CHAPTER 1

The Coming into the World of the Lord Jesus Christ

THE INTRODUCTION TO THE GOSPEL: ITS VERACITY AND PURPOSE
(LUKE 1:1–4; JOHN 20:31)

One may consider the introduction to the entire four-Gospel corpus to be the first four verses of the first chapter of the Gospel according to Luke, in which the Evangelist speaks of his careful investigation of all the eyewitness accounts and the purpose of writing the Gospel in the first place: that everyone may know the firm foundation of the Christian teaching. St John also adds: "that you may believe that Jesus is the Christ, the Son of God, and that believing you may have life in His name" (John 20:31).

Thus, St Luke began to write his Gospel because there were already several similar accounts written that were not sufficiently authoritative or convincing in their content, and he considered it his duty to write an account of the life of the Lord Jesus Christ that was fully researched, and he considered the words of "eyewitnesses and ministers of the word" in order to uphold the faith of a certain Theophilus, and of course all Christians in general. Since St Luke himself was one of the seventy disciples of Christ, and so could not have been an eyewitness of such events as the birth of John the Baptist, the Annunciation, the birth of Christ, and the meeting of the Lord, he doubtless took a significant part of his Gospel from the words of other eyewitnesses, that is, on the basis of tradition (here we see the importance of tradition, so vehemently denounced by Protestants and other sectarians!). At the same time, it is completely self-evident that the first and most important eyewitness of the early events of the Gospel narrative was the most holy Virgin Mary, about whom St Luke twice mentions, that she treasured the memory of all these events, pondering them in her heart (Luke 2:19, 51).

There can be no doubt that the superiority of Luke's account over all those many written reports that preceded him is in the fact that he wrote only after a great deal of fact checking and in his strict chronological order. The same can be said of the other three Gospels, because two of them (John and Matthew) were written by direct eyewitnesses and "ministers of the Word" (that is, members of the Twelve) and the third, Mark's, was written based on the eyewitness account of one of the nearest disciples of Christ, St Peter.

The purpose indicated by St John is especially vividly seen throughout his own Gospel, which is full of triumphant confirmations of the divinity of the Lord Jesus Christ, but of course, the other three Gospels have the same purpose as well.

THE PRE-ETERNAL BEGETTING AND THE INCARNATION OF THE SON OF GOD (JOHN 1:1–14)

While the Evangelists Matthew and Luke tell of the earthly birth of the Lord Jesus Christ, St John begins his Gospel with a summary of the teaching on His pre-eternal begetting and Incarnation, as the only begotten Son of God. The first three Evangelists begin their accounts with events thanks to which the kingdom of God had its beginning within time and space, but St John, like an eagle, rises up to the pre-eternal foundation of this kingdom, contemplating the eternal being of the One Who only in the latter days (Heb 1:1) became man.

The second Person of the Holy Trinity, the Son of God, he names "the Word." It is important to know and remember that this "Word" (*logos* in Greek) means not only a word already uttered (as in English and Russian) but also the "thought, wisdom, intelligence" expressed by a given word. Thus, by calling the Son of God "the Word," St John is identifying Him with the "Wisdom" of God (Luke 11:49; Matt 23:34). The holy Apostle Paul also calls Christ "The Wisdom of God" (1 Cor 1:24). This teaching on the wisdom of God effectively identifies Christ as the Wisdom of God in the Old Testament wisdom literature, particularly the book of Proverbs (compare the incredible passage in Prov 8:22–30). Considering this, it is strange to insist, as some do, that St John took his teaching on the *Logos* from Plato and his followers (such as Philo). St John is writing about something that was well-known already in the Old Testament, something he was taught, as the beloved disciple, by his divine Teacher and the Holy Spirit.

"In the beginning was the Word" means that the Word is coeternal with God. Later in the sentence, St John explains that this Word is not separate from God in terms of its being, and that it is consequently one in essence with God, and, finally, he openly calls the Word "God" ("and the Word was God"). Here, the word "God" in Greek is used without the article, and this was used by the Arians and Origen as proof that the Word was not as divine as God the Father. This, however, was a misunderstanding. In fact, the lack of an article actually proves the theological axiom that the Persons of the Holy Trinity should not be confused. The article, in Greek, indicates that the subject of the sentence is identical with the subject that was spoken of previously. Thus, if St John, when speaking of the Word being God, had used an article, then he would have written a theological falsehood—that the Word is equivalent to God the Father. Thus, when he speaks of the Word, the Evangelist calls him merely *theos*, not *ho theos*, indicating thus that He is divine, but underlining at the same time that the Word has its own hypostasis, and is in no way to be confused with the hypostasis of God the Father.

As Blessed Theophylact mentions, St John calls the Son of God "the Word," not "the Son," in order to avoid thinking, incorrectly, of the begetting of the Son of God in carnal and passionate terms. "This is why he calls him 'Word,' so that you may know, that as a word is born of the mind without passion, so the Son is begotten of the Father without passion."[11]

"All things were made through Him" does not mean that the Word was merely an instrument in the creation of the world, but that the world came from the First Principle and Cause for all creation (as well as God the Word), God the Father, through the Son, Who of Himself is the source of being for everything that came to be, with the exception of Himself and other Persons of the Godhead.

"In Him was life"—here the word "life" does not presuppose existence in the way we usually mean it, but rather the "spiritual life" that inspires all rational creatures to strive toward the Author of their existence, God. This spiritual life is given only by communion and unity with the hypostatic Word of God.

Thus, the Word is the source of true spiritual life for rational creation.

"And the life was the light of men"—this spiritual life that comes from the Word of God illumines the person with a complete, perfect knowledge.

"And the light shines in the darkness"—the Word Who gives mankind the light of true knowledge, does not cease to guide mankind even in the darkness of sin, but the darkness did not apprehend it, that is, people who stubbornly continue in sin prefer to remain in the darkness of spiritual blindness ("and the darkness did not comprehend it").

Then the Word undertook extraordinary measures to illumine those who remain in the darkness of sin with the light of His divinity. He sent John the Baptist, and, finally, Himself became flesh.

"There was a man … whose name was John." In the Greek, "was" in this case is *egeneto*, not *ên*, the verb used to describe the existence of the Word. In other words, John "came into existence," was born within time, and is not eternal, as is the Word.

"He was not that Light"—John was not the self-existing light, but he shone only with a reflected light of that One True Light, Who only Himself "gives light to every man coming into the world."

The world did not comprehend the Light, even though it takes its very existence from Him. "He came to His own" means that He came to the chosen nation of Israel, but "His own did not receive Him," that is, they rejected Him, though not all of them, of course.

"But as many as received Him" with faith and love, "to them He gave the right to become children of God." He gave them the chance of adoption to God, that is, He gave them the beginning of a new spiritual life, which also begins with birth; not a physical birth, but one from God, from the power on High.

"And the Word became flesh"—by "flesh" one must understand not only a human body, but the full man, as the word "flesh" is often used in the Holy Scriptures (Matt 24:22). In other words, the Word became a full and complete human being without, at the same time, ceasing to be God, "and dwelt among us ... full of grace and truth." "Grace" indicates the goodness of God as well as the gifts of this goodness that open the way to the new spiritual life, that is, the gifts of the Holy Spirit. The Word, dwelling with us, was also full of truth. In other words, He had complete knowledge of everything that has to do with the spiritual world and the spiritual life.

"And we beheld His glory, the glory as of the only begotten of the Father." The apostles truly did see His glory in the transfiguration, resurrection, and ascension, and in the glory of His teachings, miracles, deeds of love, and willful self-abasement. "As the only begotten of the Father," because only He is the Son of God in essence, according to His divine nature; these words indicate His limitless preeminence over the sons of God by grace, of whom we have spoken above.

THE CONCEPTION OF THE FORERUNNER OF CHRIST, JOHN (LUKE 1:1–25)

St Luke tells of the appearance of an angel to the priest Zacharias during his service in the temple. The angel announced the birth of his son John, who would become great in the sight of the Lord, and struck Zacharias dumb for his lack of faith. This passage also tells of St John's conception.

King Herod, who is mentioned in this passage, was by birth an Idumean, son of Antipater, who became the leader of Judea during the time of John Hyrcanus II, the last Maccabee ruler. Herod received his title of "king" from the Romans. Although he was a proselyte, the Jews did not consider him one of their own, and his reign was just that "departure of the scepter of Judah," after which the Messiah (Shiloh) was supposed to appear (compare the prophecy in Gen 49:10).

The priests were divided by David into twenty-four shifts, groups, or companies, and the head of one of these was the priest Abia. To this shift belonged Zacharias. His wife Elizabeth also came from a priestly family. Even though both of them were truly righteous, they were childless, which among the Jews was considered God's punishment for sins. Each group served in the temple twice a year, one week at a time, and the priests divided their duties among each other by casting lots. It fell to Zacharias to perform the censing, which is why he entered the second part of the Jerusalem temple, called the sanctuary, where the incense-burning altar stood, while all the people stood at prayer in their appointed places in the open-air courts.

Having entered the sanctuary, Zacharias saw the angel and he became deathly afraid, maybe because Jewish custom had it that the appearance of an angel was the harbinger of an imminent death. The angel calmed him down, saying that his prayer had been heard, and his wife would give birth to a son, who would be "great in the sight of the Lord." It is difficult to imagine that righteous Zacharias would have been praying at that moment about God granting him a son since he and his wife were already very old, and since that moment was a very solemn one in the temple service. Evidently, as one of the few exemplary people of that time, he was fervently praying to God for the quick coming of the kingdom of the Messiah, and that prayer was the one to which the angel referred. And thus, his prayer received a great reward—not only was their bitter barrenness removed, but his son would be the forerunner of the Messiah, whose coming he so passionately desired. His son would surpass all others with his unusually strict asceticism and would be filled with special gifts of the Holy Spirit from his very birth. He would have the responsibility of preparing the Hebrew people for the coming of the Messiah, which he would do through his preaching on repentance and conversion of the sons of Israel, who had a formal reverence for the Lord without dedicating their hearts and lives to Him. For this, he would be given the power and spirit of the prophet Elijah, whom he would resemble with his fiery zeal, strict ascetical life, preaching of repentance, and rebuking of ungodliness. He would have to recall the Jews from the abyss of their moral fall, return to the hearts of parents their love for their children, and confirm in a righteous mind-set all those who acted contrary to the laws of the Lord.

Zacharias could not believe the angel, since he and his wife were too old to hope for a son, and he asked the angel for a sign as proof of his words. In order to dispel the doubts of Zacharias, the angel revealed his name. He was Gabriel, which means "the power of God," the one who revealed the time of the coming of the Messiah in weeks to Daniel the Prophet (Dan 9:21–27). For his lack of faith, Zacharias was punished with muteness, and apparently deafness as well, since others later communicated with him through signs. Usually, the ritual censing took a relatively short time, and the assembled people were wondering at Zacharias's tardiness, but they understood that he had experienced a vision when he began to communicate using only signs. It is amazing that the dumb Zacharias did not abandon his shift, but continued to serve until its end. After his return, his wife Elizabeth did actually conceive, but concealed this fact for five months, fearing that people would not believe her and would ridicule her. She herself rejoiced and thanked God for removing her shame. The conception of St John the Baptist is celebrated as a church feast on September 23.

THE ANNUNCIATION TO THE MOST HOLY VIRGIN MARY (LUKE 1:26–38)

In the sixth month of Elizabeth's pregnancy, the archangel Gabriel was sent to the small town of Nazareth, which was found in the tribe of Zebulun in the southern part of Galilee, to a virgin betrothed to a man named Joseph, who was named Mary. The Evangelist does not call her a "virgin who was married," but "a virgin betrothed to a man." This means that the most holy Virgin Mary was formally considered the wife of Joseph (as far as public opinion and the law were concerned), but in reality She was not his wife. Having lost Her parents early, and having been given away by them to the service of the temple, She could not return to them when She turned fourteen, when She could no longer stay within the temple according to the law. Her only option was to marry. When the high priest and the other priests found out that She had given an oath of virginity, and not desiring that She remain without protection, they formally betrothed Her to Her relative, the eighty-year-old Joseph, known to them all for his righteous life, who had a large family from his first marriage (Matt 13:55–56) and was a carpenter by trade.

When the angel entered into the room where the Virgin Mary was, he called her "full of the grace" of God (v. 28), that is, She was full of a special love and benevolence from God, a special help from God, which is always found in saints and in those who do great deeds. The words of the angel disturbed Mary by their unexpectedness, and She began to think of their deeper significance. Having consoled Her, he told her She would soon give birth to a Son, Who would be great, not like John, but much greater, because not only will He be filled with grace-filled gifts of God, but will Himself be the "Son of the Highest." Why did the angel say that "the Lord God will give Him the throne of His father David, and He will reign over the house of Jacob"? Because the monarchy of the Old Testament had as its purpose the preparation of the people for the eternal kingdom of Christ, to be gradually transformed into it. Consequently, the kingship of David, a monarchy in which the kings were chosen by God Himself, a political system intended to be guided by the laws of God, a society in which all forms of civil life were imbued with the idea of service to God, was inextricably linked with the New Testament kingdom of God.

The question of the most holy Virgin Mary: "How can this be, since I do not know a man?" would have been completely strange and without meaning if She had not given God an oath of total virginity to the end of Her life. The angel explained that Her oath would not have to be broken, that She would give birth to a Son through supernatural means, without a husband. The seedless conception would occur through the power of the Holy Spirit. The "power of the Highest," that is, the Son of God Himself (1 Cor 1:24) would descend upon Her like the cloud that in the past would fill the tabernacle, "the swift cloud," as Isaiah describes it (Isa 19:1). The most holy Virgin Mary did not require any proof from the angel, but as proof of his words, he offered the pregnancy of Elizabeth, who conceived in her old age according to the will of God, for Whom nothing is impossible. Even though the most holy Virgin Mary knew from the books of the prophets that She and her divine Son could expect not only honor but also sorrow, She answered in perfect submission to the will of God: "Behold the maidservant of the Lord! Let it be to Me according to your word." The Annunciation is celebrated on the

25th of March. Having received this good news, She told nothing of it to Joseph, justly fearing (as St John Chrysostom explains) that he would not believe Her, but rather think that She was just concealing a terrible sin.

THE MEETING OF THE VIRGIN MARY WITH ELIZABETH (LUKE 1:42–56)

The most holy Virgin Mary hurried to share Her joy with Her relative Elizabeth who lived in Judea, as some believe in Jutta, near the priestly city of Hebron. Elizabeth met Her with the same unexpected greeting with which the angel had greeted Her, saying, "Blessed are You among women," but then added, "and blessed is the fruit of Your womb," even though, as a relative, she most likely knew of the Virgin Mary's oath. Then she joyfully exclaimed, "But why is this granted to me, that the mother of my Lord should come to me?" She then explained that the reason for her unusual greeting was that the child in her womb leaped for joy when he heard the sound of the Virgin Mary's greeting. The child of Elizabeth, of course under the inspiration of the Holy Spirit, felt the nearness of another Child, for Whose coming into the world he would have to prepare mankind, and moved in an extraordinary way inside Elizabeth's womb. Through the action of the Holy Spirit, the joy of the child in the womb passed to the mother, who immediately, with foresight given her by grace, recognized Mary's joyful news even before She said anything, and she praised her cousin as the Mother of God with the words of the archangel Gabriel. She magnified Her for Her faith, with which She accepted the angelic messenger, as if contrasting this faith with the lack of faith her husband Zacharias showed.

From all this, it became obvious to the Virgin Mary that Her secret had been revealed to Elizabeth by God Himself. With a feeling of elation and compunction at the thought that the long-awaited Messianic age and the deliverance of Israel had arrived, Mary praised God with an incredible, inspired hymn, which is now constantly sung in our services in Her honor at Matins: "My soul magnifies the Lord and my spirit has rejoiced in God my Saviour." Here, setting aside any thoughts of Her own personal worthiness, She praised God that He looked at Her humility, and prophetically declares that for this mercy of God, all generations will praise Her, and this mercy will be extended to all who fear the Lord. Later, She glorified God that the promise given to Abraham had been fulfilled; that the kingdom of the Messiah, so eagerly awaited by Israel, had come; that those followers of God who had been humiliated and despised by the world would triumph over it; and that they will be raised up and filled with goodness, while the proud and powerful will be brought down and shamed. It seems that Mary, not staying until the birth of the Forerunner, returned home.

THE BIRTH OF JOHN THE BAPTIST (LUKE 1:57–80)

When the time came for Elizabeth to give birth, all her neighbors and relatives rejoiced with her and on the eighth day they all assembled at her house for the rite of circumcision, which was established by Abraham (Gen 17:11–14) and required by the law of Moses (Lev 12:3). Through circumcision the newborn became a member of the chosen people of God, and thus the day of circumcision was considered a joyful family event. During the rite, the newborn was also given a name, usually in honor of some older relative. Thus, there was a general outcry at Elizabeth's desire to call her son John. Luke the Evangelist underlines this fact evidently because it in itself is miraculous: her desire to call him John was the fruit of the Holy Spirit's inspiration. When the assembled people then asked Zacharias's opinion, he asked for a wax-covered board on which to write, and etched out with a stick: "His name is John." Everyone was amazed at the unexpected agreement between the desires of the mother and deaf-mute father to call their son by a name that was not found in their ancestry.

Immediately, as the angel foretold, Zacharias's tongue was loosed, and he was filled with prophetic inspiration, as though he could already see the imminent kingdom of the Messiah. He praised God, Who visited His people and performed their salvation, Who "raised up a horn of salvation for us in the house of His servant David." In the same way that criminals seeking sanctuary from their pursuers could run to the altar of whole-burnt offerings and, grabbing one of the four horns on its corners, would be considered safe from any prosecution (1 Kgs 2:28), so the entire race of mankind, oppressed by sin and brought low by divine justice, could find its redemption in Christ Jesus. This salvation was not only the deliverance of Israel from its political enemies, as the majority of Jews believed at the time, especially the scribes and Pharisees, but also the fulfillment of the promise of God given to the Old Testament ancestors, which would give a possibility for all faithful Israelites to serve God in "holiness and righteousness." "Righteousness" here means justification through divine means, through the assimilation to humanity of the redemptive merits of Christ; "holiness" means the internal transformation of the person achieved by a collaboration of grace and the person's active effort.

Then Zacharias prophesies about his son's future with the words of the archangel, saying that he would be called a prophet of the Most High and would be a forerunner to the divine Messiah. He also indicated the purpose of the forerunner's mission as the preparation of the people for the Messiah's coming. He was to help the chosen nation to understand that salvation is not found in anything but forgiveness of sins. Thus, Israel must not seek worldly greatness, which is what its spiritual leaders dreamed of, but righteousness and the forgiveness of sins. Forgiveness of sins would come from the "tender mercy of our God, with which the Dayspring from on high has visited us," that is, the Messiah-Redeemer, who was given this name by the prophets Jeremiah (Jer 25:5) and Zechariah (Zech 3:8; 6:12).

According to tradition, the news of John the Forerunner's birth reached even the suspicious ears of King Herod, and when the Magi from the East came to Jerusalem, asking where the newborn king of Israel was to be found, Herod remembered

Zacharias's son, and having sent his soldiers to kill the children in Bethlehem, sent some also to Jutta. Zacharias was performing his service in the temple at that time, and Elizabeth fled and hid in the desert. Angered by the fact that the soldiers could not find John, Herod sent them to the temple to demand John's hiding place from Zacharias. Zacharias answered that he was now in service to the Lord God of Israel and did not know where his son was. He was killed between the temple and the altar, which Christ remembers in His accusatory speech to the Pharisees (Matt 23:35). The birth of John the Baptist is celebrated in the Orthodox Church on June 24.

THE GENEALOGY OF THE LORD JESUS CHRIST ACCORDING TO THE FLESH
(MATT 1:1–17; LUKE 3:23–38)

In the Gospels of Matthew and Luke, we find genealogies of the Lord Jesus Christ. They equally witness to Christ's ancestry from David and Abraham, but the names in both do not always correspond. Since St Matthew wrote his Gospel for the Jews, it was important for him to show that Christ came, as is proper for the Messiah, from Abraham and David. Thus, he begins his Gospel from the genealogy, starting from Abraham and leading to "Joseph the husband of Mary, of whom was born Jesus who is called Christ" (Matt 1:16). This leads to the obvious question. Why did the Evangelist list Joseph's genealogy, not the Virgin Mary's? This is because it was not customary for the Jews to consider the female line in genealogies, and since the Virgin Mary was without any doubt the only daughter of her parents Joachim and Anna, the law required that she be given in marriage only to another member of her tribe and family; consequently, since the elder Joseph was of the line of David, she had to be of the same line.

St Luke, who gave himself the goal of showing that the Lord Jesus Christ belongs to all mankind and is the Saviour of all mankind, brings the genealogy from Christ all to way to Adam and God. In his genealogy, however, we find some apparent contradictions with St Matthew's version. Thus, Joseph the supposed father of Christ, according to Matthew, was the son of Jacob, but St Luke has him as the son of Heli. In addition, Shealtiel, who is mentioned by both Evangelists as the father of Zerubbabel, in Matthew's version is the son of Jeconiah, but in St Luke is the son of Neri. The ancient Christian scholar Julius Africanus explains this contradiction brilliantly through the law governing childless marriages: if one of two brothers died without leaving a child, then the other brother had to accept his brother's wife, so that the seed of his brother would be restored (Deut 25:5–6). The firstborn of that particular marriage would be considered the son of the dead brother, so that the brother's line would not die and "his name may not be blotted out of Israel." This law was valid not only for blood brothers but also for half brothers. Such brothers were Jacob, the father of Joseph according to St Matthew, and Heli, the father of Joseph according to St Luke. They were born from different fathers, but one mother, who was first married to the father of Jacob, then to the father of Heli. Her name was Hesta. Thus, when one of the sons of Hesta, Heli, died without a child, the other, Jacob, took Heli's wife and restored the lineage of his brother, having given birth to Joseph. The same is true in the other discrepancy because St Luke leads Joseph's line through Rhesa, the son of Zerubbabel, and Heli, the father of Joseph, while St Matthew leads it from Zerubbabel through Abiud, the other son of Zerubbabel, and Jacob, the other father of Joseph.

The introduction in St Matthew of women into the Lord's genealogy, especially women who were either Gentiles or sinners, was done for a specific purpose— God, Who did not consider it shameful to include such women in the chosen line of the Messiah's birth, does not scorn to call the Gentile and sinner into His kingdom, for it is not because of his own righteousness that a man finds salvation, but by the power of the all-purifying grace of God.

THE NATIVITY OF CHRIST

Two Evangelists tell of events concerning the birth of Christ: St Matthew and St Luke. St Matthew tells of the revelation of the mystery of the Incarnation to the righteous Joseph, of the adoration of the Magi, of the flight of the Holy Family to Egypt, and the murder of the children in Bethlehem, while St Luke adds more details about the actual circumstances of Christ's birth in Bethlehem and the adoration of the shepherds.

THE MYSTERY OF THE INCARNATION IS REVEALED TO JOSEPH (MATT 1:18–25)

St Matthew writes that soon after the betrothal of the most holy Virgin Mary to Joseph, even before the formal legitimization of their marriage, Joseph became aware of the conception in the womb of Mary. Since he was a righteous man, that is, fair on the one hand, but merciful on the other, Joseph did not want to publicly denounce Her for Her sin because the result would be a shameful and painful death, according to the Mosaic Law (Deut 22:23–24). Rather, he intended to secretly let Her leave him without officially giving a reason. When he had this thought, an angel of the Lord appeared to him, explaining that the Child of his betrothed, whom he suspected of sin, was "of the Holy Spirit," not the fruit of sin. "She will bring forth a Son, and you shall call His name Jesus, for He will save His people from their sins." The name Jesus (or Yehoshua/Joshua in Hebrew) means "saviour." In order to prevent Joseph from doubting the truth of his words, the angel cited an ancient prophecy of Isaiah that witnessed to the fact that the great miracle of the seedless conception and the Virgin birth of the Saviour of the world was foreordained in the pre-eternal council of God: "Behold, the virgin shall conceive, and bear a Son" (Isa 7:14).

One should not think that the prophecy was not fulfilled, since it explicitly said that "they shall call His name Immanuel," but the child born of Mary was named Jesus. The name "Immanuel" is not a proper name, but rather a symbolic one that means "God with us," in other words, when this miraculous birth would occur, people would say, "God is with us," for in His person God came down to earth and dwelt among men. Isaiah's words were merely a prophetic indication of the divinity of Christ, and an indication that this miraculously born Child would not be merely a man, but God Himself. Convinced by the words of the angel, "take to you Mary as your wife," Joseph put aside his intention to send Her away from him, and allowed Her to live in his house as though She were his wife "and did not know Her till She had brought forth Her firstborn Son." This does not mean that after Christ was born, Joseph had marital relations with the most holy Virgin Mary, living with Her as husband and wife. St John Chrysostom justly remarks that it is completely impossible to think that such a righteous man as Joseph would allow himself to have relations with the holy Virgin, especially after She became a mother in such a miraculous fashion. In this case, the word "till" (*eôs*, in Greek) must not be understood as do the Protestants, who do not honor the Virgin, and say that Joseph did not have relations with Her before Jesus's birth, but afterward he did. Rather, it means he *never* had relations with Her. In the Scriptures, the word *eos* is used several times. For example, it is found in the phrase that tells of the end of the flood: "Then he sent out a raven, which kept going to and fro until [*eos*] the waters had dried up from the earth" (Gen 8:7). The point is that the raven did not come back at all. Also, in another place: "And lo, I am with you always, even until [*eos*] the end of the age" (Matt 28:20). This, of course, does not mean that after the end of the world Christ will no longer be with us![12] He will be with us more than ever before!

Here also, Jesus is called "firstborn" not because the holy Virgin had more children after Him, but because He was Her first *and only* son. In the Old Testament, God commands every firstborn male child to be consecrated to Him, regardless of whether he is the first of several or the only child. If the Gospels do make mention of the "brothers of Jesus Christ" (Matt 12:46; John 2:12), that in no way means that these were His brothers by blood. These were, as tradition tells us, the sons of Joseph from his first marriage.

The Manner and Time of the Nativity of Christ (Luke 2:7–19)

The most detailed account of the birth of Christ is found in St Luke. He dates the birth of Christ to the census of all those living in the Roman Empire, which was commanded by Caesar Augustus, that is, the Roman emperor Octavian, who received from the Senate the title "Augustus" (most holy). Unfortunately, the exact date of this census has not been preserved by history, but the dates of the reign of Augustus are well known, and give us at least an approximate date for the birth of Christ (give or take a few years), especially when considered with other historical facts. Our currently accepted way of counting from the "year of the Lord" (*Anno Domini*) was introduced in the sixth century by the Roman monk Dionysius

Exiguus ("the Small"), who calculated that the Lord Jesus Christ was born 754 years after the founding of Rome. His calculations were later shown to be quite erroneous—he indicated the birth of Christ at least five years later than it actually was. This Dionysian model, which was initially used only for the ecclesiastical calendar, became universally used in all Christian countries starting in the tenth century, and was accepted by secular historians, even though now it is generally considered to be erroneous. The actual date of Christ's birth can be determined more exactly using the following facts from the Gospel itself:

1. The time of King Herod's reign. From Matthew 2:1–18 and Luke 1:5, it is quite clear that Christ was born during the reign of Herod (714–750 years from the founding of Rome). In year 750, Herod died eight days before Passover, soon after a lunar eclipse. But according to astronomical calculations, since this eclipse happened during the night of March 13 in year 750, and Passover that year was on April 12, then, consequently, Herod died in the beginning of April in year 750 from the founding of Rome, that is, at least four years before the beginning of the Christian era.

2. The census mentioned by Luke in chapter 2 of his Gospel, announced by an edict of Augustus in year 746 from the founding of Rome, began in Judea only in the last years of Herod's reign, then was interrupted for a time because of Herod's death, to be continued and concluded when Syria was ruled by Quirinius (Luke 2:2). As a result of this census, a local insurrection began. Theudas the leader of this insurrection, was executed by Herod on March 12, 750. It is clear, then, that the census began earlier than this date.

3. The reign of Roman emperor Tiberius, in the fifteenth year of which John began his preaching and Christ was thirty years old (Luke 3:1, 23). Augustus named Tiberius co-emperor two years before his death in January 765, and thus the fifteenth year of Tiberius's reign began in August 779. Thus, Christ was born in 749, thirty years earlier.

4. Astronomical calculations show us that the year of Christ's death on the cross (which, according to the Gospel, occurred the year when Passover fell on Friday evening) could only be 783, and since Christ was thirty-three years old in that year, then according to this calculation, He was born in the year 749 from the founding of Rome.

Thus, all these facts are unanimous in declaring the year of the birth of Christ to be year 749 from the founding of Rome.

There are not enough concrete details in the Gospels themselves to indicate the actual day of the week when Christ was born. The Eastern Church at first celebrated the Nativity on the same day as the Theophany, the feast being called "Epiphany" (the appearance of God in the world), on January 6. In the Western

Church, Nativity was celebrated on December 25 since early times. From the end of the fourth century, the Eastern Church also began to celebrate the Nativity on December 25. This day was chosen for a specific reason. There are some traditions that Zacharias was the high priest, and that the angel appeared to him, behind the holy veil, in the holy of holies, not the sanctuary, where the high priest entered only on the Day of Atonement. This day, according to our calendar, falls on September 23, which became the traditional day to commemorate the conception of St John the Baptist. Six months after this, the angel visited the holy Virgin Mary, the Annunciation was thus celebrated on March 25, and nine months after that, on December 25, the Lord Jesus Christ was born. However, there are no convincing reasons to consider Zacharias a high priest. Thus, there is another, symbolic rationale for choosing this day to celebrate the birth of Christ. The ancients believed that Christ, as the second Adam, was conceived in the womb of the most holy Virgin Mary on the spring solstice of March 25, the same day that ancient tradition tells us Adam was created. Christ, the Light of the World, the Sun of Righteousness, was born nine months later on the winter solstice, when the days begin to get longer, the nights shorter. Correspondingly, the conception of John the Baptist, who was six months older than the Lord, is traditionally celebrated on September 23, the first day of autumn, and his birth on June 24 corresponds with the summer solstice, when the days begin to get shorter. St Athanasius saw the poetic justice in this, citing the Baptist's own words: "He must increase, but I must decrease" (John 3:30).

Some are disturbed by St Luke's assertion that the census, during which Christ was born, was enacted when Quirinius ruled over Syria. But according to historical accounts, Quirinius's rule over Syria began only ten years after the birth of Christ. The most likely explanation for this contradiction is that it is more correct to read the text of the Gospel not as "this taxing," but as "the taxing itself" (there are strong indications that the original Greek says precisely this). In other words, the imperial edict was issued before the birth of Christ, but because of local insurrections and the death of Herod, the census was abandoned and finished only ten years later, during the reign of Quirinius. There are certain sources that indicate that Quirinius ruled twice in Syria, and the census, begun during his first reign, was finished in his second, which is why the Evangelist indicated that the census that occurred during the birth of Christ "first occurred" during Quirinius's reign over Syria.

Every person needed to be counted in his own city, since Roman politics were always amenable to the defeated, and the Jewish practice required that any census be done by tribe, which meant that every person had to travel to the city where the founder of his bloodline had lived. As Joseph was of David's line, he had to travel to Bethlehem, the city where David was born. In this we see God's amazing providence—the Messiah had to be born in the city prophesied by Micah (Mic 5:2). According to Roman laws, women as well as men in conquered countries needed to participate in the general census. In any case, there is nothing unusual in the fact that the most holy Virgin Mary, in her expectant state, traveled with the guardian of her virginity, especially since she doubtless knew the prophecy of Micah, and could not help but see in his Roman edict the providential action of God, who was guiding her toward Bethlehem.

"And she brought forth her firstborn Son, and wrapped Him in swaddling cloths, and laid him in a manger, because there was no room for them in the inn" (Luke 2:7). Luke the Evangelist stresses the fact that the most holy Virgin Mary swaddles her newborn Son herself. In other words, it was a painless birth. Her Son is called firstborn not because there were other children afterward, but because, according to the law of Moses, any male child who opened the womb (that is, was born first) was called "firstborn," even if he was the only child. Because of the many travelers who had come earlier to Bethlehem, and because of their poverty, the Holy Family had to find shelter in one of the caves or grottos that are found all over Palestine, where shepherds would keep their flocks during inclement weather. Here the divine Messiah was born, placed in a feeding trough instead of a child's crib, from His very birth accepting on His shoulders the cross of humiliation and suffering for the redemption of mankind, and through His birth giving us a lesson of humility, that highest of virtues, about which He later constantly instructed His disciples. According to ancient tradition, during the birth of Christ, an ass and an ox were standing nearby, in order to show that "the ox knows its owner and the donkey its master's crib" (Isa 1:3).

But it was not only humiliation that accompanied the birth and earthly life of the Saviour, but also glimmers of His divine glory. The angel of the Lord, shining with divine glory, appeared to shepherds (perhaps those very shepherds to whom the caves belonged) who were sleeping in the fields because of the good weather. He declared to them "tidings of great joy" of the birth in the city of David of the Saviour, "Who is Christ the Lord." Here we must make particular note of the angel's words that this joy would be for "all people" (Luke 2:10). In other words, the Messiah came not only for the Jews, but for the entire race of mankind. The angel also gave the shepherds a "sign" through which they would be able to recognize Him: "You will find a Babe wrapped in swaddling cloths, lying in a manger." And immediately, as if in confirmation of the truth of the angel's words, the entire heavenly host appeared, singing a wonderful praise to the newborn Child—the Messiah: "Glory to God in the highest, and on earth peace, goodwill toward men!" The angels praise God, who glorified the Saviour in the world; they glorify the peace that will come down into the souls of people who believe in the Saviour, they rejoice for the people to whom God's goodwill has returned. The hosts of the heights, that is, the sinless immortal spirits who constantly praise the Creator and Lord in the heavens, especially praise Him for the incredible outpouring of His divine goodness, for the great work of the divine economy. The peace that was brought to earth by the incarnate Son of God cannot be confused with the mundane external calm and tranquility most often associated with that word. This is the peace of sinful man's conscience after he has been redeemed by Christ the Saviour. This is the peace of a conscience that has been reunited with God, with other people, which is at peace with itself. And since this peace of God, which surpasses all understanding (Phil 4:7), reigns in the souls of those who have believed in Christ, then external peace also becomes the inheritance of these believers' lives. The redemption has shown the entire greatness of God's goodwill, God's love for man. Thus, the meaning of the angel's doxology is this: "It is proper for the heavenly spirits to praise God, for salvation and peace reign on earth, since mankind has been given a special blessing from God."

The shepherds, as people apparently pious, immediately hurried to the place indicated by the angel, and were the first to be found worthy to worship the newborn Christ Child. They told everyone they could of the joyful miracle of the angel's appearance and of the chant of the heavenly hosts, and everyone was amazed. The most holy Virgin Mary, in her profound humility, retained all these things, "and pondered them in her heart."

THE CIRCUMCISION AND MEETING OF THE LORD (LUKE 2:21–39)

After eight days, the rite of circumcision was performed over the Child, according to the law of Moses (Lev 12:3), and He was named Jesus, which means "saviour," the name indicated by the angel even before the Virgin conceived.

According to the law of Moses, a woman who gave birth to a firstborn male was considered unclean for forty days (if the firstborn was a girl, the period of uncleanness was eighty days). On the fortieth day, she needed to bring a whole-burnt offering to the temple—a year-old lamb (a sacrifice for sins) and a young dove or a pigeon. In case of poverty, two doves or pigeons were acceptable. Fulfilling the Mosaic Law concerning purification, the most holy Virgin Mary and Joseph also brought the Child to Jerusalem, to dedicate the Child as a firstborn to God through the ritual payment of five shekels. This law was kept as a remembrance of the fact that on the night before Israel's flight from Egypt, the angel of the Lord destroyed all the firstborn in Egypt, and in recompense every firstborn male child needed to be dedicated to the temple. With time, when service in the temple was allotted only to the tribe of Levi, firstborns of all tribes were allowed to "pay out" their temple service with five shekels of silver (Num 18:16). It is clear from the Gospel account that the most holy Virgin Mary and her betrothed brought the sacrifice of the poor—two doves.

Why did the Lord, whose conception and birth was free of sin, have to be subjected to circumcision? Why did His most pure Mother have to be purified?

First, this was done in order to "fulfill all righteousness" (Matt 3:15) and to show an example of complete obedience to God's Law. Second, it was necessary for the future service of the Messiah in the eyes of His people. An uncircumcised man could not be a member of God's chosen people; thus, He could not enter either the temple or synagogues; uncircumcised, He would have no influence over the people, nor be acknowledged as the Messiah. The same is true for His Mother. If She were not ritually purified, in the eyes of the priests and the people, She would not be a true Israelite. The mystery of the immaculate conception and birth was known to no one except the Virgin Mary Herself and Joseph, and so everything required by the law needed to be fulfilled to the letter.

Present at the ritual sacrifice was a certain righteous and pious old man named Simeon, who awaited the "Consolation of Israel" that is the Messiah promised by God, Whose coming was supposed to bring consolation to Israel (see Isa 40:1). St Luke does not tell us anything else about him, other than the fact that the Holy Spirit told him that he would not die until he would see the long-awaited consolation, Christ the Lord Himself. However, ancient tradition tells us that Simeon was one of those seventy-two elders who, by order of Ptolemy, translated the Old Testament from ancient Hebrew to Greek. He was given the book of Isaiah, and he doubted the prophecy of the birth of Immanuel from a virgin (Isa 7:14). Then an angel appeared to him and told him that he would not die until he saw with his own eyes the fulfillment of this prophecy. Inspired by the Holy Spirit, he came to the temple, to the place where the altar of whole-burnt offerings was located, and recognized the Christ in the Child held by the most holy Virgin Mary. He took Him in his arms, and from his lips came an inspired prayer—gratitude to God for the fact that He allowed him to see in the face of this Child the salvation prepared for all people: "Lord, now You are letting Your servant depart in peace," he said. Now, from this minute, the last tie to this life has been broken, and You, My Lord, are releasing me from this life into another, new life, "according to Your word," according to the prophecy given me by the Holy Spirit, "in peace," full of inner tranquility, "for my eyes have seen Your salvation," which was promised by You to the world through the Redeemer-Messiah, whom I behold with great joy before me, "which You have prepared before the face of all peoples," not only the Jews, but all mankind. This salvation is "a light to bring revelation to the Gentiles" and "the glory of Your people Israel," since the Messiah has come from among the Jews. Joseph and the Theotokos were amazed because everywhere they went, they found people to whom God had already revealed the secret of this Child.

Having returned the Child to His Mother and blessed Her and Joseph, as is the right of a very old man on whom the Holy Spirit rested, Simeon in a moment of inspiration foretells that this Child will be the subject of much contention and argument between His followers and His enemies, "that the thoughts of many hearts may be revealed." In other words, depending on a person's attitude toward this Child, his inner disposition, the state of his soul would be revealed. Whoever loves truth and strives to do the will of God, the same will believe in Christ, while whoever loves evil and does the work of darkness, the same will hate Christ and will slander Him in any way possible, if only to justify his own hatred. This happened in actual fact with the many scribes and Pharisees who hated Him, and it continued to happen in the face of all atheists and despisers of Christ. For those who believe in Him, He is "destined for the ... rising," that is, the eternal salvation, while for those who harden their hearts against Him, He is "destined for the fall," their eternal damnation, their eternal perdition. Simeon also saw the suffering that lay before the most holy Mother as a result of the contention toward Her divine Son: "a sword will pierce through your own soul also."

Present at this meeting also was Anna, the daughter of Phanuel, whom St Luke calls a prophetess, thanks to the special activity of the Spirit of God in her and for her gift of prophecy. The Evangelist praises her as a pure widow who consecrated herself to God after she had lived with her husband only seven years. She was already eighty-four, and that entire time she never left the temple, serving God "with fastings and prayers night and day," She, like Simeon, praised the Lord and told, through prophetic inspiration, things similar to what Simeon said about the Child to everyone who awaited redemption in Jerusalem, all who awaited the coming of the Messiah.

The Evangelist further writes that, having fulfilled all according to the law, they returned to Galilee, into their own town of Nazareth. Here, Luke skips over everything that happened after the meeting at the temple, doubtless because St Matthew had already described it all in detail—the adoration of the Magi, the murder of the innocents by Herod, the flight to Egypt, and the return to Galilee after Herod's death. The Evangelists often skip over certain events in their accounts exactly in this way.

THE ADORATION OF THE MAGI (MATT 2:1–12)

When Jesus was born in "Bethlehem, in the land of Judea," Magi from the East came to Jerusalem. Bethlehem is here called "of Judea" to distinguish it from another Bethlehem, in Galilee, in the tribe of Zebulun. The newcomers who came to worship the newborn Christ were not what their name usually indicates—they were not wizards or mages who work false miracles, call on evil spirits, or awake the spirits of the dead (Exod 7:11; Deut 18:11). These were scholars, discerners of mysteries, who had great stores of knowledge, similar to those who were in Daniel's care in Babylon (Dan 2:48). They made predictions of the future based on the movement of the stars and they studied the mysterious forces of nature. These Magi in Babylon and Persia were highly regarded, and sometimes they were also priests and counselors of kings. St Matthew says that they came "from the East," without explicitly mentioning their country. Some believe they came from Arabia, while others think they were from Persia or Chaldea. The word *magos*, used to describe them in the Gospel, is Persian in origin. Thus, it is most likely that they came from

Persia or one of the countries that made up the former Babylonian Empire, since there, during the seventy-year exile of the Jews, the ancestors of these magi might have heard of the coming of the Great King, the Redeemer who will subjugate the entire world. There, in Babylon, lived the Prophet Daniel, who prophesied of the coming of this Great King. It is also possible that the ancient prophecy of Balaam (Num 24:17), which told of the coming of a star out of Jacob, was preserved there.

Studying the night sky was one of the most important activities of these Persian wise men. Thus, the Lord called them to worship the newborn Saviour of the world through the appearance in the night sky of an unusual star. In the East of that time, there was a widespread belief that the Lord of the world, before Whom all the nations of the world would bow, was to appear in Judea. Thus, having entered Jerusalem, the Magi ask with full certainty of a positive answer: "Where is He Who has been born King of the Jews?"

This disturbed Herod a great deal since he had no legal right to the Jewish throne, being an Idumean and a tyrant as well, commanding no loyalty, but instead inspiring hatred from his followers. With him, all of Jerusalem became anxious, perhaps because they feared reprisals from a disturbed and unpredictably cruel Herod. Bloody Herod, having decided to destroy this newborn upstart and rival to his throne, calls the priests and scribes together and asks them directly about the prophesied birthplace of the Messiah-King of the Jews. The scribes immediately cited the generally known prophecy of Micah, indicating Bethlehem (Mic 5:2). "Bethlehem" means "house of bread," and Ephrathah means "a fertile field"— both names indicating a land ready for harvest. It is interesting to note that in the original prophecy, Micah indicates that the Messiah will only be born in Bethlehem, but will not live there, and that His origin is "from of old," "from everlasting." For the proper fulfillment of his bloody intention, Herod also needed to know the prophesied time of the Messiah's birth, and he calls the Magi to himself, in order to secretly find out the exact time of the appearance of the star, and then he sends them to Bethlehem, using them to find out all the necessary details of the birth of this upstart newborn. When the Magi went to Bethlehem, the star, which they first saw in the East, went before them, indicating the road, until it stopped above the place where the Child was.

What sort of a star was this? There are several opinions among the Fathers. St John Chrysostom and Blessed Theophylact think that this was a manifestation of divine and angelic power that appropriated the physical appearance of a star. As for the star that they saw first in the East, many believe that this was an actual star, because events of cosmic importance are often manifested visibly in nature. It is interesting that according to astronomer Johannes Kepler's calculations, the year of Christ's birth saw an incredible convergence at one point of observation of the three brightest planets—Jupiter, Mars, and Saturn, which appeared in the night sky as an especially bright star. Such a planetary alignment coincided with the great event of the birth of the Son of God on earth, and this, of course, is a miracle and a manifestation of the providence of God, who used this natural phenomenon to call scholarly Gentiles to worship the newborn Messiah. The symbolic meaning of this wonderful arrival of the Magi from the East is given by St John Chrysostom: "Since the Jews, who constantly heard the Prophets tell of the coming of Christ, never really paid it much attention, the Lord inspired barbarians to come from a faraway land to ask about the King born among the Jews, and they learned from the Persians that, which they did not want to learn from the prophets."[13]

Of course, the star that indicated the path of the Magi from Jerusalem to Bethlehem and "came and stood over where the young child was," was not a real star or planet, but a unique miraculous phenomenon. Having seen this star, the Magi "rejoiced with exceedingly great joy," doubtless because in the appearance of this star they found further strengthening for their faith in the birth of this unique Child. It is later said of the Magi that they came into "the house" and "fell down, and worshiped Him." Consequently, this was already not the cave where Christ was born, since Mary had already had time to find a proper dwelling. "When they had opened their treasures," the Magi brought the child gifts—gold as for a king, frankincense as for God, and myrrh as for a man who would taste of death. Having received an indication in a dream not to return to Herod, who was intending to kill the God-Child, they went back to their country a different way, not through Jerusalem, probably heading south.

THE FLIGHT TO EGYPT; MURDER OF THE INNOCENTS; RETURN TO NAZARETH
(MATT 2:13–23)

After the Magi left, an angel of the Lord, appearing to Joseph in a dream, commanded him to take the Child and His Mother and flee to Egypt, which he promptly did, leaving in the dead of night. Egypt is located southwest of Judea, and they had to travel roughly seventy miles to the border. It was also a Roman province at the time, and many Jews lived there and had their own synagogues, but it was outside Herod's jurisdiction, and the Holy Family, living among other Jews, could consider themselves in relative safety. If one were to ask why Christ did not save Himself from the murderers sent by Herod, St John Chrysostom has the answer: "If the Lord began to do miracles from His earliest days, no one would believe He was fully human, as well as divine."[14] There are many fascinating traditions about the travels of the Holy Family. One of them tells the following story—when Joseph, Mary, and the Child entered a pagan temple with 365 idols, all the idols fell down to the earth and crumbled, thereby fulfilling the prophecy of Isaiah (Isa 19:1). In the fact that the Child Jesus had to flee to Egypt of all places and then return from Egypt is significant to St Matthew, who sees in it the fulfillment of the prophecy of Hosea: "Out of Egypt I called My Son" (Hos 11:1). These words in the original prophecy explicitly refer to the exodus of the Jewish nation out of Egypt, but since the chosen people were a prototype of the only Son of God, Jesus Christ, the exodus of the Jewish nation from Egypt was a type of the return of Jesus Christ Himself out of Egypt. As St John Chrysostom said, every event in the Old Testament was a foreshadowing of an event in the New Testament.

Herod was irate when the Magi did not return to Jerusalem, considering himself to be ridiculed by their actions, even though they never had the intention of mocking him, which only made him even angrier. Having found out from the Magi that the star appeared nearly a year before, he concluded that the child must be at least a year old, but younger than two, and so he cruelly ordered that all children two years or younger in Bethlehem and its vicinity should be killed, reasoning that one of them should be the Christ Child. Tradition tells us that fourteen thousand children were killed, whose memory the church celebrates every year on December 29. This cruelty was completely characteristic of Herod, who according to Josephus, had his wife strangled and three of his sons executed merely because he was suspicious of their loyalty. When Augustus was informed of this, he said, "It is better to be an animal under Herod, than a son." Even today, in the area around Bethlehem, one can find grottos in which mothers hid with their children in their arms, hoping to save them from Herod's soldiers. Many of them ended up being killed along with the children they were holding. In this murder, the Evangelist sees the fulfillment of Jeremiah 31:15: "A voice was heard in Ramah, lamentation and bitter weeping" (Jer 31:15). In these words, Jeremiah is describing the distress and sorrow of the Jewish nation as it was being led into the Babylonian captivity, as they were first herded to Ramah, a small town of the tribe of Benjamin, north of Jerusalem. A witness of the event, Jeremiah describes it as the cry of the foremother Rachel for her children, as though they were being led to their death. St Matthew sees in this event a foreshadowing of the actual murder of the children of Rachel, who was buried near Bethlehem.

There are no indications of how long the Holy Family stayed in Egypt, since we still do not know the exact year of Christ's birth. But it is clear that they returned soon after the death of Herod, and the date of his death is more or less easy to determine. According to Josephus, Herod died in terrible pain in March or early April in the year 750 from the founding of Rome. If Christ was born on December 25, 749, then the Holy Family remained in Egypt only a few months. However, if Christ was born earlier (as some maintain), in 748, then it is possible they were in Egypt for more than a year, and that the Child was nearly two when they returned. In any case, He was still a child, as the angel called Him in another dream, where he ordered Joseph to return to the land of Israel. Having reached Judea, Joseph was apparently planning to settle in Bethlehem, since it seemed proper for the Son of David, the Christ-Messiah, to reside there. But when he heard that Judea was ruled by the worst of Herod's sons, Archelaus, who was just as bloodthirsty and cruel as his father, he "was afraid to go there" and, after another dream, moved into Galilee to Nazareth, where he had lived before, plying his carpenter's trade.

In this, the Evangelist Matthew sees the fulfillment of the prophecy that the Lord Jesus Christ "shall be called a Nazarene." However, this prophecy is not found in the Old Testament. It has been suggested that this prophecy may be found in a book that has been lost by the Jews. Others think that the Evangelist is not indicating any specific prophecy, but means the general character of all the prophecies that tell of the Messiah's humble circumstances during His earthly life. At that time, to come from Nazareth meant to be humiliated, to be a pariah or an outcast. However, Old Testament Nazarenes were people who had consecrated themselves to God; it is possible that this was the reason Jesus Christ was called a Nazarene, as the Bearer of the highest oaths of the Nazarene—complete consecration of Himself to the service of God.

THE YOUTH OF THE LORD JESUS CHRIST (LUKE 2:40–52)

Before He began His service to mankind, the Lord Jesus Christ remained in anonymity. The only fact we know of this period of His life is given by the Evangelist Luke. Since he wrote his Gospel after careful research, as we have already mentioned, it can be safely assumed that there were no other important moments in Christ's early life. The general character of this period is given by St Luke in these words: "And the Child grew and became strong in spirit, filled with wisdom; and the grace of God was upon Him." This is obvious since the young Jesus was not only God but a man as well, and as a man, He subjected Himself to the usual laws of human development. The whole depth and fullness of divine knowledge within the Child Jesus, the Son of God, only revealed itself in accordance to His physical maturity.

And so, when the young Jesus turned twelve, this divine wisdom first began to be manifested. According to the law (Deut 16:16), all male Jews had to appear in Jerusalem three times a year for the feasts of Passover, Pentecost, and Tabernacles. The only exception was given for children and the sick. When a child turned twelve, he became a "child of the Law," and from that moment he had to learn all the commandments of the law and fulfill all the accompanying rites, including going to Jerusalem for the feasts. St Luke says that the parents of Jesus went to Jerusalem every year. The mystery of the divine birth remained a secret, the Virgin Mary and the elder Joseph did not consider it useful or necessary to reveal it, and in the eyes of the people of Nazareth, Joseph was the husband of Mary and the father of Jesus. The Evangelist Luke even uses these expressions, in deference to common usage. In another place (Luke 3:23), he openly writes that Joseph was only considered to be the father of Jesus (consequently, he actually was not).

The celebration of Passover lasted eight days, after which the pilgrims returned to their homes, usually in groups. Joseph and Mary, therefore, did not immediately notice that the young Jesus had remained in Jerusalem, thinking that He was somewhere in the crowd near them with family members and acquaintances.

Seeing that He took a long time joining them, they began to look for Him, and when they did not find Him, they returned to Jerusalem full of anxiety, and only found Him three days after their departure from Jerusalem, in the temple, sitting with a group of the elders, listening to them and asking them questions. This was happening, most likely, in one of the courts of the temple, where the rabbis would gather to speak with each other and the people, teaching the law to those who wished. In this conversation, the young Jesus already showed His divine wisdom, which is why all who listened were amazed at His answers. The Theotokos, having chided Him for the anxiety He had caused them, calls Joseph His father, as She could call him no other name, since in the eyes of all the people he was the father of Jesus. In response to His Mother's words, Jesus reveals His calling for the first time—to do the will of Him Who sent Him and almost corrects His Mother, indicating that God is His Father, not Joseph: "Why did you seek Me? Did you not know that I must be about My Father's business" in the temple? It is as if He is saying to them: "You should have known where I would be, since as God's Son, I have to be in God's house." They, however, did not understand His words because to them the mystery of Christ's work on earth was not yet fully revealed. Nevertheless, "His Mother kept all these things in Her heart." For Her, this was an especially memorable day, when Her Son first revealed His high calling. Since the time was not yet ripe for His preaching, He obediently followed them to Nazareth and continued to be "subject to them," as St Luke notices, probably plying His earthly father's trade. With His increased age, His wisdom also increased, and for those who were attentive, God's special love for Him was apparent, and this attracted the love of people to Him as well.

Chapter 2

The Public Ministry of the Lord Jesus Christ: Events of His Life Before the First Passover

John the Baptist and His Witness of the Lord Jesus Christ
(Matt 3:1–12; Mark 1:1–8; Luke 3:1–18; John 1:15–31)

All four Evangelists speak about the same general details concerning the public ministry of John the Baptist. Only John leaves out some specifics mentioned in the first three, emphasizing only the divinity of Christ.

The Apostle Luke gives some important information about the exact time that John the Baptist and the Lord Himself began their public ministry. He says that both began "in the fifteenth year of the reign of Tiberius Caesar, Pontius Pilate being governor of Judea, Herod being tetrarch of Galilee, his brother Philip tetrarch of Iturea and the region of Trachonitis, and Lysanias the tetrarch of Abilene, while Annas and Caiaphas were high priests" (Luke 3:1–2).

As he starts his account with the beginning of John's ministry, St Luke is effectively saying that during this time, Palestine was part of the Roman Empire, ruled by four tetrarchs in the name of Emperor Tiberius, stepson and heir of Augustus, during whose reign Christ was born. Judea was ruled by Pontius Pilate instead of the already-mentioned Archelaus. Herod Antipas, son of Herod the Great, ruled Galilee; his brother Philip ruled Iturea, the country on the eastern side of the Jordan River, and Trachonitis, situated northeast of the Jordan. The fourth part of Abilene, adjacent to Galilee at the northeast end, near Lebanon, was ruled by Lysanias. The high priests were Annas and Caiaphas, and this situation must be understood thus: the official high priest was Caiaphas, but his father-in-law Annas, or Ananus, who was relieved of his duties by the Romans, still commanded a great deal of respect and authority among the Jews and basically shared power with Caiaphas.

Tiberius began his reign after the death of Augustus in 767, but two years earlier, in 765, he became co-emperor, and his fifteenth year of rule was thus 779, during which year, most likely, the Lord turned thirty years old; this is mentioned later by St Luke where he indicates the Lord's age when He comes to be baptized by John and begin His public ministry.

St Luke witnesses that John received a special calling from God, or a revelation, that spurred his public ministry. The place where he began to preach was the "desert of Judea, according to St Matthew. This was the western bank of the Jordan and the Dead Sea, called a desert because of the dearth of settlements. After God's call, John began to appear in more settled areas of this region, closer to bodies of water necessary for baptism, for example, in Bethabara[15] (John 1:28) and Aenon near Salim (John 3:23).

The Evangelists Matthew (3:3), Mark (1:3), and Luke (3:4) called John "the voice of one crying in the wilderness: 'Prepare the way of the Lord; Make His paths straight.'" John the Baptist used this appellation to describe himself in the Gospel of John (1:23). These words are taken from the prophecy of Isaiah, where he comforts Jerusalem, saying that the time of its humiliation was coming to an end and soon the Lord would come, "and all flesh shall see it [the salvation of God] together" (Isa 40:5).

This prophecy was fulfilled when, after the seventy-year Babylonian captivity, 42,000 Jews, with the permission of the Persian king Cyrus, returned to their homeland. This return is described by the prophet as a joyful procession, led by God Himself and His harbinger. This forerunner cried out that the desert through which the Lord must walk with His people should be prepared for His coming—the valleys should be filled and the mountains and hills should be leveled. This prophecy is interpreted by both the Evangelists and John the Baptist himself (John 1:23) as a foreshadowing of future events (since all the Old Testament events are foreshadowings of events in the New Testament). The Lord Who walks at the head of His people is the Messiah Himself, and His forerunner is John the Baptist. The desert in this spiritual sense is the chosen people of Israel itself, and the valleys and hills that have to be removed, as hindrances to the coming of the Messiah, are the sins of the people, which is why the essence of the entire ministry of the forerunner can be encapsulated in one message: "Repent!" This foreshadowing in the prophecy of Isaiah is repeated directly by the last of the Old Testament prophets, Malachi, who calls the forerunner who prepares the way of the Lord an "Angel of the Lord," with which citation St Mark actually begins his Gospel (Mark 1:2; see Mal 3:1). John the Baptist explained that the reason for his penitential preaching was the imminent coming of the kingdom of heaven, that is the kingdom of the Messiah (Matt 3:2). The word of God explains that this kingdom is the freedom of man from the authority of sin and the enthronement of righteousness in his inner being (Luke 17:21; Rom 14:17). It is the drawing together of all people who have become worthy into a single organism, the Church. The eternal heavenly glory of this kingdom will be found in the future life. (Luke 23:42–43).

As he prepared the people for entry into this imminent Messianic kingdom, John calls them to repentance, and those who heeded him he baptized with the baptism of repentance for the remission of sins (Matt 3:11; Luke 3:3). This was not the Christian baptism of grace, but only an immersion in water as an expression of the desire of the penitent to be cleansed from his sins, in the same way that the water cleans him from his bodily dirt.

John, a strict ascetic who wore the roughest possible clothing made out of camel hide and who fed himself on a kind of locust and wild honey, presented a picture widely divergent from the kind of spiritual leader to which the Jews had become accustomed. His preaching about the coming kingdom of the Messiah, which at the time was especially eagerly expected by many, could not help but attract universal attention. Even the Jewish historian Josephus wrote that the "people, inspired by the teaching of John, rushed to him in great multitudes,"[16] and the authority of this man was so great over the Jews, that they were ready to follow any counsel he gave them, and even Herod the king was afraid of this authority of the great teacher. Even the Pharisees and Sadducees could not rest easily, seeing the masses of people rushing to visit John, and they themselves came to him in the desert, hardly any of them, however, with sincere desire to hear him. This is why John greets them with harshly antagonistic words: "Brood of vipers! Who warned you to flee from the wrath to come?" (Matt 3:7). The Pharisees skillfully hid their passions through an exact observance of the ritual commandments of the Mosaic Law, while the Sadducees, giving themselves up to physical pleasures, rejected everything that contradicted their epicurean manner of life—the spiritual life entirely, as well as the divine judgment after death. John accuses them for their arrogance, their sureness of their own righteousness, and tells them that the fact that they are sons of Abraham will bring them no benefit, if they bring no fruits worthy of repentance because the tree that brings not forth good fruit is useless and is chopped down and thrown into the fire. True sons of Abraham are not those who are descendants by blood, but those who live in the spirit of his faith and loyalty to God. If you do not repent, God will reject you and will call to Himself new children in the spirit of Abraham (Matt 3:9; Luke 3:8).

According to St Luke, these accusations were directed at the entire assembled crowd. This should not be seen as a contradiction since the people, or at least a majority of them, were infected with the false teachings of the Pharisees. Distressed by the severity of his words, the people asked him: "What shall we do then?" (Luke 3:10). In his answer, John indicates the necessity of doing works of love and compassion and of abstaining from any evil. These are those aforementioned fruits worthy of repentance.

That was the time of the general expectation of the coming Messiah, and the Jews believed that the Messiah, when He comes, will baptize (see John 1:25). It is thus not surprising, that many began to ask the question: "Is John the Messiah?" But John answered these questions in the negative, saying that he baptized in water for repentance (Matt 3:11), that is, as a visible sign of inner repentance, but after him will come one who is greater than he, whose sandal John is not worthy to fasten (Luke 3:16; Mark 1:7) or even to carry (Matt 3:11), as a slave would do for his lord. "He will baptize you with the Holy Spirit and fire." In His baptism, the grace of the Holy Spirit will be present, burning away all sinful impurity. "His winnowing fan is in

His hand." Christ will cleanse His people as a lord purges his harvest of the tares, keeping the pure wheat (those who believe in Him) to gather into His Church, as though in a barn, casting out all who reject Him into eternal suffering.

THE BAPTISM OF THE LORD JESUS CHRIST
(MATT 3:13–17; MARK 1:9–11; LUKE 3:21–22; JOHN 1:32–34)

All four Evangelists write of Christ's baptism. The most detailed account is given by St Matthew.

"Then Jesus came from Galilee"—St Mark adds the detail that Christ came from Nazareth of Galilee. This was, by all accounts, in the same fifteenth year of Tiberius's reign, when according to Luke, Jesus turned thirty, the minimum age for a preacher of the faith. According to St Matthew, John refused to baptize Jesus, saying: "I need to be baptized by You." According to St John, the Baptist did not recognize Jesus before he baptized Him (John 1:33), only realizing Whom he was baptizing when the Spirit of God came down on Him in the form of a dove. Again, there is no contradiction here. John did not know Jesus before the baptism in the sense that he did not know Him for the Messiah, but when Jesus came to him to ask to be baptized, he, as a prophet who could discern the hearts of those who came to him, immediately felt His holiness and sinlessness, His limitless superiority over himself, which is why he resisted baptizing Him, as we see in the Gospel of Matthew. When he saw the Spirit of God descending on Jesus, then he finally knew that before him stood the Messiah-Christ.

"For thus it is fitting for us to fulfill all righteousness." This means that the Lord Jesus Christ, as a man and as the source of the new humanity reborn in Him, must through His own example show people the necessity of fulfilling all of the divine commandments. But, having been baptized, Jesus immediately came out of the water, because since He was sinless, He did not have any need to confess His sins as all the others did, standing in the water and confessing. St Luke writes that Jesus, being baptized, prayed, doubtless asking His Father to bless the beginning of His ministry.

"And behold, the heavens were opened to Him,"—that is, they were opened above Him and for Him,—"and [h]e saw the Spirit of God descending like a dove and alighting upon Him" (Matt 3:16). In the Greek original, it is clear that "he saw" refers to John, but of course He Who was baptized and the entire assembled crowd saw it as well, because the point of this miracle was the revelation of the Son of God in the heretofore anonymous Jesus, which is why the Church sings in the *kontakion* (hymn) to the feast of the Theophany (that is, the "revelation of God"), "today He was revealed to the world." In John's Gospel, the Spirit did not just descend on Jesus, but remained on Him (John 1:32–33).

The voice of God the Father: "You are My beloved Son, in Whom I am well pleased" (with slight variations, Matt 3:17; Luke 3:22; Mark 1:11), was an indication to

St John and the assembled people of the divinity of the One being baptized, the Son of God, the only begotten One on Whom the goodwill of God the Father eternally presides. At the same time, it was an answer to His divine Son's prayer, a blessing for the great labor of the ministry for the salvation of mankind.

Our Church celebrates the baptism of Christ on January 6 from ancient times, calling this feast also the Theophany, since in this event, the Trinity was made manifest to men for the first time—God the Father in the voice from heaven, God the Son being baptized by John in the Jordan, and God the Holy Spirit descending in the form of a dove.

THE FORTY-DAY FAST AND THE TEMPTATION FROM THE DEVIL
(MATT 4:1–11; MARK 1:12–13; LUKE 4:1–13)

These events are mentioned in detail by Matthew and Luke, but Mark only mentions them in passing without any specific details.

After His baptism, Jesus "was led by the Spirit into the wilderness" located between Jericho and the Dead Sea. One of the hills in this wilderness still bears the name Mons Quarantana, or Forty-Day Mountain, since Jesus fasted there for forty days. Immediately following His baptism, the Holy Spirit led Him into the desert to prepare for the great service He was about to perform—the salvation of mankind. On that mountain, He fasted forty days and forty nights, meaning during that time He ate nothing, after which "He was hungry" and at the extreme limit of His physical strength. "When the tempter came to Him" (Matt 4:3), it was the last attack of the devil, because according to Luke he had not stopped tempting the Lord during the entire course of the forty-day fast (Luke 4:2).

What is the purpose of this temptation of the Lord from the devil?

Having come to earth in order to destroy the work of the devil, the Lord could have, of course, destroyed them at once merely with a breath from His lips. However, one must remember that the works of the devil were rooted in the delusions of man's free soul, whom the Lord had come to save without removing from man free will, that greatest gift of God. Man was created not a pawn, not a soulless automaton or an animal guided by irrational instinct, but a rational, free person. If looked at from the reference point of Christ's divinity, this temptation was a battle of the spirit of evil with the Son of God Who came to save mankind, an attempt to preserve his power over men with the help of various illusions of power and happiness. This temptation was similar to the tempting of the Lord that the Israelites allowed themselves to perpetrate in Rephidim (Exod 17:1–7), when they complained of the lack of water: "Is the Lord among us or not?" Thus, the devil begins his temptation with the words, "If You are the Son of God" (Matt 4:3). And just as the psalmist spoke of those Israelites as tempting God in the wilderness, so the devil tempted the Son of God with the intention of irritating, angering, and humiliating Him (Ps 77:40–41). For the most part, these temptations were directed at

Christ's human nature, over which the devil hoped to extend his influence, bending His will to a false path. Christ came to earth to establish His kingdom among men, the kingdom of God. Two paths could lead to this purpose. One was the path desired by most of the Jews at that time—the path of the quick and magnificent enthronement of the Messiah as an earthly king. The other was a slow and difficult path of the moral rebirth of all mankind through their free will, together with much suffering, not only for the followers of the Messiah, but for Him as well. The devil wanted to turn Christ away from the second path, showing Him the illusory ease of the first path, promising Him not suffering, but only glory.

First taking advantage of the hunger torturing Jesus as a man, the devil tried to convince Him to use His divine power to free Himself from the heavy human yoke of hunger. Indicating the rocks, he said, "If You are the Son of God, command that these stones become bread" (Matt 4:3). The devil hoped to tempt Him successfully once, ensuring that Jesus would continue to listen to him thereafter, and would surround Himself with a legion of angels against the masses of His enemies, would come down from the cross or would call Elijah to His aid (Matt 26:53; 27:40, 49), and then the work of human salvation through the passion of the Son of God would come to naught. The God-Man, who made the water into wine and miraculously increased the loaves of bread for others, rejected this evil counsel with the words of Moses spoken with reference to the manna from heaven, with which God fed His nation for forty years in the desert: "Man shall not live by bread alone; but man lives by every word that proceeds from the mouth of the Lord" (Deut 8:3). The "word" of which Moses speaks can be understood as God's goodwill toward all mankind. The Lord performed miracles for the fulfillment of the needs of others, never His own. If, instead of bearing His sufferings, He used His divine power to avoid them, then He could not be an example for us. He could have repeated this miracle often, and thus could have attracted a large mass of people who demanded "bread and circuses," but these people would not have been a good foundation for the free kingdom of God. His purpose was for people to willingly follow Him because of His words, not as slaves who are easily attracted by earthly goods gained cheaply.

Having been defeated in his first attempt, the devil immediately tried a second—he led the Lord to Jerusalem, and having placed Him at the pinnacle of the temple, he offered: "If You are the Son of God, throw Yourself down. For it is written: 'He shall give His angels charge over You,' and 'in their hands they shall bear You up'" (Matt 4:6). Again, such an action would amaze the people assembled in the temple, all of whom were intensely awaiting the Messiah. Such a miracle would have easily attracted a mass of people to Him, and of course, this action would have been completely useless for the moral improvement of the people, and the Lord rejected it with the words: "You shall not tempt the Lord your God," spoken by Moses to the nation of Israel (Deut 6:16), meaning "do not place yourself in danger without need, testing the miraculous power of God's omnipotence."

Then the devil begins his third temptation. From the top of a high hill, he showed Jesus "all the kingdoms of the world, and their glory; and he said to Him, 'All these things will I give You if You will fall down and worship me'" (Matt 4:8–9). St Luke also adds that the devil showed Jesus all the kingdoms of the earth in a moment of time and said, "All this authority I will give You, and their glory; for this has been delivered to me; and I give it to whomever I wish" (Luke 4:6). The devil revealed all the kingdoms of the earth before Jesus, over which he truly did reign as the spirit of hatred. He showed Jesus what power and means he had in this world for the war against God, Who came to the earth to save people from the grasp of the devil. Evidently, he hoped that this spectacle would distress the human spirit of Jesus with fear and doubt in His ability to effect His great work of the salvation of man. Truly, what can be more frightening than the spectacle of an entire world that had willingly given itself up to the authority of the devil? It is as if the devil is saying to the Lord: "You can see what power I have over people; do not get in my way, and in the future, I will be willing to share this power over them with You. All You have to do is enter into an alliance with me. Just bow down to me, and You will be that Messiah that the Jews are expecting." Of course, the devil promised Jesus only an external power over people, while he intended to keep his power over their souls. This is exactly what the Lord did not want, because He taught that He came not for external lordship, not so that He would be served as the lords of the earth are served (John 18:36). Rather, His kingdom is purely spiritual. Thus, the Lord answers the devil in the words of Deuteronomy: "You shall worship the Lord your God, and Him only you shall serve" (Deut 6:13) and sends the devil away from His side, saying, "Away with you, Satan!" By this, He showed that He refused to accept the devil's power over the world because the cosmos belongs to the Lord God, and to Him only is due worship.

"Then the devil left Him" (Matt 4:11), and the Evangelist Luke adds "until an opportune time," because he would soon again tempt Him through people, raising up against Him all possible obstacles (Luke 4:13).

St Mark alone makes an important point that in the wilderness the Lord was with the animals (Mark 1:13). As the New Adam, the wild beasts dared not harm Him, mutely acknowledging Him as their Lord.

THE FIRST DISCIPLES OF CHRIST (JOHN 1:35–51)

After the temptation from the devil, the Lord Jesus Christ once again went to the Jordan to John. In the meantime, before His arrival, John the Baptist gave a new, triumphant witness to Him before the Pharisees, but now speaking of Him not as imminent, but as the Messiah Who has come. Only John speaks about this in his first chapter (John 1:19–34). The Jews sent priests and Levites to John to ask whether or not he was the Christ, because according to their expectation, only the Messiah would baptize. And "he confessed, and did not deny, but confessed, 'I am not the Christ.'" When they asked him whether he was a prophet, he answered, calling himself the "voice of one crying in the wilderness," stressing that his baptism by water was only a preparation, and in order to deflect all other questions, he triumphantly declared, "there stands One among you, whom you do not know." He will begin His ministry after me, but He has eternal being and divinity, while I am unworthy even to be called His slave. This witness was given in Bethabara, where a large amount of people had gathered to be baptized by John (John 1:26–28).

On the next day, when after being tempted, Jesus once again came to the Jordan, John uttered this magnificent witness, calling him "the Lamb of God, Who takes away the sin of the world," and attesting that this is the One of Whom he preached, and that he was assured that this is the One Who will baptize with the Holy Spirit, since he saw the Spirit descending from heaven as a dove and alighting on Him (John 1:29–34).

On the next day after this personal witness, John once again stood on the banks of the Jordan with two of his disciples. Jesus was also walking there. Having seen the Lord, John once again repeats his previous witness, saying "Behold the Lamb of God!" (John 1:36). By calling him the Lamb, John refers to the wonderful prophecy of Isaiah in chapter 53, where the Messiah is presented in the form of a lamb who is led to the slaughter, a lamb who is voiceless before his shearers (53:7). Consequently, the main purpose of this witness is to indicate that Christ is a victim brought in sacrifice by God for the sins of people. But in the words "who takes away the sin of the world," this sacrificial living victim is also shown as High Priest, Who offers Himself as a sacrifice. He has taken upon Himself the sins of the world and offers Himself as a sacrifice for the world.

When they heard John's words, the two disciples followed Jesus to the place where He lived, and spent some time with Him from the tenth hour (around 4 p.m.) until the late evening, listening to His preaching. They were completely convinced that He was the Messiah (John 1:38–41). One of these disciples was Andrew, while the other was John the Evangelist himself, who never mentions himself by name in those events in which he took part. Having returned home after this conversation with the Lord, Andrew told his brother Simon that he and John had found the Messiah (John 1:41). Thus, St Andrew was not only the first-called disciple of Christ, as it is traditional to call him, but he was also the first to preach Christ to the future first among the apostles. When Andrew brought his brother to Christ, He, looking at Simon with His discerning glance, called him Cephas, which means (as the Evangelist himself explains) "rock," *petros* in Greek.

The next day after Andrew and John's visit, the Lord wanted to go to Galilee and called Philip to follow Him, and Philip, having found his friend Nathaniel, desired him to follow Christ as well, and told him, "We have found Him of Whom Moses in the law, and also the prophets, wrote—Jesus of Nazareth, the son of Joseph." Nathaniel, however, answered, "Can anything good come out of

Nazareth?" Apparently, Nathaniel shared the general prejudice that Christ, as a magnificent king, will come and reveal Himself in glory among the elites of Jerusalem. Galilee, in contrast, had a very bad reputation among the Jews, and Nazareth in particular, a small city that is never even once mentioned in the Scriptures of the Old Testament, was not imagined by anyone to be the birthplace of the Messiah promised by the prophets. However, the faithful soul of Philip did not find it necessary to contradict this prejudice. Instead, Philip offered Nathaniel to test the validity of his words for himself. "Come and see!" he said. Nathaniel, a sincere and honest man, desiring to see if his friend was speaking the truth, immediately went to see the Lord. And the Lord witnessed to the simplicity and lack of guile in his soul, saying to him: "Behold, an Israelite indeed, in whom is no deceit!" Nathaniel had no idea where the Lord could have known him, since he sees Him for the first time. And then the Lord, in order to dispel his doubts permanently, hinted at a certain mysterious circumstance whose meaning was known by no one but Nathaniel himself: ". . . when you were under the fig tree, I saw you." What happened to Nathaniel under the fig tree? This is hidden from us, and it seems that this was a mystery that no one could possibly know other than Nathaniel and God Himself. And this amazed Nathaniel so much that all his doubts in Jesus immediately melted away. He understood that before him stood not just a man, but someone gifted with divine omniscience, and he immediately believed in Jesus as the divine Messiah, expressing this by his exclamation, so full of fiery faith: "Rabbi (meaning "teacher"), You are the Son of God! You are the King of Israel!" (John 1:49). It has been suggested that Nathaniel had a custom of regular prayer under a certain fig tree, and he probably felt some especially strong emotions during prayer that he would never forget, and that no one else could have known about. This is why the words of the Lord awoke in him such a strong faith in Him as the Son of God, to Whom the hidden states of the human soul are revealed.

The Lord, answering this exclamation of Nathaniel, addressing now not only Nathaniel but all His followers, said: "Most assuredly, I say to you, hereafter you shall see heaven open, and the angels of God ascending and descending upon the Son of Man." With these words, the Lord wanted to tell His disciples that they would see His glory with their spiritual eyes, that the ancient prophecy of the ladder bringing together heaven and earth, which Jacob saw in a dream (Gen 28:11–17), was fulfilled through the Incarnation of the Son of God, who has now become the "Son of Man." The Lord calls Himself with this name often (in the Gospels, we can count at least eighty examples). Through this, Christ positively and indubitably affirmed His humanity, while at the same time underlining that His was an ideal, universal, absolute humanity, since He was the Second Adam, the source of the new humanity, which was to be renewed by Him through His passion and death on the cross. In this way, the name "Son of Man" not only indicates Christ's voluntary humility but also expresses the exalted state of His humanity, indicating that

He is the ideal manifestation of human nature, Man as His Creator and God intended Him to be.

The First Miracle at the Wedding in Cana of Galilee (John 2:1–12)

Only St John writes of the first miracle of the Lord Jesus Christ—turning the water into wine in Cana of Galilee. This miracle occurred on the third day after Philip and Nathaniel's calling. Jesus Christ was invited to a marriage feast in Cana, a small distance about two or three hours on foot north of Nazareth. This was the hometown of Nathaniel; it was called "of Galilee" to distinguish it from a different Cana, near Tyre. Jesus was invited as a mere man, an acquaintance of the family. Jesus's Mother was there, and probably She had arrived earlier. The family was most likely not well-to-do, which would explain the lack of wine during the celebration. The most holy Virgin Mary took an active part, knowing how such a circumstance could ruin everyone's simple pleasure at the family celebration. Her soul, full of compassion, showed Her first example of mediation and intercession for the sake of others before Her divine Son. "They have no wine," She said to Him, doubtless anticipating that He would help these people through a miracle. He answered, "Woman, what does Your concern have to do with Me?" It is pointless to see any lack of respect in this expression, "Woman." This was a typical mode of reference in the East. Even during His most painful moments of suffering on the cross, the Lord uses this same expression when speaking to His Mother, delivering Her care to the beloved disciple (John 19:26). "My hour has not yet come." The time was not yet ripe for the miracles to begin, perhaps because there was still some wine left. In any case, it is obvious from the subsequent words of the most holy Virgin Mary to the servants: "Whatever He says to you, do it," that She did not see the Lord's words as an outright denial of Her request. There were six stone urns that were used for ritual cleansing mandated by the law, such as washing one's hands before and after eating. They were very large in size, because the "measure" mentioned in the text would probably be the equivalent of one and a half large buckets of water. In other words, the total amount of water could have exceeded twenty-five buckets, making Christ's miracle all the more amazing. Jesus told the servants to fill these urns with water to the brim, so that they would become eyewitnesses to the miracle. "Draw some out now, and take it to the governor of the feast," in order to convince this governor as well in the truth of this miracle. This miracle, apparently, was performed by the Lord even without touching the water, at a distance, as it were, which is a vivid manifestation of His divine power.

St John Chrysostom explains it thus: "He did this in order to show that He is the One who makes water into grapes and makes the rain into wine through the root of the vine, something that in the natural world happens over a long period of time, but here is done in one instant at the wedding."[17]

Since he did not know where this new wine came from, the governor of the feast calls the groom, unwittingly witnessing to the miracle with his words and even underlining that the miraculously transmuted wine was of the best quality. However, it is completely incorrect to make the assumption that his words "when the guests have well drunk" indicates that all the people present at the wedding were drunk. This is said of a general rule, but not of this particular situation. It is well known that the Jews were remarkable for their moderation in drinking wine, which in Palestine was a common drink usually mixed with water; to become drunk was considered completely inappropriate. Of course, the Lord Jesus Christ would never have taken part in any feast where there could be a large gathering of people drinking heavily. The purpose of the feast was to give joy to these poor folk who gave all they had to celebrate a family feast, and in this we see only the goodness of the Lord. The Evangelist John explicitly says that this was the first miracle of the Lord as He began His public ministry with the purpose of revealing His glory as the Son of God, and to establish the faith of His followers. After this miracle, the entire holy family traveled to Capernaum in order to begin their journey from there to Jerusalem for the feast of the Passover.

 CHAPTER 3

The First Passover of the Public Ministry of the Lord Jesus Christ

CASTING OUT THE MERCHANTS FROM THE TEMPLE (JOHN 2:13–25)

The first three Evangelists do not speak very clearly about the Lord's travels to Jerusalem; they only give detailed accounts of His last pilgrimage for the Passover, before which He suffered. Only St John gives details about every one of the Passover pilgrimages to Jerusalem during the course of His three years of public ministry, as well as His pilgrimages for other feasts in the Jewish calendar. It was natural for the Lord to be in Jerusalem for the so-called pilgrim feasts because Jerusalem was the center of the spiritual life of the Jewish nation, and during the feasts a great multitude of people from all over Palestine and the nearby countries gathered together. Also, it was important for the Lord to reveal Himself as the Messiah in Jerusalem, in the spiritual center.

The casting out of the merchants described by John in the beginning of his Gospel is a different event from a similar casting out described by the Synoptics. The first was in the beginning of the public ministry of the Lord, before the first Passover, while the second occurred in the very end of His ministry, before the fourth Passover.

From Capernaum, the Lord, together with His disciples, went to Jerusalem for the feast of the Passover, not only because of religious duty but also to fulfill the will of Him Who sent Him, in order to continue the work of the Messiah begun in Galilee. There were no less than two million Jews in Jerusalem for the feast, and all of them were required to slaughter the Paschal lamb and to offer sacrifices in the temple. According to Josephus, in the year A.D. 63, the priests in the temple sacrificed 256,500 Paschal lambs, not counting other chattel and birds brought as ritual sacrifices. For the sake of convenience, the Jews converted the so-called Court of the Gentiles into a marketplace—they gathered all kinds of sacrificial animals, arranged cages with birds, put up stands for selling everything necessary for bringing sacrifices, and even set up money-changing stations. At that time, Roman coins were used in general circulation, but the law required that any donations to the temple must be paid by the Jewish shekel. The Jews who came to the temple needed to change their currency, and this exchange was very lucrative for the money changers. Looking for an easy profit, the Jews bartered in other objects as well, some of which had absolutely nothing to do with temple sacrifices, such as beasts of burden. The high priests themselves were breeders of pigeons, to be sold at a steep price.

The Lord, having made a whip out of rope that was perhaps used to tie the animals, herded the sheep and oxen out of the temple, threw the money on the ground, upended the tables of exchange, and said to those selling pigeons: "Take these things away! Do not make My Father's house a house of merchandise!" By calling God His Father, Jesus declared Himself the Son of God openly for the first time. No one dared to stand against the divine authority He revealed since apparently John's witness concerning Him had already reached Jerusalem, and in any case, the consciences of the merchants spoke against them. He was challenged only when He came to the doves, and by doing so dared lay His hands on the financial interests of the high priests: "What sign do You show us, since You do these things?" Jesus answered and said to them, "Destroy this temple, and in three days I will raise it up," and the Evangelist John explains, Jesus has in mind "the temple of His body." It is as if He said to the Jews: "You are asking Me for a sign? It will be given you, but not now. When you will destroy the temple of My body, I will raise it up in three days and this will be a sign to you of the authority with which I do these things."

The Jews did not understand that Jesus was foretelling His death and resurrection with these words. They understood His words literally, thinking He meant the actual Jerusalem temple, and they tried to use this to raise up the masses against Him.

As an aside, it is important to note that the Greek verb *egerô*, translated as "I will raise up" in English, actually means "I will wake up," which of course could not possibly be used in reference to a building, but makes much more sense when referring to a person in a deep sleep. It was proper for the Lord to speak of His Body as a temple, since His divinity came to dwell in His body through the incarnation. Since He was in the temple, it was especially appropriate for Jesus to speak of His Body as a temple. After that moment, whenever the Pharisees demanded a sign from Him, He answered that they would receive no other sign except the sign of the Prophet Jonah—the three-day burial and resurrection. Keeping this in mind, the Lord's words to the Jews could be understood thus:

"It is not enough for you to defile the House of my Father, made by hands, making it into a house of merchandise; your hatred results even in the crucifixion and extermination of My Body. But if you do this, you will then see the sign that will strike fear into My enemies—I will raise up My Body, dead and buried, in three days."

However, the Jews focused on the literal meaning of Christ's words in order to prove them foolish and impossible. They laughingly said that the temple was built in forty-six years. How could He raise it up in three days? Here they are speaking of the temple of Herod, the augmented Second Temple, which was begun in year 734 from the founding of Rome, or fifteen years before the birth of Christ. The forty-sixth year falls exactly on year 780 from the founding of Rome, which is exactly the year of this first Passover of Christ's preaching. Even the disciples only understood these words of Christ when He rose from the dead and "opened their understanding that they might comprehend the Scriptures" (Luke 24:45).

Later, the Evangelist John writes that during the whole course of the feast of Passover, Christ performed miracles, and many believed in Him because of the miracles, but "Jesus did not commit Himself to them." He put no trust in them, because faith that is founded only on miracles, without being warmed by love for Christ, cannot be considered true, abiding faith. The Lord knew all, and He knows what was hidden in the soul of every person, since He is omniscient God, and so He did not trust the words alone of those who confessed faith in Him after seeing His miracles.

THE CONVERSATION WITH NICODEMUS (JOHN 3:1–21)

The casting out of the merchants from the Temple and the miracles performed in Jerusalem had such a profound effect on the Jews that even one of the rulers of the Jews, a member of the Sanhedrin named Nicodemus, came to Jesus at night, evidently desiring to hear Him preach, but afraid to attract the scorn of his brothers in the Sanhedrin, who were already antagonistic to the Lord. Having come to the Lord, Nicodemus calls Him "Rabbi," thus acknowledging His right to teach, a right that the scribes and Pharisees did not ascribe to Jesus, since He did not finish a rabbinical school. This in itself already showed Nicodemus's disposition toward the Lord. He then calls Him a "teacher come from God," acknowledging that His miracles were performed by the power of God. He said this not only because this was his personal opinion but also on behalf of all the Jews who believed in the Lord, perhaps including some from among the Pharisees and the Sanhedrin, although doubtless the majority of these were already antagonistic to the Lord. This entire conversation is very interesting because it is directed at the undoing of all the false and fantastical views that the Pharisees held regarding the kingdom of God and the conditions for entry into this kingdom. The conversation can be divided into three parts: (1) Spiritual rebirth as the main condition for entry into the kingdom of God; (2) the redemption of mankind through the Passion on the cross of the Son of God, without which no man would be able to inherit the kingdom of God; and (3) the meaning of judgment over those who do not believe in the Son of God.

The Pharisee of that time was the personification of the most narrow and fanatical type of nationalism. "I am not like other men" (see Luke 18:11). The Pharisee considered himself to be a foremost and most-esteemed member of the kingdom of the Messiah just by virtue of his being a Jew, and especially thanks to his being of the Pharisee sect. The Messiah, according to the Pharisees, would be a Jew similar to them who would free the Jews from the rule of the Gentiles and would establish a universal kingdom in which the Jews would take all the ruling positions. Nicodemus apparently shared these pharisaical views, although deep in his soul he felt them to be possibly wrong. It occurred to him that Jesus, this wonderful Person of Whom so many rumors were spreading, was the long-awaited Messiah. So he decided to come to Him on his own in order to make sure. The Lord began their conversation by immediately shattering this image of the Messiah-King.

"Most assuredly, I say to you, unless one is born again, he cannot see the kingdom of God." In other words, it is not enough to be born a Jew; what is necessary is complete moral rebirth, which is given a person from above, from God. A man must be, as it were, born a second time, become a new creation (which is the entire essence of Christianity). Since the Pharisees imagined the kingdom of the Messiah to be an earthly kingdom, it is not surprising that Nicodemus understood the Lord's words in an earthly manner, as though a person would need to be physically born a second time, and expressing his frustration with these words, he said: "How can a man be born when he is old? Can he enter a second time into his mother's womb and be born?"

Jesus explained that He was not speaking of physical birth, but of a special spiritual birth, which differs both in purpose and in fruits from birth in the flesh. This is the birth in water and the Spirit. The water here is the means, and the Holy Spirit is the Power that effects a new birth, since He is the Source of the new creation: "Unless one is born of water and the Spirit, he cannot enter the kingdom of God." This new birth is also different from the physical in its fruits: "That which is born of the flesh is flesh"; when a man is born from his parents, he inherits from them Adam's ancestral sin which is hidden in the very flesh, he thinks carnally and he feeds his carnal lusts and desires. That which is lacking in the physical birth is healed in the spiritual rebirth. Whoever receives rebirth from the Spirit enters a new, spiritual life that raises him above all that is fleshly and sensible.

Seeing that Nicodemus still did not understand, the Lord began to explain to him what the birth from the Spirit consists of, comparing the possibility of this rebirth with the wind: "The wind blows where it wishes, and you hear the sound of it, but cannot tell where it comes from and where it goes. So is everyone who is born of the Spirit." In other words, the spiritual rebirth of man is evident only in the change that occurs within the actual person, while the power that effects the rebirth and the ways in which it does so are all mysterious and beyond a person's comprehension. This is similar to a situation when we feel the wind in our face and hear its "voice," but where it comes from and where it is going we have no idea because its ways are completely outside our will and desire. In the same way, the action of the Spirit of God that gives us new life is apparent and palpable, but at the same time mysterious and inexplicable.

Nicodemus persisted in his lack of comprehension, and in his question ("How can these things be?") there is a note of doubt in the words of Jesus, as well as his pharisaical pride in his expectation that he should be able to understand and explain everything. The Lord immediately strikes down this pharisaical arrogance with full force in His answer, so much so that Nicodemus no longer dared to argue, and in this moral humiliation little by little his heart was preparing the soil where later the seeds of the Lord's salvific teaching would sprout and bear fruit. "Are you the teacher of Israel, and do not know these things?" With these words, the Lord is accusing not so much Nicodemus as the entire sect of the Pharisees, which, taking the keys of understanding the kingdom of God, neither use them to enter nor allow anyone else to enter. How could the Pharisees not know the teaching of the necessity for spiritual rebirth, when even in the Old Testament we constantly encounter the idea of the necessity of the renewal of a person, of God giving man a heart of flesh instead of a heart of stone (Ezek 36:26). Even David prayed: "Make me a clean heart, O God, and renew a right spirit within me" (Ps 50:12).

The Lord then continues to the revelation concerning Himself and His kingdom, and tells Nicodemus that He Himself and His disciples preach a different faith, one that is established in the direct knowledge and contemplation of the truth: "We speak what We know and testify what We have seen, and you do not receive Our witness," meaning the Pharisees, the teachers of Nicodemus.

"If I have told you earthly things and you do not believe, how will you believe if I tell you heavenly things?" By "earthly things," He means the already-mentioned spiritual rebirth, since its necessity and its results are both evident in the person and can be experienced, while "heavenly things" refer to the highest mysteries of God that are higher than any human vision or understanding, including the pre-eternal council of the Trinity, the redeeming labor of the Son of God, taken upon Himself, the union between divine mercy and divine justice in this work of redemption. What happens within man, one is at least partially able to understand. But who among people can raise himself up to heaven and enter the mysteries of the divine life? No one but the Son of Man, Who came down to earth without leaving the heavens: "No one has ascended to heaven but He Who came down from heaven, that is, the Son of Man Who is in heaven."

With these words, the Lord reveals to Nicodemus the mystery of His Incarnation. His intention is to convince Nicodemus that He is greater than a mere prophet of God, that His appearance on earth in the form of the Son of Man is a self-abasement from a higher state to a lower, humble one, because His eternal being is not on earth, but in heaven.

Then the Lord reveals the mystery of His redemptive work to Nicodemus: "And as Moses lifted up the serpent in the wilderness, even so must the Son of Man be lifted up." Why must the Son of Man be lifted up on the cross for the salvation of men? This is exactly that "heavenly thing" that cannot be understood by a carnal mind-set. The Lord indicates the bronze serpent raised by Moses in the desert as a foreshadowing of His suffering on the cross. Moses raised up this serpent so that the Hebrews, as they were being bitten by poisonous snakes, could be healed by looking up at the serpent. In the same way, all of mankind, stricken by the wound of sin living in its flesh, receives healing when it looks with faith at Christ, who came "in the likeness of sinful flesh" (Rom 8:3). The death that the Son of God suffers upon the cross is grounded in God's love for mankind: "For God so loved the world that He gave His only begotten Son, that whoever believes in Him should not perish but have everlasting life." Eternal life is wrought in the person through the grace of the Holy Spirit, while access to the altar of grace (Heb 4:16) is given the people by the redemptive death of Jesus Christ.

The Pharisees thought that the work of Christ would be judgment over all the other nations. The Lord explains that He is now sent not to judge, but to save the world. Those who do not believe will condemn themselves because this lack of faith will reveal their love for the darkness and hatred for the light, which come from their love for evil deeds. Those who do the works of the truth, moral and upright souls, go toward the light of their own accord, not fearing to be condemned for their actions.

The Last Witness of St John the Baptist Concerning Jesus Christ (John 3:22–36)

After the conversation with Nicodemus, which occurred in Jerusalem during the Passover, the Lord left Jerusalem and came "into the land of Judea; and there He remained with them and baptized." Here we see an important indication from the Evangelist John about Christ's rather lengthy stay in the southernmost part of Palestine—the region called Judea. This entire sojourn is not mentioned in any of the Synoptic Gospels. We can safely calculate the length of the stay based on subsequent words of Christ to His disciples, when they were already in Samaria: "Do you not say, 'There are still four months and then comes the harvest'?" (John 3:35). From these words, one can conclude that the Lord returned to Galilee four months before the harvest, and since harvest in Palestine usually occurs in April, then the Lord left Palestine no earlier than November. Thus, He stayed in Judea no less than eight months, from April to November. The first three Evangelists say nothing of this first period of the public ministry of the Lord Jesus Christ, and having begun with His baptism and temptation in the wilderness, they all proceed to speak of His preaching in Galilee. St Matthew, since he was called by the Lord much later, was naturally not a witness of any of the events that occurred in Judea. It is also likely that St Peter was not present during this period, from whose words we know St Mark wrote his Gospel. Apparently, St Luke did not have enough eyewitness accounts to include this period in his Gospel either. St John thus found it necessary to add these events, since he was present at all of them. There is nothing to suggest that the Lord lived only in one place in Judea during this time; rather, one must assume that He traveled throughout the region, preaching.

"And [he] baptized." Later, in the fourth chapter of his Gospel, St John explicitly mentions that Jesus did *not* baptize, but His disciples did (John 4:2). This baptism was in no way different from the baptism of John. It was a ritual cleansing, not a baptism of grace, since the disciples did not yet have the Holy Spirit: "for the Holy Spirit was not yet given, because Jesus was not yet glorified" (John 7:39). They received the instruction to perform Christian baptism—in the name of the Father, the Son, and the Holy Spirit—directly from the Lord after He had risen from the dead (Matt 28:19).

During this time, St John the Baptist continued to baptize in Aenon near Salim, in a place that is hard to determine precisely, but apparently was not near the Jordan; otherwise, there would have been no reason to add the words: "because there was much water there" (John 3:23). The disciples of John soon noticed that fewer people were coming to hear their master, and in their blind and irrational attachment to him, they were sorrowful and began to envy Him Who had more success with the people, the Lord Jesus Christ. Doubtless these unkind feelings were only stoked by the Pharisees when they began an argument about purification, which led to a comparison between the worth of John's baptism and the worth of the baptism performed by the disciples of Jesus. Desiring to tell their master of their envy of Christ, the disciples of John came to him and said: "Rabbi, He who was with you beyond Jordan, to whom you have testified—behold, He is baptizing [meaning on His own, not together with John], and all are coming to Him!" ("all" here is obvious hyperbole, intended to provoke envy in John).

Of course, John was foreign to any envy toward Christ, and in his answer he directly begins to reveal the greatness of Christ compared to his own, and gives a new, a last, triumphant witness to the divinity of Christ. While upholding Jesus's right to baptize, John said that no one of those sent by God can ever ascribe to himself anything that is not given to him from heaven, and so if Jesus baptizes, then He has the authority to do this from God Himself. John reminds his disciples of what he said from the beginning, that he was not the Christ, calling Jesus "the bridegroom," and himself "the friend of the bridegroom" who does not envy the bridegroom his joy, but stands with Him, ready to serve, and rejoices with great joy when he hears His voice. The union of God with His faithful in the Old Testament as well as in the Church of the New Testament is often described through the image of a marriage feast (Isa 54:5–6; 62:5; Eph 5:23–27). Christ is the Bridegroom of the Church, while John is His friend, His trusted one, who can only be full of joy at the success of the Bridegroom. Among the Jews, the groom's friend, the "best man," if you will, was a very important figure in the days before the wedding, and as soon as the wedding was performed, and the groom had become a husband, his friend no longer had a position to play. The same happened to John. He was the most important figure in the time of preparation for the coming of Christ. When Christ began the work of His public ministry, the role of John was diminished. This is why he said, "He must increase, but I must decrease." The light of the morning star slowly fades away as the sun rises.

Confessing Christ's greatness in reference to himself, John said that Christ is "He who comes from above" and so "is above all." He is greater than all other people and even other chosen ones of God, such as John himself. Since John had an earthly birth, he could witness to divine truth only as much as any human being could, but the Christ who comes from heaven can witness to the heavenly and the divine, since these things He sees and hears directly, and no mortal man is capable of accepting His testimony without the grace of God (Matt 16:17; John 6:44).

With sorrow at his disciples' ill will, John praises those who accepted the testimony of Christ, for Christ announces the words of God Himself to mankind, and whoever accepts His words as true, accepts as true the words of God the Father. God the Father gave His Son Jesus Christ the gifts of the Holy Spirit in abundance, more than can ever be measured, for He loves His Son and gives everything into His hands. Thus, whoever believes in His Son, the Lord Jesus Christ, will have eternal life, while whoever does not believe in Him will not see eternal life, but "the wrath of God abides on him."

Thus, having completed his ministry, John for the last time witnessed triumphantly to the divinity of Christ, exhorting all to follow after Christ. These words can be seen as the last testament of the greatest of the prophets.

St John Is Imprisoned (Matt 14:3–5; Mark 6:17–20; Luke 3:19–20)

Soon after this, John was seized and imprisoned because he rebuked King Herod Antipas for his unlawful cohabitation with Herodias, the wife of his brother Philip. This is only mentioned in the Synoptics. Herod Antipas, the son of Herod the Great, ruled over Galilee and Perea. He was married to the daughter of the Arabian King Aretas IV, but he began an affair with Herodias, who was unhappy with her marriage to Philip. She openly went to live in Herod's palace, sending away his lawful wife. The dishonored Aretas gathered an army to punish Herod. Herod himself had to leave to the fortress at Machaerus to the east of the Dead Sea, where he personally commanded his armies. There he heard of John as a prophet who attracted great multitudes, and hoping to find John willing to support his cause, he sent for him. But instead of the expected support, he heard an unpleasant accusation: "It is not lawful for you to have your brother's wife." These words were especially hateful to Herodias, who used all her influence to convince Herod to kill John. But Herod, afraid of the people, decided not to kill John, only to keep him in the fortress of Machaerus. According to St Mark, Herod even respected John as a righteous and holy man, and acted according to his counsel in many situations.

Apparently, as is the case with all weak-willed people, he was trying to buy off his conscience, hoping to lessen his great sin by fulfilling some small good deeds. He even listened to John with pleasure, but he refused to stop sinning with Herodias, and in the final reckoning, to please evil Herodias, he imprisoned John permanently. Thus ended the ministry of John, the last of the Old Testament prophets.

THE DEPARTURE OF THE LORD TO GALILEE AND HIS CONVERSATION WITH THE SAMARITAN WOMAN (MATT 4:12; MARK 1:14; LUKE 4:14; JOHN 4:1–42)

All four Evangelists write of the Lord's departure to Galilee. Saints Matthew and Mark note that this was done after John was put in prison, while St John adds that the reason he left was the widespread rumor that Jesus was gathering even more disciples than John and baptizing, although, as St John clarifies, the disciples did the baptizing, not Jesus. After John was imprisoned, all the enmity of the Pharisees was directed at Jesus, Whom they now considered more dangerous than John. Since it was not yet time for Jesus to suffer, He left Judea and went into Galilee in order to avoid the persecution of His envious enemies. The conversation He had with the Samaritan woman on the way to Galilee is only found in the Gospel of John.

The Lord's path lay through Samaria, north of Judea, land belonging to three tribes of Israel—Dan, Ephraim, and Manasseh. The city of Samaria used to be the capital of the Kingdom of Israel. The Assyrian king Shalmaneser defeated this kingdom, led the Israelites into captivity and, instead of them, he settled the region with pagans from Babylon and other places. These people intermarried with the remaining Jews, and their descendants were the Samaritans, who accepted the Pentateuch of Moses and worshipped the God of Abraham, but also continued to worship their pagan gods. When the Hebrews returned from the Babylonian captivity and began to rebuild the temple in Jerusalem, the Samaritans wished to take part in the project, but they were barred by the Jews. So they built themselves another temple on Mount Chorazin. Having accepted the Torah, the Samaritans rejected the writings of the prophets and all oral tradition. For this, the Jews considered them worse than pagans, scorning any sort of association with them and despising them.

As they walked through Samaria, the Lord and His disciples stopped to rest near a well which, according to tradition, was dug by Jacob, near the city of Shechem, called Sychar by the Evangelist John. It is possible that this discrepancy in names comes from a Jewish pun on the word *shichar*, meaning "he made him drunk," or *shecher*, meaning "falsehood." The Evangelist writes that it was near the sixth hour, which is midday, the time of the worst heat, necessitating their stopping to rest.

"A woman of Samaria came" to take water from the well. The disciples of Jesus in the meantime had gone into the city to buy food, and He addressed the woman with a request: "Give Me a drink." Recognizing that He was a Jew by His manner of speaking and His clothing, the Samaritan woman expressed her surprise at being addressed by a Jew, since the Jews hated and despised the Samaritans so much. But Jesus, Who came into the world to save all, not only the Jews, explained to her that she would not have been surprised if she knew Who it was that was speaking to her, and what a joy (the gift of God) God was sending her in this chance meeting. If she knew Who it was that asked her to drink, then she herself would have asked Him to satisfy her spiritual thirst, to reveal to her that truth that all men seek, and He would give her "living water," which one must understand to mean the grace of the Holy Spirit (see John 7:38–39).

The Samaritan woman did not understand the Lord. By "living water," she understood Him to mean the source at the bottom of the well, and so she asks Jesus where He could have this living water, since He had no vessel with which to draw the water, and the well was very deep. "Are You greater than our father Jacob, which gave us the well, and drank from it himself, as well as his sons and his livestock?" With pride she remembers the Patriarch Jacob, who left this well for the use of his descendants. Then the Lord calls her to a higher understanding of His words: "Whoever drinks of this water will thirst again, but whoever drinks of the water that I shall give him will never thirst. But the water that I shall give him will become in him a fountain of water springing up into everlasting life." In the spiritual life, the water of grace has a different effect than physical water on the body. Whoever is filled with the grace of the Holy Spirit already feels no spiritual thirst because all of his spiritual needs have been completely satisfied. But he who drinks earthly water, and one who satisfies his earthly needs, satisfies his thirst only for a time, and soon thirsts again. Moreover, the living water will remain inside the man, making him a source that rushes (literally, from the Greek "leaps") into eternal life, allowing the person to partake of life eternal.

But the woman continued to misunderstand the Lord. Thinking that He was still speaking of plain water but with some unusual qualities that quench thirst permanently, she asks the Lord to give her this water so that she would no longer need to come to the well. Desiring to help her understand that she was not speaking to a mere man, the Lord at first told her to call her husband, then openly accuses her of living in sin with a man, after already being married five times. Seeing that this man was a prophet who knows those things that are hidden, she takes the opportunity to ask Him the question that bothered the Samaritans most of all during that time. Who was right in the eternal argument with the Jews? Who was right about the proper place for worshipping God? Was it the Samaritans, who worshipped God in the temple they built on Mount Gerizim, or was it the Jews, who insisted that worship was only proper in the temple at Jerusalem? The Samaritans chose Chorazin, citing the words of Moses in Deuteronomy, that blessings should be uttered in this mountain (Deut 11:29). And although their temple, built on top of the mountain, had been destroyed by Hyrcanus in 130 B.C. before the birth of Christ, they continued to bring sacrifices to the place of the destroyed temple. The Lord answered this controversial question with the assertion that it is incorrect to think that God can only be worshipped in one place. This question would soon lose all meaning because both the Jews and Samaritans would cease their worship in the near future. This happened historically when the Samaritans, ravaged by wars, finally abandoned Chorazin as a holy site, and Jerusalem was destroyed in A.D. 70 by the Romans, the Temple razed to the ground. However, the Lord does give preference to the Jewish religious observance, meaning of course that the Samaritans, who only accepted the Torah, rejected the prophets in which the teaching of the person and kingdom of the Messiah is described in such detail. Even salvation itself "is of the Jews," since the Redeemer of mankind would come from the nation of Israel.

Then the Lord, developing this thought, indicates that soon the time will come (and indeed, it has come already, since the Messiah has appeared) for a new, higher form of worship, which will not be limited by any specific place but will be everywhere, for it will be performed in spirit and in truth. Only such worship is proper since it corresponds to the nature of God Himself, Who is Spirit. To worship God in spirit and in truth means to strive to fulfill His will not only externally, through the bringing of sacrifices as did the Jews and Samaritans both, thinking that this was the essence of worship, but truly and sincerely striving toward God as to a Spirit, with all the powers of one's spiritual being, to know God and to love God, to guilelessly and genuinely desire to please Him through the fulfillment of His commandments. Worshipping God in spirit and in truth of course does not disregard the external ritual, as some false teachers and sectarians try to prove, but rather it places such worship first in importance. There is nothing reprehensible in the external, ritual form of worship; it is necessary and unavoidable since man is created not only as a soul but also as a body. Jesus Christ Himself worshipped God the Father with His body, praying on His knees and prostrating His face to the ground, and He did not reject a similar form of worship of Himself during His earthly life (see Matt 2:11; 14:33; 15:22; John 11:21; 12:3; and many other places).

Seemingly beginning to understand the meaning of Jesus's words, the Samaritan woman said, deep in thought, "I know that Messiah is coming" (who is called Christ). "When He comes, He will tell us all things." The Samaritans also expected the Messiah, whom they called Taheb, citing certain passages in the Pentateuch, including Genesis 49:10, Numbers 24, and especially Moses's words in Deuteronomy 18:18. Their understanding of the Messiah was not as distorted as that of the Jews. They believed He would be a prophet, unlike the political leader expected by the Jews. Thus Jesus, who for a long time would not refer to Himself as the Messiah before the Jews, directly says to this simple-hearted Samaritan woman that He is that promised Messiah: "I Who speak to you am He." In ecstatic joy at seeing the Messiah, the Samaritan woman left her vessel behind at the well and hurried into the city to tell everyone of the coming of the Messiah, Who, as the knower of hearts, told her everything, "all things that I ever did."

Meanwhile, the disciples who had returned from the city were amazed that their Teacher was speaking to a woman, since this was forbidden by the rules of the Jewish rabbis, who taught, "Do not speak for a long time with any woman," or "No one may speak with a woman on the street, even with one's lawful wife," or "It is better to burn the words of the Law than to teach them to a woman." However, since they honored their Teacher, the disciples did not express their astonishment in words, only asking Him to eat the food they brought from the city. But His natural hunger had been stilled by the joy of the conversion of the Samaritans and His desire for their salvation. He was joyful that the seed that He sowed was already bearing fruit, and so, in answer to His disciples' suggestion that He eat, He answered them that true food for Him is the fulfillment of the work of the salvation of mankind, given to Him by God His Father. The residents of Samaria who were coming to Him were like a field that was ready for the harvest, while in actual fact the fields would only be harvested in four months. It is usual for the one who sows to reap his own wheat; however, the harvest of spiritual seed is usually reaped by someone other than the sower, but the sower still rejoices together with the harvesters, for he sowed not for himself, but for others. Christ says this because He will send the apostles to harvest the spiritual field that was originally harrowed and sowed not by them, but by others—the Old Testament prophets and Christ Himself. During this conversation, the Samaritans came to the Lord. Many believed in Him thanks to the words of the woman, but an even greater number were converted based on His words, when He stayed with them for two days after their invitation. Hearing the teaching of the Lord, they were convinced that He truly was "the Christ, the Saviour of the world."

The Coming of Christ the Saviour into Galilee and the Beginning of His Preaching There (Matt 4:13–17; Mark 1:15; Luke 4:14–15; John 4:43–45)

Christ's arrival in Galilee is described by all four Evangelists. When He arrived, He left His childhood home of Nazareth, thereby witnessing to the fact that no prophet is welcome in his own country, and settled in Capernaum by the sea, in the region of Zebulun and Naphtali, which St Matthew interprets as the fulfillment of the prophecy of Isaiah 9:1–2. The Galileans accepted Him warmly because many of them had been in Jerusalem for the feast and saw all that Jesus had done there. Soon His fame spread all over the land, and He taught in all their synagogues, beginning His preaching with the words, "Repent, for the kingdom of heaven is at hand!" These were the exact same words that John the Baptist preached at the beginning of his ministry. The new kingdom and the new order that the Lord had come to institute was so much more exalted than the sinful state of man, that people truly needed to leave behind everything and be reborn through repentance, through complete internal change. Repentance is just such a complete change of thoughts, feelings, and desires.

From the time of the Lord's return to Galilee from Judea, Galilee became the usual place of His ministry. It was not a very large region, but it was densely settled by not only Jews but also Phoenicians, Arabians, and even Egyptians. The exceptional fertility of the land always attracted a large number of immigrants who were usually quickly assimilated into the local population. The main faith was that of the Jews, but there were many pagans living there as well, which is why it was known as "Galilee of the Gentiles." All this was a reason, on the one hand, of the great religious ignorance of the Galileans, but on the other hand, it also meant that they were free of the religious prejudices of the Judeans, especially when it came to the person of the Messiah. The disciples of the Lord were all from Galilee, and many of His other followers found it easy to travel with Him throughout this small, fertile land. These are some of the reasons why the Lord chose Galilee as the major place of His ministry. And we see that the Galileans truly were more receptive of His preaching than the proud Judeans.

THE HEALING IN CANA OF THE SON OF THE NOBLEMAN (JOHN 4:46–54)

On the way to Capernaum, the Lord came to Cana, where He had performed His first miracle of transforming the water into wine. One of the inhabitants of Capernaum, a former courtier of Herod's, hearing of Christ's arrival, hurried to Cana to ask Jesus to come with him to heal his son, who was near death. "Then Jesus said to him, 'Unless you people see signs and wonders, you will by no means believe.'" Faith that is dependent on seeing miracles is put by the Lord on a lower level than faith based on understanding the purity and greatness of His divine teaching. Faith born of miracles requires increasingly more miracles to be sustained since they become habitual and lose their ability to astonish. At the same time, the person who only accepts the teaching that is confirmed by miracles can easily fall into delusion because there are such things as false and demonic miracles. Thus, the word of God warns us to be careful with miracles (Deut 13:1–5). The Lord, in this case, is somewhat sorrowful that the Galileans rely so much on miracles to support their faith. However, the nobleman answers this rebuke with insistence, showing the firm foundation of his faith. Jesus, however, does not follow him, but heals his son from a distance, saying, "Go your way; your son lives." At that same moment, the fever left his son, and the servants of the nobleman, amazed at the instantaneous healing of the dying young man, hurried to their lord to inform him of this joyous news. The father, having believed the words of the Lord, but still thinking that the healing would occur gradually, asked at what hour the sick boy became better. They told him that it was the exact hour, when "Jesus said to him, 'Your son lives.' And he himself believed, and his whole household." Perhaps this was that very Chuza, whose wife Joanna later followed after Christ, serving Him. This was the second miracle that Christ performed in Galilee.

THE CALLING OF THE FISHERMEN-APOSTLES: PETER, ANDREW, JAMES, AND JOHN (MATT 4:18–22; MARK 1:16–20; AND LUKE 5:1–11)

The calling of the first apostles is narrated by the Synoptics. Matthew and Mark tell of this quickly, almost in passing, as if just to establish the fact of this calling, while St Luke gives a detailed account, describing the miraculous catch of fish that preceded the call. As St John the Evangelist tells us, the first apostles Andrew and John already followed Christ when they were still near the Jordan, then Simon, Philip, and Nathaniel came after them. But after they returned with Jesus to Galilee, they gradually returned to their previous occupation—fishing. Now, the Lord is calling them to constant discipleship, ordering them to leave behind their fishing nets to dedicate themselves to a new work—catching souls for the kingdom of God.

The rumors of the Messiah's appearance quickly spread throughout Galilee, and masses of people gathered to hear His teaching. They all huddled around Him, and thus, one time, when He was on the banks of the Lake of Gennesaret (which was also called a sea, probably because of the fierceness of its storms), He was forced to board a boat in order to be able to speak to the assembled crowd. When He finished speaking, He told Simon, whose boat He was sitting on, to go out into deeper water and cast out his fishing nets. Peter was an experienced fisherman who had toiled all night without success, and so was sure that he would not catch any fish this time either; however, there were so many fish in his nets that the nets began to tear. Peter and Andrew had to call some of their friends on another boat to help them pull out the fish. There were so many fish that both boats began to sink from the weight. Filled with pious fear, Peter fell at the feet of Jesus, saying, "Depart from me, for I am a sinful man, O Lord!" With these words, he wanted to express his own sense of unworthiness before the greatness and power of the Miracle Worker. With a meek word, the Lord calms Peter and foretells his future high calling. According to the witness of the Evangelists Mark and Matthew, the Lord called both Peter and Andrew with the words, "From now on you will catch men," only later calling James and John, the sons of Zebedee. Leaving behind their nets and their father, they followed after Christ.

THE POWER OF CHRIST'S PREACHING AND THE HEALING OF THE POSSESSED MAN IN THE SYNAGOGUE OF CAPERNAUM (MARK 1:21–28; LUKE 4:31–37)

Christ's most frequent place of residence in Galilee was Capernaum, so much so that it began to be called "His city," and He was even taxed as a resident (Matt 9:1; 17:24). Capernaum is on the border of two regions, Ituraea and Galilee; it was remarkable for its mild climate and material wealth, and it was perfectly situated for the masses of people who came to hear Jesus. Since He lived in Capernaum, Christ would preach at the local synagogue on the Sabbath. Synagogues were houses where Jews assembled for prayer. Worship and the sacrificial offerings occurred only in the Jerusalem temple, but during the Babylonian captivity, the

Jews felt a great need to gather together to pray and read the books of the Law. Synagogues became the places for such gatherings. When the Jews returned from captivity, every Jewish settlement established its own synagogue, both in Palestine and in all the other places of the Jewish Diaspora. Each synagogue had an ark that would contain the books of the law, a raised platform from which they read the Law and the prophets, and places to sit. Anyone who considered himself capable could read and interpret the Law and the Prophets. The reader would usually stand, but when he began to interpret what he read, he would sit. Being accustomed to constantly hearing the dead words of their teachers the scribes and the Pharisees, the Galileans were amazed when they heard the living word of the Lord. The former spoke as servants of the Law, but Jesus spoke as one who had authority. The scribes and Pharisees, themselves little comprehending the Law, distorted its meaning, and so spoke without conviction or power. Jesus spoke the word of God that He heard from His Father, and so spoke with authority, with conviction, and an ability to convince, which left a strong impression on the listeners.

As the Lord was teaching in the Capernaum synagogue, a certain man possessed by a demon was sitting among the assembled. Unexpectedly for all the assembled, he loudly cried out: "Let us alone! What have we to do with You, Jesus of Nazareth? Did You come to destroy us? I know who You are—the Holy One of God!"

This unwilling confession of the truth, forced out by the presence of the Son of God, was the cry of a slave-like fear affectedly and flatteringly attempting to avoid the coming judgment, the cry of a man without his own will, who, upon seeing his lord, imagined in his mind the terrible pain and torture awaiting him. Perhaps the enemy hoped to weaken the people's faith in Him, and we do see that the Lord categorically forbade him to witness to Him, saying: "Be quiet, and come out of him!" The possessed one fell down in the middle of the synagogue and got up already completely healed, for the demon, heeding the command of Jesus, went out of him. Both Evangelists underline the strong impression left on all the assembled by the healing of the possessed man.

Healing Peter's Mother-in-Law and Many Others
(Matt 8:14–17; Mark 1:29–34; Luke 4:38–41)

This miracle is located in immediate proximity to the previous one by the Evangelists Mark and Luke. When He came out of the synagogue, the Lord entered Peter's house, most likely to partake of food. Peter's mother-in-law was found to be gravely ill, and St Luke explains, as a doctor, that it was "a high fever." After only one word from the Lord, the fever immediately left her, and she even felt strong enough to rise up and minister to all of them. These two miracles left such an impression on the people that after the setting of the sun (most likely because it was a Sabbath), people started to bring the sick and possessed right to Peter's door, so that the entire city was soon assembled there, and the Lord healed many of them who were suffering from various diseases and He expelled many demons. St Matthew, who wanted to show through his Gospel that the Lord was the Messiah promised by the prophets, explains that this mass healing was the fulfillment of the prophecy of Isaiah, who said, "He Himself took our infirmities and bore our sicknesses." Not wanting to accept the witnesses of the evil spirits, the Lord forbade them to proclaim through the lips of the possessed that He was Christ, the Son of God.

PREACHING IN GALILEE (MATT 4:23–25; MARK 1:35–38; LUKE 4:42–44)

As a man, Christ the Saviour Himself suffered from exhaustion after all His labors, and in this sense, one can also say that He took upon Himself our weaknesses and He carried our diseases. And so on the next day, early in the morning, in order to rest and strengthen Himself by solitude and prayer, He left the city for a deserted place. But the masses were once again at Peter's house, and when they found out that the Lord was not there, they began to search for Him. Seeing this, Simon and those with him—Andrew, James, and John—also went to seek Jesus, and finding Him, called Him to the city where all were waiting for Him. The Lord said to them, however, that He had to go into other cities and towns to preach, for that is why He came, that is why He was sent, to give the good news to everyone. Leaving Capernaum, Jesus went throughout Galilee, preaching and performing miracles. Rumors of His coming spread even far beyond Galilee, to Syria, and the sick were brought to Him even from Decapolis, from Judea, Jerusalem, and from beyond the Jordan, and He healed them all. Many were the people who followed Him, hearing His teaching.

JESUS CHRIST PREACHED IN THE SYNAGOGUE IN NAZARETH (LUKE 4:14–30)

This event in St Luke is mentioned in the beginning of the Gospel, before the events we have previously described, but there is an important preface: "And news of Him went out through all the surrounding region. And He taught in their synagogues, being glorified by all." Keeping this in mind, it is obvious that the Lord came to Nazareth not at the beginning of His public ministry, as one might think, but much later, after the many miracles done in Capernaum. Nevertheless, the Evangelists Matthew and Mark seem to refer this event at a much later time, but such trustworthy exegetes of the Gospels such as Bishop Theophan the Recluse consider that the visit of the Lord to Nazareth, spoken of in Matthew 13 and Mark 6, is different from the one mentioned in Luke's account. Indeed, despite all the external similarities, there are some very important differences in these two accounts. In general it must be said that an exact, unquestionable chronology of the events of the Gospel is impossible to determine because every Evangelist has his own system of narration, corresponding with a specific goal, and exact chronology was never one of their guiding principles.

Having entered the synagogue of Nazareth, the Lord began to read that part of the book of Isaiah where the prophet, speaking as if from the person of the coming Messiah, describes the purpose of His coming. The Messiah says that He was sent by God to tell all the poor, downtrodden, and miserable that the kingdom of God is coming for them—the kingdom of love and mercy. The Jews did not doubt that this prophecy referred to the Messiah, and so when the Lord Jesus Christ said, "Today this Scripture is fulfilled in your hearing," they had nothing left to do, only to accept Him as the Messiah. And many were indeed ready to accept Him, knowing of the miracles He had performed. But among those in the synagogue were many who were antagonistic to the Lord—scribes and Pharisees, who had an incorrect understanding of the coming Messiah, imagining Him to be an earthly king, a national leader who would subject all the nations of the earth under the Jews, and would place the scribes and Pharisees, as His counselors, in all the positions of power. The teaching of the Lord of the kingdom of the destitute and the poor in spirit was completely unacceptable to them. In addition, many of the others, while they gloried in the grace-filled words of the Lord, knew Him from childhood, the son of a poor carpenter, and were not ready to proclaim Him the Messiah, but were only amazed at His wisdom and miracles. And instead of believing in Him, they were offended by Him.

Then the Lord, not wishing to resort to grand miracles to bolster the lack of faith of His unbelieving countrymen, mentions two Old Testament stories of Elijah and Elisha, which vividly express to the hearers their lack of worthiness to see those miracles that they expected to see. When they heard this bitter truth from One Whom they considered their own, and when they understood that Jesus ranked them lower even than the pagans, they were "filled with wrath," cast Him out of the city, and immediately tried to murder Him by throwing Him off a high mountain, on which Nazareth was situated. However, the mysterious power of God miraculously kept them from accomplishing this evil deed.

THE HEALING OF THE LEPER (MARK 1:40–45; LUKE 5:12–16)

The healing of the leper is mentioned also in Matthew (Matt 8:1–4), but such authoritative exegetes as St Theophan the Recluse find that the miracle in Matthew is a unique event, performed after the Sermon on the Mount, while St Luke explicitly mentions this happening in the city. Among all the diseases found in the East that are explicitly mentioned in the Bible, leprosy is the worst. Its symptoms are red spots first on the face, near the nose and eyes, which gradually spread to the whole body, which becomes covered in open sores. The face becomes puffy, the nose dries up and becomes deformed, the sense of smell fades, the eyes begin to constantly ooze liquid, the vision becomes dim, the voice becomes raspy, the hair falls out, the skin becomes lumpy and starts to crack, the sores begin to rot and stink, and the disfigured mouth oozes odorous saliva. The hands and legs lose their feeling and the entire body withers; then the feet, fingers, and other appendages begin to fall off until death finally ends the sick person's terrible torture. Those who have been afflicted from birth can sometimes live for thirty, forty, even fifty miserable years. Moses in the book of Leviticus gave specific instructions about those suffering from leprosy. A priest had to examine the disease, and to avoid contamination, the leper was separated from the society of the chosen nation.

This particular leper, evidently full of deep faith, boldly transgresses the law that forbids him to come into the society of those not infected, because he felt that here was the very Lord of the Law. His request to be healed is full of humility and equally full of faith in the miraculous power of the Lord. As He healed, the Lord touched him, showing that He was not limited by the Law that forbade touching lepers, that the Pure One knows no impurity, and expressing with this gesture a feeling of deep compassion for the afflicted leper. His words "I am willing; be cleansed" show His divine authority. He orders the healed man to show himself to a priest, in fulfillment of the law of Moses, and to tell no one of the miracle. The main reason why the Lord forbade others to speak of His miracles was the humility according to which the Son of God belittled Himself and accepted the form of a slave for the sake of our salvation. He did not want to walk the way of earthly glory (see John 5:41), especially since the glory surrounding a miracle worker could only encourage the unnecessary dreaming among the people of a warrior Messiah, an idea with which the Lord constantly battled. The Lord ordered him to go to the priest "as a testimony to them," in that sense, that the priest had to witness lawfully the fact of healing from leprosy, and also to show that the Lord does not destroy the law, but fulfills it Himself.

THE HEALING OF THE PARALYTIC IN CAPERNAUM (MATT 9:1–8; MARK 2:1–12; LUKE 5:17–26)

The three Evangelists, Matthew, Mark, and Luke, all speak of this miracle, while Mark clearly designates the place as Capernaum, while Matthew says that the Lord performed this miracle, having come into "His own city," which we have already mentioned to be Capernaum. St John Chrysostom has this to say about His native city: "He was born in Bethlehem, raised in Nazareth, but He lived in Capernaum."[18] The paralytic was brought to the Lord on a litter, and obviously was unable to move by his own power. Saints Mark and Luke add that because of the number of people surrounding Jesus in the house, those who brought the paralytic could not bring him into the house and so they lowered him in through the opening in the roof, meaning that this was a temporary roof made either of leather or boards, placed over an open courtyard in the middle of the house, surrounded on all sides by flat-roofed buildings onto which one could easily climb using ladders. Only strong faith could inspire those who brought the paralytic to such a bold action. Seeing their faith, as well as the faith of the paralytic himself since he allowed himself to be lowered in such a manner, Jesus said to him, "Your sins are forgiven you," indicating by these words that there is a connection between his disease and his sins. The word of God clearly teaches that diseases are the consequences of sin (John 9:2; Jas 5:14–15) and are sent sometimes by God as chastisement for sins (1 Cor 5:3–5; 11:30). Often there is an obvious connection between sin and diseases, such as those that result from drunkenness and wanton living. Thus, in order to heal the disease, the sin needs to be taken away, forgiven. Apparently, the paralytic considered himself to be such a great sinner that he had almost despaired of his sins being forgiven, which is why the Saviour emboldens him with His words.

Some scribes and Pharisees who were in attendance began to judge the Lord mentally for blasphemy, seeing in His words unlawful appropriation of God's exclusive authority to Himself. The Lord, knowing their thoughts, showed this by saying: "Which is easier, to say to the paralytic, 'Your sins are forgiven you,' or to say, 'Arise, take up your bed and walk'?" It is obvious that one and the other require divine power. "'But that you may know that the Son of Man has power on earth to forgive sins'—He said to the paralytic, 'I say to you, arise, take up your bed, and go to your house.'" How wonderfully St John Chrysostom interprets these words: "Since the healing of the soul is invisible, while the healing of the body is obvious, I unite to the first the latter as well, which is lower, but more obvious, so that through this visible sign you may believe in that which occurs invisibly."[19]

The miracle of healing that followed these words of Christ confirmed that Christ, mantled in divine power, did not speak these words lightly: "Your sins are forgiven you." Of course, it would be wrong to think that the Lord performed the miracle only to convince the Pharisees of His divine omnipotence. This miracle, as with all His miracles, was primarily the work of His goodness and mercy. The paralytic witnessed to his complete healing by taking up his own bed, on which he had been carried before. The result of the miracle was that the people were brought into a state of amazement, praising God who gave such power to men. In other words, not only the Pharisees, but the rest of the people also did not come to believe in Jesus as the Son of God, but only as a man.

THE CALLING OF MATTHEW (MATT 9:9–17; MARK 2:13–22; LUKE 5:27–39)

While all three Synoptics mention this event, only Matthew calls himself by this name, while the other two call him Levi. As the Lord left the house where He had just healed the paralytic, He saw a man who sat at the tax collector's stand, named Matthew (or Levi), and said to him, "Follow Me!" And he immediately got up and followed after Jesus. It needs to be said that the publicans, or tax collectors, one of whom Matthew was, were considered among the Jews to be the most sinful and despicable of people, for they collected taxes for the hated Roman government. In addition, each one was given full power to collect as much as was needed, and desiring to make a profit, the publicans would often take much more than was needed, which only increased the people's hatred of them. Such was the power of the Lord's word, that this publican, a prosperous man, dropped everything and followed the Lord, Who did not even have a place to lay His head. But this proves also that sinners who acknowledge their sinfulness and are ready to sincerely repent, are closer to the kingdom of heaven than those, such as the Pharisees, who exalt themselves with their apparent righteousness. In the joy of his calling, Matthew invited the Lord and the disciples to his home to a feast in their honor. According to the Eastern custom, those who ate at the table did not sit in chairs, but reclined around a low table on special couches, leaning with their left arm on a cushion. Apparently, many friends of Matthew, fellow publicans (whom the Pharisees considered to be sinners), also came to this feast and reclined together with the Lord and His disciples. This gave the Pharisees another opportunity to judge the Lord for His association with sinners. "Why does your Teacher eat with tax collectors and sinners?" they asked His disciples. St John Chrysostom explains: "They slander the Teacher before His disciples with the evil intention of turning them away from Him,"[20] suggesting that He was a man who sought out "the wrong crowd." "Those who are well have no need of a physician, but those who are sick," Christ Himself answers this accusation. It is as if He said, "Only so-called righteous people such as the Pharisees do not feel the need for a Saviour, but sinners do feel this need. The place of a physician is at the side of those who are sick; My place is by those who are sick with the knowledge of their own spiritual diseases, and I am a physician to them, to the publicans and the sinners."

"But go and learn what this means: 'I desire mercy and not sacrifice.'" The Pharisees considered that righteousness consisted of bringing the proper lawful sacrifices, but they forgot the Word of God speaking through the Prophet Hosea, "For I desire mercy and not sacrifice, and the knowledge of God more than burnt offerings" (Hos 6:6). It is as if the Lord said, "Understand that your sacrifice, all your external ritual piety means nothing in the eyes of God without love for your neighbor, without deeds of mercy." "For I did not come to call the righteous, but sinners, to repentance," in other words, "I came so that sinners would repent and be converted. I did not come to call to repentance those who already consider themselves to be righteous and imagine that they do not need repentance, but those who humbly admit themselves to be sinful and ask God for mercy." Yes, the Lord came to call and save everyone, including self-delusional, so-called righteous people, but until they leave behind their delusions of personal righteousness and admit themselves to be sinners, calling them would be pointless, and salvation for them would be impossible.

Defeated at every step, the Pharisees transfer their accusations to the disciples of the Lord, and in this they were joined by the disciples of John the Baptist, who, as we already mentioned, considered their teacher greater than Jesus and were envious of the ever-increasing prestige of the Lord. St John the Baptist was a strict ascetic, and, of course, he taught his disciples in the same spirit. It is likely that by this time, John was already in prison, and his disciples probably had intensified their fasting for this reason. The Pharisees directed their attention to the fact that the disciples of Christ did not fast as strictly, asking the Lord, "Why do we and the Pharisees fast often, but Your disciples do not fast?"

The Lord answered them with the words of their own teacher: "Can the friends of the bridegroom mourn as long as the bridegroom is with them? But the days will come when the bridegroom will be taken away from them, and then they will fast." This means: "Your own teacher called Me the Bridegroom, and himself the friend of the Bridegroom, who must be joyful in the presence of his friend. Thus also My disciples, as friends of the Bridegroom, rejoice while I am with them, and such a joy is not compatible with a strict fast, because fasting is an expression of grief and sorrow. When those days will come, and they will be alone in the world, then they will fast."

And so, in remembrance of these words of the Lord, the Holy Church established the fasting period of Passion Week adjoining the holy forty days of Lent, as well as the fasts on Wednesdays and Fridays, the days when the Bridegroom was taken away, the days of His betrayal and death on the cross. When He said that the time had not yet come for His disciples to fast, Christ expands the thought with these words: "No one puts a piece from a new garment on an old one; otherwise the new makes a tear, and also the piece that was taken out of the new does not match the old. And no one puts new wine into old wineskins; or else the new wine will burst the wineskins and be spilled, and the wineskins will be ruined. But new wine must be put into new wineskins, and both are preserved." St John Chrysostom interprets these words thus: The new cloth and the new wineskins are strict fasting and strict asceticism in general, while the old garment and the old wineskins are the weakness, inability of the disciples, who are not yet ready to attempt great labors. "I do not find it timely," the Lord says to us, "to lay the burden of the ascetic life and heavy commandments on My disciples, who are yet weak, until they have been renewed, reborn in the grace of the Holy Spirit." Here the Lord protects His disciples from accusation with true Fatherly love and condescension.

 CHAPTER 4

The Second Passover of Public Ministry of the Lord Jesus Christ

HEALING THE PARALYTIC NEAR THE POOL OF SILOAM (JOHN 5:2–16)

Only St John tells of this event, St John who takes special care to narrate every visit of the Lord to Jerusalem for the feasts. In this case, it is not clear for which feast the Lord came to Jerusalem, but it was probably either the Passover or Pentecost because only thus does the public ministry of Christ last three and a half years, following the ancient tradition of the Church, which takes the chronology of the fourth Gospel as the standard. Nearly half a year passed from the Lord's baptism to His first Passover, mentioned in John 2, then another year passed until the second Passover mentioned in the fifth chapter, another year passed until the third Passover mentioned in chapter 6, and a third year until the fourth Passover, the one before which the Lord suffered and died.

At the Sheep Gate, known thus because the sheep intended for sacrifice were herded through there, or because there was a market for such animals nearby, at the northeastern side of the city walls on the way to Gethsemane and the Mount of Olives, there was a pool of water known in Hebrew as Bethesda, which means "house of compassion" or of God's mercy, since the water from that pool came from a healing source. According to Eusebius, even in the fourth century A.D. there were five porches near this source. It attracted a great multitude of sick people. It was not a typical spring—its healing power was exhibited only occasionally, when the angel of the Lord would come down into the waters and disturb them, and only he who would descend into the water first would be healed. In other words, it seems that the water would have its healing properties only for a short period of time; then it would revert to normal water. Near this pool lay a paralytic who was paralyzed for thirty-eight years, and who had nearly lost all hope for healing, especially because, as he explained to the Lord, he did not have anyone to help him reach the water, and he himself was powerless to take advantage of the water's healing properties. Having compassion on him, the Lord immediately healed him, with His word alone: "Rise, take up your bed and walk" (John 5:8), thereby showing the primacy of His saving grace over the ways of salvation available in the Old Testament.

However, since it was the Sabbath, the Jews, under which name St John usually means the Pharisees, Sadducees, and elders who were antagonistic to the Lord Jesus Christ, instead of rejoicing or marveling at the healing of the paralytic, who had suffered for such a long time, were disturbed that he dared to break the commandment not to work on a Sabbath (which he broke by carrying his bed), and they rebuked him. The healed man, however, not without a measure of brazenness in his tone, justifies himself with the command of the One Who healed him, and Who in his eyes had enough authority to free him from following the excessively trivial rules concerning the Sabbath. With disdain, the Jews asked him Who was the Man that dared to allow him to carry his bed on a Sabbath.

Blessed Theophylact wonderfully interprets this event: "This is the very meaning of hatred! They do not even ask who healed him, but who commanded him to carry his bed. They do not ask about the thing that arouses wonder, but the thing that they found lacking." They could not know for sure, but they must have suspected that the Healer must be the hated Jesus from Nazareth, and so they did not even want to hear about the miracle. The healed one could not give them an exact answer, for he did not know Jesus. It is likely that the healed one soon came to the temple to thank God for his healing. Here Jesus accosted him with the remarkable words: "See, you have been made well. Sin no more, lest a worse thing come upon you." From these words, it is especially vividly evident that disease comes as a punishment for sins, in order to prevent an even worse punishment later. When he found out who his Healer was, the paralytic came and announced Him to His enemies, of course not with any ill intention, but to show the authority under which he had acted. This only inspired more hatred from the Jews against Jesus, and they "sought to kill Him, because He had done these things on the Sabbath."

THE LORD'S TEACHING REGARDING HIS EQUALITY TO GOD THE FATHER AND THE UNIVERSAL RESURRECTION AND JUDGMENT (JOHN 5:17–47)

In answer to the Jews' plans to kill Him for breaking the Sabbath, "Jesus answered them, My Father has been working until now, and I have been working." In these words is the Lord's witness to Himself as the Son of God, One in essence with the Father. All the subsequent works are only a development of this most important thought in the Lord's answer to the Jews.

As the Son of God, it is natural for Him to follow not the commandment given to Adam and his descendants, but to follow the example of God the Father. And God the Father, though He rested on the seventh day from the work of creation, did not cease the work of providence. Correctly understanding these words of the Lord that He equated Himself with God the Father, the Jews began to see in Him a double crime, worthy of death—breaking the Sabbath and blasphemy.

Jesus develops the teaching of His oneness in action with God the Father (John 5:19–20), comparing it to people's usual understanding of the son as emulator of his father, and of the father who loves his son and teaches him how to act. In the words: "The Son can do nothing of Himself," one cannot see a justification of Arianism, but only that, in St John Chrysostom's words, "the Son does nothing against His Father, nothing contrary to Him, nothing incompatible with the will of the Father."[21] "And He will show Him greater works than these"; that is, not only can He raise the paralytic from his bed, but He can raise the dead.

The Lord speaks first of spiritual resurrection, of the spiritual awakening of the spiritual dead man into a true, holy life in God, and only then does He speak of universal resurrection, but both of these are interconnected (John 5:21). A person's reception of the true life, the spiritual life, is already the beginning of his victory over death. Just as the fall into sin serves as the reason for death in the first place, so does true spiritual life lead one to eternal life that defeats death.

Spiritual resurrection is connected by the Lord explicitly with His other great work—judgment (John 5:22–23). Here, He first means moral judgment in this life, which will lead inexorably to the final universal fearful judgment. Christ came as Light and Life into a spiritually dead and dark world. Those who believed in Him resurrected into a new life and themselves became light. Those who rejected Him remained in the darkness of sin, in spiritual death. This is why the judgment of the Son of God continues through the course of a person's entire life, and this judgment will end at the Final Judgment. Since the eternal fate of mankind is thus in the complete authority of the Son, then He should be equally honored with the Father: "He who does not honor the Son does not honor the Father who sent Him."

A further illustration of the life-giving work of the Son of God is contained in John 5:24–29. Obedience to the words of the Saviour and faith in the fact that He was sent is the main condition for the acceptance of eternal life, in which is the pledge also of blessed immortality of the body. He "shall not come into judgment … the hour is coming, and now is, when the dead will hear the voice of the Son of God; and those who hear will live." Here again we hear of the spiritual vivification of a person as a result of the preaching of Christ, for the Son is the source of life, "For as the Father has life in Himself; so He has granted the Son to have life in Himself."

The Son also has the authority of the judge because for this purpose He became man by nature, being in essence the Son of God (John 5:27). This authority of the Son of God as Judge will be fully realized in the end of ages during the universal resurrection and righteous retribution (John 5:28–29). This will be a righteous judgment, for it will be the result of the total agreements of the will of the Judge with the will of the heavenly Father (John 5:30).

Christ with full conviction witnesses to His own divinity (John 5:31–39). He cites the witness of John the Baptist, whom the Jews respected greatly, but at the same time says that He has a witness greater than that of John's—the witness of God the Father, Who witnesses to His Son's divinity through the signs and miracles that the Son performs, as though by order of the Father, for they all comprise the divine plan for the salvation of mankind, which was given to Him by the Father to accomplish. God the Father witnessed to His Son in the moment of His baptism, but He gave an even greater proof of His Messianic dignity through the Old Testament prophets; however, the Jews did not listen to their own Scriptures, because the word of God did not find a home in their hearts. They did not hear the voice of God in His Scriptures, and they do not see the face of God in His revelation to them. "Search the Scriptures" and you will see that "these are they which testify of Me."

Later, Christ chastises the Jews for their lack of faith (John 5:40–47), saying that He has no need of their glory or honor, for He does not seek the glory of men, but He sorrows for them because by not believing in Him as God's Messiah they reveal their lack of love for God the Father Who sent Him. Since they do not love God, they do not accept Christ Who came with His commands, but when another comes, the false Messiah, with his own delusional teachings, they will accept him even without signs and miracles. From the time of Christ, there have already been more than sixty such false messiahs, and the last of them will be the Antichrist, whom the Jews will accept also as their Messiah. The reason for the Jews' lack of faith is that they seek human glory, and they do not respect the one who reveals their sins, even if he is right, while the one who praises them (even if he lies), they accept as their own. In conclusion, the Lord denies the Jews even the last hope for their false expectations. He tells them that even Moses, on whom they rely, will accuse them at God's Judgment. He will accuse them for their lack of faith in Christ, for he wrote of Him. Here, Christ has in mind both direct prophecies and the promise of the Messiah's coming in the books of Moses, including Genesis 3:15; 12:3; 49:10; Deuteronomy 18:15; and the entire Law, which was a shadow of the imminent good things of the kingdom of Christ (Heb 10:1) and the guardian before Christ.

PLUCKING THE HEADS OF GRAIN ON A SABBATH (MATT 12:1–8; MARK 2:23–28; LUKE 6:1–5)

After this, Jesus left Judea for Galilee. On the way to Galilee, on a Sabbath day (which St Luke calls "the second Sabbath after the first," or the first Sabbath after the second day of Passover), He was walking with His disciples through a field of wheat. His disciples, being hungry from the journey, began to pluck the stalks and rub them in their hands to take out the seeds. This was allowed by the law of Moses, which only forbade one to use a sickle in a neighbor's field on a Sabbath (Deut 23:25). But the Pharisees considered this to be breaking the law of rest on a Sabbath, and they did not let this opportunity slip by to rebuke the Lord for allowing His disciples to do this. In order to protect His disciples, the Lord reminds the Pharisees of a certain occurrence involving King David in the first book of Samuel (chapter 21), when David, fleeing from Saul, came to a priestly city and asked the priest Abimelech to give him five breads or whatever could be found, and the priest gave him the breads of offering which, according to the Law, could only be eaten by the priests. The effectiveness of this example is the following—if no one judged David for eating these breads when he was tortured by hunger, then the disciples of the Lord also do not deserve to be judged for breaking the Sabbath in such an insignificant manner, since while serving the Lord, they sometimes did not even have time to eat.

Having justified His disciples' actions, the Lord then reveals the source of the unfair judgment of the Pharisees. This is a false understanding of the requirements of the law of God. If the Pharisees had understood that compassionate love to a hungry man is higher than traditions and rites, then they would never have judged the faultless who plucked a bit of wheat for the sake of filling their hungry bellies. Man was not created for the sake of the law; rather, the law was given to man for his benefit, and thus preserving man from death and weakness is far more important than the law about the Sabbath. In addition, it is clear that the Sabbath prohibitions did not actually mean complete lack of activity, which is seen in the fact that the priests killed sacrificial animals on a Sabbath, skinned them, prepared them for the altar, and burned them, while never being considered in violation of the Sabbath's rest. If the ministers of the temple are not at fault when they work on a Sabbath, then how much more faultless are the servants of Him Who is greater than the temple and Who is Himself the Lord of the Sabbath, with authority to abrogate the Sabbath, since He established it in the first place.

HEALING THE MAN WITH THE WITHERED ARM ON A SABBATH
(MATT 12:9–14; MARK 3:1–6; LUKE 6:6–11)

With this healing, the Lord once again provoked the anger of the scribes and Pharisees, who were apparently traveling everywhere with Him only in order to accuse Him of breaking the law of Moses. When He asked the Pharisees the question: "What man is there among you who has one sheep, and if it falls into a pit on the Sabbath, will not lay hold of it and lift it out?" The Lord showed that in His eyes deeds of mercy are more important than keeping the Sabbath rest, and that it is permissible to break it for the sake of doing good.

A GREAT MULTITUDE OF PEOPLE GATHERS AROUND THE LORD, HIS MANY MIRACLES: THE LORD AVOIDS GLORY AND THE PROPHECY OF HIS HUMILITY
(MATT 12:15–21; MARK 3:7–12)

When the Lord left the synagogue in which He healed the man with the withered arm, a large multitude followed Him from Galilee, Judea, and even from lands beyond the Jordan and the Gentile regions, and He performed a great many miraculous healings, always, however, forbidding people to speak openly about these healings. St Matthew sees this occurrence as the fulfillment of the prophecy in Isaiah regarding the beloved Servant of God (Isa 42:1–4). In this prophecy, which obviously refers to the Messiah, the prophet praises the meekness and humility of Christ. By referencing this prophecy, St Matthew tries to show the Jews that their expectations regarding the Messiah as a warrior-king who will raise up the Jewish kingdom and will rule with great majesty and pomp on the throne of David are wrong, that the Old Testament prophets spoke of a meek and humble Messiah, whose kingdom would not be of this world, but Who would nonetheless give the law to all nations, and in Whose name all would come to trust.

Choosing the Twelve Apostles (Matt 10:2–4; Mark 3:13–19; Luke 6:12–16)

After praying all night (most likely for the foundation of His Church) on a mountain that tradition says may have been Tabor, the Lord called His disciples to Himself and chose twelve from among them, who would constantly attend Him and would later witness to Him. These would be like the heads of the new twelve tribes of Israel. The number twelve has a mystical meaning in the Scriptures, since it is a multiple of three and four. Three is the eternal uncreated Essence of God, and four indicates the four directions of the world. The number twelve thus symbolically means the incursion of the divine into humanity and the world. The first three Evangelists and the Book of Acts give us lists of names for the Twelve. It is interesting to note that in every one of these lists, the apostles are divided into three groups of four, and the first person in each group of four is the same in all accounts. These are the names of the Apostles: (1) Simon-Peter, (2) Andrew, (3) James, (4) John, (5) Philip, (6) Bartholomew, (7) Thomas, (8) Matthew, (9) James the Son of Alpheus, (10) Levi or Thaddeus, as Judah son of James was named, (11) Simon the Canaanite or the Zealot, and (12) Judas Iscariot. Bartholomew is the same man whom St John called Nathaniel. "Canaanite" is a Jewish translation of the Greek "zealot." The Zealots belonged to a party that actively tried to restore the independence of the Jewish kingdom. The word "Iscariot" some consider to be made up of two words: "ish" or "man," and "Kerioth," the name of a city. The word "apostle" in the Greek means "messenger," which is appropriate for the calling of the chosen—to be sent to preach. In order to give them more success in their preaching, the Lord gave them the power to heal diseases and cast out demons.

The Sermon on the Mount (Matt 5–7; Luke 6:12–49)

In its fullness, the Sermon on the Mount is only given to us by Matthew. St Luke gives a summary version, and certain passages from it are also found in later events of St Luke's Gospel. The Sermon on the Mount is remarkable in that it contains the entire essence of the Gospel teaching. Not far from the Sea of Tiberias between Capernaum and Tiberias, tourists are still shown the "Hill of the Beatitudes," from which the Lord spoke the Sermon on the Mount, so that many would be able to hear Him. The Jewish nation, proud in its chosen status and unable to come to terms with the loss of its political independence, began to dream of a Messiah who would free them from the lordship of foreigners, who would avenge his people against all their enemies, who would become the king of the Jews who would enslave all the nations of the world, and who would give the Jews a purely fairytale-like blessedness—he would order the seas to reveal all the pearls and treasures that it contained, he would put royal garments shining with jewels on all his people, and he would feed them manna even sweeter than the manna given to them in the desert. With such false hopes of earthly blessedness, they surrounded Jesus, expecting that any moment He would declare Himself to be the true King of Israel and that blessed age would begin. They thought that their suffering and humiliation would end, and they would be forever joyful and blessed.

In answer to these thoughts and emotions, the Lord instead develops His evangelical teaching of the Beatitudes, which completely uprooted and destroyed all their false hopes. He taught them of the same things He told Nicodemus—of the need to be reborn spiritually in order to build the kingdom of God on earth—that Eden, which was lost by mankind—and thereby prepare for themselves the blessedness of eternal life in the kingdom of heaven. The first step is to acknowledge one's own spiritual poverty, sinfulness, and nothingness, to humble oneself. This is why "Blessed are the poor in spirit, for theirs is the kingdom of heaven." Blessed are those who, when they see and admit their own sins, which hinder their entrance into the kingdom, weep over them, for they become reconciled to their conscience and are consoled. Those who weep for their sins reach such an inner calm that they are no longer able to become angry and instead become meek. Meek Christians truly did inherit the earth, which used to be under the dominion of the pagans, but they will also inherit the earth in the future life, a new earth, which will be revealed after the destruction of this perishable earth, a "land of the living" (Exod 26:13, Rev 21:1).

"Blessed are those who hunger and thirst for righteousness," those who are zealous to do God's will, "For they shall be filled," they will reach that righteousness and justification from God that gives true zeal to fulfill in all things the will of God. God requires His people also to be merciful, a virtue that is given to those who strive to live according to God's will. This is why "Blessed are the merciful, for they shall obtain mercy" from God, just as the opposite is true as well: "For judgment is without mercy to the one who has shown no mercy" (Jas 2:13). Sincere works of compassion cleanse the human heart from all sinful uncleanness, and those who have pure hearts are blessed because they will see God with their heart, as with a spiritual eye. Those who see God strive to emulate Him, to be like a son to Him Who united man with God, Who brought peace to the human soul. They hate strife, and so become peacemakers, desiring to bring peace wherever they are. Thus they are also blessed, for they shall be called "the sons of God." Those who reach such spiritual heights have to be ready because the sinful world that lies in sin (1 John 5:19) will hate them for this truth of God, whose bearers they have become, and will persecute them and revile them, slander them, and in all possible ways oppress them for their loyalty to the Lord Jesus Christ and His divine teaching. Those who suffer much here on earth for Christ can expect a great reward in heaven.

These nine New Testament commandments, called the Beatitudes, are a synopsis of the entire Gospel. Their difference from the Decalogue is characteristic. The Old Testament speaks mostly of the importance of the external actions of a man, and strict prohibitions are put on these actions in very categorical forms. Christ speaks first and foremost of the internal disposition of a human soul and so does not categorically list prohibitions, but only the conditions that make eternal blessedness possible for mankind.

St Luke adds to St Matthew's account regarding the Beatitudes. He tells of Christ's words that warn those people who see blessedness merely as satisfaction with earthly good things. "Woe to you who are rich!" says the Lord, contrasting those rich to those who are poor in spirit. Christ has in mind not only those who have much material wealth, of course, but those who put all their trust in their money, who are proud and conceited and look down on other people. "Woe to you who are full, For you shall hunger." In contrast to those who hunger and thirst after righteousness, these people do not seek for the righteousness of God, but are content with their own false righteousness. "Woe to you who laugh now, for you shall mourn and weep." In contrast to those who weep for their sins, such people are without care or attention to the sinful kind of life that they lead. The world that lies in sin loves those who live according to its own sinful ways, so, "woe to you, when all men speak well of you," for this is a clear sign that your moral state is fallen.

Later, the Lord says that all of His followers who fulfill these commands will be the salt of the earth. Salt preserves food from spoiling and makes it healthy, pleasant to taste. In the same way, Christians must protect the world from moral rot and help it improve. Salt gives its saltiness to everything that comes near it, and in the same way Christians must pass on the spirit of Christ to all other people who have not yet become Christian. Salt does not change either the essence or the external appearance of the substance in which it is dissolved, but only gives it its flavor. In the same way, Christianity does not cause any disruption in a person or society, but only beautifies the soul of man and through this transforms all aspects of human life, giving it a special Christian character.

"If the salt loses its flavor, how shall it be seasoned?" (Matt 5:13). In the East, it is actually possible to make salt lose its flavor, thanks to the extreme effects of rain, sun, and the air itself. You cannot return the savor to such salt. In the same way, those people who, having once tasted of the grace-filled communion with the Holy Spirit, fall into the terrible sin of rejecting Him and become incapable of being renewed spiritually, outside the extraordinary help of God.

The Light of the world is the Lord Jesus Christ Himself, but since those who believe in Him take this light and reflect it in the world, they also become "the light of the world." Such are especially the apostles and their successors, whose very calling is to be lights that shine forth the light of Christ, pastors of His Church. They have to live in such a way that people, seeing their good deeds, glorify God.

Intending to show how His new law referred to the Old Testament, the Lord at first calms the zeal of the Jews for their law, underlining that He did not come to destroy it, but to fulfill it. Christ truly did come to earth so that in Him the entire Old Testament word of God might be fulfilled, in order that He might reveal, embody, and confirm the entire power of the law and the prophets, and to show the true meaning and spirit of the entire Old Testament.

"How did He fulfill the Law?" asks Blessed Theophylact. "First of all, He accomplished all that was foretold of Him by the prophets. He fulfilled all the commandments of the Law, for He never did evil and there was no hypocrisy in His mouth. He fulfilled the Law by completing it fully, meaning that He filled out empty spaces, which the Law only suggested in shadows."[22] He gave a more full and spiritual understanding of all the Old Testament commandments, teaching of the insufficiency of fulfilling only the external, formal aspects of the law. When the Lord said, "one jot or one tittle will by no means pass from the law," He underlined that even the smallest aspects of God's Law will not be left unfulfilled. The Pharisees divided the commandments into "large" and "small" ones, and did not consider it a sin to break the small ones. Incidentally, in their understanding, these "small" commandments included the ones regarding love, mercy, and justice. "Shall be called least in the kingdom of heaven," by the sense of the original Greek phrase, means "will not enter in the kingdom of heaven at all." The righteousness of the scribes and Pharisees was characterized only with external fulfillment of laws and rites of the law, and most of these were trivial. Therefore, it survived perfectly well with their internal conceit and arrogance, with no traces of the spirit of humility and meek love and was consequently external and hypocritical, while passions and sins hid underneath the mask, something for which Christ rebuked them many times. The Lord warned His followers against such external, ostentatious righteousness.

In the rest of Matthew's fifth chapter, beginning with the twenty-first verse, the Lord shows in what ways specifically He has come to fulfill the Old Testament law. He teaches here a deeper and more spiritual understanding and fulfillment of the Old Testament commandments. It is not enough only not to murder someone physically; one must avoid killing him morally by becoming angry at him without reason. "Whoever is angry with his brother without a cause shall be in danger of the judgment: and whoever says to his brother, 'Raca!' shall be in danger of the council. But whoever says, 'You fool,' shall be in danger of hell fire." Here, condescending to the Jewish division of large and small sins, the Lord illustrates different levels of anger toward one's neighbor. Small crimes were usually dealt with by the city council. More serious crimes were adjudicated by the Sanhedrin, the high court and council of the Jewish people in Jerusalem, consisting of seventy-two members chaired by the high priest. "Raca" means "empty man" and is an expression of extreme scorn. "You fool" is meant to express the limit of hatred or disdain for one's neighbor, not just a stupid man, but a man considered wholly without honor or conscience. The punishment for this worst level of anger is "hell fire" or the "fires of Gehenna." Gehenna was a valley southwest of Jerusalem in which impious kings brought sacrifices to the god Moloch (2 Kgs 16:3; 2 Chr 28:3), where young men were led through a fire ritual and children were killed on the altar. After the end of paganism, this valley became an area of taboo and revulsion. All the filth of Jerusalem began to be dumped there, including the bodies of the unburied, and sometimes executions were held there as well. The air in that valley was so foul that fires were constantly fed to purify the air; this is why the place was called the valley of fire and became an image of the eternal suffering of sinners.

The meek love of a Christian for his neighbor must be so great that he must not only never be angry at anyone, but neither should he even do anything to cause his brother to be angry with him. Anger prevents us from praying with a pure heart to God, and so we must hurry to make peace with our brother. Using an image taken from Roman law, according to which a creditor may forcefully drag his debtor to court, Christ calls our offended brother our "adversary," with whom we must make peace while still "on the way" of this passing life, so that he does not drag us before the Judge, God Himself, lest we bear our just punishment. St Apostle Paul also told the offender to make peace, before the sun sets on his anger (Eph 4:26).

In exactly the same way, it is not enough to only externally fulfill the seventh commandment of the Decalogue: "You shall not commit adultery" by preventing the crude falling into sin by action. Raising up this commandment to a higher level, the Lord teaches that not only the action of fornication is sinful, but even the desire for it; even a lustful glance at a woman is a sin. "He fornicates with a woman in his heart," said St Athanasius the Great, "who internally agrees with the sin, but who is externally prevented from it either by place or time or fear of civil laws."[23] Not every glance at a woman is sinful, but only a glance that is a result of an inner desire to commit fornication. In cases of such temptations to sin, one must show such a conviction to cut off this temptation that one would not even be afraid to sacrifice the dearest things—even to pluck out eyes and cut off hands. In this case, the eyes and the hands are not meant to be understood literally; rather, they are symbolic of everything that is most dear to us, everything that we must sacrifice in order to uproot this passion from our souls and avoid falling into it in the future.

In connection with this, the Lord forbids a husband to divorce his wife, "for any reason except sexual immorality." The Old Testament law (Deut 24:1–2) allowed a man to divorce his wife, having given her a letter, a written pledge that she was his wife and that he was releasing her from him for that or another reason.

The situation of women was quite difficult at that time since it depended entirely on the man.

In another place (Mark 10:2–12), the Lord says that this permission for divorce was granted by Moses because of the Jews' hard-heartedness, but that it was not so from the beginning. Marriage was established by God as an unbreakable union. It breaks only when one of the spouses commits adultery. If a man divorces his wife for no reason, he is pushing her toward adultery, and so becomes equally guilty as the one who will take her for his own.

The Old Testament law forbade using the name of God as an oath in trivial matters, and of course when swearing falsely. The third commandment of the Decalogue forbids using the Lord's name in vain, and forbids a flippant attitude to swearing by the name of God. The Jews of Jesus's time, literally following the law prohibiting swearing by God's name, took oaths by the sky or the earth, by Jerusalem, by their head, and thus, without actually using the name of God, they still constantly made oaths, even when they lied. Such oaths are forbidden by the Lord Jesus Christ, for everything is created by God, and swearing by a creation still means that you are swearing by the Creator, and to make a false oath by Him is to blaspheme the holiness of the oath. A Christian must be so honorable and truthful that he should be believed only by his word. If he says yes, it means yes. If he says no, it means no, without any oaths. But in important matters, a lawful oath is not forbidden. The Lord Jesus Christ Himself confirmed the validity of oaths on His judgment before the Sanhedrin, when the high priest adjured Him by the Living God, and He answered, "It is as you said," for that was the Jewish form of a legal, binding oath (Matt 26:63–64). The Apostle Paul swore that He spoke truth, calling God as His witness (Rom 1:9; 9:1; 2 Cor 1:23; 2:17; Gal 1:20; and others). Only an empty, thoughtless oath is forbidden.

In the ancient world, vengeance was such a widespread phenomenon that even limiting it somewhat was significant, which is what the law managed to do. The Law of Christ completely forbids vengeance, instead preaching love for one's enemies. However, the words "I tell you not to resist an evil person" should not be understood as complete passivity before evil, as Leo Tolstoy and other false teachers do. The Lord forbids us to answer evil for evil, but a Christian can be in no way reconciled to any form of evil, and he must fight against evil with all the means available to him, however never allowing evil into his own heart. Also, it is useless to understand these words literally: "Whoever slaps you on your right cheek, turn the other to him also," for we know that Christ Himself acted otherwise when the servant at the judgment of Annas struck Him on the cheek (John 18:22–23). We must strive to correct not only those who do evil in general but also those who do evil to us personally. There is a direct commandment to do this in Matthew chapter 18. What is forbidden is the evil emotion of the desire for revenge, but not the battle against evil. Swindling others is also forbidden; on the contrary, Christ calls us to fulfill our neighbor's needs: "Give to him who asks you." This, of course, does not include those situations when giving to your neighbor is not only unbeneficial, but may be even harmful. A true Christian who loves his neighbor will not give a murderer a knife or poison to a man who wishes to commit suicide.

In the Old Testament, we do not find the commandment: "you shall hate your enemy," but apparently the Jews themselves extrapolated this commandment from the commandment to love one's neighbor. They considered as their "neighbors" only those people who were of the same faith or blood. Everyone else, such as those of different faiths, nations, and those who did not agree with them, they considered "enemies," whom it was completely inappropriate to love. Christ, however, commands that we be as our Heavenly Father, Who is foreign to any anger and hatred and loves all people, even the evil and unrighteous. We, who desire to be worthy sons of the Heavenly Father, must love as He does, including our enemies. The Lord desires that His followers in a moral sense would be higher than the Jews and Gentiles, whose love was essentially founded upon the love of oneself. Love for the sake of God, for the sake of God's commands, is worthy of reward, but love based on natural inclination or personal benefit is not worthy of any reward. Thus, moving ever higher on the ladder of Christian perfection, the Christian will finally reach the highest commandment of love for one's enemies, most difficult to understand for the natural man, yet to be reborn. With this highest commandment, the Lord concludes the first half of the Sermon on the Mount.

As if desiring to show how this commandment makes the weak and incomplete man like unto God, He confirms that the ideal of Christian perfection is found in acquiring the likeness of God: "Therefore you shall be perfect, just like your Father in heaven is perfect." This conforms perfectly to the divine plan expressed even before the creation of man: "Let Us make man in Our image" (Gen 1:26). Divine holiness is of course inaccessible to us, and so here we do not mean equality with God, but a certain inner likeness, a gradual approach of the immortal human soul to its Archetype with the help of divine grace.

In the second part of the Sermon on the Mount (the whole of Matt 6), the Lord develops His teaching on almsgiving, prayer, and fasting, with an admonition to strive toward the most important goal of human life—the kingdom of God. Having told His disciples what they must and must not do to be blessed, the Lord continued to the question of *how* one must do what He commanded. Neither works of mercy nor the worship of God nor prayers or fasting should be done for show, to receive praise from others, because in that case the praise of men will be our only reward. Vainglory, like a moth, eats away all our good deeds, and therefore it is better to do all our good deeds in secret so that we do not lose the reward from our Father Who is in heaven. Of course, giving alms openly is not forbidden here, but giving alms with the express purpose of attracting attention to oneself is forbidden. Also, praying in churches is of course not forbidden, but praying in a way that attracts praise is. But St John Chrysostom elaborates, saying that it is even possible to pray with vainglory in a closed room, and in that case, "the closed doors will bring absolutely no benefit."[24]

"Vain repetitions" here refer to the pagan understanding of prayer as incantation, which is the more effective the more times you repeat it. We do not pray in order for God to know our needs, but to purify our hearts through prayer, and to become worthy of the mercies of God, to enter with our spirit into inner communion with God. This communion with God is the goal of prayer, and this goal is not accomplished by a large quantity of uttered words.

While He forbids such long-windedness, Christ nevertheless in many places commands to pray unceasingly and not to despair (Luke 18:1). He Himself spent many nights in prayer. Prayer has to involve the reason; we have to approach God with the kind of requests that are worthy of Him and whose fulfillment would be salvific for us. In order to teach us this kind of prayer, the Lord gives us, a model, the prayer "Our Father," which is also known as the "Lord's Prayer." As a model, this prayer does not exclude other prayers; Christ Himself prayed in the Gospels using other words (John 17). When we call God our Father, we recognize ourselves to be His children, and that means that we are all brothers to each other, and we pray not only from ourselves and for ourselves, but on behalf of all and for all. When we say, "Who art in heaven," we reject all that is earthly and raise up our minds and hearts to the world on high. "Hallowed be Thy name": May Your name be holy for all people, may all mankind glorify God's name with their words and their deeds. "Thy kingdom come": The Kingdom of the Messiah Christ, the expectation of all pious Jews, was not a material one, as they expected. Here we pray that the Lord would reign in the souls of all people, and after this temporary earthly life, we would all be found worthy of the eternal blessed life in communion with Him. "Thy will be done on earth as it is in heaven": May everything in this world occur according to the all-good and all-wise will of God, and may we fulfill the Lord's will here as joyfully as the angels fulfill it in heaven.

"Give us this day our daily bread": Give us for this day everything that we need for our sustenance. What will be tomorrow, we do not know; we only need our daily bread, only what is necessary to sustain our life. "And forgive us our debts, As we forgive our debtors": These words are given deeper explanation by St Luke, who transmits these words thus: "forgive us our sins" (Luke 11:4). Our sins are our debts, because when we sin, we do not do that which was necessary, and we thus remain debtors before God and before men. This petition powerfully shows us how necessary it is to forgive others all their offenses. When we do not forgive one another, we have no right to ask God to forgive our sins; we have no right to pray with the words of the Lord's Prayer. "And lead us not into temptation": Temptation here means a test of our moral strength when we are inclined to do something sinful. We ask God to protect us from falling into sin if such a test of our moral strength is inevitable. "But deliver us from the evil one," from all evil and the source of evil, the devil. The prayer ends with certainty in the fulfillment of all that was asked, for to God belongs the eternal kingdom, eternal power, and glory in this world. The word "Amen" in Hebrew means "it is so," "truly," "verily," or "so be it." It was spoken in synagogues by those who prayed as an affirmation of a prayer read by an elder.

The Lord's teaching on fasting, which must also be done for the sake of God, not to receive praise from men, clearly shows how incorrect those people are who say that the Lord never intended His followers to fast. When you fast, you should not change your external appearance so much that it begins to attract attention to yourself. Rather, you should appear before people in the same way that you always do—in the East, this meant covering your body and hair with oil after washing. On the contrary, the Pharisees did not wash during fasting periods, did not brush their hair, and did not pour oil on their heads, thus attracting general attention to their ascetic feats by their unusual appearance. This is what the Lord decries.

Later (from Matt 6:19), the Lord teaches us to first seek the kingdom of God and not to be distracted from this striving by any cares. We should not worry about acquiring and hoarding earthly treasures, which do not last long and will soon rot. Wherever one puts the things he treasures, that is where his mind constantly will be in thoughts, feelings, and desires. Thus, a Christian, who must be in heaven with his heart, should not be diverted by earthly things but should strive to acquire heavenly treasures, which are virtues. In order to do this, one must preserve one's heart as though it were one's eye. We have to guard our heart from earthly desires and passions, so that it will not cease to be a conduit of spiritual, heavenly light, as the physical eye is the conduit for earthly light.

Whoever imagines he may simultaneously serve God and mammon (Mammon is a Syrian divinity who was a patron of all wealth, as Pluto was for the Greeks) is like a servant who wants to please two masters who have different characters and conflicting expectations from him, which is obviously impossible. The Lord calls us to the heavenly and the eternal, while riches tie us down to the earthly and perishable. Thus, in order to avoid being pulled in two directions at once, which hinders the work of our salvation, we must reject all extraneous, troubling, tiring worries about food, drink, and clothing—all the things that take up our time and attention and distract us from the care for our salvation. If God takes such care with irrational creatures that He gives birds food and adorns the flowers beautifully, then of course He will not leave man without everything necessary for his earthly life, since man was created in God's image and called to be the heir of the kingdom of God. All our life is in the will of God, and it does not depend on our cares. Can we ourselves add even one inch of height to our bodies by worrying? All this of course does not mean that a Christian must cease all work and live a lazy life, as some heretics have tried to interpret this passage from the Sermon of the Mount.

Work was commanded for man while he was still in Eden, even before the Fall (Gen 2:15), which was confirmed after Adam was expelled from Eden (Gen 3:19). Here it is not work that is condemned, but an excessive, overwhelming worry about the future, about tomorrow, which is completely outside of our power and which we may not even live to see. This is only an admonition for a proper prioritization of values: "Seek *first* the kingdom of God and His righteousness" (emphasis added). As a reward, the Lord Himself will care for you, so that you will have all you need for this life, and the cares of this life should not torture you and depress you, as they do those pagans who do not believe in the providence of God.

This part of the Sermon on the Mount (Matt 6:25–34) shows us a remarkable vision of the providence of God Who takes care of His creation. "Therefore do not worry about tomorrow, for tomorrow will worry about its own things." It is unwise to worry about the next day because tomorrow is outside our control, and we do not know what it will bring. Tomorrow may bring worries that we could not even imagine today.

The third part of the Sermon on the Mount (Matt 7) teaches us not to judge our neighbor, to protect the sacred from those who would blaspheme it, to be constant in prayer. Christ speaks of the wide and narrow path, of false teachers, of true and false wisdom.

"Judge not, that you be not judged." Judgment in this case does not refer to "making a judgment call" about someone or something, but condemning your neighbor, in the sense of finding fault with him, which is most often a result of self-love, vanity, and pride. Christ here forbids speaking ill of another, angrily rebuking the sins of others, especially when this is done with a sense of anger or hatred for that person. If all manner of judging were here forbidden, Christ would not have said later, "Do not give what is holy to the dogs; nor cast your pearls before swine," and Christians would not be able to fulfill their responsibility to rebuke and correct those who have sinned, something that is commanded by the Lord (Matt 18:15–17). What is forbidden here is the evil feeling of superiority over others, the joy in the misfortune of others, but not the mere assessment of the actions of one's neighbor, for if we do not call evil what it is, we may become indifferent to good and evil, and we may lose the sense of distinguishing between the two. St John Chrysostom has this to say on the subject: "If anyone performs adultery, shall I not say that adultery is an evil, must I not correct the sinner? Yes, I must correct him, but not as though he were my enemy, not as a physician who punishes, but as a physician who gives medicine. We must not accuse, not decry, but we must enlighten. We must not denounce, but advise. We must not attack with pride, but correct with love."[25]

Here, Christ forbids rebuking people for their sins with an evil feeling in one's heart without noticing our own, maybe even greater sins. However, there is nothing here spoken about civil law, as some false teachers interpret, just as judging the actions of people in principle is also not forbidden. These words of the Lord have in mind the Pharisees, who mercilessly condemned others, considering only them-selves to be righteous. Immediately after this, the Lord warns His disciples that the preaching of His divine word, that true pearl, should not be given to those who, like dogs and pigs, are incapable of receiving it due to their extreme incorrigibility in evil, and who hate anything to do with the good because they have wallowed deeply in the filth of debauchery, passions, and evil deeds.

Later, in His words, "Ask, and it will be given to you," the Lord teaches con-stancy, patience, and zeal in prayer. A true Christian who remembers the admoni-tion to seek first the kingdom of God and its righteousness will not ask for useless things in his prayer, nothing harmful for the salvation of the soul, and so he can be sure that by his prayer, what he asks will be given to him and revealed to him, as the Lord promises those who zealously pray. In Matthew's Gospel, Christ says, "How much more will your Father who is in heaven give good things to those who ask Him," while in St Luke, He says, "He will give the Holy Spirit to those who ask Him" (Luke 11:13). This is an explanation of what kinds of things one should ask in prayer. The Father will not give His Son anything harmful, and so the Lord gives a person only that which is truly beneficial to him.

As a conclusion to His teaching about our relationship with other people, the Lord gives a rule, which is called the Golden Rule: "Whatever you want men to do to you, do also to them, for this is the Law and the Prophets," for love for other people is a reflection of love for God, in the same way as love for one's brothers is a reflection of one's love for one's parents.

Christ warns that following His commandments is not easy. This is the difficult way, and the "narrow gate," but this path leads into eternal, blessed life, while the broad, easy way, attractive to those who do not like to fight their sinful passions, leads to destruction.

Here the Lord also warns His followers about various false teachers and false prophets, who can turn one away from this narrow path. In our time, these words appropriately describe all the many sectarians who speak so temptingly about the ease of salvation, completely avoiding the narrow gate and difficult path. These false teachers have the appearance of meek lambs, but inside they are ravening wolves who feast on the true sheep. These false teachers can be known "by their fruits," by their life and works. As if the Lord were speaking directly to Protestants who deny the need for good works preaching justification by faith alone, He says, "Not everyone who says to Me, 'Lord, Lord,' shall enter the kingdom of heaven, but he who does the will of My Father in heaven." Here it is clear that faith in Jesus Christ on its own is not enough; a life that reveals this faith is also necessary, and one must fulfill the commandments of Christ and do good works. In the early days of Christi-anity, many did perform miracles with the name of Christ, even Judas, who received this authority together with the rest of the Twelve, but this by itself does not save, unless such people constantly work on fulfilling the commandments of God.

The Lord repeats the same thought in the conclusion of His Sermon on the Mount. Whoever hears the words of Christ, but does not fulfill them, who does not do good works, he is like a man who builds his house on the sand, while only the man who does the will of Christ's teaching in action is like one who builds his house on rock. This comparison was easily understandable to the Jews, because Palestine occasionally saw torrential rains that would tear down houses that were built on a sandy foundation. Only he who fulfills the commandments of Christ in actual fact can remain standing when temptations attack him like a storm. He who does not fulfill the commandments will easily fall to despair and perish, rejecting Christ. This is why our Church in its hymnography asks Christ to establish us "on the rock of His commandments."[26]

St Matthew finishes his account of the Sermon on the Mount saying that the people were astonished at the teaching of Christ, for Christ taught them as one having authority, not as the scribes and Pharisees. The teaching of the Pharisees was mostly a collection of useless minutiae, in pretentious and long-winded words. The teaching of Christ was simple and exalted, for He spoke as the Son of God, as no one before Him spoke, and He spoke as Himself, not citing the authority of others. In His words they could vividly sense divine power and authority.

Healing the Leper (Matt 8:1–4)

When the Lord Jesus Christ came down from the mountain after His Sermon on the Mount, many people followed Him, doubtless overwhelmed by what they had just heard. And once again, as had happened before in the accounts of Mark and Luke (Mark 1:40–45; Luke 5:12–16), a leper approached Him and asked to be healed of his horrible disease. Of course, this was in no way the only example of Christ healing a leper, especially if we keep in mind all of the healings that Christ performed during His public ministry that are only mentioned in passing. It is not surprising that this event is similar in its telling to the ones in Mark and Luke, or that the Lord commanded this leper to appear before the priest so that he, according to the law, could officially witness the fact of his healing. Without doing this, the leper would not be able to reenter the society of the people of Israel because all would fear him and avoid him, knowing him to be sick with leprosy. The Lord ordered the healed man to be silent about his healing, but to immediately appear before the priest. Some exegetes point out that if the healed man did not immediately go to Jerusalem to the priests, but rather had begun to tell everyone about the miracle done to him, the priests who were antagonistic to Christ could have just made the claim that the healed man had never been stricken with leprosy in the first place.

Healing the Servant of the Centurion of Capernaum (Matt 8:5–13; Luke 7:1–10)

After this, the Lord returned to Capernaum, where He performed the miracle of healing the servant of the Roman centurion at a distance. This soldier was apparently the head of a local Roman garrison of one hundred soldiers. Such garrisons were usually stationed in problematic Palestinian cities. This centurion was a pagan by birth, but was sympathetic to the Jewish religion, which he proved by building several synagogues. His servant, according to St Matthew, was in great pain and was totally paralyzed, while St Luke even goes as far as to say that the man was near death. The account given in St Luke is more detailed, relating that the local Jewish elders were sent to Jesus first with a request to come and heal the servant, and then he later sent his friends, after which, apparently, as St Matthew says, he himself came out to meet the Lord as He approached the house. These words he said to the Lord: "Lord, I am not worthy that You should come under my roof. But only speak a word, and my servant will be healed."

This speech was so remarkably full of faith and humility, unusual for such a pagan, that the Lord (according to both Evangelists) "marveled" at him and found it necessary to underline such faith before all who surrounded Him, saying that He had not found such faith among those who considered themselves the chosen nation of God. Later, as St Matthew alone relates, the Lord, countering the false opinion that many Jews had as being the only members of the coming kingdom of the Messiah, said that many of the Gentiles "from east and west" would be found worthy, together with the Old Testament forefathers, to inherit this kingdom. But the sons of the kingdom, the Jews, for their lack of faith in the Messiah Who had already come, would be cast out into the outer darkness, where there will be weeping and gnashing of teeth. In these words of the Lord, the kingdom of heaven, as in many other of His words and parables, is presented through the image of the feast. Those guests who were in some way found to be rude or out of order were led out of the main room where the feast was taking place, and would be left in an outer dark room in the cold, so obviously contrasting with the light and warmth of the chamber of the feast. These pariahs would gnash their teeth from cold and sorrow. This was a universally understandable image, and here Christ uses it to vividly describe the eternal suffering of the sinner in hell. The faith and humility of the pagan centurion were immediately rewarded. His servant was healed in the exact moment that the Lord told him it would be, according to his faith.

THE RAISING OF THE SON OF THE WIDOW OF NAIN (LUKE 7:11–17)

Only St Luke describes this event, connecting it with the embassy from John the Baptist that immediately followed. From Capernaum, the Lord went into the city of Nain, near the southern border of Galilee on the northern side of the mountain called Little Hermon, in the region of the tribe of Issachar. The name Nain, which means "pleasant," referred most likely to the beautiful and fertile area found in the valley of Hesdrelon. The Lord was accompanied by His disciples and many other people. In the ancient world, many cities were surrounded by heavy walls for protection, so entry was possible only through the central gates, and it was at these gates of Nain that the Lord encountered the funeral procession of a young man, the only son of his widowed mother. Seeing the mother despondent in her grief, the Lord took pity on her and said, "Do not weep." Then He touched the funeral bier, indicating that He wanted them to stop. He called to the dead youth, "Young man, I say to you, arise!" and He immediately raised him and returned him to his mother. All those assembled were terrified, and yet these eyewitnesses still did not accept this great Miracle Worker as the Messiah, but only a "great prophet," and this was the rumor that spread concerning Him throughout all Judea and the surrounding areas.

JOHN THE BAPTIST SENDS HIS DISCIPLES TO THE LORD JESUS CHRIST, AND THE LORD'S WITNESS CONCERNING JOHN THE BAPTIST (MATT 11:2–19; LUKE 7:18–35)

St John the Baptist could not possibly have doubted the divinity of the Lord Jesus Christ (see John 1:32–34). Nevertheless, since he was already in prison, he sent two of his disciples to ask Jesus Christ the following question: "Are You the Coming One or do we look for another?" John did not need to hear the answer, but his disciples did, since they had heard of all the miracles that the Lord performed and could not understand why He did not proclaim Himself the Messiah openly, if He truly was the Messiah. But the Lord did not give a direct answer to the question, because even these disciples still clung to the incorrect notions of the earthly Messiah-King. Only he whose soul had been cleansed from all earthly things by the teaching of Christ could become worthy of knowing and truly understanding that Jesus in truth was the Messiah, the Christ. Therefore, instead of answering, He, as if citing the prophecy of Isaiah (Isa 35:2–6), directed their attention to the miracles that He performed as proof of His divinity. He added, "Blessed is he who is not offended because of Me," who shall not doubt that I am the Messiah, seeing My humble state.

The Lord, in order to make sure that no one would think that John the Baptist himself doubted in Jesus, began to speak to the people of the high dignity and service of John the Baptist, who was the greatest of the prophets. The words "but he who is least in the kingdom of heaven is greater than he," show the superiority of Christianity, even over the highest righteousness of the Old Testament. "And from the days of John the Baptist until now the kingdom of heaven suffers violence, and the violent take it by force." Here the Church of Christ in the New Testament is deliberately opposed to the "Law and Prophets" of the Old Testament Church. St John, who stood at the boundary separating the two covenants, ended the time of the Old Testament, which had a merely preparatory importance. After him, the kingdom of Christ begins, and all who force themselves can enter into it.

Citing the prophecy of Malachi (Mal 4:5), which obviously refers to the Second Coming of Christ, the Jews expected that the prophet Elijah would come before the Messiah. But concerning John, Malachi prophesied that he would be the angel who prepared the way of the Lord (Mal 3:1). The angel who foretold John's birth to Zacharias also said that John would walk before the Lord with the spirit and power of Elijah, but would not be Elijah himself. Even John himself when asked by the Jews, said that he was not Elijah. Then, the meaning of Christ's words, "And if you are willing to receive it, he is Elijah who is to come" is this: if you literally understand the prophecy of Malachi to mean that Elijah must come himself before the Messiah, then know that he who must prepare the way for the Messiah has already come. He is John. Thus, pay special attention to My witness of John: "He who has ears to hear, let him hear!"

"But to what shall I liken this generation?" meaning the scribes and Pharisees. They are like spoiled children who are never content with anything. St John, the great ascetic, who called them to sorrow and compunction regarding their own sins, was not good enough for them, since they waited for the great King, the Conquering Messiah. Neither was Jesus Christ, Who, contrary to John, did not scorn to eat at table with sinners in order to save them. "But wisdom is justified by her children." These enigmatic words are explained by Blessed Theophylact thus: "It is as if Christ is saying to them: 'when neither My life, nor John's life pleases you, and you reject all paths to salvation, then I, the Wisdom of God, will be justified not before the Pharisees, but before My children.'"[27] These "children of Wisdom" are the simple Jewish people, the repentant publicans and sinners, who believed in Christ and with their whole hearts accepted His divine teaching. They have "justified" God and His Wisdom, or in other words, they showed by their own examples that the Lord truly and wisely works out the salvation of all men. To them, the Wisdom of God was revealed, but It remained inaccessible to the proud Pharisees.

REBUKING THE SINFUL CITIES, PRAISING GOD FOR REVEALING THE TRUTH TO CHILDREN, AND A CALL TO ALL WHO ARE WEARY AND HEAVY LADEN
(MATT 11:20–30; LUKE 10:13–16, 21–22)

With sorrow in His heart, Christ declares His "woes" to the cities of Chorazin (north of Capernaum) and Bethsaida (south of Capernaum) since they did not repent, even though they saw many of Christ's miracles. The Lord compares these cities to the pagan cities of Tyre and Sidon in nearby Phoenicia, saying that the judgment proclaimed over those cities will be better at the final judgment than the judgment over the Jews who were given the opportunity for salvation. But they did not want to repent, as long ago Nineveh repented in sackcloth (a crude hair shirt that deliberately inflicts pain on the body) and ashes (sprinkling ashes on one's head and sitting on ashes were external signs of profound grief) after the prophecy of Jonah. The Lord also prophesies destruction for Capernaum for its extreme degree of arrogance, a result of its material wealth. He compares its sinfulness with that of Sodom and Gomorrah, which were destroyed by God with fire and brimstone. All these cities truly were visited by the anger of God—they were completely destroyed by the Romans during the same war that saw the destruction of Jerusalem.

The scribes and Pharisees, proud in their so-called wisdom and knowledge of Scripture, did not understand the words of Jesus, or His teaching. Due to their spiritual blindness, His teaching remained dark to them, and so the Lord praises His Father in heaven that the truth of His teaching, inaccessible to these "wise and prudent," was revealed to "babes"—simple and guileless people such as the apostles and His other close disciples and followers, who felt in their hearts, not their minds, that Jesus was truly the Messiah, the Christ. "All things have been delivered to Me by my Father," everything submits to My authority, both the physical, visible world, and the spiritual, invisible world, given not to the Son of God, Who always had such authority, but to the God-Man and Saviour of mankind, so that through Him all of mankind could be converted to salvation. "And no one knows the Son except the Father. Nor does anyone know the Father except the Son, and the one to whom the Son wills to reveal Him." All the majesty and goodness of the Son is inaccessible to any person, and the same is true of the Father. Only the Son in Himself can reveal the Father to those who come to Him. And He calls all to Himself: "Come to Me all you who labor and are heavy laden [those who are exhausted by the troubles and fruitless suffering under the lordship of sinful passions coming from pride and self-love], and I will give you rest." I will give you peace from your passions. "Take My yoke upon you," the yoke of the law of the Gospel, learn from Christ's meekness and humility, and you will find peace for your soul. This yoke of the law of the Gospels, compared with the yoke of the passions, "is easy and My burden is light," for the Lord Himself gives one the strength to bear it through the grace of the Holy Spirit, and His own personal example inspires us to bear this yoke.

FORGIVING THE SINFUL WOMAN IN THE HOUSE OF SIMON THE PHARISEE (LUKE 7:36–50)

A certain Pharisee named Simon, who apparently loved the Lord but lacked true faith in Him, invited Him to dine at his house, perhaps in order to better understand His words and actions. A woman who was well known in the city as a prostitute unexpectedly walked in and humbly stood behind Jesus. Seeing that His feet were not yet washed after the road, she began to weep over them, washing them with her tears instead of water, and wiping them with her hair. Kissing His feet, she began to anoint them with precious ointment. The Pharisees taught that even the touch of a prostitute defiles one, and so Simon, in no way moved by her apparent fervent repentance, only condemned the Lord for allowing these kisses, thinking to himself that Jesus could not possibly be a prophet; otherwise, He would have known what sort of a woman was touching Him, and He would have cast her off. Answering the hidden thoughts of the Pharisee, the Lord rebukes him by telling him the parable of the two debtors, one of whom owed five hundred denarii, another fifty. Since neither had the money necessary to pay off their respective debts, the creditor forgave them both. It was easy to answer the Lord's question regarding which of them came to love the creditor more—the one who was forgiven more. Having confirmed the Pharisee's correct answer, the Lord added, "to whom little is forgiven, the same loves little."

These last words, judging by their context, were directed at Simon, who was poor in his love for Christ and poor also in the works of love. From this parable, Simon was intended to understand that the Lord placed this repentant prostitute on a higher moral level than him, in order to help him understand that since he did not even perform the customary actions of hospitality and love for Christ (washing His feet and greeting Him with a kiss), even if he was the one who invited Christ, then he is forgiven less, even though his debt is still forgiven by Christ, for he was still somewhat inclined toward the Lord. The others who reclined with Simon, most likely also Pharisees, however, refused to accept Christ's rebuke, and they murmured at Christ's words of forgiveness to the woman, which is why He sent her away, saying "Go in peace."

HEALING THE POSSESSED MAN AND REBUKING THE PHARISEES FOR BLASPHEMING THE HOLY SPIRIT (MATT 12:22–37; MARK 3:20–30; LUKE 11:14–23)

The Lord healed a possessed man in whom lived an evil spirit that caused blindness and lack of speaking ability, and all assembled were amazed at this miracle. The Pharisees, desiring to cut short any talk among the people that Jesus was the Messiah, began to say that He cast out demons through the power of Beelzebub, prince of demons, that He had an unclean spirit with Himself (Mark 3:30), and some even called Him Beelzebub directly (Matt 10:25). The Lord's answer, in other words, means the following: "Can it be possible that Satan himself has begun to destroy his own kingdom?" In conjunction with this thought, one finds the inevitable truth that "He who is not with Me is against Me." In the kingdom of Christ, whoever is not with Christ is already His enemy, for he brings division into the one kingdom under one authority, where there can be no place for division. It is a different situation when a person is still outside the kingdom of Christ, is yet to be called to it. In that case, at least allow him not to be against Christ, not in union with the world that is antagonistic to Christ. Such a person is already Christ's and will soon become one with Christ by entering into His kingdom. Using this example of His own kingdom, the Lord explains that even in the kingdom of the devil there must be oneness of authority and action, and so devil cannot act against devil.

"By whom do your sons cast them out?" Here, He may mean the apostles to whom He gave this power, and the disciples of the Pharisees, who practiced exorcisms, and that man of whom the apostles said that he cast out demons by the name of Christ, but did not follow Christ (Mark 9:38; Luke 9:49). "They shall be your judges"; in other words, at the final judgment, their own sons will reveal them for the distorters of truth that they are. "But if I cast out demons by the Spirit of God, surely the kingdom of God has come upon you." The kingdom of God has come to you in place of the kingdom of Satan, who runs from the world, cast out by Christ. By casting out individual demons, the Lord shows that He has already tied down the "strong man," that is, Satan. "He who is not with Me is against Me, and he who does not gather with Me scatters abroad," for whoever knows and hears the teaching of Christ, but does not take His side, is already His enemy. So much more is he an enemy if he openly acts against Christ. The conclusion of this thought: "Every sin and blasphemy will be forgiven men, but the blasphemy against the Spirit will not be forgiven men."

The mercy of God is endless, and there is no sin that could be greater than God's mercy. But whoever stubbornly rejects this mercy, whoever acts against the saving grace of God, puts himself outside God's mercy, and his sin remains unforgiven, and this person perishes. This intentional antagonism against the saving grace of God, which is the grace of the Holy Spirit, Christ calls blasphemy against the Holy Spirit. The Pharisees' antagonism is vividly expressed in the fact that they dare to call the almighty works of God the works of the devil. Why will this sin not be forgiven in this age or the next? Because if a person rejects the obvious activity of the grace of the Holy Spirit, then he is incapable of repentance, without which there can be no salvation. He cannot repent! Whoever blasphemes Christ, seeing His humble state, that person will be forgiven because this is a sin of ignorance, easily washed away by repentance. This is not the same as the stubborn battle against the obvious manifestation of the power of God, which the Pharisees had, and which is far from a state of repentance. The Lord explains the Pharisees' slander against His works with the following words: "out of the abundance of the heart the mouth speaks." He warns them that they will have to answer for every idle word on the Day of Judgment, for false and evil words indicate the reality of an evil heart.

THE LORD'S ANSWER TO THOSE WHO SOUGHT A SIGN FROM HIM
(MATT 12:38–45; LUKE 11:24–26, 29–32)

The Jews were offended by Christ's humble station, and they required that He would show them a kind of sign that would definitely prove His divine authority, His Messianic dignity. They did not consider all the miracles already performed as being enough; they wanted to see a special "sign from heaven" (Matt 16:1). They ask it as enemies and hypocrites, and so the Lord calls them an "evil and adulterous generation," meaning their lack of faithfulness to God, an image used already by the prophets repeatedly when rebuking Israel for their idolatry, comparing their falls into paganism with unfaithfulness to the Bridegroom, God (see Isa 57:3; Ezek 16:15; 23:27). The Lord said that such a miracle will not be given to them, and He indicates only that great sign in the past, the type of the greatest miracle that would yet be performed—the miracle of Jonah's preservation for three days in the belly of the whale, which was a foreshadowing of the resurrection of Christ after his three-day death.

Christ was actually in the tomb only a full day and two nights, but in the East there is a custom of counting even a part of a day as a whole day or night (see 1 Sam 30:12; Gen 42:17–18; 2 Chr 10:5–12; and others). The Ninevites, inhabitants of the city of Nineveh, the capital of the Assyrian Empire, built on the shores of the Tigris, north of Babylon, who repented as a result of Jonah's prophecy, will judge the Jews at the final judgment for not hearing the preaching of their own Messiah and not desiring to repent in their stubbornness. The queen of the South, the Queen of Sheba, who came to Solomon from Arabia (1 Kgs 10), will also judge the Jews, for they came from far away only to hear the wisdom of Solomon, but the Jews do not want to listen to the Wisdom of God incarnate, Who is "greater than Solomon." Then the Lord tells the parable of the unclean spirit that left a man and then came back later together with seven other spirits, even more evil than he. The Lord means to say that even if He forced them to believe in Him through some kind of overwhelming sign from above, their moral decay was so profound that after the passage of some more time, their lack of faith would return with even greater vehemence, and they would become even worse morally. Their lack of faith and their moral decay are like the evil spirit in the possessed man. If a person remains lazy and inattentive to himself, then the evil spirit and his passions, which were once cast out of him, will return to him in even greater strength.

A Woman Praises the Mother of Christ, and Christ Answers Her: Spiritual Relation to the Lord (Matthew 12:46–50; Mark 3:31–35; Luke 8:19–21; 11:27–28)

The words of the Lord so amazed a certain woman (according to tradition, this was Marcella, a servant to Martha, which is why this excerpt is always connected in the lectionary with the reading concerning Christ's visit to Martha and Mary) that she could not contain her elation and openly glorified the Lord and His all-holy Mother, who together with His acknowledged brothers was in the crowd, only outside the house (see Matt 12:46). "Blessed is the womb" (Luke 11:27), Blessed is She who gave birth and raised such a great Teacher. Here we saw the beginning of the glorification of the Mother of God, the fulfillment of Her own prophecy: "All generations will call me blessed" (Luke 1:48). Christ answered that blessed also are all those who hear the word of God and fulfill it. St Matthew indicates that during this precise moment, Mary and His brothers were standing outside the house, and they sent someone to tell the Lord that they were there, since they were not able to come near Him because of the many people surrounding Him. The Lord always had gentle love for His mother, and even when hanging in terrible pain on the cross, He gave her over to the care of His beloved apostle. But here, during His preaching to the people, He showed everyone that fulfilling the will of the heavenly Father for Him is even higher than His love for His Mother: "Whoever does the will of My Father in heaven, is My brother, and sister, and mother."

The brothers here mentioned are named in differed places of the Gospel: James, Josiah, Simon, and Judas (Matt 13:54–56). It is also clear from putting together the events in all four Gospels (concerning the women who stood at the cross of Jesus and then later came to the tomb on the day of His resurrection) that the mother of these "brothers of Jesus" was Mary, the wife of Cleopas, whom St John calls the "sister of His Mother" (John 19:25). Apparently, Mary, Cleopas's wife, was a cousin to the Mother of God, since Mary was the only daughter of Joachim and Anna. According to tradition, Cleopas was the father of these "brothers of Jesus." Another possible explanation is that these "brothers of Jesus" were other children of Joseph from his first wife. It is entirely possible that both these traditions are, in fact, correct. In any case, "brothers" in the Jewish sense could include cousins and second cousins, and even relatives in general.

THE LORD'S PARABLES REGARDING THE KINGDOM OF GOD

THE PARABLE OF THE SOWER (MATT 13:1–23; MARK 4:1–20; LUKE 8:4–15)

A parable is a story that hides its meaning behind symbols taken from everyday life to indicate higher spiritual truth. The parables in Matthew's thirteenth chapter and in the parallel passages in the other Synoptics were spoken before such great multitudes of people that the Lord had to speak from a boat in the Sea of Tiberias so that they could better hear Him.

As St John Chrysostom explains, "The Lord spoke in parables to make His preaching more expressive, the better to leave a deep impression in the memory and the mind's eye."[28] The parables of the Lord are symbolic stories, images, and examples, which used situations and objects from the everyday life of the people and the nature surrounding them. In His parable of the sower, He vividly called to the minds of His hearers their own fields, through which an occasional road would cross, in places covered in thick weeds, in some places rocky, in some places barely covered by a thin layer of earth. Sowing is a wonderful image for the preaching of the word of God, which, when it falls on the heart, depending on the state of the heart, either gives no fruit or yields a small or large harvest. Christ indicates the sower to be Himself and the ground on which the seed falls to be the hearts of those who hear Him.

When His disciples asked Him why He spoke in parables, the Lord answered: "Because it has been given to you to know the mysteries of the kingdom of heaven, but to them it has not been given." The disciples, as future preachers of the Gospel, through a special illumination of grace, were given understanding of certain divine truths, even if not completely, at least until the descent of the Holy Spirit, while all the other people were incapable of understanding these truths by reason of their moral primitiveness and false expectations of the Messiah and His kingdom, a fact prophesied by Isaiah (Isa 6:9–10). If one were to show such morally rotten, spiritually ignorant people the truth as it is, without disguising it behind veils and images, then even though they have eyes, they would not see it, and even though they have ears, they would not hear it. Only by covering up the truth, so to speak, by using images and objects recognizable to everyone, could the truth become accessible to the understanding. Without being forced, the thought of such people then naturally moved up from the visible image to the invisible reality, from the external sign to the inner spiritual meaning.

"For whoever has, to him more will be given, and he will have abundance; but whoever does not have, even what he has will be taken away from him." These words were repeated more than once by the Lord in various places in the Gospels (Matt 25:29; Luke 19:26). It means that he who is rich can become even richer with increased effort, while he who is poor, if he is lazy, will lose what little he already has. In the spiritual sense, Christ tells the apostles that they, who have already been given understanding of certain truths of the kingdom of God, can go ever deeper into these mysteries, understanding them ever more profoundly. The people, however, would lose even the little knowledge they do have if these higher truths were not given to them in symbolic fashion, in a way more appropriate to their level. St John Chrysostom interprets this place thus: "Whoever desires and tries himself to acquire gifts of grace, to him God gives everything. But whoever does not have this desire and effort, he will not be benefited even by the small gifts that he imagines he already has."[29]

Whoever has a mind already so darkened, a heart so hardened by sin, that he cannot understand the word of God, it is as though the word falls only to the surface of his mind and heart, without giving any deeper roots, like a seed on the road where everyone constantly walks by; and the evil one (the devil) easily catches him and makes his hearing the word pointless. The ground full of stones is symbolic of those kinds of people who are attracted by the words of the Gospel as an interesting new idea. Sometimes this interest is even sincere and genuine, but their hearts are cold and hard as stone, unable to be changed. They are not capable, as the Gospel requires of them, to radically change their usual way of life, to reject their beloved friends the passions, to battle temptations, or to bear for the sake of the Gospel's truth any sort of sorrow or suffering. As soon as such people begin to battle temptations, they fall, lose heart, and betray their faith and the Gospel.

The ground full of weeds is symbolic of people who have been snared by countless passions—love of money, love of sinful pleasures, and in general all the pleasant things of the world. The good ground indicates people with kind, pure hearts, who, having heard the word of God, firmly decide to make it their guide in life and therefore bear the fruits of virtues. "There are many kinds of virtues, as well as different levels of success in spiritual wisdom" (Blessed Theophylact).[30]

THE PARABLE OF THE TARES (MATT 13:24–43)

"The kingdom of heaven," the earthly church established by the heavenly Founder that leads people to heaven, "is like a man who sowed good seed in his field; but while men slept," meaning at night, when one can act in secret without anyone seeing, an indication of the cunning of our enemy, "his enemy came and sowed tares among the wheat." Tares are weeds that may visibly resemble wheat while they are small, but when they mature, it is difficult to tear them out without also damaging the roots of the good wheat. Christ's teaching is sowed all over the world, but the devil through his temptations also sows evil among men. In the huge noetic field of the world, thus, the worthy sons of the Heavenly Father (the wheat) and the sons of Satan (the tares) live together. The Lord patiently bears them, leaving them until the reaping, the Final Judgment, when the reapers, the angels of God, will collect the tares, that is, all those who do evil, and will cast them into a fiery furnace, into eternal hellish tortures. The wheat (the righteous) will be gathered and placed in the barn of the Lord, that is, the kingdom of heaven, where the righteous will shine as the sun.

THE PARABLE OF THE SEED THAT GROWS INVISIBLY (MARK 4:26–29)
The kingdom of heaven is like a seed that was once dropped in the ground and begins to grow by itself without anyone noticing. The inner process of this growth is invisible and not easily explained. How an entire plant can grow from a small seed, nobody can say. In the same way, the spiritual transfiguration of the soul of man, effected by the power of the grace of God, is a process that is invisible and difficult to explain.

THE PARABLE OF THE MUSTARD SEED (MATT 13:31–32; MARK 4:30–32; LUKE 13:18–19)
In the East, the mustard plant can grow to an astonishing size, even though its seed is incredibly small. Thus, the Jews of that time had a saying, "small as a mustard seed." The meaning of this parable is that although the beginning of the kingdom of God is apparently small and without glory, the power that is hidden within it can defeat all hindrances and it will transform into a great and universal kingdom. St John Chrysostom has this to say about the parable: "With this parable, the Lord wants to give an image of the spread of the preaching of the Gospel. Although His disciples were the least powerful of all men, the most humble, the power hidden in them was so great that their word spread throughout the entire known world."[31] The Church of Christ, at first small and unnoticed by the world, spread through the earth so much that a great number of nations, like the birds in the parable, are able to fit under its shadow. The same thing happens in the soul of every person. The fragrance of God's grace, at first barely noticeable, begins to inundate the soul more and more, and the soul then becomes the dwelling place of all manner of virtues.

THE PARABLE OF THE LEAVEN (MATT 13:33–35; MARK 4:33–34; LUKE 13:20–21)
This parable has the same meaning as the previous one. In the words of St John Chrysostom: "As leaven has the effect of diffusing its power throughout a large volume of flour, just so did the Apostles transform the entire world."[32] In the same

way, in the soul of every individual member of the kingdom of Christ, the power of grace is invisible, but it truly overcomes all the powers of his soul and transforms them, sanctifying them. Under the three measures, some believe the three powers of the soul are indicated—the mind, the emotions, and the will.

The Parable of the Treasure Hidden in the Field (Matt 13:44)

A certain man learned of treasure buried in a field that did not belong to him. In order to use this treasure, he ensured that the treasure would not be found, sold all that he had, and bought the field, becoming the owner of the treasure. A wise man would consider the kingdom of God to be equally precious, especially if we are to understand the treasure as spiritual gifts and inner sanctification. Hiding within himself this precious treasure, the follower of Christ sacrifices everything and rejects everything in order to keep it.

The Parable of the Pearl of Great Price (Matt 13:45–46)

The meaning of this parable is the same as the previous one. In order to gain the kingdom of heaven, that greatest treasure a man can have, one must sacrifice everything, all one's goods, everything one owns.

The Parable of the Net Cast into the Sea (Matt 13:47–50)

This parable has the same meaning as the parables of the wheat and the tares. The sea is the world, the net is the teaching of faith, and the fishermen are the apostles and their successors. This net gathered all kinds—barbarians, Greeks, Jews, fornicators, publicans, thieves. The shore and the sifting of the fish indicates the Last Judgment and the end of the world, when the righteous will be separated from the sinner, as the good fish in the nets are separated from the bad. It must be mentioned that Christ the Saviour often takes advantage of a given situation to indicate the difference in the future life between the righteous and the sinners. Therefore, it would be incorrect to agree with the opinions of those (such as Origen) who think that in the end all will be saved, even the devil.

When we interpret the parables of the Lord, we must keep in mind that when the Lord taught with parables, He used examples that were not especially unusual, but rather from the everyday, mundane life of His listeners. St John Chrysostom explains that He did this in order to make His words more vivid and more easily absorbed by the memory. Therefore, it is very important to find the meaning only in general, not in the minute details themselves, not trying to find significance in every single word taken separately. Of course, every parable must also be understood in its reference to the other parables that are similar in content, as well as in reference to the general spirit of Christ's teaching.

It is important to note that in His preaching and parables, the Lord Jesus Christ makes a very clear distinction between the kingdom of heaven and the kingdom of God. The kingdom of heaven is that blessed state of the righteous which will be revealed to them in the future life, after the Final Judgment. The kingdom of God is the kingdom, on earth, of those who believe in Him and strive to do the will of His Father in heaven. This kingdom of God, which began with the coming of Christ the Saviour to earth, invisibly enters the souls of men and prepares them on earth to inherit the kingdom of heaven, which will be revealed after the end of time. The aforementioned parables are all dedicated to illustrating this distinction.

St Matthew sees Christ's preaching in parables as a fulfillment of the prophecy of Asaph: "I will open my mouth in parables" (Ps 77:1–2). Even though Asaph refers to himself, as a prophet, he effectively became a prototype of the Messiah, which is seen in the following words: "I will declare hard sayings of old," saying things that could not be known by a mortal man, but only by the all-knowing Messiah. The "hard sayings," or the hidden things, of the kingdom of God are known, of course, only to the hypostatic Wisdom of God.

When He asked the disciples if they understood all that He had said, they answered affirmatively. He then calls them "scribes," not in the pejorative sense of the Jewish scribes—elders who only knew the old law and even what they knew, they twisted and interpreted incorrectly. Rather, these are scribes who have been taught the kingdom of heaven, are capable of becoming preachers of this kingdom of heaven. Taught by the Lord Jesus Christ, they now know both the "old" prophecies and the "new" teaching of Christ regarding the kingdom of heaven. In the forthcoming work of spreading the Gospel, they will be able to, like the master of the house, bring forth from this treasury both new and old things, using both whenever they are necessary. Thus, all the successors of the apostles in the work of preaching must use both the Old and the New Testaments, for the truth in both is God-inspired.

THE LORD ANSWERS THOSE WHO ARE HESITANT TO FOLLOW HIM
(MATT 8:18–22; LUKE 9:57–62)

The people pressed around the Lord so much that He had no place where He could be alone (Luke 4:42) for prayer and conversation with His apostles. There was not even time to have a bit of bread to eat (Mark 3:20); so on one occasion, the Lord ordered His disciples to sail to the other side of the Sea of Tiberias. When they had already gathered in the boat, a certain scribe came up to the Lord, desiring to follow Him, wherever He would go. Desiring to warn him that he would be placing on himself a very difficult burden, which could be too heavy for him to bear, the Lord described the kind of life He was leading: "Foxes have holes and birds of the air have nests, but the Son of Man has nowhere to lay His head." He had no place where He would be able to rest from His constant work. Calling Himself the Son of Man, the Lord humbly underlines His humanity, but at the same time, those who know the book of Daniel (Dan 7:13–14) will recognize the implied hint to His Messianic dignity.

This answer apparently had a strong effect on those disciples of Christ who were already following Him. Desiring to test their readiness to follow Him everywhere with total self-denial, the Lord said to one of them, "Follow Me," showing by this that He desired to be in more intimate communion with him and to show him the good things of the kingdom of God. But the disciple began to waver, citing that he first had to go bury his father. The Lord answered: "Follow Me, and let the dead bury their own dead." Two times he uses the word "dead" to indicate two different states. The first word indicates them who are dead spiritually, and only the second refers to those physically dead. The Lord means to tell His follower that one must leave everything behind for the case of this most important work of preaching the kingdom of God. "Leave those dead who are deaf to My Word, to My work. Let them who are completely tied to this earthly world bury their corpses, but you, who have heard the words of life, follow Me."

Through this somewhat confusing prohibition to fulfill a son's last duty to his father, Christ is apparently either testing the character and loyalty of His follower or is warning him against his other relatives, who perhaps wanted to distract him from following Christ. Another disciple, not waiting to be called, himself said that he wanted to follow Christ, but first asked to say good-bye to his family. But the Lord answered him, "No one, having put his hand to the plow, and looking back, is fit for the kingdom of God." In other words, whoever has already made the decision to follow Christ should not look back at the world with its family relations and worldly attachments, for any kind of attachment to the world hinders one from wholeheartedly giving himself to Christ.

CALMING THE STORM ON THE SEA (MATT 8:23–27; MARK 4:35–41; LUKE 8:22–25)

When they had cast off, Jesus, physically exhausted from all His day's work, fell asleep. A terrible storm suddenly appeared, which is not unusual for the Sea of Tiberias, since it is surrounded by mountains on all sides (it is for this reason that a mere lake was called by the impressive name of "sea"). The disciples, nearly all of whom were fishermen of this very lake, were used to these sudden storms; nevertheless, they began to lose control of the boat, and in despair woke up their Teacher, "Lord, save us! We are perishing!" On the one hand, this was an obvious expression of concern for their lives, but on the other hand, it was a call to the power of the Lord. According to St Mark, the disciples even dared to rebuke the Master: "Do You not care that we are perishing?" For this, the Lord rebuked them for their lack of faith, and then calmed the waves with the power of His word. Both the disciples and some other people (perhaps in nearby boats) were amazed: "Who can this be, that even the wind and the sea obey Him!"

Casting Out the Legion of Demons in the Country of the Gadarenes
(Matt 8:28–34; Mark 5:1–20; Luke 8:26–40)

Having crossed to the other side, Jesus and His disciples came to a region on the eastern side of the Sea of Tiberias, which Saints Mark and Luke call the country of the Gadarenes, while St Matthew calls it the country of the Gergesenes, named after another city of Gorges; but both of these cities were part of a more generally named "Decapolis." On the shore, they were met by one demoniac according to Mark and Luke, while St Matthew mentions two demoniacs. It is probable that one of these two was a rather famous person in Gadara, and was in an especially terrible state of possession, while the other, in comparison, was hardly noticeable.

Possession, in its essence, is a state where a man loses his personal consciousness and becomes enslaved to the reason of the demon, which then has full control of his body and the powers of his soul, resulting in indescribable suffering inflicted by the man's own actions. The greatness and power of the Son of God, hidden to the eyes of men, were obvious to the demons that have a more complete spiritual vision, and so they were in a state of horror and trepidation. The possessed men began to scream, confessing Jesus to be the Son of God and imploring Him not to torture them with His near presence. According to Mark and Luke, the more obvious demoniac answered the question about his name by calling himself "Legion," indicating the huge number of demons possessing him. The demons asked permission of Jesus not to be cast out into the abyss and not be forced to leave this country, but instead to enter a herd of pigs that was grazing nearby.

We do not know enough about the nature of the evil spirits to understand why they asked to enter these animals, but it is typical that of all the animals they could have chosen, they asked for the animals most despised and considered most unclean in the law, rather than be forced to leave that country and not be able to continue their "work" there. The Lord allowed them to enter the herd of swine, and the crazed pigs threw themselves off a nearby cliff and drowned in the sea. The Lord apparently allowed this to happen in order to remind the Gadarenes that they raised swine contrary to the law of Moses, especially since there were so many of them, according to St Mark—nearly two thousand pigs. At the same time, this circumstance immediately drew the attention of all the inhabitants of the region, who saw the well-known possessed man suddenly in his right mind and healthy, sitting at the feet of Jesus. But by all accounts they were not enlightened by what they saw; rather, they were merely horrified and probably were afraid that Jesus's continued presence would mean more serious financial losses. Their distress at losing the pigs apparently overwhelmed any feeling of gratitude they may have had at the miraculous healing of a man who had terrorized the countryside, and they asked the Lord to leave their country.

What madness these people had to desire the absence of a man who had so obviously destroyed the power of the devil! Interestingly, instead of His usual prohibition of speaking about miracles, Jesus here tells the healed demoniac to return home and tell everyone what God had done to him. This is likely because the Lord did not have the same worries that He did in His own country and Judea, where the general misunderstanding concerning the Messiah was so rampant. In addition, as is immediately obvious, the Gadarenes were especially ignorant religiously speaking, and the Lord wanted to reach their hearts through the healed demoniac's preaching concerning Him. And truly, as St Mark tells us, the man did begin to preach Christ through all of Decapolis, and through this, he prepared the ground for future preaching by the apostles and for the conversion of many people to Christ.

HEALING THE WOMAN WITH AN ISSUE OF BLOOD AND RESURRECTING THE DAUGHTER OF JAIRUS (MATT 9:18–26; MARK 5:21–43; LUKE 8:41–56)

Jesus Christ and His disciples returned to the western shore of Lake Gennesareth, where Capernaum was situated. A crowd was already there, waiting for Him, and among them was a ruler of the synagogue named Jairus, whose only daughter of twelve was near death. Although the rulers of synagogues were generally of the party antagonistic to Jesus (John 7:47–48), this man, hearing of Jesus's many miracles, and perhaps himself being a witness of the healing of the centurion's servant, began to hope that Jesus may also heal his daughter.

Not having the kind of faith that Christ praised in the centurion, he asked the Lord to come and lay His hands on her, so that she would become well. Seeing this, the people followed after the Lord with extreme curiosity to the house of Jairus, and since everyone wanted to be near the great Miracle Worker, they were crowding Him from all sides. During this procession, a certain woman who suffered for twenty years from constant bleeding and who by now had lost all hope of being healed, approached Jesus from behind and unnoticeably touched His garments.

According to the law of Moses, a woman who suffered from such a disease was considered unclean, was required to remain at home, and was forbidden from touching anyone (Lev 15:25–28). But this poor woman had such a burning faith in the Lord Jesus Christ that she decided to secretly touch only His clothes, completely sure that this touch would be enough to heal her. And her faith was justified. She was immediately healed, and "she felt in her body that she was healed of the affliction" (Mark 5:29).

St Mark gives the most detailed account of this healing, and according to him, Jesus felt that power had gone out of Him and He turned to the people, asking "Who touched My clothes?" Of course, He knew who had touched Him, but He asked it in order to show everyone what faith this woman had that the miracle would be performed. The woman understood that she could no longer remain hidden, and she fell before Him and revealed the whole truth before everyone. According to the Jews, she had committed a crime by entering the crowd, having made everyone unclean by her mere presence, and so with fear and trembling she awaited her just condemnation for her actions. But the Lord calmed her with the words: "Daughter, your faith has made you well. Go in peace, and be healed of your affliction."

During this healing, the daughter of Jairus died, and someone came from the house to tell them not to bother the Teacher. Seeing the despair of the girl's father, the Lord comforted him: "Do not be afraid; only believe." Having entered the house, they found there some "mourners," professional weepers who were invited to cry over the bodies of the dead, according to the Eastern tradition. This weeping, which would continue for eight days for a simple dead man, a month for those of more exalted standing, was accompanied by depressing music on strings or flutes. "Why make this commotion and weep?" said the Lord to them, "The child is not dead, but sleeping." Of course, these words must not be literally interpreted because even Lazarus, who lay for four days in the tomb and was already stinking, was referred to by Jesus as "sleeping" (John 11:11–14). Truly, the death of the girl was so obvious to all who attended her that they even began to laugh at Jesus.

Only worthy people, who could appreciate the great mystery of God's omnipotence, could be eyewitnesses of the great miracle of resurrecting the dead, and so the Lord ordered all of them to leave, keeping only Peter, James, and John and the parents of the dead girl near His side. Having approached the dead girl, the Lord took her by the hand and spoke two powerful words: "*Talitha, cumi,*" which means "Little girl, I say to you, arise!" Immediately she was raised from the dead, and her body was so strong that she was not hindered from immediately getting up and walking like a healthy person. Everyone was amazed, and the Lord ordered that the resurrected girl be given food, in order to fully convince the parents that this was truly their daughter, not a ghost. As was His custom, He forbade them to speak of the miracle.

HEALING THE TWO BLIND MEN AND THE DUMB DEMONIAC (MATT 9:27–34)

When Jesus walked out of Jairus's house, the crowd followed Him, and in the midst of them were two blind men shouting, "Son of David, have mercy on us!" The Lord continued to walk, as though He were paying no attention to their cries, apparently testing the faith of the blind men, who were calling Him "son of David," that is, the Messiah. When He came to a house (it is not clear which house), and the blind men had come closer with the same request for healing, Jesus asked whether they believed in His power to heal them. When they answered affirmatively, Christ touched their eyes so that they could feel the moment of healing, and their eyes were opened. Jesus strictly forbade them from speaking of the miracle, but they could not contain their joy and gratitude to their Healer and "spread the news about Him in all that country."

The moment they left, someone led a speechless demoniac before Jesus. He could not ask to be healed, because the demon had bound his tongue. Therefore, the Lord did not ask him about his faith, as He usually did in such cases. He ordered the demon to leave, and the dumb man began to speak again. The amazed crowd began to say that nothing like this had ever been seen in Israel, but the Pharisees, desiring to lessen the effect of the miracle on the people, said that Jesus cast out demons by the power of the prince of demons, Satan.

THE SECOND VISIT TO NAZARETH (MATT 13:53–58; MARK 6:1–6)

Then Jesus once again came "to His own country," Nazareth, the home of His Mother and worldly father Joseph, the place where He was raised. There, He taught at the local synagogues so that "they were astonished, and said, 'Where did this man get this wisdom and these mighty works?'" This was not the same amazement that we read about in a previous visit, but rather a wonder connected with annoyance: "Is this not the carpenter's son?" The Nazarenes either did not know or did not believe in the miraculous Incarnation and birth of Jesus Christ, considering Him a mere son of Joseph and Mary. But this is not meant to excuse them, for even in a previous time, there were many cases when simple parents gave birth to exalted sons. Such were David, Amos, Moses, and others. It would have been more appropriate for them to respect Christ for this since He, born of simple parents, was able to find such wisdom that it was obvious it did not come from human learning but from the grace of God.

This was of course, due to typical human envy, which is always evil. People often look with envy and hatred at their own countrymen who develop unusual talents and are raised up to a higher level. Here, there were perhaps His close acquaintances who knew Him in various everyday circumstances, and so did not want to see in Him anything out of the ordinary. "A prophet is not without honor, except in his own country." This is not how it should be, but many times it is exactly like this, for people often pay more attention not to what is being preached to them, but *who* is doing the preaching. And if a person who has been found worthy to be chosen for a divine calling is someone they have grown used to seeing in everyday contexts, his acquaintances continue to see him as they always have, without giving credence to his words as being prophetic. The Lord adds to this adage the phrase, "and in his own house," meaning that even His brothers (see John 7:5) did not believe in Him. Nowhere does Christ find so many barriers to Himself and His teaching as in His own city, where they even tried once to throw Him off a cliff (Luke 4:28–29). "Now He did not do many mighty works there because of their unbelief," since the performance of miracles does not only depend on the miraculous power of God but also on the faith of the people who receive the miracles.

CHRIST WALKS THROUGHOUT GALILEE WITH HIS DISCIPLES AND CERTAIN WOMEN: HIS SORROW AT THE LACK OF WORKERS FOR THE HARVEST (MATT 9:35–38; MARK 6:6; LUKE 8:1–3)

The crowds of people whom Christ sees as He walks through the cities and villages are compared by Him to a herd of sheep who are wandering aimlessly without a shepherd. The image is especially understandable in Palestine, a pastoral country. The spiritual teachers of this nation were not true pastors and teachers. They themselves were blind and not only did not illuminate the people with true teaching, but led them into worse sin. "The harvest truly is plentiful, but the laborers are few." The field, covered in ripe wheat, has to be harvested before the crop fails, but there are very few workers. The meaning of His words are this: there are a great number of people who desire to enter the kingdom of the Messiah and who are ready to accept it, but there are very few teachers of the nation who are prepared for this great work. "Pray the Lord of the harvest," that is, God Himself, that He would deign to make new teachers, not in the spirit of the Pharisees, but for the work of preaching the coming kingdom of the Messiah. During these travels of the Lord throughout Galilee, He was accompanied by a few women whom He had helped in one way or another, who from a feeling of gratitude served Him out of their financial resources. They ended up following the Lord even to Golgotha and then became that choir of myrrh-bearing women whom the Church glorifies to this day.

CHRIST SENDS THE TWELVE TO PREACH (MATT 10:1–42; MARK 6:7–13; LUKE 9:1–6; 12:11–12)
Pitying this mass of people who had no pastors, and it being physically impossible to lead all of them Himself, the Lord sends His disciples to preach the kingdom. This sending out of the apostles is markedly different from the preaching after the resurrection. During the latter, the Lord sends the apostles to the whole world, to preach the Gospel to all nations and to lead all of them into His kingdom through the mystery of baptism. But in the former, Christ only sends them to the lost sheep of the house of Israel, to the Jews alone. He ordered the apostles only to preach the coming of the kingdom of heaven, but not yet to lead them into this kingdom. This is intended to be a preparatory mission, for the apostles themselves have yet to be clothed in power from on high, given them later through the descent of the Holy Spirit, the Comforter. The Lord sends them two by two, in order that they can support each other physically, but also to give more credence to their preaching, because the law of Moses required there to be two in order to establish the veracity of a witness (John 8:17, Deut 19:15).

Knowing that people would demand to see signs as proof of the truth of their word, the Lord gave the apostles power over unclean spirits and the power to heal the sick and resurrect the dead. In order to ensure the success of their mission, He warns them of the danger of love of money and of any care for food, clothing, and lodging, saying that "a laborer is worthy of his wages" (Luke 10:7). God did not allow His servants, who rejected all care for themselves for the sake of their service, to be denied anything necessary for their sustenance. In every town or village, they were instructed to stay only in one house, a house that would not bring their mission into disrepute, so that, according to Blessed Jerome, "the dignity of the preaching would not be lessened by the evil reputation of those who housed the Apostles."[33] Also, they could not move from house to house, which is typical of a frivolous character. "And when you go into a household, greet it. If the household is worthy, let your peace come upon it." This was a typical greeting for the Jews, but of course desiring peace is not the same as bringing it. So the Lord further explains that their invocation for peace will truly bring peace to that house or town that will accept them with joy and with a pure heart. In the contrary situation, their invocation will remain without effect, and "let your peace return to you."

And if someone will deny hospitality to the apostles, they must shake the dust off their feet. The Jews believed that even the earth and dust on which the Gentiles walked was unclean, and it had to be shaken off. Giving this command, Christ wanted to show that such Jews were like the Gentiles, for "it will be more tolerable for the land of Sodom and Gomorrah," those cities that were destroyed for their extreme sinfulness and depravity, "in the day of judgment, than for that city!" Those who reject the preaching of Christ as the Law of God are more criminal than those who, having never received the Law of God, rejected merely the requirements of the natural law of the conscience, which is not so obvious or categorical.

The Lord sends His apostles first to only the Jews because the Jews were the chosen nation of God, to whom the Messiah was promised by the Old Testament prophets, and among whom He appeared in the flesh. Later, Christ gives instructions regarding the apostolic calling in general. The Lord warns the apostles of those dangers that will greet them. He says that they will feel as helpless as sheep surrounded by ravenous wolves. "Therefore be wise as serpents," meaning be careful not to put your lives into unnecessary danger, be discerning where it would make sense to sow the word of God and where to avoid it, according to the commandment not to cast pearls before swine. At the same time, they are admonished to be "harmless as doves," or of such character that no man would be able to accuse them of anything criminal. The Lord warns that the apostles will have to witness to Him before lords and kings, keeping in mind not only this temporary mission, but the future worldwide preaching that became the hallmark of the apostolic calling. They were to be subjected to many persecutions from unbelievers.

However, they must not worry and begin to doubt their calling, or to wonder about what words to use in various situations, for the Holy Spirit Himself would inspire them with the necessary words. Hatred for the Gospel preaching and its preachers and confessors would be so strong in the people of this world, already given the name "wolves," that even the closest familial ties would mean nothing. All this happened exactly as the Lord predicted in the age of persecutions, when truly brother would betray brother to execution, and when all the true followers of Christ were subjected to the worst and most inhuman hatred of the enemies of Christianity.

Those who will bear all these persecutions patiently to the end, that is, until death, and will not reject Christ, will be saved. They will be found worthy of eternal blessedness in the kingdom of heaven. The apostles should not, however, pointlessly throw away their own lives, which were so necessary for the salvation of many. If they are to be persecuted in one city, Christ tells them to flee to another. "You will not have gone through the cities of Israel before the Son of Man comes." In another parallel passage, Christ adds these words as well, "in His Kingdom" (Matt 16:28). Here, Christ is speaking not of His second glorious coming to judge the world. The coming of Jesus Christ into His kingdom is the same as the beginning of this kingdom, which occurred after the resurrection and the descent of the Holy Spirit on the apostles, after which they went into the whole world preaching the beginning of this kingdom. Thus, the Lord here is telling them that they will not have time to cover even all of Palestine with their preaching because the hour will come for the beginning of the kingdom, the passion, resurrection, and descent of the Holy Spirit.

By sending out the apostles to this preliminary mission, which could be beneficial to them as a kind of "school of preaching in which they would prepare themselves for the labors of the evangelical mission for the whole world" (St John Chrysostom),[34] the Lord indicates the short amount of time that they have at their disposal, for already the hour of His suffering and death was coming. For their work, the apostles were not to expect any honors; on the contrary, they were to prepare themselves for maltreatment, for if the Jews called the Lord Himself Beelzebub, then of course they will persecute His disciples even more. "A disciple is not above his teacher, nor a servant above his master.... Therefore do not fear them. For there is nothing covered that will not be revealed"; that is, their faith and innocence will eventually become known to all. "Whatever I tell you in the dark, speak in the light; and what you hear in the ear, preach on the housetops." In other words, that which I have spoken to you in solitude in the small corner of the world that is Palestine, you will have to preach to the entire world, to all the nations, from the proverbial housetop.

The apostles are told not to fear those "who kill the body but cannot kill the soul." For without the will of God, nothing will happen to them, since God's providence reaches out and covers everything, even birds and the hair on a man's head. "Are not two sparrows sold for a copper coin?" The point here is their low price, indicating the apparent insignificance of these birds.

Whoever will firmly confess Christ before men, despite all slander and persecution, him Christ will also confess as His faithful servant, at the judgment of the heavenly Father. But whoever will deny Christ, Christ will deny him.

"I did not come to bring peace but a sword." Of course, this must not be understood literally, but in the sense that disagreement and quarrels are the inevitable result of the coming of Christ to earth, since the hatred of people will begin a terrible war against the kingdom of God, its preachers and followers. "He who loves father or mother more than Me is not worthy of Me." These words and the words immediately following indicate that service to Christ necessitates the sacrifice of all earthly attachments, even family love.

"And he who does not take his cross and follow after Me, is not worthy of Me." This image is taken from the Roman practice of forcing convicted criminals to carry their own cross to the place of their execution. This means that we, when we have become the disciples of Christ, must in His name bear all manner of temptations and suffering, even the heaviest and most humiliating, if this is what God intends for us.

"He who finds his life will lose it, and he who loses his life for My sake will find it." Whoever prefers earthly goods to the kingdom of heaven, whoever sacrifices future good things for the sake of those on earth, whoever goes as far as to actually reject Christ in order to preserve his earthly life, that person will destroy his soul eternally. Whoever sacrifices everything for the sake of Christ, even including his own life, that person preserves his soul for eternal life.

As He instructed and consoled the apostles, the Lord Jesus Christ reminded them of that reward that awaits everyone who receives them in His name: "He who receives you receives Me, and he who receives Me receives Him who sent Me." Christ says that whoever receives the apostles as prophets or righteous men, will receive the same rewards as await the prophet and the righteous. Whosoever even gives a follower of Christ a mere cup of water to quench his thirst will not remain unrewarded.

Having finished His instruction to the twelve, Jesus went to preach in the cities of Galilee, while the apostles, divided into groups of two, went through the towns preaching repentance. They cast out many demons and anointed many sick with oil and healed them. Later, at the Mystical Supper, it becomes obvious from the answer to the question given the Lord that during this preaching they lacked nothing for their daily needs. Apparently, they all returned to the Lord when He heard of John the Baptist's death.

THE BEHEADING OF JOHN THE BAPTIST (MATT 14:1–12; MARK 6:14–29; LUKE 9:7–9)

The introduction to this event in the Gospels is the fact that Herod Antipas the tetrarch began to wonder whether Jesus Christ was John the Baptist risen from the dead. As St Luke explains, Herod was not the first to have this thought, but rather was influenced by conversations among his courtiers (Luke 9:7–9).

The Jews did not have a custom of celebrating their birthdays, but Herod, emulating other Eastern monarchs, decided to throw a feast in honor of his day of birth, inviting all the important people in Galilee. According to the practices of the East, women were not allowed to take part in the feasts of men; only slave girls were allowed to dance. But Salome, a fitting daughter for the prodigal Herodias, who lived in sin with Herod, ignored all customs and decency, walked into the hall of the feast wearing the skimpy outfit of a slave dancer, and began to dance. Her seductive dance so aroused the already drunk Herod that he swore an oath to give her anything her heart desired. Salome walked out and asked her mother, who was not taking part in the feast, what she should request. Not stopping to think even for a moment, Herodias knew the answer. The greatest gift she could ask for was the death of her hated accuser John the Baptist. She answered, "The head of John the Baptist!"

But she was afraid that such a promise would not be fulfilled by Herod, since Herod on the one hand feared the people, and on the other hand respected John himself as a "just and holy man," and even "when he heard him, he did many things, and heard him gladly" (Mark 6:20). She told her daughter to demand the immediate death of the prophet, and even gave her a platter, on which they were to bring her the head of the dead man. The girl did exactly as her mother told her, immediately. She walked back into the hall of the feast and told the king, "I want you to give me at once the head of John the Baptist on a platter."

Both Evangelists mention that Herod was saddened by this request, not desiring, obviously, to execute John. But at the same time, he was ashamed to break his own oath due to his pride and false sense of honor before his guests. So he sent an executioner, probably his own bodyguard, who immediately beheaded St John and brought the head back on a platter. This feast most likely did not occur in the usual residence of Herod in Tiberias, but in his residence beyond the Jordan, Julia, which was not far from the fortress of Makhera, where John was held prisoner, or perhaps the feast occurred in the fortress itself.

Tradition tells us that Herodias mocked the head for a long time, pierced his tongue with needles, the tongue that had accused her in sin, and finally ordering that the head be dumped into a rubbish heap near Makhera. The disciples of John took his headless body and put him in a tomb, as St Mark writes. According to tradition, this was a cave in which the Prophets Obadiah and Elisha were buried, near the city of Sebastian, built on the place of the former capital of Samaria. The Church celebrates this tragic event every year on August 29 as a strict fast day. Herod later received his just reward. His army was routed in battle, and being forced to return to Rome, he was stripped of all his titles and wealth and was exiled to Gaul, where he died together with his wife Herodias in prison. Salome's death was even more gruesome. One day in winter, she was walking on an icy river when the ice beneath her broke and she fell in. Her head was then sliced off by a piece of ice.

Having buried their master, the disciples of John told of all that had happened to the Lord Jesus Christ, on the one hand desiring consolation in their sorrow, and on the other hand desiring to warn Him of the possible danger to Him from Herod as well, in whose region He was preaching. St Mark also mentions that at the same moment the apostles all returned from their travels and told Him of all that they had done and taught.

When the Lord heard of St John's execution, He departed (according to all the Synoptics) into a desert place with His disciples. Apparently, when He heard the news, He was somewhere near the Sea of Tiberias, because they left by boat. This desert place was near Bethsaida, according to St Luke, who also adds that Herod, thinking that Jesus Christ was John risen from the dead, sought to find Him.

THE MIRACULOUS FEEDING OF THE FIVE THOUSAND WITH FIVE BREADS
(MATT 14:14–21; MARK 6:32–44; LUKE 9:10–17; JOHN 6:1–15)

All four Evangelists tell of this event, and St John even indicates that this was the instigating event for Christ to reveal before the Jews His teaching of the bread from heaven and of the mystery of the communion of His Body and Blood. In addition, St John gives the very important chronological detail that this all occurred right before the Passover, the third Passover of Christ's public ministry.

After hearing of John the Baptist's death, Jesus Christ left Galilee together with the apostles, who had just returned from their journeys, on a boat to the eastern side of the Sea of Tiberias, to a deserted place near Bethsaida. Since there was a city called Bethsaida located on the western bank near Capernaum, this was apparently a different city, east of the point where the Jordan River flowed into the Sea of Tiberias, called Bethsaida-Julia. According to St Mark, the crowds saw that He was making His way there, and many ran there on foot from all the cities and arrived there even before the boat, so that when Christ arrived, there was already a crowd waiting for Him.

Seeing the multitude, the Lord had pity on them, for they were "as sheep without a shepherd," and He began to teach them many things (Mark 6:34), telling them of the kingdom of God (Luke 9:11), and healing their sick (Matt 14:14). After some time had passed, He, according to St John's account, climbed up to a hill to sit with His disciples and saw that even more people were coming to Him. The day was already turning to evening. Then the apostles began to say to Him, "This is a deserted place, and the hour is already late. Send the multitudes away, that they may go into the villages and buy themselves food." But the Lord did not want to send them away and said to His disciples, "You give them something to eat." Testing the faith of the Apostle Philip, the Lord asked Him directly, "Where shall we buy bread, that these may eat?" Philip answered, "Two hundred denarii worth of bread is not sufficient for them, that every one of them may have a little." The other disciples agreed with him.

Then the Lord asked how much bread they had, and Andrew, when he found out, said, "there is a lad here [probably a merchant who followed the crowds with food] who has five barley loaves and two small fish, but what are they among so many?" Then Jesus said, "Make the people sit down." He ordered that the people be divided by groups of fifty, or as St Mark says, "they sat down in ranks, in hundreds and in fifties," so that everyone could be counted. There were nearly five thousand men, not counting the women and children.

Having taken the five breads and two fish, the Lord looked up at heaven, gave thanks (John 6:14), blessed them (Luke 9:16), broke them, and gave them to the disciples to give out to the people. Also the two fish were "divided among them all" (Mark 6:41), "as much as they wanted" (John 6:11). "So they all ate and were filled." When they were full, the Lord ordered the disciples to collect the remaining bits, so that nothing would be lost. There were nearly twelve baskets of remnants.

"Then those men, when they had seen the sign that Jesus did, said, 'This is truly the Prophet who is to come into the world.' Therefore when Jesus perceived that they were about to come and take Him by force to make Him king, He departed again to the mountain by Himself alone" (John 6:14–15). Evidently, the people wanted to take advantage of the coming Passover to take Christ with them to Jerusalem, there to crown Him king before all of Israel. But the Lord, of course, did not want to countenance such false expectations of the Messiah as an earthly king. He told His disciples to go ahead of Him to the western bank of the Sea of Galilee, while He Himself, having calmed down the people, went to a hill to pray.

THE LORD WALKS ON WATER AND HEALS MANY SICK
(MATT 14:22–36; MARK 6:45–56; JOHN 6:16–21)

The disciples listened to Christ and embarked on the boat to go to the western bank. It became dark (John 6:17), a violent wind blew (Matt 14:24), and the disciples were in great distress (Mark 6:48), but the Lord was not with them. He was alone on the land, but He saw their danger (Mark 6:48). They were twenty or thirty furlongs out into sea (John 6:19). The time was nearly the fourth watch of the night; in other words, it was near dawn. And suddenly, they saw Jesus, who was walking toward them on the waves, but according to Mark, it seemed that He intended to walk past them. Seeing Him walking on water, they thought that He was a ghost and began to scream in fear, but the Lord calmed them saying, "It is I; do not be afraid."

St Peter, who had a fiery temperament, had a sudden desire to walk to the Lord, and asked His permission to walk to Him on the waters, and the Lord said, "Come!" Peter climbed out of the boat, and such was the power of his faith that he walked on water. But the fierce wind and stormy waves distracted Peter's attention from Christ, to Whom he walked, and his fear weakened his faith, and he began to sink, and in despair cried out, "Lord, save me!" Immediately, the Lord extended His hand in order to raise him up, and said, "O you of little faith, why did you doubt?" Only St Matthew tells of Peter's walking on the water.

As soon as they had entered the boat, the waves immediately calmed down, and the boat quickly reached the shore. All who were in the boat came up to Christ and fell at His feet, saying, "Truly You are the Son of God." As soon as Jesus walked on dry land, immediately the inhabitants of that land surrounded Him. They recognized Him and hurried to tell all the surrounding villages, and brought all their sick. Their faith in His healing power was so strong that the inhabitants of that place asked only the permission to touch the hem of His garments, and those who touched Him were healed.

CONVERSATION ABOUT THE BREAD FROM HEAVEN (JOHN 6:22–71)

The miraculous crossing of the Lord Jesus Christ over the Sea of Galilee amazed the people who had just been fed by the miraculously increased loaves. Only St John speaks of this event, telling of the amazing speech of the Lord about Himself as the Bread, which came down from heaven, revealing in these words how necessary for salvation is the communion of His Body and Blood. The people sought the Lord throughout the desert, knowing that He was not in the boat with His disciples. Having found Him already on the other side, teaching in the Capernaum synagogue, they asked Him when He had the opportunity to make His way back to Capernaum. Without answering their question, the Lord took it as an opportunity to speak of Himself as of the Bread of Life.

He begins His preaching by rebuking the Jews for remaining slaves to their physical needs, and even their following Him is proof of that fact. They seek Christ not because in His miracles they sensed the grace of God, which would give them eternal heavenly blessings, but because in the miracle that had happened the day before, their hunger was satisfied, in the same way as other miracles had ended other kinds of physical suffering. But none of them were taking care of satisfying the needs of the spirit, for which reason Christ came in the first place. "You seek Me ... because you ate of the loaves and were filled." This rebuke the Lord directs at anyone who considers Christianity to be useful only because it helps with the arrangements of this temporal life.

"Do not labor for the food which perishes," which is destroyed together with the body, "but for the food which endures to everlasting life," the food that will remain eternally and will last even to the eternal life. This food "the Son of Man will give to you," the Lord said, "because God the Father has set His seal on Him" as proof that He is the Giver of Life, who can give them this food. This "seal" can be understood to indicate the signs and miracles that Christ performed according to His Father's will.

Stung by the accusation, the Jews ask, "What shall we do, that we may work the works of God?" They understood that the Lord's words implied the requirement of moral action from them, but they were not sure which ones. Instead of listing a long series of external actions of the law of Moses that they expected to hear about, He only indicates one action: "This is the work of God, that you believe in Him whom He sent." This is the most important God-pleasing action a man can accomplish, without which a God-pleasing life is essentially impossible, for it contains, as in a seed, all the good deeds that one can do to please God. Understanding that Jesus is calling Himself the "chosen One of God, the Jews answer that for such faith, the faith that the Israelites had in Moses, more signs are needed than the ones

He had already performed. This is yet another proof of the fact that faith based on miracles is utterly unreliable—it requires increasingly more miracles. And so the Jews did not find it sufficient that the Lord Jesus fed five thousand people with five loaves, and required that He show them an even greater miracle, something like the manna that God sent through Moses during the forty-year wandering in the desert.

The Lord answered that the miracles that God did through Moses were less important than the miracle that God was performing now through Him, the Messiah, giving them not illusory bread, as was manna, but "true bread from heaven." This bread gives life to the world. They understood Christ to mean actual physical bread with miraculous properties, and they asked to receive this magical bread. This only proved the entirely carnal direction of their spirit, their completely temporal expectations of the Messiah.

Then the Lord openly, with conviction, declares His teaching of Himself as the "bread of life," saying that this bread, which comes down from heaven and gives life to the world, is He Himself. Whoever comes to Him will not hunger and whoever believes in Him will not thirst ever again. The Lord, however, noticed with sorrow that the Jews did not believe in Him; nevertheless, this fact would not prevent the actualization of the Father's will through Him. All who seek salvation through Him, all who "come to Him" will become the inheritors of the kingdom of the Messiah, founded by Him. All such people will be raised by Him on the last day and will be found worthy of eternal life. The Jews become upset at this saying, and begin to complain among themselves how it is that Jesus can say that He came from heaven when they know His earthly background.

The Lord explains that their complaining is only further proof of their not being in the number of those chosen by God, whom God the Father calls to Himself with the power of His divine grace. Without this calling, accomplished by grace, no one can believe in the Son, the Messiah, sent to earth for the salvation of all mankind. This thought in no way destroys the free will of a person. St Theophylact interprets these words thus: "The Father calls those who have the ability, according to the free will of each person; while those who have made themselves incapable, are not called to faith. As a magnet attracts not all substances, but only metal, so God comes close to all, but attracts only those who are able and have already found a certain affinity with Him."[35]

It is as if Christ is saying, "Do not complain about Me, but rather about yourselves for your inability to believe in Me as in the Messiah," for all the Old Testament books witness to the coming of Christ, and whoever carefully studies them cannot but see the lessons of God and accept the Messiah-Christ, Whom He sent. Being thus taught by God is not the same as seeing God, for only He Who is Himself of God (that is, Christ Himself) has seen Him. Anyone who assiduously, faithfully studies the Scriptures will be taught directly by God Himself, for the main theme of all the Scriptures is the Christ.

"I am the bread of life," Christ then says of Himself; living bread, not simple, lifeless bread as was manna. Manna fed only the body, and so those who ate it eventually died. The bread that comes supersubstantially, not only visibly, from heaven itself, has the characteristic that "if anyone eats of this bread, he will live forever." This bread that came down from heaven is the very Lord Jesus Christ Himself. Then the Lord speaks even more definitely that this bread is His Body, which He gives for the life of the world, by which He means the imminent death on the cross at Golgotha for the redemption of the sins of all mankind. Here, in connection with the coming feast of Passover, the Lord teaches of Himself as the true Paschal Lamb, Who took upon Himself the sins of the whole world. The traditional Paschal lamb was only the foreshadowing of this Lamb-Christ. The Lord let them understand that the time of foreshadowing has passed, for Truth Himself has appeared. Eating the Paschal lamb in the New Testament is replaced with eating the Body of Christ, brought as an offering for the sins of the whole world.

The Jews, having correctly understood the Lord's words, became confused and started to argue with each other: "How can this Man give us His flesh to eat?" Obviously, they understood these words literally, not metaphorically, as some contemporary Protestants think, who themselves reject the mystery of the Eucharist as a sacrament that can give grace-filled union with Christ. And here, in order to put an end to their arguing, Christ categorically and firmly repeats: "Most assuredly, I say to you, unless you eat the flesh of the Son of Man and drink His blood, you have no life in you. Whoever eats My flesh and drinks My blood has eternal life, and I will raise him up at the last day."

Here the Lord reveals, in its complete fullness and lucidity, His teaching on the necessity of communing of His Body and Blood for eternal salvation. During the Exodus, the blood of the sacrificed lamb was wiped on doorways as a sign of the preservation of the Jewish firstborns from the destroyer-angel (Exod 12:7–13). In the temple, the blood of the lamb was sprinkled on the horns of the altar, in remembrance of the aforementioned doorways. During the Paschal meal, the blood of the lamb was symbolically replaced by wine. Thus, in the same way that the Paschal lamb prefigured Christ, as the Exodus prefigured the salvation of all mankind, so Christ's Body replaces the lamb and His Blood replaces the symbolic wine. This is the New Passover (Pascha), which the Lord prophetically foretells in His preaching. The meaning of Christ's words here, consequently, is that whoever wants to be saved by Christ's death on the cross must eat His Body and drink His Blood. Otherwise, he will not be a partaker of Christ's redemptive sacrifice, he will not have within himself eternal life, and will remain in separation from God, which is eternal death. The Body and Blood of the Lord, according to His own words, is true food and true drink, for only they can give eternal life to a man. This is because they give the communicant the closest possible communication with Christ—a mystical union with Him (John 6:56).

Through this mystery, fallen, sinful man is grafted into new life. Just as a gardener grafts a fruit-bearing branch onto a barren tree to help it bear fruit, Christ Himself, desiring to make us participants of divine life, enters into our body darkened by sin and lays the foundation for inner transformation and sanctification, making us a new creation. It is not enough for our salvation merely to believe in Christ; one must become one with Him, to abide in Him, so that He may abide in us, and this is only possible through the great mystery of the communion of His Body and Blood.

These words of the Lord, however, were so strange to the ear, that this time not only His enemies, but even some of His disciples were offended at Him, saying: "This is a hard saying; who can understand it?" The Lord heard their thoughts and said, "Does this offend you? What then if you should see the Son of Man ascend where He was before?" Here, the Lord means that they will be offended so much more when they see Him crucified on the cross. Later, the Lord explains how His words must be properly understood: "It is the Spirit who gives life; the flesh profits nothing. The words that I speak to you are spirit, and they are life." This means that the words of Christ must be understood spiritually, not crudely, in the fleshly way, as though somehow He were actually offering us His flesh like the meat of some animal, which we eat to satisfy our physical hunger.

It is as if He is saying, "My teaching is not about meat or food that satisfies the life of the body, but it concerns the divine Spirit, grace and eternal life, which is given to mankind through the grace of the Spirit." When He said, "The flesh profits nothing," He did not have in mind His own Body—of course not! But rather, He meant those who understand His words carnally, that is, to look at something simply and not to imagine anything other than the external reality. But we must not judge what we see in this way; with our inner eyes we must look into all the mysteries of creation. This is what it means to understand spiritually (St John Chrysostom).

The Body of Christ, separated from His Spirit, could not give life. Of course, it is obvious that Christ is not speaking of His lifeless, fleshly body, but of His Body inseparably united with His divine Spirit. "But there are some of you who do not believe." Of course, it is difficult to believe in self-abased divinity without the help of the grace of God. As we discuss later, these words are Christ's first indication of Judas's betrayal. And it is true that the teaching of the Holy Eucharist was and always will be a stumbling block for true faith in Christ. There are many people who are amazed by the moral laws that Christ gives, but who do not understand the necessity of uniting with Him in this great mystery. But the truth is that without this mystical union with Christ, following His moral law in one's life is impossible, for it is beyond mankind's power to fulfill.

This is why, as the Gospel mentions, many stopped following Him after these words, especially since this particular teaching contradicted everything they believed about the coming Messiah. Then the Lord, testing the faith of His closest disciples, the twelve, asked them if they did not also want to leave Him. But in answer, Simon Peter (speaking, of course, for all the twelve) uttered a great confession of faith in Him as "the Christ, the Son of the living God," a confession that we now always pronounce as we read the prayer before communion, "I believe O Lord and confess that Thou art the Christ, the Son of the Living God."

In answer to this amazing confession, the Lord only said that not all the twelve believed in this way, since one of them is "a devil," not literally, but as an enemy of Christ and His work. Thus the Lord warned Judas, knowing as the Knower of Hearts that Judas was already thinking of betraying Him. This time, the Lord did not go to Jerusalem for the feast of the Passover, since the Jews were seeking to kill Him (John 7:1), and the time for His suffering and death had not yet come.

 CHAPTER 5

The Third Passover of the Lord Jesus Christ's Public Ministry

REBUKING THE TRADITION OF THE PHARISEES (MATT 15:1–20; MARK 7:1–23)

The Lord Jesus Christ did not go to Jerusalem for the feast of the Passover, but the Pharisees of Jerusalem never left their close watch over Him, and so, not finding Him in Jerusalem, they went to Galilee. Finding Him together with His disciples, they renewed their previous condemnation of the disciples for not following the traditions of the elders. The reason for this was the fact that the disciples of the Lord ate without first washing their hands. According to the pious rituals of the Pharisees, one must wash the hands before and after eating, and the Talmud even gives the exact amount of water to be used, at what times, and the order in which to wash in case there are more (or less) than five people in attendance at the meal. These rules were given such importance that whoever did not follow them was cast out of Israel by the Sanhedrin. For some reason, the Jews believed that Moses received two laws on Mount Sinai—one that was written down, and another oral law that was passed down from parent to child and was only later written down in the Talmud. This law was called the "tradition of the elders," the ancient rabbis. This tradition is especially remarkable for its many niggling rules.

Thus, the rite of oblation, which was originally intended to encourage hygiene, which of course is perfectly good and right in itself, became a stumbling block, along with other similar rules, which effectively put the more important aspects of God's law on a second plane. Thus, the rite of oblation became an empty and even harmful ritual. Therefore, the disciples, together with their divine Teacher, labored for the great work of building the kingdom of God on earth and sometimes did not even have enough time to sit down and eat properly (Mark 3:20), while the Pharisees demanded that they strictly follow all these minute rituals. So the Lord answers their rebuke thus: "Why do you also transgress the commandment of God because of your tradition?" St John Chrysostom explains that "Christ thus shows that whoever is guilty of heavy sins should not waste time noticing small sins in others."[36]

The Lord indicates that the Pharisees, in the name of their tradition, were breaking the categorical and direct commandment to honor their parents.

Their tradition allowed children to legally stop giving material help to their parents if they declared their money to be "corban," that is, dedicated to God. And one could declare anything to be "dedicated to God"—one's home, field, pure and impure animals—and the one who dedicated it can still continue to use it for himself, as long as he pays a certain "buyout" tax to the temple treasury. But at least he could consider himself free of any need to take care of his parents, even when denying them food necessary for survival. For this, the Lord calls the Pharisees hypocrites, thereby referring to the prophecy in Isaiah (Isa 29:13), insisting that they serve God only superficially, while their hearts are far from God. In vain do they think to please God with such a life, in vain do they teach others to do likewise.

Turning to all the assembled people, the Lord accuses the Pharisees: "Hear and understand: Not what goes into the mouth defiles a man; but what comes out of the mouth, this defiles a man." The Pharisees did not understand the distinction between bodily and moral uncleanness, and so they thought that unclean food or even food taken with dirty hands could result in moral uncleanness, making a man odious in the eyes of God. Criticizing the absurdity of this thought, the Lord instead maintains that a man is only defiled in a moral sense by what comes out of his impure heart. It is completely ridiculous to use these words, as some Protestants and all enemies of fasting do, against the fasts established by the Church. Of course, what enters a person's mouth does not defile him in and of itself, but only when accompanied by lack of temperance, lack of obedience and other sinful inclinations of the heart. We do not fast because we are afraid that meat will defile our bodies, but to help us battle our sinful passions, to battle against carnality in general, to teach ourselves to cut off our will through obedience to the rules of the Church. When we declare drunkenness to be a great evil, for example, we are not saying that drinking wine defiles a man.

The Pharisees, however, were offended that the Lord did not consider the tradition of the elders to be valid, even suggesting that He had the same disdain for the whole Mosaic Law, which had strict dietary laws. The Lord calmed His disciples, saying that the Pharisees were the "blind leaders of the blind," and so there was no need to follow their made-up teachings, and any such teaching that does not come from God will be rooted out.

Later, the Lord explains to the apostles that the food that enters the mouth does not touch a person's soul, eventually being cast out without leaving a sinful imprint on a person's soul. But sins, which come from within a person, his mouth and his heart, do defile him.

HEALING THE DAUGHTER OF THE CANAANITE WOMAN (MATT 15:21–28; MARK 7:24–30)

Having left Galilee, the Lord went into the country of Tyre and Sidon, the main cities of the pagan country of Phoenicia to the northwest of Galilee. From St Mark's words that Christ "entered into a house and wanted no one to know it," one can assume that His purpose in coming to this pagan and foreign land was temporary solitude, to rest from the masses of people constantly surrounding Him in Galilee, and also perhaps to hide from the constant hatred of the Pharisees. "But He could not be hidden," for a certain woman, whom St Matthew calls a "Canaanite," while St Mark, a "Syro-Phoenician," heard of Him. St Mark also calls her a "Greek," but this does not refer to her nationality, rather to her pagan religion (the Scriptures often call the pagans in general "Greeks"; see Rom 1:16 and 1 Cor 1:22). Her daughter was possessed by an unclean spirit, and she began to ask the Lord that He cast out the demon from her daughter. Also, knowing from the Jews of the coming Messiah, she called the Lord "Son of David," showing by this her faith in His Messianic dignity.

Testing her faith, the Lord did not answer her with a single word, so that even His disciples began to ask on her behalf, indicating her persistence and insistence. "But He answered her and said, "I was not sent except to the lost sheep of the house of Israel," for the Jews were the chosen nation of God, and to them was promised the divine Redeemer, and to them He must come first, to save them and to perform miracles among them. It is possible that the Lord said these words, using the typical Jewish disdain toward the pagans, in order to fully reveal the full power of the faith of this pagan woman before His disciples, for their instruction. Finally, according to St Mark, the Canaanite woman fell at the feet of Jesus, begging Him to cast out the demon from her daughter. Knowing, of course, the strength of her faith and continuing to test her, the Lord rejects her using words that could appear to be extremely cruel, if they were not uttered by the lips of the Lord who was filled with love for suffering mankind: "It is not good to take the children's bread and throw it to the little dogs." In other words, Jesus did not leave the country of the chosen nation, the sons of the kingdom (Matt 8:12) and take away His grace and miracle-working power in order to waste it in the land of the pagans. Of course, these words as well were spoken only to reveal the full power of her faith and to show that even the pagans, since they also believe, are worthy of God's mercies, contrary to the disdain that was common among the Jews toward the pagans.

And the Canaanite woman truly showed the depth of her faith and the incredible profundity of her humility, accepting the insulting title of "dog" and even finding in this a further reason to continue her pressing petition to the Lord. "Yes, Lord, yet even the little dogs eat the crumbs which fall from their masters' table." This incredible faith and humility were immediately rewarded. "O woman, great is your faith!" said the Lord. "Let it be to you as you desire." And her daughter was immediately healed. Just like the healing of the servant of the centurion of Capernaum, also a pagan, this healing was done at a distance, as a sign of the special favor of the Lord.

Healing the Deaf with a Speech Impediment and Many Other Sick
(Mark 7:31–37; Matt 15:29–31)

From Phoenicia, the Lord went through Decapolis to the Sea of Galilee. This country, the combination of ten cities, was almost entirely to the east of the Sea of Galilee (except for Scythopolis), and from the time of the Assyrian captivity of the Jews, it was inhabited mostly by pagans. Here, along the way, the Lord healed a deaf man with a speech impediment, a miracle only mentioned by St Mark. Usually the Lord healed only with His word, but here He took the sick man to the side, apparently to avoid the idle curiosity of the masses, many of them pagan, put His fingers into the ears of the sick man, and, having spit, touched his tongue. These physical actions were doubtless meant to arouse the man's faith, an absolutely necessary condition for healing, because to ask him about his faith would have been impossible.

Then, looking up at heaven, the Lord prayerfully sighed, so that those surrounding Him would see that He was healing with the power of God, not the power of demons, as the Pharisees were constantly saying of Him. He healed him, forcefully speaking the Syrian word "Ephphatha," which means, "be opened." As usual, He forbade those around to speak of the miracle in order to avoid excessive agitation in the crowd and not to provoke the Pharisees more than necessary at that time. But, amazed by the miracle, they talked of it everywhere, no matter that He forbade them. Having crossed Decapolis, the Lord, according to St Matthew, came to the Sea of Galilee, probably from the east or northeast, and here, as always, the crowds followed Him, other crowds met Him, and wherever He stopped immediately many people gathered. They brought Him their lame, blind, dumb, and others suffering from all manner of sicknesses. Their faith in Christ's healing power was so strong, that they did not even ask Him for anything, only silently brought the sick to His feet, and "He healed them." They, seeing the miracles, praised the God of Israel, considering, as the chosen nation, that God was exclusively their own.

THE MIRACULOUS FEEDING OF THE FOUR THOUSAND (MATT 15:32–39; MARK 8:1–9)

The Lord remained here, at the banks of the Sea of Galilee, for three days. Their stores of bread were completely emptied, and there was no food to be bought anywhere, so the Lord once again performed the miracle of feeding the crowd. This time there were four thousand, fed by seven breads, and there were seven baskets of leftovers. Having fed the people, the Lord sent them away, while He and His apostles traveled across the lake to Magdala, or, according to St Mark, Dalmanutha, a small village near the city of Magdala on the western bank of the Sea of Galilee.

REBUKING THE PHARISEES WHO ASKED FOR SIGNS AND WARNING AGAINST THE LEAVEN OF THE PHARISEES AND SADDUCEES (MATT 16:1–12; MARK 8:11–21)

As soon as Jesus came to shore, He was immediately accosted by the Pharisees and Sadducees, who were apparently waiting for Him there. These two sects were rivals, the Pharisees being conservative and the Sadducees, broadly speaking, liberal. However, when it came to Jesus, they worked together against their common enemy as never before. Tempting Him, they insincerely asked for a sign from heaven, a kind of miracle that would be a clear indication, both for them and the people, that He was the Messiah. In answer, the Lord sharply rebukes the Pharisees, calling them hypocrites since they, knowing how to predict the weather using clear atmospheric signs, refuse to accept the obvious signs that already prove His Messianic dignity, and once again He said that no sign was to be given them, except the sign of Jonah the Prophet (see Matt 12:38–45).

Not desiring to continue this conversation with hypocrites, the Lord, even though He had only just arrived on this shore, again cast off in the boat with His disciples and sailed to the other side. This haste did not give the apostles time to buy bread. Christ, sorrowing over the spiritual blindness of the Pharisees and Sadducees, and desiring to warn His disciples not to fall into a similar state, said to them, "Take heed and beware of the leaven of the Pharisees and the Sadducees!" St Mark, instead of the Sadducees, mentions Herod, but the meaning is the same, since Herod Antipas was of the sect of the Sadducees. The apostles did not understand what He was saying, thinking that with these words the Lord was rebuking them for not buying enough bread. Then the Lord truly rebuked them for their little faith, lack of understanding, and tendency to forget everything quickly, reminding them of the recent miraculous feeding of the several thousand with only a few loaves. Only after being thus reminded did the disciples understand that Jesus was warning them against the teaching of the Pharisees and Sadducees.

HEALING THE BLIND MAN IN BETHSAIDA (MARK 8:22–26)

This miracle is told only by St Mark, and was performed by the Lord after He and His disciples had returned to the eastern shore of the Sea of Galilee, on the road to Caesaria Philippi in the city of Bethsaida, also known as Julia, given this name by the local tetrarch Philipp in honor of his daughter Augusta Julia. A blind man was brought to the Lord to be healed by His touch. Apparently, this man was not born blind, since after the Saviour's first touch, he said that he could see the people like trees, meaning that at some point in his life he had seen both people and trees. The Lord, healing him, acted in the same way as with the dumb man with a speech impediment. He took him out of the village, spit in his eyes and restored his sight not immediately, but gradually, laying His hands on him twice, evidently inspiring faith in the man thus. Again, after the healing, He sent him home with the injunction not to speak of the miracle.

THE APOSTLE PETER CONFESSES, ON BEHALF OF ALL THE APOSTLES, THAT JESUS CHRIST IS THE SON OF GOD (MATT 16:13–20; MARK 8:27–30; LUKE 9:18–21)

From Bethsaida-Julia, the Lord went with His disciples to the countryside around Caesaria Philippi. This city was named Panea previously, and was situated on the northern border of the tribe of Naphtali, at the source of the Jordan River under Mount Lebanon. It was enlarged and enriched by the tetrarch Philip and called Caesaria in honor of Caesar Tiberius. In contrast to the other Caesaria in Palestine, which was found on the shores of the Mediterranean Sea, this Caesaria was also named after its benefactor, Philip.

The time of Christ's work on earth was nearing its end, but those chosen by Him for spreading the message of the Gospel throughout the world were not ready for their high mission. Thus, the Lord increasingly sought more opportunities to speak to them privately, in order to prepare them for the reality of the Messiah—that He was not an earthly king who would subjugate all peoples under the Jews, which is what they dreamed of, but a king whose kingdom is not of this world, a king who will Himself suffer for this world, be crucified, and rise again. Thus, during these distant travels, remaining alone with His apostles, Christ asked them, trying to direct their thoughts to the proper way: "Who do men say that I, the Son of Man, am?"

The apostles answered that there were different opinions heard among the people. The court of Herod Antipas thought that He was John the Baptist who rose from the dead, the people generally considered Him to be one of the Old Testament prophets and, not considering Him to be the Messiah, generally thought He was a forerunner of the imminent Messiah. But when Christ asked: "But who do you say that I am?" Peter answered on behalf of all the apostles. St John Chrysostom called him "the always fiery Peter, that mouth of the Apostles." "Thou art the Christ, the Son of the Living God!"[37] The Evangelists Mark and Luke stop their account with these words, adding that the Lord forbade them to speak thus of Him to anyone, but St Matthew adds that the Lord praised Peter for his words, saying, "Blessed are you, Simon Bar-Jonah, for flesh and blood has not revealed this to you, but My Father Who is in heaven."

In other words, Peter's confession was not the result of a faith that came from his own reason, but a faith that was given as a gift from God. "And I also say to you that you are Peter, and on this rock I will build My church, and the gates of Hades shall not prevail against it." The Lord gave Simon the name Peter (meaning "stone" in Greek) during their first meeting, and now it is as if He is saying that Simon truly deserved the name given him before, that he is truly a rock in his firm faith. Can one understand these words to mean that Christ founded the Church on the person of Peter, as do the Catholics, in order to justify their false teaching of the primacy of the pope of Rome over the whole Church, as the successor of St Peter? Of course not! If, in these words of the Lord, Peter himself is meant for the Church's foundation, then Christ would have said something like: "You are Peter, and on you I shall establish my Church," or at the very least, "You are Peter, and upon this Peter I shall establish my Church." But Christ speaks quite differently, which is especially evident in the Greek text, which should always be consulted in such controversial passages. The word "Petros" is not repeated, even though the word itself does mean both "rock" and "Peter," but another word, *petra* is used, which means "cliff." Here it is obvious that in these words directed at Peter, the Lord promises to establish His church not on Peter, but on the confession of faith that Peter uttered, on the great truth that "Christ is the Son of the living God." This is how St John Chrysostom and other great Fathers of the Church understood this passage, understanding the "Rock" to be the confession of faith in Jesus Christ as the Messiah, the Son of God, or even Jesus Christ Himself, Who is often called the Rock in Scriptures (see, for example, Isa 28:16; Acts 4:11; Rom 9:33; 1 Cor 10:4). It is interesting to note that the Apostle Peter himself, in his First General Epistle, calls not himself the Rock, but Jesus Christ, instructing the faithful to approach the Lord as the "Living Rock, rejected indeed by men, but chosen by God and precious" (1 Pet 2:4) and to become themselves living stones that would build the spiritual house. Here, Peter obviously teaches all Christians to walk the same way that he did himself, when he became "Petros" after confessing the name of the Rock, Christ.

Thus, the meaning of this amazing and profound utterance of the Lord is this: "Blessed are you, Simon, son of Jonah, because you did not come to know this truth due to human means, but it was revealed to you by My Heavenly Father. And I tell you that it was not by accident that I called you Peter. Be established in that which you have confessed, as on a cliff, and you will remain truly the rock, and my Church will be built and remain undefeated, so that no power of the enemy will be able to overcome it." The phrase "gates of Hades" is characteristic of Eastern phraseology. The gates of a city or a fortress are always especially guarded in case of attack by enemies, and the gates were the place where leaders would come to parley, where judgment and conviction was doled out to criminals, where all important social events were held.

The later promise, apparently given to Peter alone: "And I will give you the keys of the kingdom of heaven, and whatever you bind on earth will be bound in heaven; and whatever you loose on earth will be loosed in heaven," is later repeated and given to all the apostles (Matt 18:18), and consists of the right of all the apostles and their successors the bishops to judge and punish those who sin, even to cast them out of the Church if need be. The power to loose is the power to forgive sins, to accept the sinner into the Church through baptism and repentance. This grace was received by all the apostles equally after His resurrection (John 20:22–23). The Lord forbade the disciples to speak of Him as the Christ, in order to not agitate the people with further false hopes regarding the Messianic kingdom.

THE LORD FORETELLS HIS DEATH AND RESURRECTION, AND TEACHES OF THE NECESSITY TO BEAR ONE'S CROSS (MATT 16:21–28; MARK 8:31–38; 9:1; LUKE 9:22–27)

Having inspired the confession of His divinity in the apostles, the Lord tells them of the sufferings awaiting Him in Jerusalem, in order to prepare them for the thought of the earthly fate of the Messiah, to destroy their false ideas about the Messiah, and to consecrate them into the great mystery of His redemptive sufferings. Deeply committed to the Lord, but not yet free from the false Jewish ideas of the Messiah as the earthly king, fiery and forceful Peter could not bear to hear such things of his beloved Teacher, and not desiring to contradict Him before all the others, he took Him aside and said, "Far be it from You, Lord; this shall not happen to You," meaning something along these lines: "God forbid! It cannot be that this will happen to You!" To Peter's mind, the idea of the dignity of the Lord Jesus Christ as Messiah and Son of God was incompatible with the idea of His suffering and death. "Get behind me, Satan!" the Lord answered heatedly, clearly sensing that Peter was trying to dissuade Him from the coming suffering, and through Peter, Satan himself was taking advantage of the pure emotion of Peter to inspire fear in the human nature of Christ before the great suffering of man's redemption.

It is interesting that the Lord, who had just called Simon "Peter," in only a short period of time calls him "Satan," which especially vividly refutes all the Roman Catholic ideas of the Church being founded on the person of Peter. Can the establishment of Christ's Church, which will not be overcome by the gates of hell, be founded on such a fickle, unstable personality as Peter's? And if one is to understand all the words of the Lord literally, which in the first case the Catholics do without any scruples, then the latter words also should be understood literally, which is absurd and impossible. But that would mean that the Church was founded on Satan!

The Lord then says to Peter, "You are an offense to Me, for you are not mindful of the things of God, but the things of men." Euthymius Zigabenos interprets these words to mean that Peter, "by going against Christ's will, becomes a hindrance to Him if he desires that Christ's purpose in coming to earth, that which has been determined from before the ages, should not be fulfilled."[38] Peter is not thinking of that which is pleasing to God, not considering His sufferings in the light of man's redemption, but rather is still clinging to the desires of the Jews, the human hopes that the Messiah would be their great earthly conqueror-king. It is proper for man to protect his own life, to avoid suffering, and to strive for a pleasant and easy life. This path is the path offered people by the devil, who desires their perdition. This is not the path of Christ and His true followers.

"If anyone desires to come after Me," to be His true follower, "let him deny himself," let him cut off his natural will and striving, "and take up his cross," let him be ready for the sake of Christ to suffer any deprivations, even death, "and follow Me," emulating Christ in His labors of self-denial and self-rejection. "For whoever desires to save his life" in the sense of seeking after all manner of comforts and pleasures, "will lose it, but whoever loses his life for my sake," whoever will not pamper himself and instead seek a harder path for the sake of Christ, "will find it." Only he who preserves his soul for eternal life shall truly live.

"For what profit is it to a man if he gains the whole world," if he finds all the honors and pleasures that the world offers, if he has all its perishable treasures at his own disposal, "and loses his own soul?" The soul of a man is more precious than all the treasures of the world, and a lost soul is impossible to redeem with any earthly wealth. "What will a man give in exchange for his soul?"

The Lord connects this thought of the eternal perdition of those people who try to preserve themselves only for this world with the thought of His terrible Second Coming, when everyone will receive a reward according to one's deeds. This is an important thought, and it speaks against the Protestant teaching regarding the lack of necessity of deeds for salvation. The Evangelists Mark and Luke, in connection with this thought, add the following words of the Lord: "For whoever is ashamed of Me and of My words in this adulterous and sinful generation," whoever will consider it shameful to be considered a follower of Christ and to fulfill His commandments, "of him the Son of Man also will be ashamed when He comes in the glory of His Father with the holy angels." Christ will refuse to admit such a person into His company at the Final Judgment.

The Lord finished this important conversation with His disciples with the following words: "There are some standing here who shall not taste of death till they see the Son of Man coming in His kingdom." These words gave rise to the opinion that the Second Coming of Christ would come very soon, and when it did not, some began to doubt. Two other Evangelists, Mark and Luke, explain how these words must be properly understood: "till they see the kingdom of God" (St Luke) and "till they see the kingdom of God present with power" (St Mark). From this it is evident that Christ is not speaking of His Second Coming, but of the revelation of the kingdom of God, that is, His grace-filled power on earth among the faithful, the foundation of the Church of Christ. The Church is the kingdom of God come in power, which is the Church established by the Lord, whose extension over the entire face of the earth was witnessed by many of the disciples and contemporaries of Christ.

THE TRANSFIGURATION OF CHRIST (MATT 17:1–3; MARK 9:2–13; LUKE 9:28–36)

All three Synoptics relate this event, and it is worthy of mention that all of them connect this event with Christ's preceding prophecy six days earlier (eight, according to St Luke) of His own suffering, the carrying of the cross, and of the imminent revelation of the kingdom of God, come in power. The Lord took His closest and most trusted disciples, who were always with Him during the most majestic and important moments of His earthly life—Peter, James, and John—and He took them up to a high mountain alone. Even though no Evangelist mentions this hill by name, ancient Church tradition unanimously agrees that this was Mount Tabor in Galilee, south of Nazareth, in the beautiful valley of Jezreel. This majestic hill is almost three thousand feet high, covered with flora from the bottom to about halfway up, and offering breathtaking views of the surrounding valley.

And "He was transfigured before them." He appeared before the disciples in His heavenly glory, from which His face grew bright as the sun, and His clothes became "as white as the light" (St Matthew), "like snow" (St Mark), "glistening" according to St Luke. St Luke also adds an important point, indicating that the point of the ascent to the hill was to pray, and that the Lord transfigured during prayer: "As He prayed, the appearance of His face was altered, and His robe became white and glistening." He also notes that the apostles were heavy with sleep during prayer, and only when they awoke did they see Him transfigured and flanked on either side by Moses and Elijah, who were speaking to Him about His forthcoming death in Jerusalem. St John Chrysostom explains that Moses and Elijah appeared because some among the people considered Jesus to be Elijah or one of the other Old Testament prophets, and so the most important of these prophets appeared in order to underline the distinction between master and slave. Moses appeared to show that Jesus was not a destroyer of his law, as the scribes and Pharisees said. Neither Moses, through whom the law was given, nor Elijah, that great zealot of the glory of God, would have come and submitted themselves to one who was not truly the Son of God. The appearance of Moses, already dead, and Elijah, who did not die but was taken alive into the heavens, indicated the Lord's power over both life and death, over heaven and earth.

St Peter expressed the especially grace-filled state that had ravished their souls: "Master, it is good for us to be here," and offered to set up three tents there. It would be better, he said, not to return to the evil world full of hatred and cunning, the world that was threatening the Lord with death and suffering. St Mark even adds that Peter was in such a joyful state that he did not know what he was saying. The miraculous cloud, the evident indication of God's presence, surrounded them (this is the cloud, the "shekinah" that always remained in the holy of holies; see 1 Kgs 8:10–11), and out of this cloud they heard the voice of God the Father: "This is My beloved Son. Hear Him!" These are the same words heard during the baptism of Christ, but with the added "Hear Him!" which should have immediately reminded the apostles of the prophecy of Moses concerning the Christ (Deut 18:15) and the fulfillment of the prophecy in Jesus.

The Lord forbade the apostles from telling anyone of what they saw, until He would be risen from the dead, again not to agitate the carnal expectations of the Messiah among the Jews. St Mark adds the following detail, doubtless from the testimony of Peter himself: "so they kept this word to themselves," still wondering why the Lord had to die in order to be raised up again. By now completely convinced that their Teacher was the true Messiah, they asked Him: "Why do the scribes say that Elijah must come first?" The Lord confirms that Elijah must indeed come before the Messiah and "restores all things," or *apokatastisi* in the Greek, referencing the prophecy of Malachi: "and he will turn the hearts of the fathers to the children, and the hearts of the children to their fathers" (Mal 4:5–6). In other words, he would restore in the souls of people the primordial good and pure states of the heart, without which the work of the Messiah would be impossible, for He would not find good soil in the hearts of any man, since they had become hardened and petrified from a long, sinful life.

"But I say to you that Elijah has also come, and they did to him whatever they wished." By this He means that St John the Baptist was His Elijah because he was filled with the strength of Elijah and a similar spirit, but the people did not see this and imprisoned and killed him: "Likewise the Son of Man is also about to suffer at their hands" (Matt 17:12). In the same way that they did not recognize Elijah and killed him, they will not recognize the Messiah either, and will also kill Him.

HEALING THE POSSESSED YOUTH: ON THE IMPORTANCE OF FAITH, PRAYER, AND FASTING (MATT 17:14–23; MARK 9:14–32; LUKE 9:37–45)

All three Synoptics speak of this event, indicating that it happened immediately after the transfiguration. During this time, a large crowd surrounded the disciples of Christ who were waiting for Him at the bottom of Tabor. According to St Mark, they were arguing with the scribes. St Mark also indicates that all the people, when they saw Jesus, "were greatly amazed," probably because His face and entire appearance still retained a shade of His former glory on Tabor during the transfiguration. A certain man approached the Lord with a request to heal his son, who was a lunatic, meaning that the devil in him would go into fits of rage on a full moon, casting him alternatively into the fire or the water. He also added that he had already brought the boy to the disciples, and they could not heal him.

Hearing that the disciples could not heal him, even though He had given them power over the unclean spirits, the Lord exclaimed: "O faithless generation, how long shall I be with you?" Some exegetes interpret these words as directed toward the disciples since they did not have enough faith to heal the possessed boy, while others refer them to the whole nation of Israel. St Matthew merely says that after this exclamation, Jesus had the boy brought to Him, and He "rebuked the demon, and it came out of him." Saints Mark and Luke add certain other details. When the boy was brought to Him, he had a demoniac fit. When the Lord asked the father how long the child had been afflicted with this devil, the father said that it was from early childhood, adding: "but if You can do anything, have compassion on us, and help us." The Lord answered him: "If you can believe, all things are possible to him who believes." And straightway the father of the child cried out, and said with tears, "Lord, I believe; help my unbelief." With humility, he admitted that his faith was not sufficient, incomplete. For this humble confession, the Lord rewarded him. His son was healed.

When His disciples asked why they could not cast out the demon, the Lord answered: "Because of your unbelief." It is possible that having heard of the strength, duration, and stubbornness of this possession, they began to doubt their own ability to cast out this particular demon, and so they could not, just as Peter began to sink even after he had begun to walk on the water, when he was faced with the ferocity of the winds and waves and doubted his ability to walk to Jesus. "I say to you, if you have faith as a mustard seed, you will say to this mountain, 'Move from here to there,' and it will move; and nothing will be impossible for you." Even the smallest amount of faith is capable of performing great miracles, because in this faith is hidden a great power, similar to the power that is hidden in the minuscule mustard seed that later grows into a large tree.

However, it would be wrong to think that faith has power in and of itself; no, faith is merely the necessary precondition for the action of God's power. God can, of course, perform miracles even when faith is insufficient, as Christ showed with the father of the possessed youth. "All things are possible to him who believes" (Mark 9:23). This means that the Lord is ready to do anything for a person, contingent on his faith. Faith is like a conductor for the grace of God, which performs miracles. In conclusion, the Lord utters some very important words: "However, this kind" meaning this kind of demon, "does not go out except by prayer and fasting." This is because true faith cannot be had without labors of prayer and fasting. True faith gives birth to prayer and fasting, which themselves help and, even more, strengthen faith. Thus, our hymnography praises both prayer and fasting as a double-edged sword against the demons and the passions. St Theophan the Recluse writes: "The demons sense the fasting and prayerful man from a distance, and they run far from him, in order not to receive a painful blow. Can one say that where there is *no* prayer and fasting, there are demons? Yes, one can."[39]

During this sojourn in Galilee, the Lord again "taught His disciples, and said to them, "The Son of Man is being betrayed into the hands of men, and they will kill Him. And after He is killed, He will rise the third day" (Mark 9:31–32). The Lord saw that now more than ever, His disciples needed to know about the nearness of His suffering, death, and resurrection, and so He repeats His prophecy several times, in order for them to better remember it when the time came and to prepare them for it. But they still clung to the Jewish expectations of the Messiah, and these words remained for them something incomprehensible.

THE MIRACULOUS PAYING OF THE TEMPLE TAX (MATT 17:24–27)

Those who collected the taxes for the temple required that the Lord Jesus Christ also pay, as if paying to God Himself. Of course, as the Son of God, He should have been free of any need to pay this tax, but in order to avoid any more accusations of breaking the law, He, not having any money on His person, directed the Apostle Peter how to find the necessary four drachmas for the tax for two people. This miracle, mentioned only by St Matthew, vividly shows His divinity. As Bishop Michael in his Gospel commentary said, "If He knew that the four drachmas would be in the mouth of the fish that Peter caught, then He is all-knowing. If He formed the drachmas in the mouth of the fish, then He is all-powerful."[40]

Who Is Greatest in the Kingdom of Heaven? The Lord Uses a Child as an Example to the Disciples (Matt 18:1–5; Mark 9:33–37; Luke 9:46–48)

After the miraculous paying of the temple tax in Capernaum, the disciples, arguing among themselves about who is the greatest, meaning who would be in the most important positions of power in the coming earthly kingdom of the Messiah, came to Jesus with the question: "Who then is greatest in the kingdom of heaven?" The answer of the Lord, that whoever would be first should be last, and the servant of all, openly and convincingly deflated all of their preconceptions about primacy in the earthly kingdom. He tells them not to strive to be first in His Church, for primacy is connected with the heaviest labors and the greatest self-denial, not rest and glory, as they imagine.

Calling to Himself a child, who according to the witness of Nikephoros Kallistos Xanthopoulos (fourteenth cent.) later became the hieromartyr Ignatius the Godbearer, Bishop of Antioch,[41] the Lord placed him among the disciples and indicated to him, saying, "Whoever humbles himself as this little child is the greatest in the kingdom of heaven." In other words, whoever humbles himself, acknowledges himself to be unworthy of the kingdom of heaven; whoever will consider himself to be worse than others, only he will end up the greater. Thus, whoever rejects his own imagined greatness, whoever turns from ambition and pride to humility and meekness, whoever becomes as apparently insignificant as this little child, he will have the greater importance in the kingdom of heaven.

The Lord is giving the disciples simultaneously a lesson about the proper relationship among the members of His Church: "Whoever receives one little child like this in My name receives Me." Whoever treats such small children—or all humble and meek people, who are like children—with love in the name of Christ, in the fulfillment of His commandment to love all such downtrodden and weak, the same will be doing it to Christ Himself. In Saints Mark and Luke, this section is interrupted by the words of John concerning the man who was casting out demons in the name of Christ.

Miracles Were Performed in Christ's Name Even by Those Who Did Not Follow Him (Mark 9:38–41; Luke 9:49–50)

The Lord's words, that whoever accepts a weak, humble, meek person in His name accepts Christ Himself, reminded John about a man they had seen, who was casting out demons using the name of Jesus, but was not a formal disciple of Jesus, and so they had forbidden him from using the Lord's name. With his gentle, sensitive heart, St John apparently felt that in this situation, the apostles had acted contrary to Christ's instruction. Since they all had left everything behind and followed after Christ and were chosen by Him into the circle of the twelve closest and most trusted disciples and were even given the grace of healing, they concluded that they were greater than others, and had a right to forbid the man to use the name of Christ in casting out demons, since he was not one of them. In the meantime, considering the open antagonism of the rulers of the Jewish nation, it was not safe to be an open follower of Christ and walk with Him in all places. Thus, the Lord had many secret followers, among whom, as we know, was Joseph of Arimathea. It is probable that the man whom the apostles encountered was one of these secret disciples who did not dare to follow Him openly.

The apostles did not want to consider him one of them, and so forbade him to continue acting thus, motivated by the fact that he did not walk with them after Christ. The Lord Jesus Christ did not sanction their action. "Do not forbid him," said Jesus, for whoever performs a miracle in My name cannot be My enemy, at least in this present time and in the near future. "For he who is not against us is on our side." Therefore, do not forbid anyone from doing good deeds in My name just because they, for whatever reason, are not openly among My disciples. On the contrary, act together with them, and know that whoever will do any good deed to My follower in My name, even if it is only giving them a cup of cold water, "will by no means lose his reward."

The Lord says the exact opposite about people who are like a field of wheat that is worked on constantly and watered a great deal, yet brings no fruit. If such people are not for Christ, if they are cold and not hot, then it means that inside they are already against Him (see Matt 12:30).

THE TEACHING CONCERNING BATTLING AGAINST THE PASSIONS
(MATT 18:6–10; MARK 9:42–50; LUKE 17:1–2)

All these previous events inspired the Lord to direct His conversation to the need for defending all the weak and small against temptations from the powerful of this world. "But whoever causes one of these little ones who believe in Me to sin, it would be better for him if a millstone were hung around his neck." It would be better for the one who tempts one of the followers of Christ to die, for with this temptation he could destroy the soul of a person for whom Christ died and, consequently, this man commits the greatest crime, worthy of the severest punishment. The Lord continues with sorrow, "Woe to the world because of offenses! For offenses must come," because the world cannot avoid these temptations, for it lies in sin (1 John 5:19), its people are in a state of sinful damage, and the devil constantly searches among them for new prey. However, this does not mean that tempting others is permissible. Quite the contrary: "Woe to that man by whom the offense comes!" Woe to that person who consciously, due either to his disdain or lack of affection for his neighbor, leads him to sin. In order to show what a terrible evil is done by the one who leads the other to sin, the Lord once again uses an expression of the Sermon on the Mount about the hand or the foot that offends one, and the need to cut it off.

These expressions concerning cutting off and throwing away the tempting arm or leg, or to pluck out the offending eye, mean that there is nothing worse for a person than sin, and in order to avoid falling into sin, it may be necessary to sacrifice that which is most near and dear, just to avoid sinful temptation and not allow oneself to fall into this sin. St Mark's expression "where 'Their worm does not die'" is an expression calling to mind the dead, rotten body being eaten by worms and maggots. The worm here is a symbol of the conscience because it constantly tortures a person with the remembrance of his sins (Isa 66:24).

"For everyone will be seasoned with fire"—every person needs to be subjected to suffering. Thus, whoever did not suffer in this life, mortifying and belaboring his body (1 Cor 9:27), will suffer in the fires of eternal tortures. Just as any lawful sacrifice brought to God according to the law (Lev 2:13) had to be salted, so the salt of calamities, temptations, and enmity were intended to prepare the apostles and all followers of Christ as worthy sacrifices to God.

"Have salt in yourselves," meaning follow those moral rules and commandments that purify the soul and preserve it from moral decay, have within yourself the salt of true wisdom and true teaching (see Col 4:6). "And have peace with one another," peace, which is the fruit of love, an expression of the perfection reached by total self-rejection. It is not proper to think about who is greatest in the kingdom of heaven because this can lead to divisions, offenses, and antagonism. Rather, it is better to be the "salt of the earth" and remain in peace and unity of love among one another.

THE PARABLE OF THE LOST SHEEP, OF CORRECTING THOSE WHO ARE LOST, AND THE MEANING OF THE JUDGMENT OF THE CHURCH (MATT 18:10–20; LUKE 15:3–7)

In this parable, Christ draws a picture of the limitless love and mercy of God for fallen man. "Take heed that you do not despise one of these little ones." Do not despise—this means almost the same thing as "do not tempt"; in other words, do not consider them so worthless that tempting them means nothing. "Little ones" refers to those who have belittled themselves for the sake of the kingdom of heaven, that is, true Christians. Each of these receives a guardian angel from God; thus, if God Himself takes such care of them, is it right to disdain them?

"For the Son of Man has come to save that which was lost." This is a renewed instruction not to disdain "these little ones," for God Himself came down to earth for their salvation. In order to show more vividly just how precious the salvation of man is in the eyes of God, the Lord compares Himself to a shepherd who leaves his entire flock (in this case, the countless hosts of the angels) to go and search for one lost sheep (here meaning fallen mankind).

The meaning of the parable, according to Blessed Theophylact, is that "God takes care of the conversion of sinners, and rejoices over a converted sinner more than over one who has long been established in virtue."[42] Later, the Lord instructs us how we must correct our neighbor, which is closely connected with the prohibition to tempt him. If it is contrary to the law of love to tempt our neighbor, to incline him to sin, then it is no less contrary to the law of love to leave him in his sin and not care about his conversion when he does. But this must be done carefully, with brotherly love. First, one must chide him one-on-one, and if he recognizes his sin and condemns himself, then "you have gained your brother," who had been separated from the Church because of his sin. If he does not listen to your brotherly rebuke, remaining stubbornly in his own sin, then one must bring another or two other people who could then be witnesses of the sin of the brother who remains in his sin, and perhaps they would be more able in numbers to convince him of the error of his ways and inspire repentance (the law of Moses required two or three witnesses in a court case; see Deut 19:15). If the brother will remain deaf to their entreaties, then he must be committed to the Church. Here, "Church" does not mean the entire group of assembled faithful, but whoever is the leader of a local community, the hierarchy, the pastors to whom the authority is given to bind and loose.

"But if he refuses even to hear the church, let him be to you like a heathen and a tax collector." In other words, if he is so mired in his sin that he does not even consider the authority of the pastors of the Church, then let him be cast out of communion with the Church, as the pagans and publicans who had no fellowship with the Jews, as they were considered to be the worst kinds of pariahs. The practical meaning of this injunction is this: you should no longer consider a person who ignores the authority of the Church as your brother, and you should cease to have brotherly Christian association with him so that you are not infected by his disease. Such stubborn sinners who reject the authority of the Church's leadership are completely cast out of the Church, based on the example given by St Paul (1 Cor 5). The Church's practice of anathematizing heretics, dating even to apostolic times, is firmly based on these words of the Lord (and corroborated by 1 Cor 16:22).

Anathema is not a curse, as many in our time think, and use this as a reason to condemn the Church, as if it allowed itself to act in a way contrary to Christian love. Quite the opposite, anathema is a very sobering measure for the stubborn sinner who refuses to be corrected and also for the protection of those who might follow him in his madness. The Lord Himself gave the Church hierarchy the authority to commit sinners to anathema, saying, "Assuredly, I say unto you, whatever you bind on earth will be bound in heaven; and whatever you loose on earth will be loosed in heaven." That which was initially promised only to Peter is now given to all the apostles. The apostles, in their turn, gave this power to bind and loose sins to their own successors, the pastors of the Church, installed by them for the continuation of their work on the earth. Also, in any other situation, when the apostles of Christ come together in prayer for whatever need, the Lord promised to fulfill their petitions, saying: "Where two or three are gathered together in My name, I am there in the midst of them."

ON FORGIVING OFFENSES AND THE PARABLE OF THE MERCILESS CREDITOR
(MATT 18:21–35; LUKE 17:3–4)

The Lord's instruction about forgiving the sinner who repents inspired a question from Peter about how many times one should forgive a brother. The reason Peter asked this question is that the Jewish scribes taught that one should only forgive one's offending brother three times. Desiring to surpass the Old Testament's righteousness and at the same time to appear generous, Peters asks if one should forgive him seven times. Then Christ answers that one must forgive "seventy times seven" times, meaning that one must always forgive, without limiting oneself to a number. In order to better explain this need for constant and limitless forgiveness, the Lord tells the parable of the merciless creditor.

In this parable, God is imagined as an earthly king whose slaves owe him a certain amount of money. Thus, mankind is a debtor before God because good deeds are not done and time is instead wasted on sin. "To settle accounts" in the parable refers to God's final reckoning at the Last Judgment, as well as the partial reckoning at the particular judgment after each person's death. The debtor owed the king ten thousand talents, and as such, is an image of every sinner who before the face of God's righteousness is truly a debtor who has not paid. Ten thousand talents is a huge sum, to be counted in the millions in our currency. According to the laws of Moses (Lev 25:39, 47), a king has the right to sell a debtor who does not pay into slavery, and the king in the parable was prepared to do that. But he was compassionate to him after his repeated entreaties, and forgave him his entire debt. This is an amazing image of the compassion of God for repentant sinners.

The forgiven debtor found a person who owed him one hundred denarii, an inconsequential amount of money (especially compared to the previous amount; only several dollars in our currency). When the man could not pay, he began to choke him (according to Roman law, a creditor had the right to torture a debtor until he paid in full), demanding that the man pay him his debt. He had no compassion on him, even though the man begged him to wait, and he had him placed in prison.

The friends of the debtor, seeing what had happened and obviously upset for their friend, told the king everything they saw. The king was furious at the evil servant, called him to his side, and, after chiding him severely for not acting in the same way as the king did to his own debtor, gave him up to the torturers until he would pay his huge debt of ten thousand talents, that is, his tortures were to be until he died, for he would never be able to pay back such a huge sum (a sinner is saved only by the compassion of God; he is incapable to satisfy the justice of God with his own powers).

The meaning of the parable is best expressed in St Matthew's Gospel: "So My heavenly Father also will do to you, if each of you from his heart, does not forgive his brother his trespasses" (Matt 18:35). The Lord teaches us here that all of us have sinned so much that we, before God, are debtors unable to pay our huge debt. However, our neighbors' sins against us are insignificant compared to our debt to God, but God still forgives us all our sins in His limitless compassion if we, in our turn, find the compassion to forgive our neighbors their sins against us. If we remain intransigent and merciless to the offenses of others and do not forgive them, then the Lord will not forgive us, but will condemn us to eternal suffering. This parable is a very effective illustration of the petition in the "Lord's Prayer": "and forgive us our debts, as we forgive our debtors."

CHRIST REFUSES TO GO TOGETHER WITH HIS BROTHERS TO JERUSALEM FOR THE FEAST OF BOOTHS (JOHN 7:1–9)

The Evangelist John, after describing in chapter 6 the conversation about the bread of life, says that "after these things," Jesus walked only in Galilee. This long sojourn in Galilee and His activity there is described in detail by the Synoptics, as we have already seen. The Lord did not want to go yet into Judea because "the Jews sought to kill Him," and it was not yet the time of His suffering. "Now the Jews' Feast of Tabernacles was at hand," one of the three pilgrim feasts of the Jewish calendar (Passover and Pentecost are the other two), celebrated for seven days from the fifteenth day of Tishri, at the end of September/early October according to our calendar. It was founded as a remembrance of the forty-year wandering in the desert. During all seven days, people leave their homes and live in specially built tabernacles or tents. Since the feast occurred soon after the harvest, it was celebrated with much revelry and drinking of wine, so much so that Plutarch even compared it to a Bacchanalia.

Before this feast, Christ had not been in Jerusalem for nearly a year and a half (He did not attend His third Passover after He began His public ministry, and the time from Passover to the feast of booths is roughly half a year), and His brothers were pressuring Him to go with them to Jerusalem for the feast. They wanted the Lord to enter Jerusalem triumphantly, as the Messiah, in the full manifestation of His power. The Lord's refusal to accept worldly power and glory was not understandable to them. "For even His brothers did not believe in Him," said the Evangelist. They were unsure about their brother and wanted their state of anxious waiting to be resolved. On the one hand, they could not deny the incredible deeds He was performing, many of which they had seen with their own eyes, but on the other hand, they were not ready to accept as the Messiah a man with whom they had been in close familial ties since childhood. With this in mind, they offered Him to stop being in what they considered to be an ambiguous position and to take a stand. If He was truly the Messiah, they thought, why is He afraid to appear as the Messiah before the whole world in Jerusalem? He *must* appear there in His full power and glory. In answer, the Lord explains that going to Jerusalem for Him does not have the same meaning as for everyone else, His brothers included. If His brothers go to Jerusalem, they will not be met with hatred since the world does not hate them because they are of the world. Christ, however, will be met with hatred because He accuses the evil deeds of the world. Thus, they can always go there, but He cannot go at any time, but only when the time for His sufferings has been determined from on high. Letting His brothers go, the Lord remained in Galilee, intending to come to the feast in Jerusalem in secret, with only His closest disciples.

CHRIST GOES TO JERUSALEM WITH HIS DISCIPLES: THE SAMARITAN TOWN REFUSES TO TAKE HIM IN (LUKE 9:51–56)

The Lord was already known in Samaria, but such was the enmity between the Jews and Samaritans that He did not expect to be kindly greeted by them, so He sent a few disciples ahead of them to warn the Samaritans of their coming. It is unclear to which Samaritan town the disciples came, but it was probably in north Samaria, closer to Galilee, within a day's journey from the border. Since the Lord intended to travel to Jerusalem, the Samaritans refused to take Him in, evidently because of their deep-seated hatred of the Jews. James and John, whom the Lord called "Sons of Thunder" (Mark 3:17) because of their spiritual strength and energy and their frequent outbursts of religious zeal, became full of righteous anger for the sake of their Lord's honor. Remembering how Elijah the prophet sent fire from heaven to consume those who had come to seize him (1 Kgs 1:9–12), they asked their Teacher whether He wanted them to do the same and destroy these Samaritans with fire from heaven.

They had already performed many miracles with the power the Lord had given them, and so they did not think it impossible for them to perform this miracle as well, if it were pleasing to their all-powerful Teacher. But the Lord answered them that they did not realize of what spirit they are—the spirit of the New Testament is not the same as the spirit of the Old. That was a spirit of severity and divine anger; here, there is a spirit of love and compassion, since the purpose of the Son of Man's coming is not to destroy, but to save (Matt 18:11). In addition, the Lord wanted to show the zealous apostles that, in this case, they were less motivated by love for Him than by hatred for the Samaritans, and this Old Testament spirit of hatred for those outside the chosen nation must be abandoned by the servants of the New Testament. Since this was the reception in Samaria, Christ most likely went back to Galilee and traveled to Judea a different way, the way the Jews normally traveled, through the region of Perea beyond the Jordan. From the subsequent account in St Luke, we see that the Lord was in Galilee and Perea for a while longer, and only later went to Judea.

CHRIST SENDS THE SEVENTY TO PREACH (LUKE 10:1–16)

When the Lord decided to go to Judea, leaving Galilee behind for the last time (since the time for His sufferings was nigh), He chose seventy other disciples in addition to the chosen twelve, and sent them also two by two, so that in the eyes of the world their witness to Christ would have more validity, into all the places that Christ planned on visiting, in order to prepare the people for His coming. The number seventy was a sacred number for the Jews, as were forty and seven. The Sanhedrin had seventy members, for example. We do not know the names of all those seventy.

"The harvest truly is great, but the laborers are few." Samaria and Judea were still little acquainted with the preaching of Christ, and there were many souls there ready, like ripe wheat, for the storehouses of Christ, for His Church. The instructions given to the seventy were quite similar to the ones given to the Twelve, already mentioned by Matthew in chapter 10 of his Gospel. The prohibition to greet those on the road is once again repeated. This prohibition is explained thus—for the Eastern peoples, a greeting on the road was not a simple affair, a nod or a shake of the hand, but with bows to the earth, embraces, kisses, and long expressions of well wishing, all of which required time. By prohibiting this, the Lord wanted to inspire in His disciples the haste that was needed for the spread of the Gospel. In the Old Testament, the Prophet Elisha gave exactly the same instruction to his disciple Ghazi when he sent him with a staff to raise the son of the widow from the dead (2 Kgs 4:29).

The "son of peace" here mentioned (Luke 10:6) is any person who in his heart is ready to accept the peace that will be given by the messengers of peace, the disciples of the Lord. By ordering them to eat what was offered to them, the Lord instructs the disciples in a proper lack of specific requirements and personal desires, as well as decrying the usual disdain with which the Jews viewed the Samaritans, which would be improper in a preacher of the kingdom of peace and love. The Lord concluded His instruction with a threat of divine wrath for those cities in which His power was revealed, but which refused to repent. He also shows what great significance all this preliminary preaching of His disciples had: whoever rejected them rejected Him, and whoever rejects Him, rejects Him Who sent Him, God the Father.

THE LORD IN JERUSALEM FOR THE FEAST OF BOOTHS (JOHN 7:10–53)

Having let His brothers leave for Jerusalem, the Lord Himself came there slightly later, but secretly. He arrived not in triumph, as He would before the final Passover when He would come to suffer, and not accompanied by masses of people who normally followed Him, but quietly and unnoticeably. Bishop Michael notes the following:

It is remarkable how the Lord's visits to Jerusalem get progressively sadder, not inspired, of course, by His own actions, but by the ever-increasing antagonism of

His enemies. During His first Passover, He triumphantly appeared in the Temple as the Messiah, the Son of God clothed in authority (John 2), during the second, He comes as a traveler, but His actions and words inspire hatred against Him and even leads to one of the several attempts to kill Him; for which reason He did not even come to Jerusalem for the third Passover, staying far from Jerusalem for a year and a half, after which He is forced to come to Jerusalem in secret![43]

Verses 11–13 of St John's chapter 7 give a vivid representation of what was going on in Jerusalem during that time. Everyone was speaking of Christ. It is evident that His enemies kept a watch over Him and followed all of His actions, which is why they asked the question, "Where is He?" Among the people there were many rumors concerning Him of the most varying kinds, but everyone spoke quietly, fearing "the Jews," who in St John's Gospel generally indicate the party of the Jewish leaders with members of the Sanhedrin and the Pharisees at its head. St John Chrysostom and Blessed Theophylact together believe that the people generally spoke well of Christ, with the real antagonism limited to the leaders: "The leaders said that He was lying to the people, while the people said that He was a good man."[44] This is seen from the fact that the leaders separated themselves from the people, saying that "He deceives the people." Only on the fourth day of the feast, more than halfway through, did Jesus finally appear in the temple and teach, meaning that He probably interpreted the Scriptures, as was customary for the Jews.

Knowing that the Lord did not have any formal learning from any of the more or less known rabbinical schools, the Jews were amazed at His knowledge of the Scriptures. It is characteristic that they were deaf to the content of His teaching, only paying attention to the fact that He was not formally trained. This indicates their disdain and enmity to the Lord. Jesus immediately explained to them that "My doctrine in not Mine, but His Who sent Me." With these words, the Lord is saying to them: I did not finish any of your rabbinical schools, but I have a perfect Teacher, My heavenly Father, Who sent Me."

The means to be assured in the divine origin of this teaching is the personal decision to do the will of God. Whoever willingly decides to do the will of God will be assured by an inner feeling that this teaching is from God. By "will of God" Christ means the entire moral law of God—both the law of the conscience and the written Old Testament law. Whoever would wish to walk the path to moral perfection by fulfilling this law will understand with an inner conviction that the teaching of Christ is the teaching of God. The Lord underlines this, saying that He preaches for the glory of the One Who sent Him, not for His own glory, as someone presenting his own new teaching.

Having in mind the Jewish leaders, the Lord then says that they seek to kill Him for breaking the law that they themselves do not follow. Not knowing of these secret assassination plans of their leaders, the people thought Christ was speaking of them and were offended, and among them was heard the following: "Who seeks to kill You? Perhaps an evil spirit is inspiring such thoughts in You? Perhaps You are possessed?" From the subsequent words of the Lord, it is clear that the healing of the paralytic, performed on a Sabbath, continued to be a subject of many conversations, especially His disagreement with the Pharisees' meticulous observance of the law of the Sabbath rest. The Lord tells the people that one can do good works on a Sabbath, which is why the rite of circumcision is performed on a Sabbath in order not to break Moses's law concerning circumcision on the eighth day after birth. Consequently, it should not be shocking to anyone that He healed a man on a Sabbath.

The Lord concluded His speech with a call to judge concerning the law not by the letter, the external aspects, but by the spirit, in order to properly judge what the law intends: "If a man receives circumcision on the Sabbath, so that the law of Moses should not be broken, are you angry with Me because I made a man completely well on the Sabbath?" – as Blessed Theophylact beautifully analyzes these words.[45] Bishop Michael adds: "If you had judged My actions not superficially, but from a moral point of view, then you would not have condemned Me. Then your judgment would have been proper and unbiased."[46]

This powerful speech of the Lord made a serious impression on the people who knew of the leaders' plot to kill the Lord, and they wondered how those who seek to kill Him are allowing Him to speak so boldly without contradicting Him. Not knowing how to explain this anomaly, some of them suggest that this is perhaps because they have decided "indeed that this is truly the Christ." But at the same time, there were those who expressed their doubts. According to the teachings of the rabbis, the Messiah had to be born in Bethlehem, then disappear from them without being noticed, then He would appear again suddenly, in a way that no one would be able to tell how and from where He came. According to the people, Jesus could not be the Christ, because they knew where He came from. Then the Lord, raising His voice, answered with emphasis that even though they say that they know where He came from, they are mistaken. "You only think you know Me, and you say that I came of My own volition, that I am a self-proclaimed Messiah. But I do not come of Myself, but I am a true messenger of the One Who sent Me, Whom you do not know, God Himself."

These words were perceived as especially offensive to the proud Pharisees, and "they sought to take Him," but since "His hour had not yet come," this effort was futile, and "no one laid a hand on Him," most likely because His enemies were still afraid of the people who were well-disposed to Him. Perhaps their consciences did not yet allow them to reach such a low point as they did later. Many of the people believed in Him as in the Messiah, and they were correct to say, as if contradicting the enemies of Christ, "When the Christ comes, will He do more signs than these which this Man has done?" In other words, they wanted to say that the miracles and signs that Jesus performed were strong enough proof of His Messianic dignity.

Having heard such words among the people, the Pharisees met secretly with the chief priests and decided to wait no further to put in action their intention to kill Christ, and they sent soldiers to take the Lord and bring Him to them. In answer to their plotting, Jesus said, "I shall be with you a little while longer, and then I go to Him who sent Me," thinking of His imminent death, and He implores the Jews to take advantage of the time He still has with them to learn from Him. The subsequent words of the Lord can be rephrased thus: "Now you are persecuting Me, but there will be a time when you will look for Me, as the all-powerful Miracle Worker who can remove all your troubles and cares, but it will then be too late." But the coldhearted Jews were not inspired by these words and some even started to mock Him: "Where does He intend to go that we shall not find Him? Does He intend to go to the Dispersion among the Greeks and teach the Greeks?" Here, they unwittingly prophesied the spread of Christ's teaching among the pagans.

"On the last day, that great day of the feast," on the eighth day, which was added to the regular seven days of celebrating the feast of booths (Lev 23:36), and was celebrated with especial pomp, "Jesus stood and cried out, saying, 'If anyone thirsts, let him come to Me and drink.'" In these words and those subsequent, the Lord used the rites performed during the feast as points of departure for His preaching. After the morning sacrifice in the temple, the people walked in procession to the pool of Siloam, where the priest would fill a golden urn with water. Accompanied by the joyful cries of the people and the music of cymbals and trumpets, he carried it to the temple and poured the water onto the altar of whole-burnt offerings, performing the sacrifice of oblation that was intended to remind the people of how Moses made the water pour from the side of the rock during the Hebrew wandering in the wilderness.

During this procession, the people chanted the words of Isaiah that referred to the Messiah (Isa 12:3). The Lord Jesus Christ compared Himself to the rock that parched the thirst of the Israelites in the desert, calling Himself the Source of goodness, whose prototype was the rock. He also indicates that whoever believes in Him will himself become a source of grace, which will quench the spiritual thirst of all who seek salvation. John the Evangelist gives an explanatory note that the Lord here was speaking of the grace of the Holy Spirit, which was going to be sent to people after the glorification of Christ, that is, His resurrection and ascension.

This speech of the Lord immediately had a tremendous effect on the crowd—many of the people took the Lord's side, calling Him "Prophet," and some even said openly, "This is the Christ!" The Pharisees immediately countered to those who did not know that Jesus was born in Bethlehem that He could not be the Messiah: "Will the Christ come out of Galilee?" And there was a division among them.

The soldiers who were sent to bring Him to the Sanhedrin tried to take advantage of this situation to seize Him, but every time they tried, their hands refused to obey them. They dared not do it; evidently, their consciences were hinting that it would be a great sin to even touch such a Man. In this same confusion, they returned to their masters and confessed that the power of Jesus was so great and irresistible that they could not fulfill their command. This answer had the most irritating effect on the members of the Sanhedrin: "Are you also deceived?" They tell their soldiers that the wise "rulers" and Pharisees do not believe in Christ, while only the commoners are ignorant enough to be fooled. "But this crowd that does not know the law is accursed," with such an expression of irrational hatred, the Jewish leaders attack even their own people who believed in Christ. This faith they try to discredit by calling it ignorance of the law.

But here Nicodemus, himself a Pharisee and a member of the Sanhedrin, decided to bravely show them that they were guilty of the same ignorance of the law: "Does our law judge a man before it hears him and knows what he is doing?" The law in Exodus (Exod 23:1) and Deuteronomy (Deut 1:16) requires the chosen nation not to give credence to empty rumors and to look into the case of the one who is denounced as a vain babbler. But these wise words of Nicodemus only inspired further irritation: "Are you also from Galilee?" meaning that only a Galilean (the term here is clearly used pejoratively) can think this way. They did not notice that in this moment even their vaunted historical memory failed them, since the Prophet Jonah, to give one example, was a Galilean by birth.

CHRIST'S JUDGMENT OVER THE WOMAN CAUGHT IN ADULTERY, BROUGHT BEFORE HIM BY THE PHARISEES (JOHN 8:1–11)

Only St John tells of this episode. After spending the night in prayer on the Mount of Olives, situated east of Jerusalem beyond Kidron, where the Lord often went during the nights of His Jerusalem visits, in the morning, He came once again to the temple to teach the people. The scribes and Pharisees, wishing to find an occasion to accuse Him of a concrete crime against the law, brought a woman to Him who was found in the act of adultery, and "They said to Him, 'Teacher, this woman was caught in adultery, in the very act. Now Moses, in the law, commanded us that such should be stoned. But what do You say?'"

If the Lord had answered, "Let her be stoned," they would have accused Him before the Roman rulers, because the Sanhedrin was deprived of the right of execution by Roman law. If the Lord had said instead, "Let her be released," they would take the opportunity to denounce Him before the people as a transgressor against the law of Moses.

Instead, the Lord, leaning down to the ground, began to write with His finger on the ground, "as though He did not hear." John the Evangelist does not say what He wrote, and the various theories offer little more than that. The most widespread of these theories is that the Lord was writing His answer to the Pharisees by writing down the specific sins of which each of them was guilty. Since they continued stubbornly to demand an answer from Him, He raised His head and said, "He who is without sin among you, let him throw a stone at her first."

These words had a tremendous effect on the not-yet-completely deadened conscience of the Pharisees. As each remembered his own sins, many of them probably of a similar nature to the woman's, and as each one's conscience accused him, they started to leave, one by one, until there was no one left except the woman and Jesus Himself. In this way, the Lord, in answer to the cunning of the Pharisees, wisely moved the question of the woman's guilt from the strictly juridical sphere to the moral sphere, and thus put the accusers in a difficult position with regard to their own consciences. The Lord acted in this way because the Pharisees who brought the woman before Him were themselves not a lawful court with any legal right to condemn her. They brought her to Jesus with ill will, desiring to humiliate her, speaking evil of her and condemning her, forgetting at the same time their own sins, of which the Lord reminded them.

It is interesting to note that the woman remained, even though she had ample opportunity to take advantage of this unexpected turn of events to run away and hide herself. Apparently, her own conscience was accusing her and she was on her way to repentance. In this light, the words of Christ make sense: "Neither do I condemn you; go and sin no more." In these words, however, it would be wrong to see a lack of condemnation of her sin. The Lord did not come to judge but to find and save the lost (Matt 18:11; Luke 7:48; John 3:17; 12:47). Thus, He condemns the sin, but not the sinner, desiring to inspire the sinner to repentance. If rephrased, His words could sound like this: "I also do not punish you for this sin, but I want you to repent; therefore, go and do not sin anymore." The crux of His pronouncement is the last phrase. This passage teaches us to avoid the sin of condemning our neighbor, offering us instead to judge ourselves for our own sins and to repent of them.

CHRIST SPEAKS WITH THE JEWS IN THE TEMPLE (JOHN 8:12–59)

In this conversation, apparently occurring on the next day after the end of the feast of booths, the Lord took another image from Jewish sacred history and applied it to Himself—the image of the pillar of fire that miraculously lit the way for the Hebrews through the desert at night. In this pillar was the angel of the Lord, in whom many holy Fathers see the Second Person of the Holy Trinity. The Lord begins His preaching with the words "I am the light of the world." As in the Old Testament, where the pillar of fire lit the way for the Hebrews from Egypt to the better life in the Promised Land, so Christ in the New Testament indicates the way out of sin and toward the eternal blessed life not only for the Jews, but for all mankind.

The Pharisees, citing the generally accepted rule that no one can be a witness to his own case, accused Him that such a proclamation regarding Himself cannot be accepted as truthful by definition. The Lord answered with authority, saying that such a carnal mind-set is not applicable to His situation, that one cannot judge "according to the flesh" about Him, as the Pharisees do, who consider Him to be a mere man. "I know where I came from and where I am going." According to St John Chrysostom, these words mean the same thing as "I know that I am the Son of God and not a mere man."[47] In this knowledge of His own pre-eternal birth from the Father is contained the full right for self-witness and at the same time the impossibility of self-deception. The Lord adds that His witness is also true from a formal point of view, because it is not He alone who bring witness, but "the Father who sent Me bears witness of Me."

Having heard the Lord speak many times of the Father as the One Who sent Him, they nonetheless pretended ignorance and asked the question: "Where is Your Father?" The Lord answers that they do not know the Father because they do not want to know the Son. Here, there is a hidden indication that the Father and the Son are one in essence, especially in the fact that the Father revealed Himself to men through the Son. John the Evangelist mentions that this was spoken in the temple treasury, which was located near the hall of deliberation of the Sanhedrin, and even though He declared His Messianic dignity within hearing of the entire group of antagonistic leaders, "no one laid hands on Him, for His hour had not yet come." Once again we see how the people never had authority over Him, and even when they took Him later, in Gethsemane, it was due to His own permission and will, not their power.

Once again the Lord reminds them of the dilemma they all will face after His departure from this world if they will not believe in Him as the Messiah: "Where I go you cannot come." These words only inspired irritation and mockery: "Will He kill Himself?" Not responding to their rude taunt, the Lord instead addresses their moral state, which leads them to such crude mockery of Him: "You are from beneath." In other words, they have lost the ability to understand the divine completely. They interpret everything carnally, guided by their own sinful, earthly ideas, and so, if they do not believe in Him ("that I am He," meaning the Messiah), "you will die in your sins."

The Lord did not at any one time call Himself the Messiah; but so clearly and understandably did He express this truth about Himself that of course the Pharisees understood His meaning. However, they continued to feign ignorance since they wanted to hear the words "I am the Messiah" come out of His mouth, and they asked Him, "Who are You?" But even now, the Lord refused to accommodate their desires, instead saying, "Just what I have been saying to you from the beginning," meaning that He had repeatedly referred to Himself as the Son of God in the past.

Continuing His words about the sorry moral state of the Jewish people, the Lord explains that He must do this, because the One Who sent Him is Truth Himself, and He must witness to the truth that He hears from Him. Once again, His listeners do not understand the allusion to the Father. So the Lord tells them of the coming time when they will learn of the truth concerning Himself and the Father Who sent Him, when they will raise Him up on the cross, for the crucifixion is the beginning of the glorification of the Son of God and the calling of all the nations. The events subsequent to His crucifixion, such as the resurrection, the ascension, and the descent of the Spirit on the apostles—all this showed the truth of Christ's teaching and His divinity. These words once again impressed many who listened, so that "many believed in Him," apparently even from among those who were unfriendly to Him. To them does the Lord direct these subsequent words.

He teaches them how they can become and remain His true disciples. For this, they must "abide in My word." Only then will they know the truth, and the truth will give them freedom from sin, which is the only kind of true freedom. Among the listeners we then hear the sounds of nationalistic pride: "We are Abraham's descendents," and the sons of Abraham were promised lordship over the nations and the consecration of the world through them (Gen 12:7; 22:17), "and have never been in bondage to anyone." In this passionate, sickly cry of strident nationalistic pride, they seemed to have forgotten about their Egyptian bondage, the Babylonian captivity, even the current lordship of the Romans! The Lord answers them that He was speaking of a different kind of bondage, the bondage to sin, which is the fate of every man who sins: "whoever commits sin is the slave of sin."

The one who is enslaved to sin cannot remain in the kingdom of the Messiah, where there must be total moral freedom and where all must acknowledge themselves to be exclusively children of the Heavenly Father. "A slave does not abide in the house forever," for a displeased master can either sell him or send him away. This slavery is the opposite of sonship because the son as heir of the house cannot be sold or sent away, and remains the son forever. "You who commit sins are slaves to sin, and you can receive true freedom and become sons of God only if you believe in the Son of God, remain in His words, and He will free you from slavery to sin."

Later, the Lord tells them that He does not reject their being sons of Abraham, but He does not acknowledge them to be true sons of Abraham in spirit, because they seek to kill Him only because "My word has no place in you." His word did not find good soil in which to grow in their hearts. Since Abraham was not as stone-hearted as they were, then their father was not Abraham, as they insist, but the devil, who "was a murderer from the beginning," for he brought death-dealing sin into the nature of mankind. Speaking of the devil, the Lord connects the idea of his being a murderer with his being an enemy of truth and "a liar and the father of it." Consequently, speaking of Himself, the Lord also connects His sinlessness and truthfulness. If the Jews do not accept His teaching as true, then let them show the sinfulness of His life: "Which of you convicts Me of sin?" If no one can accuse Him of a sinful life, then one must admit as a logical extension the truth of His preaching. By their lack of faith, the Jews clearly show that they are not of God.

This angered His listeners greatly: "Do we not say rightly that You are a Samaritan and have a demon?" This they say because only those who hate the chosen nation (that is, possessed people or Samaritans) can deny their descent from Abraham. The Lord calmly ignores this insult and says that by speaking in the way they call demon-possessed, He is actually giving praise to the Father in heaven. He speaks thus because "I honor My Father," while they disparage the One Who gives them the Father's truth. "I do not seek my own glory; there is One who seeks and judges," the Heavenly Father, Who will condemn all those who rejected His Son.

Once again addressing those who believed in Him, the Lord said, "If anyone keeps My word, he shall never taste death," meaning, of course, "shall receive eternal life." But those who did not believe in Him interpreted these words literally, as referring to physical death, and in this they once again found a reason to accuse Him of demonic possession: "Now we know that You have a demon! Abraham is dead, and the prophets ... Are You greater than our father Abraham? ... Whom do You make Yourself out to be?" The Lord answers that He is not praising Himself, but the Father praises Him, Whom He knows and Whose word He keeps, and then shows them His superiority over Abraham. It is as if He said, "Yes, I am greater than your father Abraham, for I was the source of strivings when he was still alive, and the reason for his joy after his death, in heaven." Jesus continued: "Your father Abraham rejoiced to see My day, and he saw it and was glad."

Once again the Jews understood the Lord's words in the earthly, literal sense, as though Christ had seen Abraham while he was still alive. And they rebuked Jesus: "You are not yet fifty years old, and have You seen Abraham?" To this rebuke, the Lord gives a final answer, whose meaning could not be misinterpreted even by the Pharisees, blinded by their hatred. "Most assuredly, I say to you, before Abraham was, I AM." In these words, the Lord is clearly saying so that everyone immediately understood that He is the Eternal God. And it is obvious that the Pharisees understood, but instead of believing in Him, they became incensed because they considered such words coming from a mere man to be the worst kind of blasphemy, and they took up stones to kill Him. But Jesus, triumphantly finishing this testimony regarding Himself and surrounded by His disciples and the people, hid from them in the masses of people surrounding the temple, and "and so passed by."

HEALING THE MAN BLIND FROM BIRTH (JOHN 9:1–41)

This great miracle, performed apparently in the temple right after the conversation with the Jews about His divinity, is described with great detail only by the Evangelist John. When the disciples saw a certain blind man begging, about whom it was well known that he was blind from birth, they asked Jesus, "Who sinned, this man or his parents, that he was born blind?"

The Jews believed that the worst calamities in a person's life were nothing other than divine punishment for their own sins or the sins of their parents, grandparents, and great-grandparents. This belief is based on the Law of Moses, which says that God will punish the children for the faults of their fathers until the third and fourth generation (Exod 20:5). The rabbis also taught that the child can sin even in the womb because he has good and evil feelings from his very conception. When the Lord answers, He shows them not the cause of his blindness, but its purpose: "Neither this man nor his parents sinned," not meaning that they were sinless but that their sin was not the cause of blindness, "but that the works of God should be revealed in him." In other words, this miracle would reveal that Christ truly is the "light of the world," that He came into the world to illumine mankind, which remained in spiritual darkness, a good symbol of which is physical blindness.

"I must work the works of Him who sent Me while it is day," meaning while Christ is still visible for all on earth, but "the night is coming," the time of His departure from the world, when the work of the Saviour in the world as Miracle Worker will not be as obvious to all as it is now. "As long as I am in the world, I am the light of the world"; even though Christ always was and will be the light of the world, His visible activity on earth only lasts as long as His earthly life, which is already coming to its end.

The Lord performed many miracles only with His word, but sometimes He also used special preliminary actions. Thus, He does on this occasion: "He spat on the ground and made clay with the saliva; and He anointed the eyes of the blind man with the clay. And He said to him, 'Go, wash in the pool of Siloam.'" One can say that all this was necessary for inspiring faith in the one being healed, to help him understand that an extraordinary miracle was about to be performed over him. The pool of Siloam was situated on the spring of Siloam, pouring out from beneath the holy mountain of Zion, a place of God's special presence in Jerusalem (and the Temple), and so it was called, as the Evangelist writes, "which is translated, Sent," a special blessing given by God to His people. Did the Lord Jesus Christ want to express by this that He is truly the One sent from God, the fulfillment of all the blessings that were symbolized for the Jews by the pool of Siloam? Having washed in the holy water, the man blind from birth began to see.

This miracle had an immediate effect on the blind man's family and neighbors, so much so that some of them even began to doubt his identity. But he confirmed that he was indeed the man blind from birth who had begged at the temple, and he told everyone how the miracle was accomplished. Those who heard him led him to the Pharisees in order to fully investigate this unusual account and to learn their opinion of the matter, for the miracle was performed during the Sabbath when, according to law, one could not even receive medical aid from a physician.

The healed man told the Pharisees all he knew of his healing. Immediately there was a division among the Pharisees regarding his case. Some, and we can assume that it was the majority, said, "This Man is not from God, because He does not keep the Sabbath." But others were quite fair in their rebuttal: "How can a Man Who is a sinner do such signs?"

The Pharisees who did not believe in the Lord then asked the healed man about his healer. They apparently hoped to find something in his account that would allow them to accuse Christ directly with breaking the law, or at least to find a reason to invalidate the miracle or reinterpret it somehow. But the healed man said with conviction: "He is a prophet." Not finding the blind man helpful at all, the hate-filled Jews called the parents of the man to inquire into his case further. Fearing to be cast out of the synagogue, the parents gave an evasive answer. They confirmed that this was their son who was born blind, but for some reason now he could see. They claimed ignorance and offered that they ask their son directly since he was already of age and could speak for himself.

The Pharisees called the healed man in a second time and tried to tell him that they had made detailed inquiries into the Man Who had healed him and had determined, without a doubt, that the Man was a sinner. Instead, he should "give God the glory," by which they meant that he should agree with them that Jesus was a sinner who broke the Sabbath law. In other words, they wanted him to speak the truth under oath. But the healed man gave an answer full of truth and deep irony with reference to the Pharisees: "Whether He is a sinner or not I do not know. One thing I know: that though I was blind, now I see." Having achieved none of their goals so far, the Pharisees once again asked the healed man to give an account of his healing, perhaps hoping to find a new detail that would help them condemn Jesus.

But the healed man was only irritated by their repeated request: "I told you already, and you did not listen. Why do you want to hear it again? Do you also want to become His disciples?" This bold jibe resulted in a stern rebuke to this brave confessor of the truth: "You are His disciple, but we are Moses' disciples. We know that God spoke to Moses; as for this fellow, we do not know where He is from." The leaders of the Jewish people should have found out where this Man had come from, because so many people followed Him, but they lied when they said they did not know who He was. This lie only irritated the former blind man even more, and gave him added boldness to defend the truth. "Why, this is a marvelous thing, that you do not know where He is from," he said to them, for they really should bother to find out who had performed such an unheard-of miracle. Sinners cannot perform such miracles; it is therefore evident that this is a holy Man, sent by God.

Stricken by the unbending logic of the simple, direct man, the Pharisees did not have the strength to continue losing the discussion, and having rebuked him for being born "altogether in sins," they cast him out of their presence. When Christ heard of this, He desired to open the man's spiritual eyes as well, and having revealed Himself to the man as his healer, He began to lead him to faith in Him as the Son of God. All that had already happened gave the Lord an opportunity to express the thought that His coming into the world had as an inevitable consequence the sharp division between those who believed and did not believe in Him. "For judgment I have come into this world, that those who do not see may see; and that those who see may be made blind."

"Those who do not see" are those who are humble and poor in spirit, who believed in Christ. "Those who see" are those who consider themselves already illumined and wise and so do not feel the need for faith in Christ, the so-called wise men such as the Pharisees who rejected Christ. The Lord calls them "blind" because they have become spiritually blind, not able to see the divine truth, which He brought to the earth.

To these words, some Pharisees who were with Him answered, "Are we blind also?" But they heard an unexpected answer: "If you were blind, you would have no sin; but now you say, 'We see.' Therefore your sin remains." The meaning of these words is this: If you had been one of those whom I called unable to see, then you would not have any sin because in that case, your lack of faith would be a forgivable sin of ignorance and weakness. But since you say that you can see, you consider yourselves to be knowledgeable about the divine revelation and able to interpret it correctly, and you have the law and the prophets at your disposal, your sin is nothing less than a sin of stubborn and merciless rejection of divine truth, and such a sin is not forgiven, for this is the sin of blasphemy against the Holy Spirit (Matt 12:31–32).

SERMON REGARDING THE GOOD SHEPHERD (JOHN 10:1–21)

This sermon is a continuation of the accusatory speech of the Lord directed at the Pharisees in connection with the healing of the man born blind. Having explained to them that they are responsible for "seeing, but not being able to see" (Matt 13:13), the Lord indirectly tells them that they are not true leaders of the religious life of the people as they imagine; they are not "good shepherds," for they think more of their personal gain than of the good of the people, and so end up leading the people not to salvation, but to perdition. This wonderful speech, whose meaning the Pharisees only understood at the very end of it, uses an image taken out of the pastoral life of Palestine.

The Lord compares the people to a flock of sheep, and the leaders of the people are the shepherds. The flocks were often rounded up at night and hidden from thieves and wolves in caves or specially built pens. It was not unusual to round up flocks belonging to several different masters into one pen. In the morning, the gate-keepers would open the pen and the shepherds would walk in and call their own sheep by name. The sheep would recognize their own shepherd's voice (something that still can be seen in the rural life of Palestine) and follow them out to the pastures. Thieves and robbers, of course, dared not enter through the gates into these pens, because they were guarded. So instead, they climbed over the walls.

Taking this accessible image, the Lord used the sheepfold as the symbol of the chosen nation of Israel, the Old Testament Church, which later developed into the New Testament Church. The shepherd is an image of any true religious leader. The "thieves" and "robbers" are all false, self-proclaimed prophets, false teachers, heretics, and so-called religious leaders who actually only think of themselves and their own interests, such as the Pharisees, accused by the Lord. The Lord called Himself both the "door" and the "Good Shepherd," who would lay down His life for the sheep to protect them from the wolves. The Lord calls Himself the door in the sense that He is the only true mediator between God and mankind, the only way both for the shepherds and the sheep. One cannot enter His kingdom of God, which is symbolized by the sheepfold, except through Him. All those who avoid Him and try to climb over the walls are "thieves and robbers," not true shepherds, but impostors who seek to fulfill their own needs, but not the good of the sheep. The sheepfold is the earthly church, while the pasture is the Church in heaven.

The Pharisees failed to understand the first part of the parable. Then, in the second part, He fully disclosed His teaching of Himself as the "Good Shepherd." In this second part, the "hireling" is symbolic of all those unworthy shepherds who, in the words of the Prophet Ezekiel, "pasture themselves"[48] and leave behind the sheep to their own devices, as soon as any danger presents itself. The wolf is symbolic of the devil and his angels, who seek to destroy the sheep. As the most important characteristic of the true shepherd, the Lord indicates two things: (1) self-denial even unto death for the sake of the sheep, and (2) knowledge of the sheep by name. This knowledge belongs to him in the superlative sense—this mutual knowledge between shepherd and sheep must be similar to the mutual knowledge shared by Father and Son: "As the Father knows Me, even so I know the Father."

By the other sheep, "which are not of this fold," but whom also "I must bring," the Lord means, of course, the pagans, who are also called into the kingdom of Christ. The Lord finishes this parable with the words that He would willingly "lay down My life for the sheep.... No one takes it from Me, but I lay it down of Myself. I have power to lay it down, and I have power to take it again." This is an expression of total freedom, meaning that His own death was something Christ chose for Himself and it is a voluntary means for the salvation of His sheep. These words once again incited division among the Jews because once again some listened sympathetically to His words, while others continued to declare Him demon possessed.

THE DISCUSSION DURING THE FEAST OF PURIFICATION (JOHN 10:22–42)

This feast was established by Judas Maccabeus around 160 B.C. in honor of the renewal, purification, and blessing of the temple in Jerusalem after it was defiled by Antiochus Epiphanius. This feast took place every year for eight days starting on the twenty-fifth day of Kislev (near the middle of December). It was cold, and so the Lord walked in the portico of Solomon, which was a covered gallery. Here the Jews surrounded Him and said to Him, "How long do You keep us in doubt? If You are the Christ, tell us plainly." Telling them this "plainly" was exactly what the Lord would not do because the word "Messiah" or "Christ" inspired incorrect ideas of the earthly, political leader, who was supposed to free their country from Roman lordship. The Lord wisely answered them by indicating all of His previous testimony concerning Himself, His works, and His relationship to His Father in heaven. From all this, they should have long ago understood that He is the Messiah, but not in the way that they incorrectly imagine it. The reason they do not understand this is "because you are not of My sheep" and they do not recognize His voice.

Having remembered about His sheep, the Lord gives them a promise concerning the gift of eternal life. No one will be able to take them out of His hands because "I and My Father are one." There can be no more obvious proof of the divinity of Christ than these words. Once again, the Jews understood His words as blasphemy, and took stones with which to stone Him as a blasphemer, but the Lord disarmed them with a simple, meek question: "Many good works I have shown you from my Father. For which of those works do you stone Me?"

The unexpectedness of the question confused the Jews and against their will they showed that they do acknowledge the greatness of His miracles because they put down their stones and began to justify themselves. They said that they wanted to stone Him not for His good deeds but for "blasphemy." In answer, the Lord cites Psalm 81, where people are called to protect the weak from the cruelty of the strong, and are called thus "gods," of course not in the literal sense. By bringing this citation, the Lord tells the Jews that they cannot accuse the psalmist for blasphemy; and so, if he called those worthy to bear divine authority "gods," then how can they accuse Jesus of blasphemy when He calls Himself Son of God and performs miracles that only God could perform? "You would be free to disregard My claims if I did not perform miracles that proved My divinity, but since I do such works, you must understand that I and the Father are one, 'that the Father is in Me and I in Him.'"

The Jews once again tried to seize Him, but He "escaped out of their hand." He left in such a way that no one dared to touch Him, and He went beyond the Jordan to Perea. There, many had already heard of Him from John the Baptist, and were convinced by Christ's own preaching and believed in Him.

THE RETURN OF THE SEVENTY (LUKE 10:17–24)

The Evangelist Luke speaks of the return of the seventy disciples immediately after he speaks of them being sent, but of course between the sending and the return there had to be some passage of time, either long or short. Some believe that this return happened in Perea, where He had not yet preached, while others believe that they returned to the same place from which they were sent, Galilee. Seeing the Lord, they first expressed their joy regarding the fact that the demons were under their authority due to the name of Jesus. In these words, one can see their humility. The Lord told them that they should not be surprised that the demons listen to them because long ago their leader had fallen to the power of God: "I saw Satan fall like lightning from heaven." The shining of lightning here indicates immediacy and quickness. In other words, the Lord tells the apostles how He saw the king of demons defeated and fallen in the blink of an eye, and if their prince is so defeated, that means his hosts are equally defeated. The Lord, as the victor over the power of the enemy, gives the same victorious power to His disciples, calling the demons symbolically "serpents and scorpions."

However, it is not the greatest of things that they can defeat the demons, but rather it is greater that they have been found worthy of salvation and blessedness in the heavens. In the Scriptures, God is often described as holding a book in which He writes the names and deeds of His faithful servants. Thus, to be written in the heavens means to be a citizen of the heavenly kingdom. This should give them more joy than any earthly deed, even the most incredible ones like casting out demons.

The subsequent praise given to God the Father in Luke's chapter 10, verse 21, the words regarding the mutual knowledge of Father and Son and the blessing of the disciples, are also found in Matthew, but uttered in different circumstances (see Matt 11:25–27; 13:16–17). Perhaps the Lord repeated these words several times. But in Luke the chronology is carefully established, which is indicated by the words "in that hour," and in the concrete actions of the Lord: "Then He turned to His disciples and said privately ..."

By the words "wise" and "prudent" the Lord means those who consider themselves to be so. It is likely that in this case the Lord had in mind the scribes and Pharisees, who were drunk with pride in their own knowledge of the law of Moses. The "babes" are simple people who are not learned in human wisdom in schools or who were not worthy of learning with a famous rabbi. In this case, the Lord means His apostles, to whom the mysteries of the kingdom of God have been revealed. Of course, when Christ says that God "hid these things," it does not mean (according to St John Chrysostom) that God Himself was the reason for this knowledge being hidden, in the same way in which St Paul speaks: "and seeking to establish their own righteousness, [they] have not submitted to the righteousness of God" (Rom 10:3). As Blessed Theophylact says, "God hid these great mysteries from those who considered themselves wise because they became unworthy of this knowledge by considering themselves wise."[49]

"All things have been delivered to Me by My Father." The rule of the world is given to the Christ as the Mediator between God and Man, the Redeemer of the human race. The divine nature is not accessible for any mortal being, but God reveals Himself in the Son (John 14:6–8) and through the Son (Heb 1:1), as much as a person through faith and love shows himself capable of receiving such revelation. Later, the Lord calls the apostles blessed because they had been found worthy to see Him, the incarnate Son of God, something that many prophets and righteous men did not see, instead contemplating Him only through faith, but not with their physical eyes, as did the apostles.

THE PARABLE OF THE MERCIFUL SAMARITAN (LUKE 10:25–37)

This parable is only found in Luke, as an answer of the Lord to a lawyer who wanted to "tempt" Him, meaning to find fault with His teaching when he said, "What shall I do to inherit eternal life?" The Lord forces the cunning lawyer to answer his question himself with the words of Deuteronomy and Leviticus regarding the love for God and neighbor (Deut 6:5; Lev 19:18). Having shown the lawyer the requirements of the law, the Lord wanted him to delve deeper into the power and meaning of these requirements and to fully understand how far this lawyer was from fulfilling the tenets of the law. The lawyer apparently felt this, which is why Luke mentions that he was "wanting to justify himself," and asked, "Who is my neighbor?" In other words, he wanted to show that if he did not fulfill these requirements, it is because they are unclear. For example, how is one to understand who exactly is "one's neighbor"?

In answer, the Lord told a wonderful parable about a man who was attacked by robbers, and whose bloodied body was ignored by a priest and a Levite. Only a Samaritan had compassion on him, a person who was hateful to all Jews and despised by them. This Samaritan understood better than the priest and the Levite that the law of mercy admits no discrimination of persons—all people are equal in the sense that all people are neighbors to each other. As we see, the parable does not quite answer the question of the lawyer. He asked, "Who is my neighbor?" while the parable describes how one of the three, seeing the unfortunate man's plight, became his "neighbor." Consequently, the parable does not teach us whom we must consider our neighbor, but how to become good neighbors ourselves to every single person who needs compassion. The distinction between the question and the answer has a very important significance, because in the Old Testament, in order to protect the chosen nation from evil influence, clear distinctions were set up between them and all others, and a "neighbor" for a Hebrew was only his fellow Jew. The New Testament law removes all such distinctions and teaches universal evangelical love to all people. The lawyer asked, "Who is my neighbor?" as if he were afraid he might end up showing compassion to the wrong kind of people. The Lord, however, teaches him that he himself must become a neighbor to the one who needs it, rather than asking the question of whether or not that person is his neighbor. One must not look at other people, but at one's own heart, so that there he would not find the coldness of the priest and the Levite but the mercy and compassion of the Samaritan. If you begin to distinguish with your mind between who is your neighbor and who is not, then you will not be able to avoid cruelty and coldness toward people, and you will walk past suffering people who need your help, as did the priest and the Levite, even though the man was a Jew and was "their neighbor" according to the law. Compassion is the condition for inheriting eternal life.

THE LORD JESUS CHRIST IN THE HOME OF MARTHA AND MARY (LUKE 10:38–42)

Then the Lord entered a "certain village," most likely Bethany, a town situated on one of the slopes of the Mount of Olives, near Jerusalem. The Martha and Mary who receive Him are easily recognized as the same Martha and Mary who were sisters to the beloved Lazarus, whose resurrection is recounted in John, chapter 11. Both of these women appear with the same character traits as in St John— Martha is an active woman, while Mary is quiet, contemplative, and sensitive. Having received the Lord, Martha began to rush about in preparation for the meal; Mary, on the contrary, sat at Jesus's feet and listened to Him. Martha was not managing well in the kitchen, and so she spoke to the Lord almost in rebuke, which vividly shows how close their relationship was: "Lord, do You not care that my sister has left me to serve alone? Therefore tell her to help me."

Justifying Mary, the Lord answered Martha with the same playful rebuke: "Martha, Martha, you are worried and troubled about many things. But one thing is needed, and Mary has chosen that good part, which will not be taken away from her." The meaning of the rebuke is that the assiduity of Martha is directed at things that quickly pass by, without which one can easily survive, while Mary chose to direct her energies to the only thing that is truly necessary for mankind—attention to the divine teaching of Christ and following it. That which Mary receives for her attention in hearing Christ will never be taken from her.

This short passage is read during the liturgy of nearly every feast of the Mother of God because the image of this Mary corresponds very much to the image of His Mother, who also chose "that good part." Added to this passage is Luke 11:27–28, where the Mother of God is openly praised and the Lord blesses those "who hear the word of God and keep it."

THE PARABLE OF THE INSISTENT REQUEST (LUKE 11:5–8)

Similarly to the holy Evangelist Matthew, St Luke also gives the text of the "Lord's Prayer" in his eleventh chapter, and immediately afterward, he gives the Lord's teaching of the necessity of constancy in prayer. In His incomprehensible providence, God does not always give what is asked, even if the petition would seem to be according to His will. By telling of the friend who asks for bread, and only receives it after insistently asking for it, the Lord tries to inspire the necessity of constancy in prayer.

DENUNCIATION OF THE SCRIBES AND PHARISEES (MATT 23:1–39; LUKE 11:37–54)

Matthew and Luke give two very similar denunciations of the scribes and Pharisees, with the distinction that in St Luke, the Lord denounces the Pharisees at a lunch to which He was invited by a certain Pharisee in reference to the rite of washing hands, while in St Matthew, the Lord gives this speech in the Jerusalem temple, not long before His crucifixion. One can safely assume that the Lord gave similar speeches in various places and circumstances. It is very probable that St Luke, while he did not tell of Christ's speech in the temple, took some phrases from St Matthew and put them in the Lord's mouth, so to speak, during His denunciation of the Pharisees at the lunch that only he, out of the four Evangelists, describes. In both speeches, the Pharisees are denounced for their excessive attention to external purity, at the expense of seeking internal purity and cleansing their souls from sinful passions and lusts. In both speeches, the Lord compares them to tombs that on the outside look beautiful but inside are full of the bones of the dead and all sorts of filth. In both speeches, the Lord condemns the Pharisees for their love of honors, for laying unbearable burdens on others while they do not lift a finger to put anything on their own shoulders; for their formal and exact adherence to the external requirements of the law concerning tithes, coupled with their ignoring the more important matters of judgments and mercy and faith, that is, faithfulness to God and His moral law. The Lord further condemns them because they "have taken away the key of knowledge" (Luke 11:52). In other words, they have taken into their own keeping, so to speak, the entire Old Testament law, which should lead people to Christ, and having taken this key, they themselves do not enter the kingdom of Christ, and prevent others from doing so as well through their incorrect interpretations of the law. The Lord even accuses the Pharisees of killing the prophets, sent by the "wisdom of God," meaning Christ Himself, for He is the hypostatic Wisdom of God that is cited in the eighth chapter of Proverbs. In conclusion, the Lord declared them guilty of the blood of all the righteous, starting from Abel, killed by his brother Cain, until the blood of Zechariah, son of Berechiah, killed between the altar and the temple. This Zechariah is apparently the one killed with stones in the court of the house of the Lord by order of King Joash (2 Chron 24:20). Some, however, believe this is Zacharias, the father of John the Baptist.

THE PARABLE OF THE FOOLISH RICH MAN (LUKE 12:13–21)

A certain person, seeing what great authority the Lord commanded among the people, approached Him with a request to settle a dispute between him and his brother regarding their inheritance. The Lord refused to do this, for He came to earth not to resolve petty disputes regarding money, all of which are based on the passions. In addition, He preached rejection of one's inheritance, and in any case, any decision He would have made would naturally result in the disappointment of one of the parties and possible further legal inquiries, all of which the Lord wanted to avoid. However, it is not the case that the Lord was foreign to people's interests in general; rather, it was not His intention to use any external means for enforcing general order and law. He came to earth to transform people's hearts and wills.

This is a good example for all preachers of the Gospel and servants of the Church. In answer to the inappropriate request, the Lord told another parable to warn against the disease of avarice, the passion to gather the good of this world for pleasure alone. "One's life," that is, his joy and happiness, "does not consist in the abundance of the things he possesses." A certain man had a very rich harvest. Not thinking at all about the future life, he only limited his thoughts to the best way to use these riches for pleasures gained here and now. He has no thought either for God or the spiritual life, nothing except animal, sensual pleasures: "Take your ease; eat, drink, and be merry." He does not even suspect that this is the last day of his earthly life, and he will have no opportunity to enjoy these collected riches: "Fool! This night your soul will be required of you; then whose will those things be, which you have provided?"

If rephrased, His words could sound thus: "You will receive no pleasure or benefit from these things you have collected, and you care nothing for what will happen to it all after you die." Instead of collecting things and money for oneself, one should become rich in God, or take care to acquire eternal, undying riches—the virtues, which can be acquired by using one's earthly riches not for base physical pleasures, but for various good deeds.

Parables on Awaiting the Second Coming of Christ: Of the Slaves Who Wait for the Coming of the Lord and of the Good and Faithful Servant (Matt 24:42–51; Luke 12:35–48)

One must be ready always, for no one knows when the Second Coming of Christ will be or when death will come, which for a person should have the same meaning, for in either case, the person will have to give account to God for how he lived his earthly life. "Let your waist be girded"; this image references the wide, loose clothing worn in the East. When something needed to be done with speed or hard work, this wide and long clothing was tied up by a belt, so it would not be a nuisance. Thus, this expression means: "Be ready!" "And your lamps burning," expresses the same thought—the slave must always be ready to meet his master with lit candles when the master returns home at night. In the same way as good servants must expect their master at any hour of the night, even if in the second or third watch of the night, the true follower of Christ always must be morally ready to meet His Second Coming. For this spiritual vigilance, the Lord promises a reward: "Blessed are those servants," He says.

This blessedness is vividly portrayed by the image of the master who himself girds his waist and serves meat to the faithful servants as though he were the servant and they the masters. When Peter asks whether this parable refers just to the apostles or to everyone, the Lord does not give a direct answer, but from His subsequent words, it is clear that His instructions are directed at all followers of Christ. In this second parable, the Lord blesses the good and faithful servant who was put by his master as head of the household in his absence for the diligent fulfillment of his duties—"to give them their portion of food in due season." He also foretells the tragic fate of the servant who, not awaiting the quick return of his master, began to avoid his responsibilities and instead to wreak havoc, "to beat the male and female servants, and to eat and drink and be drunk." Such a servant will be subject to heavy punishment: the master will "cut him in two," the worst form of death used for the direst criminals. St Luke also adds that the punishment for the lazy servants will not always be equal—those who knew the will of their master will receive "many stripes," while the one who was ignorant of the will of his master will receive "few stripes"; however, even he will be punished because he never bothered to find out what the will of the Lord was. Whoever was given more opportunities to fulfill this will, the same will be punished more heavily for not fulfilling it.

THE LORD PREDICTS DIVISION AMONG PEOPLE ON ACCOUNT OF HIS TEACHING (LUKE 12:49–53)

"I came to send fire on the earth; and how I wish it were already kindled!" This fire is interpreted by the Holy Fathers as spiritual zeal, which the Lord came to plant in the hearts of men and that will inevitably give rise to divisions and enmity among people, for some will accept the teaching of Christ with their whole heart, while others will reject it. Since this fire of zeal must especially come to blaze only after the crucifixion, resurrection, ascension, and descent of the Holy Spirit on the apostles, the Lord expresses His desire to quickly be baptized with that baptism with which He must be baptized, meaning He wishes to quickly suffer His imminent death and redemption of mankind, as a result of which the fire of zeal will blaze forth.

As a result of the redemptive sacrifice of the Lord, there will no longer be that evil peace that unites all in the doing of sin and separates them from God, but instead there will arise a salvific division—the followers of the teaching of Christ will be separated from the enemies of Christ. The war that will arise on the basis of this essential division, even within families, was especially evident in the time of the great persecution of Christians by the Roman pagans, but it is always inevitable, for evil hates good and strives to destroy it completely.

A CALL TO REPENTANCE, INSPIRED BY THE DEATH OF THE GALILEANS AND THOSE WHO WERE CRUSHED BY THE TOWER OF SILOAM (LUKE 13:1–5)

Those who came from Jerusalem told the Lord about a group of Galileans whose blood Pilate mixed with their sacrifices. The Jews often revolted against the Roman authority, and this was probably one of those unsuccessful revolts that occurred in the temple during one of the great feasts, when armed Roman soldiers stood in the temple to keep the peace. Based on this account, it seems Pilate ordered the rebellious Galileans to be killed in the temple at the same time as the sacrifices were being offered, and their blood was thus mixed with the blood of the sacrificed animals.

Jesus Christ explained that this horrific execution in such a holy place cannot be explained by saying that these Galileans were more sinful than everyone else. Thus, it also would be wrong to think that those who were not killed are automatically more righteous than the Galileans. If the Lord chooses not to punish some so cruelly, it is because He is waiting for their repentance. The meaning of the Lord's words is this: "You are all just as sinful as they are, and you will die in the same horrible way if you do not repent. Those have already received God's judgment, but you will also receive it sooner or later, if you do not repent."

It is possible that the Lord concretely meant the divine judgment in the form of the destruction of Jerusalem at the hands of Titus Flavius, when a huge number of Jews were killed in the same way in the temple as Pilate killed the Galileans. In addition, the Lord himself remembers another tragic case when eighteen people in Jerusalem were crushed by the falling tower of Siloam. Some people could make the same incorrect inference that those eighteen were somehow more sinful than all the rest of Jerusalem's residents. But the Lord offers a different explanation—these are reminders to those still alive that they must repent because if they do not, they will all perish likewise. The Lord further develops this thought in the next section.

The Parable of the Fruitless Fig Tree (Luke 13:6–9)

The lord of the vineyard in this parable is meant to symbolize the Lord God, who lives in expectation of the repentance of the Jewish nation, which is symbolized by the fig tree that bore no fruit. To plant a fig tree in a vineyard is definitely out of the ordinary, but here the Lord is expressing the important thought that the Jewish nation had the exalted status of the chosen people of God, the only such nation on earth, in the same way that one single fig tree stood in a huge sea of vines. The gardener symbolizes the Lord Jesus Christ, who came to the chosen nation of God and for three years did everything possible to convert the Jewish nation to the saving faith in Himself as the Messiah. In other words, He waited for His work on this fig tree to bear fruit.

"And if it bears fruit, well. But if not, after that you can cut it down." These terrible words foretell the punishment of God that eventually came down on the Jewish nation because they did not all turn to God, they did not bring the expected fruit, and in the fourth year of Christ's public ministry, they put Him to death on the cross. For this, they were rejected by God and punished by an incursion of

Romans and the total destruction of Jerusalem and the temple. The Son of God, the gardener of the parable, is shown here as the Mediator for mankind who begs God to grant mercy for their lack of fruit.

HEALING THE WOMAN WHO WAS BENT OVER (LUKE 13:10–17)

During His time in Galilee, the Lord, while teaching in one of the synagogues, healed a woman who for eighteen years was bent over and could not straighten herself. The leader of the synagogue became angry that the healing was performed on a Sabbath day, when, according to the law, no work should be done, and he expressed his irritation aloud, speaking to the people. The Lord called him a hypocrite for this, as He usually called the Pharisees, showing by this that the synagogue leader's irritation was not a result of his zeal for the law, but merely from envy for Christ the Miracle Worker. In addition, the Lord explained that the law does not forbid anyone to do good deeds on the Sabbath, especially if certain daily work is allowed, such as the daily care for cattle.

"Ought not this woman, being a daughter of Abraham, whom Satan has bound—think of it—for eighteen years, be loosed from this bond on the Sabbath?" In other words, it is even more proper to do good deeds to people who need them on a Sabbath than on other days. By "daughter of Abraham" the Lord meant that this woman was a Jew, and the leader of the synagogue, who had the responsibility to take care of the needs of all those who attended his synagogue, should have rejoiced at this miracle of the Lord's, but instead he was angry. Satan's bonds are interpreted differently by different Fathers. Some think that the woman's disease was a result of demonic activity, while others believe that the disease was directly a result of her sinful life. St Gregory the Dialogist believes that the fig tree and this woman are both intended as images of depraved humanity.

When the leader of the synagogue heard the Lord's words, he was ashamed since naturally he could not contest the truth of His words, while all the rest of the people, the commoners, "rejoiced for all the glorious things that were done by Him."

ON THE NARROW PATH TO THE KINGDOM OF GOD (LUKE 13:22–30)

Along the way, when the Lord was walking from Galilee to Jerusalem, someone asked Him a question: "Lord, are there few who are saved?" Apparently, the question referred to some of the strict requirements that Christ the Saviour had for those who wished to enter the kingdom of the Messiah. The Lord answered this question quickly and definitively, not only to him personally, but for everyone: "Strive to enter through the narrow gate." This image is often used by Him. The kingdom of the Messiah, or the Church of Christ, is here imagined as a house that has a wide, large entrance, but also has a smaller, narrow door, through which only some are allowed to enter. Many seek to enter through this narrow door, but they will not be able to because they are so morally corrupt and they have so many false preconceptions regarding the kingdom of the Messiah.

The meaning of this image is that for the Jews of that time, the only real entrance to the kingdom of the Messiah was the narrow door of repentance and self-denial, for which they were unfortunately little suited due to the aforementioned prejudices so widely propagated by the Pharisees.

"When once the master of the house has risen up ...." God here is described as a host who sits at dinner and awaits his guests, who at a certain point gets up to lock the door to his feast. This is an image of the judgment of the Lord over every person and all people after His Second Coming. All will be judged outside the comforts of the house, where the feast of the Lord is occurring with His friends, since they are not worthy of blessed communion with God, even though they now acknowledge their sins and still strive to enter there, but it will already be too late. After death, there is no repentance. These rejected ones will say, "We ate and drank in Your presence, and You taught in our streets." In other words, the unworthy ones will remind the Master that they are His acquaintances, that they were superficial followers of Christ's teaching, but they were not true Christians, and so they will be cast out. These words are especially appropriate if we take them literally to indicate the Jews of Christ's time, since they rejected their Messiah and so lost the right to enter into His kingdom. They will recognize their mistake during the Second Coming, but then it will already be too late, and they will hear God's answer: "I do not know you, where you are from. Depart from Me, all you workers of iniquity."

Instead of the rejected Jews, those pagans who believed in Christ will enter the kingdom from the "east and the west, from the north and the south," from all the corners of the earth. "There are last who will be first, and there are first who will be last." The Jews considered themselves to be "first," but since they rejected the Messiah, they will be "last," while the first to enter the kingdom of the Messiah will be those pagans whom they considered to be the "last," the dregs of humanity. In this same way, all those who consider themselves to be "first," but in actual fact do not fulfill the commandments of Christ as they should, will be "last" in the Final Judgment, while those whom they despise will be "first."

CHRIST ANSWERS THE THREATS OF HEROD AND LAMENTS THE DESTRUCTION OF JERUSALEM (LUKE 13:31–35; MATT 23:37–39)

Seemingly motivated by friendship and concern for His well-being, the Pharisees counseled the Lord to leave the lands ruled by Herod Antipas. From the fact that the Lord calls Herod a fox, one can assume that these Pharisees were sent by Herod himself in order to encourage the Lord to leave Galilee. Since the Lord was constantly surrounded by masses of people, Herod was apparently worried that some sort of nationalistic insurrection would occur. He did not want to dirty his hands by dealing with the Lord himself, and so he tried this method to encourage Him to leave, showing all the cunning and guile usually associated with foxes.

"Behold, I cast out demons and perform cures today and tomorrow, and the third day I shall be perfected." In other words, Christ is saying: "I will do My work, regardless of any threats, until the appointed time." These were, in fact, the last days of the Lord's sojourn in Galilee, for He was already going toward Jerusalem (Luke 13:22), where His passion awaited Him.

"For it cannot be that a prophet should perish outside of Jerusalem." This is a deeply tragic and ironic statement, for truly, as history has shown, the prophets were most often murdered in Jerusalem. This inspired deep sorrow in the Lord for the sake of this holy city, according to St John Chrysostom: "a voice of mercy, co-suffering, and great love."[50] Here, Christ also foretells the terrible punishment of God that would be visited upon Jerusalem in A.D. 70, when the Romans razed it to the ground. "You shall not see Me until the time comes when you say, 'Blessed is He Who comes in the name of the Lord!" Here, Christ refers to the day of the Second Coming, when the unfaithful will unwillingly worship the Lord.

HEALING THE MAN SICK WITH DROPSY (LUKE 14:1–6)

When the Lord was in the house of one of the rulers of the Pharisees on a Sabbath, a certain man sick with dropsy (considered untreatable) came before Him. Since the Pharisees were closely scrutinizing Him, looking for an opportunity to accuse Him of something, the Lord asked them before healing the man: "Is it lawful to heal on the Sabbath?" They did not answer in the negative since the law truly does not forbid it, only the traditions of the elders. Then the Lord healed the man with a mere touch, and to the Pharisees He directed His instruction regarding the ass or the ox who fell into a pit, which clearly shows that one may perform deeds of mercy on the Sabbath. This was so convincing that they "could not answer Him regarding these things."

THE PARABLE OF THOSE WHO LOVE TO BE FIRST (LUKE 14:7–15)

When a feast began, the Pharisees always hurried to be there early, to take the best places at the table. The Lord began to boldly and frankly accuse them for their love of praise and even told them a parable; not a "parable" in the strict sense, but an admonition taken from the parabolic, frequently used image of the marriage feast, as the largest kind of feast in their culture. "When you are invited by anyone to a wedding feast, do not sit down in the best place." With these words, the Lord was not merely giving an axiom of behavior; here He is speaking of the internal disposition of the heart, which is why the Lord finished the parable with the words "whoever exalts himself will be humbled; and he who humbles himself will be exalted."

This was said regarding the guests, but the Lord gives a special instruction to the host. Noticing that he invited only his friends, the Lord told him that it is not right to invite only those from whom he can later receive equal recompense. On the contrary, one should invite the poor, the lame, and the blind who in no way can pay back the honor of being invited to the feast. It is not good to disdain the poor, as the Pharisees did; rather, one must look at a meal as an action that can have a moral dimension, an act that can become a good deed. If one does this, the reward from God will be great in the future life, in the "resurrection of the just." The general meaning of the instruction is the same as the Sermon on the Mount: "If you love those who love you, what reward can you expect?" (see Luke 6:32).

Hearing this, one of the guests exclaimed: "Blessed is he who shall eat bread in the kingdom of God!" Blessed Theophylact has this to say: "Evidently this man was not spiritual enough to understand; he was still guided by human reasoning."[51] In other words, he once again expressed the majority opinion regarding the earthly kingdom of the Messiah. But perhaps he was merely trying to express his astonishment at how blessed those will be who participate in the kingdom of the Messiah.

THE PARABLE OF THOSE CALLED TO THE FEAST (LUKE 14:16–24)

In answer to the aforementioned exclamation of one of the guests, the Lord told a parable in which He uses the image of the supper to describe the kingdom of the Messiah, or the Church of Christ. The host of the supper is the Lord God, Who through the law and the prophets, His servants, invited the entire Jewish nation to enter the kingdom, and when the kingdom itself approached, He repeated the invitation through the Messiah-Christ Himself (who in several prophecies, such as Isaiah 52:13, is called the "slave of the Lord," appearing in the form of a man). The Messiah appeared first to the "called"—the Jews—with the news that the kingdom of heaven is at hand: "Come, for all things are now ready."

But those among the Jews, first among which are the ones listening to this parable since they are experts in the Old Testament law—the scribes, Pharisees, and other leaders of the chosen nation of God—all began to make excuses, as if they had conspired about it in advance. The reasons for their excuses were motivated by their earthly, physical needs, which made them deaf to the divine call, and they rejected the Messiah-Christ Who came to them. Then the Lord commanded the Messiah to call the publicans and sinners, and since there was room even after this, the Lord called even the pagans into His kingdom. All who responded to the evangelical preaching entered the kingdom of the Messiah, the kingdom of God, while those who disdained it, the scribes and Pharisees, remained outside it.

THE TEACHING REGARDING TRUE FOLLOWERS OF CHRIST (LUKE 14:25–33)

"If anyone comes to Me and does not hate his father and mother, wife and children ... he cannot be My disciple."

Blessed Theophylact warns: "Be careful not to be offended at these words, for the Lover of Mankind is not teaching lack of love towards mankind, but He wishes that His sincere disciple would come to hate his relatives only when they hinder the work of honoring God, and when he, in association with them, finds it difficult to do good."[52] If earthly attachments become a real hindrance to following Christ, then one must hate them for the sake of Christ and to cut ties with them all. Hatred then ceases to be immoral when it is directed to all those things that definitively turn a man away from his highest calling—the salvation of his soul.

The Lord bolsters this instruction regarding self-denial, indispensable for every true Christian, with parables regarding those who want to build a tower, the two kings at war with each other, and the parable about the salt (Luke 14:34–35). This is the meaning of the parable of the tower—whoever has decided with his whole being to follow Christ must calculate his strength in advance and prepare himself properly for the coming labor; otherwise, he will become a laughingstock. The same meaning applies to the second parable. Whoever wants to follow Christ must find the spiritual means for it, the first of which is self-denial. Otherwise, he will not be able to finish his well-intended work and may even find himself in the dangerous situation of a defeat at the hands of spiritual enemies. Desiring "conditions of peace" of course is only used for the purposes of the structure of the parable, but it does not mean that one should make peace with the spiritual enemies. In the parable, not all aspects of the story are appropriate for a metaphorical interpretation; some details are used without any second, spiritual meaning, only to make the story more lively and realistic.

The followers of Christ are finally compared with salt, which preserves any food it is mixed with from decomposition. But the disciples of Christ who do not have the moral strength to deny themselves are useless, just like salt that has lost its savor, its power to preserve.

THE PARABLE OF THE PRODIGAL SON (LUKE 15:11–32)

This parable, only given by St Luke, is preceded by two short parables of the lost sheep (Luke 15:1–7) and the lost drachma (Luke 15:8–10). The Pharisees and scribes condemned the Lord Jesus Christ because He welcomed sinners and ate with them. For this reason, the Lord told them these parables, in which He illustrates the joy in heaven when sinners, who already appear to be lost for the kingdom of heaven, repent. The ninety-nine righteous who do not have need of repentance are usually interpreted by exegetes of the Gospel to mean the angels of God, or the righteous who have already entered eternity and have been found worthy of blessedness. The drachma is a small silver coin, worth very little. In these parables, the Lord uses for His illustration man's natural joy at finding a lost object, which is greater than finding something that was not lost, no matter how expensive it may be.

Later, in the parable of the prodigal son, the Lord compares the joy of God after the repentance of a sinner to the joy of a loving father to whom his profligate son has returned.

A certain man had two sons—the man is a symbol of God, while the two sons are a sinner on the one hand, and so-called righteous men on the other, the scribes and Pharisees. The younger, evidently of age but lacking yet in experience and wisdom, asks his father for his portion of his inheritance—one-third, according to the law (Deut 21:17), leaving the other two-thirds to the elder son. After receiving it, the younger son decided to live independently, according to his own whims, and left to a faraway country where he wasted his inheritance in a profligate life. In the same way a person who is given spiritual and physical gifts by God, once he feels inclined to sin, begins to feel God's law to be burdensome, and gives himself up to lawlessness, and he wastes all the gifts he received from God in spiritual and physical profligacy.

"There arose a severe famine in that land." Thus, often the Lord sends external calamities to a sinner who has become mired in his sinful life, to force him to become sober. These misfortunes are at the same time both the punishment of God and His call to repentance. To herd swine is the most demeaning of work for a true Israelite, for the law declared swine to be unclean. In the same way, when the sinner becomes attached to some object through which he satisfies his sinful passion, he will demean himself to the lowest state possible. The "pods" that he would have gladly eaten are the fruit of a certain tree that grows in Syria and Asia Minor, which is fodder for pigs. This is another indication of the absolutely catastrophic state of the sinner.

And so he "came to himself"—a very expressive phrase. Just as a sick man who is recovering from a severe illness often loses his consciousness for a certain time and then regains it, so the sinner, mired in sin, can be compared to such a sick man in a coma, for he no longer recognizes the requirements of God's Law and his conscience seems to be dead. The heavy consequences of sin, together with external calamities, force him finally to wake up, and his sober reason comes back to him. He begins to see and understand the hopelessness of his situation, and he searches for ways to get out of it. "I will arise and go to my father"—this is the decision of the sinner to leave his sin and repent. "I have sinned against heaven," that is, before the holy place of God's presence and the pure sinless spirit, "and before you," by disdaining his loving father, and "and I am no longer worthy to be called your son." This is an expression of profound humility and a confession of his unworthiness, both of which always accompany true repentance in a sinner. "Make me like one of your hired servants" is an expression of deep love for the house and the hearth of the father and agreement to submit to the heaviest conditions for reception into the father's house.

The remainder of the parable is meant to illustrate the limitless love of God to a repentant sinner, His forgiveness of all, and that joy which, according to Christ, is heard in heaven at the repentance of even one sinner. The father, seeing his son returning from a distance, and not even knowing what his inner disposition is, runs to meet him, embraces him, and kisses him, not even allowing him to finish his words of repentance. Instead, he orders him to be dressed and shod in the best clothes instead of his rags, and prepares a feast in honor of his return. All these are symbols taken from everyday life that illustrate how God, with love for every repentant sinner, mercifully accepts his repentance and gives him new spiritual goods and gifts, instead of those he wasted through sin.

For the sinner "was dead and is alive again." The sinner who turns away from God is no different from a dead man, for true life depends only on the source of life—God Himself—while the conversion of a sinner to God is thus described as a resurrection from the dead. The elder brother, angry at his father for his mercy to the younger brother, is a vivid image of the scribes and Pharisees, proud in their exact and strict fulfillment of the Law, but cold and heartless in their soul when it comes to loving their brothers; praising themselves in doing the will of God, but not desiring to have any communication with the repentant publicans and sinners. Just as the elder brother "was angry and would not go in," so the meticulous fulfillers of the law were angry at the Lord Jesus Christ for His close association with repentant sinners. Instead of rejoicing with the father and the younger brother, the elder begins to announce his own merits, not even desiring to call his younger sibling "brother"; instead, disdainfully calling him "this son of yours."

"You are always with me, and all that I have is yours." With these words, the Lord indicates that the Pharisees, in whose hands the Law is kept, always had free access to God and His spiritual benefits, but they cannot receive the good will of the Heavenly Father when they have such a twisted and cruel spiritual and moral disposition.

THE PARABLE OF THE UNJUST STEWARD (LUKE 16:1–17)

This is a parable that upsets many people without any reason. Blessed Theophylact brilliantly explains that "any parable uses symbols and images to explain the essence of some subject, but not all elements relate directly to the subject discussed. Thus, it is pointless to try to explain every single aspect of a parable in the minutest detail."[53] In a parable, only the main thought is important. In this parable of the unjust steward, many people are confused by the fact that the master, who is obviously a symbol of God, apparently praised his steward for using unlawful means to make it seem that his master's debtors owed less than they actually did. He did this in order to be "received in their houses," that is, to find support among them for himself, should he be cast out by his master. But the master praised the steward not for his unlawful act per se, but for the resourcefulness he showed when put in a difficult position.

The meaning of the parable is this—we are all merely temporary stewards of our earthly wealth and possessions, which are given to us only because the Lord entrusted them to us for the time of our earthly life. And we must use these earthly goods in such a way that by their help we may make provisions for the eternal life. However, we often do not do this; we do not use the kind of adroitness that the unjust steward exhibited, which is why the Lord said that "the sons of this world are more shrewd in their generation than the sons of light." At the same time, we, like the steward in the parable, should be making "friends for yourselves by unrighteous mammon [unrighteous riches], that when you fail, they may receive you into an everlasting home." Earthly prosperity is called "unrighteous mammon" because it is often obtained unlawfully and it often makes a person act unfairly toward others and never justifies all the hopes and cares that are wasted on it. Thus, the only wise way to use riches is to use it to help those who are needy, to use it for all possible good deeds, so that in this way even money can become a means to acquire the kingdom of heaven. Because after all, we will lose our riches one way or another, since no one will take his possessions with him to the other world; while the good deed done by means of riches will always remain with us and will serve to justify us at the Final Judgment of God.

In conclusion, the Lord said, "He who is faithful in what is least is faithful also in much; and he who is unjust in what is least is unjust also in much. Therefore if you have not been faithful in the unrighteous mammon, who will commit to your trust the true riches? And if you have not been faithful in what is another man's, who will give you what is your own? In other words, if you were unfaithful even with earthly riches and were not able to use them wisely, for the good of the soul, then how can you possibly deserve to be given spiritual riches, the riches of the gifts of the Holy Spirit?

In answer to this, the avaricious Pharisees began to laugh at the Lord, apparently refusing to agree that the passion for earthly riches can be a hindrance to acquiring spiritual gifts. In order to accuse them, the Lord tells a whole parable regarding the incorrect use of riches—the parable of the rich man and Lazarus.

THE PARABLE OF THE RICH MAN AND LAZARUS (LUKE 16:19–31)

The main idea of this parable is that the wrong use of riches can result in the loss of the kingdom of heaven and eternal suffering in hell. A certain rich man liked to dress in purple and fine linen. Purple (*porphyra* in Greek) is a Syrian outer garment made out of expensive purple cloth. This rich man lived sumptuously and completely hedonistically, feasting every day. At his gates lay a poor man named Lazarus. The name Lazarus literally means "God's help," suggesting that this poor man had no one to help him but God alone. The dogs made him suffer even more because they licked open his sores, but he apparently did not have enough physical strength to drive them off. In this poor man, the rich man could have found himself a friend who would lead him after death into the eternal habitations, if we follow the logic of the previous parable, but the rich man was evidently heartless and cruel, and he gave nothing to the poor man, though he spared little expense on his own feasting.

After Lazarus's death, his soul was carried by the angels to Abraham's bosom. Christ does not say "to heaven" because heaven was only opened after the suffering and death of Christ, but being in "Abraham's bosom" expresses the thought that Lazarus, as a true son of Abraham, shared the same after-death state as Abraham, a place full of consoling hopes for future blessedness, the place of the expectation of all the righteous of the Old Testament. Lazarus deserved these eternal habitations without a doubt through his difficult and uncomplaining suffering.

"The rich man also died and was buried." The funeral is explicitly mentioned here, most likely because it was extravagant, while the body of Lazarus was merely thrown away for the wild animals to eat. But the rich man found himself in the tortures of hell. And from there he could see, from a distance, Lazarus and Abraham. Thus, the contemplation by sinners of the blessedness of the righteous increases their suffering in hell, and maybe encourages them to hope for eventual consolation, even though any such hope is futile. Just as Lazarus in life desired only to have a few crumbs from the rich man's table, so now the newly poor rich man asks only for a few drops of water to cool his burning tongue.

However, the rich man is refused even this small consolation. Lazarus now has consolation for the terrible sufferings he bore in life, and the rich man now suffers as much as he was consoled in the previous life. In addition, Abraham gives another reason for his refusal—the finality of God's judgment, symbolized by the deep chasm separating the place of blessedness and the place of suffering, a chasm that is related to the moral chasm between sinners and those who are righteous. Abraham also refuses the rich man's request to send Lazarus to the house of his father to warn his brothers, lest they follow his example into the suffering of hell. "They have Moses and the prophets," the Law of God, from which they can easily learn how one must live in order to avoid eternal suffering. The rich man admits that his brothers, like him, are deaf to the Law of God, and only an extraordinary appearance of a dead man could sober them up and force them to change their manner of life for the better. Abraham, however, countered that if they reached such a moral low point that they did not hear the voice of God, expressed in His Word, then any other assurances would be useless.

A man with no faith, even when faced with the incredible sight of a man raised from the dead, later will rationalize the vision in some way and remain in the same moral state. This is very vividly seen in the fact that the unfaithful Jews were not in any way convinced by the countless signs and miracles performed by Christ. They did not even believe when they saw Lazarus raised from the dead, and even conspired to kill Lazarus a second time! The fact is that the heart corrupted by sin stubbornly refuses to believe in the future sufferings that await sinners, and no miracles can convince it otherwise.

The Teaching on the Holiness of Marriage and on Virginity
(Matt 19:3–12; Mark 10:2–12; Luke 16:18)

Every time the Pharisees came to Jesus Christ with some question, they did this not to learn from His answer, but to "tempt" Him, to see if He would say anything contrary to the Law, so that they might accuse Him. Thus, they asked Him: "Is it lawful for a man to divorce his wife for just any reason?" The question referred to a dispute between the Pharisees and the people. Some, following the teaching of Rabbi Hillel, said that divorce was allowed in all cases; others, following Rabbi Shammai, said that divorce is permissible only in cases of adultery. The Pharisees awaited Christ's opinion only as an opportunity to agitate one of the sides against Him, it did not matter which one.

According to the law of Moses (Deut 24:1), a letter of divorce may be given to a wife if, after the marriage, "it happens that she finds no favor in his eyes because he has found some uncleanness in her." Without referencing the various opinions held among the rabbis, the Lord instead cites the scriptural account of the creation of man and woman by God, explaining the true meaning of marriage as an institution given by God and at the same time avoiding the trap set by the Pharisees. God created one man and one woman; consequently, it was the intention of the Creator that the man have only one wife and that he would not leave her. This bond of marriage is closer even than the ties of blood between a man and his mother and father, whom he leaves for the sake of his wife. Two people become one flesh in thoughts, feelings, intentions, and actions. If they are thus united into one, according to God's original intention, then they must not be separated. Only one exception is allowed in cases of adultery, but this is only because adultery in and of itself destroys the idea of marriage, and the union between man and wife ceases to exist.

Moses allowed divorce merely for the hardness of their hearts because men were abusing the wives they did not love. In other words, he allowed a lesser evil in order to avoid the greater. Christ, however, restores the original significance of marriage, calling it indissoluble. His disciples, shocked at the strict requirements put forth by the Lord, said, "If such is the case of the man with his wife, it is better not to marry." In other words, better to avoid marriage altogether than having to bear a nagging and angry wife without the possibility of sending her away.

The Lord, in His answer, corrects the erroneous reasoning of the disciples. On the one hand, He does say that it is better "not to marry," but on the other hand, he indicates that the state of remaining single and unmarried, united with a preservation of virginity is not only no easier than married life, but is altogether so difficult that not every person is capable of it: "All cannot accept this saying." Thus, the Lord raises virginity to the same moral height as the highest and most perfect states of spiritual life, for all the greatest things that man can acquire are always presented by Him as the precious gifts of the heavenly Father (see Matt 13:11; 16:17; and so forth).

"To whom it has been given" does not mean, however, that this gift of God does not depend on our own personal will and desire. St John Chrysostom explains that gifts are given to those who desire them. Whoever begins the great labor of virginity has great need of God's help, and he receives it if he seeks it with a pure conscience. Later, the Lord compares virginity with willful castration, which of course must not be understood literally, in the crude physical sense, as is evident from the context. This is spiritual castration, not physical. "There are eunuchs who were so born thus from their mother's womb, and there are eunuchs who were made eunuchs by men." This is why the contrast is effective—those who have been castrated cannot be said to have accepted the labor of virginity willingly, for they are incapable of marriage by their nature. To cut oneself off for the sake of the kingdom of heaven means to completely cut off all physical desires, to kill lust within oneself, and to decide to lead a virginal life for the sake of better serving God and to acquire the kingdom, which is greatly hindered by the cares of family life.

"He who is able to accept it, let him accept it." No one is forced to such a life, but whoever feels himself capable of lifting this heavy burden must take it up. St John Chrysostom says: "With these words, the Lord showed that this virtue is indeed possible, in order to arouse in the will the desire to live in this way."[54]

ON THE POWER OF FAITH AND ON THE NECESSITY OF FULFILLING THE COMMANDMENTS (LUKE 17:5–10)

The apostles approached the Lord with a request that He would increase their faith, for they felt that their faith was not sufficient for the works to which they were called (compare with Matt 17:19–20). The apostles believed in the Lord Jesus Christ, without a doubt, but since they had not yet completely rejected the false pharisaical assumptions regarding the Messiah and His kingdom, their faith sometimes fell short, and they were troubled by this. In answer to their request, the Lord repeated His words regarding the power and strength of true faith, even if it be as small as a mustard seed. From the small seed grows a large tree—such a great power is hidden in the miniscule mustard seed; in the same way, even the weakest faith, if it be genuine, if it truly be in the apostles, will grow and become stronger in them so that they will become capable of performing extraordinary miracles. This passage in Luke does not have the negative connotation as does Matthew 17:20, where the words of the Lord sound like a rebuke. Here they sound comforting and hopeful for the apostles, being a kind of testament as well as a means to inflame their faith.

The subsequent words: "And which of you, having a servant plowing ..." have the following meaning: When your faith grows to such a level that you are able to perform miracles, beware of pride and arrogance in order not to lose these fruits of faith. These miracles, this faith, are gifts of God, which must be used with great humility, because through humility faith grows even greater. Thus, without directly answering the request to increase their faith, the Lord through parables shows them the means to increase it in themselves through humility, while at the same time warning them of the dangers that destroy faith. This warning was especially needed for the apostles at that moment because they were still motivated by petty concerns—they argued about primacy in the kingdom of the Messiah, expected worldly praise and rewards, and so forth.

The Lord offers the example of the relationship between master and servant: if a servant plows the field, does the master consider it worthy of special praise? When the slave comes home tired after a day of work, does the master show solicitation for his fatigue and invite him to his own table to rest and eat? No! The master still orders the slave to serve him first. Will the master then thank the servant when he has done all that the master commanded? "I think not," said the Lord and makes the following conclusion: "So likewise you, when you have done all those things which you are commanded, say, 'We are unprofitable servants. We have done what was our duty to do.'"

This does not mean that the Lord will not praise His servants or give them rest, but rather that we ourselves should look at our good works as our duty, and at ourselves as slaves who can bring our Lord nothing more than the fulfillment of our duty. In other words, a person can have no merits before God.

HEALING THE TEN LEPERS (LUKE 17:11–19)

The Lord performed this miracle during His last journey from Galilee to Jerusalem to the last Passover, during which He was to be crucified. A group of ten lepers "stood afar off" because the law forbade them to come near healthy people, and with a loud voice they begged the Lord to have mercy on them. The Lord told them to go and show themselves to the priests. These words in and of themselves mean that He was healing them because He sent them to the priests so they could witness their being made whole, according to the requirements of the law, after which they would be given permission to reenter the society of God.

Their willingness to listen to His words shows their living faith. And along the way, they realized that they were truly healed of their disease. Having received this healing, however, they forgot (as so often happens!) about the One Who healed them, and only one of them, a Samaritan, returned to the Lord to thank Him for His healing. This situation shows us that even though the Jews despised the Samaritans, the latter were sometimes morally superior to them. The Lord asked him with a meek rebuke and sorrow: "Were there not ten cleansed? But where are the nine? Were there not any found who returned to give glory to God except this foreigner?" These "nine" are a vivid example of the ingratitude of men to their Benefactor, God.

ON THE COMING OF THE KINGDOM OF GOD AND THE SECOND COMING OF CHRIST
(LUKE 17:20–37)

When the Pharisees asked the Lord about the coming of the kingdom of God, the Lord answered: "The kingdom of God does not come with observation; nor will they say, 'See here!' or 'See there!' For indeed, the kingdom of God is within in you." There is no specific place in the world for the kingdom of God, for it is not material—the essence of the kingdom of God is the internal renewal and sanctification of people. The Pharisees understood the "kingdom of God" to mean the earthly kingdom of the Messiah, whose arrival, along with freedom from the hated Romans, they awaited eagerly. The Lord tells them rather that it is a spiritual inner kingdom, not an external earthly one, and that it has already come.

"Within you" can be understood in two ways: (1) the kingdom of God has already come—it is already among you, the Jewish nation, even though you cannot see it due to your spiritual blindness; and (2) the kingdom of God is invisible for the physical eyes, for it is found in the soul of a person. Having spoken about the coming of the kingdom of God, which at first will only be a kind of spiritual yeast that will transform the world from within, the Lord goes on to speak of the calamities that await the Jews who did not notice the coming of His kingdom (that is, the destruction of Jerusalem in A.D. 70), as well as of the visible revelation of the kingdom, which will occur after His Second Coming, in its full glory, like lightning that flashes from one end of the sky to the other.

Equally unexpected as the flood in Noah's day or the destruction of Sodom and Gomorrah during Lot's time will be the coming of Christ to judge Jerusalem during its destruction, as well as the Second Coming to judge all the nations of mankind at the end of the world. Then one will have to go to meet the Lord, not looking back at the condemned world as did Lot's wife, for then the final separation of the righteous and sinners will occur, even if on that night they were sleeping in the same bed or working the same occupation. The disciples, amazed at this teaching, asked where all this would occur. The Lord answered them with a proverb: "For wherever the carcass is, there the eagles will be gathered together" (Matt 24:28). In other words, just as birds of prey gather in the place where dead bodies lie, so will the dread judgment of God show itself there, where the inner life has died and spiritual decomposition has begun.

THE PARABLE OF THE UNRIGHTEOUS JUDGE (LUKE 18:1–8)

The time preceding the Second Coming of Christ will be grievous; however, one should not despair, but rather "pray and not lose heart." How one should pray is vividly described by the Lord in the parable of the unrighteous judge, who did not want to hear the just complaints of a persecuted widow, but finally fulfilled her petition only because she refused to stop bothering him. The Lord, of course, does not mean to compare God to an unrighteous judge (yet another example of the fact that not all details of a parable should be interpreted spiritually), but only uses this comparison for purposes of logical extension. In other words, if an unrighteous man will listen to constant petitions, how much more will the all-good and all-righteous God defend His chosen ones, if they will cry to Him day and night, even if at first His protection seems to be dilatory.

"Nevertheless, when the Son of Man comes, will He really find faith on earth?" Despite the incontrovertible truth that God will defend His chosen, will He find such faithful servants who would have such constancy and insistence in prayer, as is required? In other words, one should not be afraid that God will not defend His faithful from the coming calamities and misfortunes, but rather one must fear that by the Second Coming there may be no such faithful left in the world.

THE PARABLE OF THE PUBLICAN AND THE PHARISEE (LUKE 18: 9–14)

As an example of the kind of prayer the faithful followers of Christ should practice with constancy to attract God's help and protection, the Lord tells a parable of how two very different people prayed in the temple. A Pharisee prayed with a feeling of personal pride and self-aggrandizement, laying before God all his good deeds as worthy merits, and at the same time demeaning others. A publican, in contrast, prayed with a vivid sense of his own sinfulness and worthlessness. As a result, he went back to his home justified "rather than the other," for, as the Lord expresses in the conclusion of the parable: "Everyone who exalts himself will be humbled, and he who humbles himself will be exalted." Consequently, one must pray with humility, with compunction in the heart over one's own sins. The prayer of the publican: "God, be merciful to me a sinner!" has become a model prayer for general use.

BLESSING THE CHILDREN (MATT 19:13–15; MARK 10:13–16; LUKE 18:15–17)

St Mark gives the most detailed account of this event, saying that the Lord was "greatly displeased" at His disciples that they did not allow children to come to Him. It must be a very great love that the Lord has for children, if He who meekly and patiently endured much human falseness was so angered at His disciples. The Lord explains His love for children by indicating their worthiness, and this worthiness He gives as an example for emulation to all who desire to enter the kingdom, saying, "Whoever does not receive the kingdom of God as a little child will by no means enter it." In other words, one must receive the kingdom of God in one's heart with the same kind of pure, innocent, and incorrupt spiritual disposition that children have before they have been corrupted by sin.

"Let the little children come to Me, and do not forbid them; for of such is the kingdom of God." Here we can safely infer that those parents and role models who do not lead children to Christ and do not teach them the Christian faith are committing a great sin. An even greater sin lies upon those who purposely push children away from the path of faith.

THE RICH YOUTH (MATT 19:16–26; MARK 10:17–27; LUKE 18:18–27)

All three Synoptics speak of this young man (or nobleman, in Luke) who asked the Lord Jesus Christ what he should do to inherit eternal life. This conversation, as well as those that follow, occurred on the way to Jerusalem, when the Lord was already on His way to the Passion. The young man called the Lord "Good Teacher," to which the Lord answered, "Why do you call Me good? No one is good but One, that is, God." In other words, Christ says that if the young man is merely speaking to Him as to a teacher, then, consequently, he should not call a mere man with a name that is appropriate only for God. As for the answer to his question, the Lord suggested that he should follow the commandments. The young man then thought that the Lord had some new commandments that he did not know about, and so asked him, "Which ones?"

But the Lord only indicated the well-known commandments of the Decalogue, naming only some of them (6, 7, 8, 9, and 5), then the general commandment of love for one's neighbor. The young man answered that he had followed all these commandments from his youth. It must be assumed that he understood the fulfillment of the commandments as the Pharisees did; otherwise, he would not have dared to answer the Lord in this way. But it is still important to note that he believed himself to be deficient in the fulfillment of all the requirements for salvation. Apparently, his conscience hinted to him that a mere external fulfillment of the stipulations of the law is not sufficient. Then the Lord revealed to him the mystery of Christian perfection in these words: "If you want to be perfect, go, sell what you have and give to the poor, and you will have treasure in heaven; and come, follow Me."

In answer to this call to perfection, the youth walked away from the Lord in sorrow, for he had a great deal of money. Consequently, his riches had become such an idol for him that he was unable to part from them. This idol he preferred even to eternal life, to which, it would seem, he was sincerely striving. Referring to this passion, which takes hold of the entire person (and not to riches in themselves), the Lord said, "Assuredly, I say unto you that it is hard for a rich man to enter the kingdom of heaven."

The Evangelist Mark says that the disciples were horrified at these words. This is understandable because riches are something that every person wants, and according to the law, riches are a sign of God's blessing on a person, while the Lord suddenly makes it into a huge hindrance to remaining on the path to the kingdom of God. In order to calm His disciples and explain to them what He actually meant, the Lord said, "Children, how hard it is for those who *trust* in riches to enter into the kingdom of God!" (emphasis added). As St John Chrysostom writes: "Christ is not denouncing riches, but rather those who have become passionately attached to them,"[55] because for the sinful nature of man, riches provide a wealth of temptations and stumbling blocks to fulfilling the Law of God. "It is easier for a camel to go through the eye of a needle than for a rich man to enter the kingdom of God."

This is a folk saying, still used in the East, indicating a task either impossible or very difficult to accomplish. Some have understood "camel" to indicate the ropes used on a ship, sometimes made from camel hide. Others interpret the "eye of the needle" as very low and narrow gates, through which a camel could pass only with great difficulty.

Riches in themselves are not dangerous; they only become so if a person puts all his trust in them and makes all his happiness dependent on them, making them a kind of idol. But the apostles were still astonished and worried by His words: "Who then can be saved?" The Lord looked at them, calming them even with His mere glance, and said, "With men it is impossible, but not with God; for with God all things are possible." The merciful and salvific grace of God is strong enough to do what a man cannot do with his own strength. God can heal the rich man from his wound of avarice, which prevents him from reaching salvation.

THE APOSTLES, WHO LEFT EVERYTHING FOR CHRIST'S SAKE, WILL INHERIT ETERNAL LIFE (MATT 19:27–30; MARK 10:28–31; LUKE 18:28–30)

In connection with the conversation with the young man, the Apostle Peter, on behalf of all the apostles, asked the Lord what their reward would be, since they left everything to follow after Christ. They were poor people with little property—nets, lines, boats, and poor houses—but these few things were everything they had, and they truly did leave them all behind to follow Christ, thereby showing true self-denial. Perhaps the apostles doubted that they could become perfect while still remaining poor. But the Lord calmed them, saying that not only they but anyone who for His sake and the Gospel's would leave everything to which his soul is tied will receive a great reward, and not only in the future life but even in this life.

Whoever leaves his house or family will receive houses and relatives a hundred-fold in the persons of true Christians and their homes. Truly, in the first centuries of Christianity, during the epoch of persecutions, these words of the Lord were literally fulfilled—all the Christians were like one family, all were truly brothers and sisters in Christ, and the house of every one of them was always open for any Christian, which he could consider as his own home instead of the one he left for the sake of Christ. Here, the Christian would find a new family—a new mother, father, brothers, sisters, children. But the most important reward, of course, will be in the coming age—eternal life.

The "regeneration" Christ speaks of refers to the renewal of the world, which will occur at the resurrection of the dead, after the general judgment and transformation of the heavens and the earth. Then the apostles will participate in the glorification of the God-Man Jesus Christ, taking part in His judgment over the Jewish nation and all nations of the world through their witness and mediation.

The Jews, as the chosen nation of God, considered themselves "first" among others. They also believed they would be first in the age to come. But the Lord said that many of them, of course for their lack of faith in Him as the Messiah, would in the eternal life find themselves to be last, while the repentant publicans and sinners, as well as the Gentiles, will find themselves to be first.

THE PARABLE OF THE WORKERS IN THE VINEYARD WHO RECEIVED EQUAL PAY (MATT 20:1–16)

This parable has as its purpose to explain how it could be that the last could become the first. This will come about as a result of God's mercy and goodness. The kingdom of God is here imagined as a master of a vineyard who hired workers to harvest the grapes. When he agreed with the first workers he hired in the morning, he agreed to pay them one denarius a day. At the end of the day, he paid the same amount to every worker, even those who came to work at the third, sixth, ninth, and even the eleventh hour. The ones who worked the longest began to complain, considering their pay to be unfair, but the master countered: "Friend, I am doing you no wrong. Did you not agree with me for a denarius [penny]? Take what is yours and go your way: I wish to give to this last man the same as to you. Is it not lawful for me to do what I wish with my own things? Or is your eye evil because I am good?"

A denarius was roughly worth a day's wages for a common laborer. The day in Hebrew reckoning was divided into twelve hours, which were counted from the morning, beginning with sunrise. The meaning of this parable is that the Lord Himself rewards those who serve Him. People cannot make deals with God or expect to demand of Him any conditions. The Lord rewards people only according to His goodness. It is necessary also to know that in the work of man's salvation so little is done by the person himself that there can be no talk of fair exchange. The Lord does not reward because of a debt that needs to be paid, but by grace, with full freedom, according to His Own providence.

Thus, whoever labors less might receive the same as he who labors more. In this is contained all the hope of sinners, who can attract God's mercy and the grace to wash them of their sins with one repentant sigh, coming from the depths of the soul. What was the purpose of telling this parable? Peter had just asked about the reward the apostles should expect for following Christ. The Lord did not immediately rebuke this pride of an immature mind; quite the opposite—He promised them great rewards, but now through this parable He shows them that their reward does not depend on their own merits but only on the mercy of God. It may end up being thus: the ones with the most merits may receive the least reward, while those who had the fewest merits, calling on the Lord in the last moments of their life, could receive the greatest reward.

In conclusion, the Lord said, "For many are called, but few chosen." In other words, although many, even *all*, are called to eternal blessedness in the kingdom of heaven, those who will be chosen for this blessedness will end up being only a few.

Of course, as in all parables, one should not find hidden meaning in every aspect of this parable either. The main idea is the most important thing, the essential thought behind it: that a person is rewarded by God not based on how many good things he has done but only by the mercy of God.

THE LORD REPEATS HIS PROPHECY OF HIS IMMINENT SUFFERING AND RESURRECTION AND ANSWERS THE SONS OF ZEBEDEE REGARDING PRIMACY IN HIS KINGDOM (MATT 20:17–28; MARK 10:32–45; LUKE 18:31–34)

All three Synoptics agree that the Lord, on the way to Jerusalem, once again began to speak to the disciples about His forthcoming suffering, death, and resurrection. St Mark's account is most detailed and vivid, since he heard it all firsthand from the Apostle Peter. He said that the Lord walked ahead, evidently as one going to His own suffering willingly, desiring to accomplish the will of God (compare with Luke 12:50). His disciples, however, still burdened with human reasoning, were thinking only of the earthly glory of the Messiah, "and they were amazed. And as they followed they were afraid." Having called the Twelve to Himself, apparently because there was a multitude walking with Him, the Lord told them about everything that would occur in Jerusalem, everything the prophets wrote about Him—that He would be submitted to mocking, condemned to death, and given to the Gentiles (the Romans), who, after beating Him and mocking Him, would kill Him, and on the third day He would be raised up. St Luke adds that the disciples understood nothing, for the meaning of His words was hidden from them.

Then the mother of the sons of Zebedee came up to the Lord, with her sons James and John (see Mark's account), with a request to place one of her sons at the right hand and the other at the left hand of His kingdom. In other words, she was asking her sons to be second and third in importance after Him in the Messianic kingdom. But the Lord answered, "You do not know what you ask." Truly, the apostles did not know that primacy in His kingdom meant primacy in self-denial and martyrdom in the name of Christ; they thought that they were only asking for honors, power, and joy. Therefore, the Lord indicates with His question: "Are you able to drink the cup that I drink?" that being near Him in the kingdom will mean emulating Him in suffering. Sufferings here are spoken of as a cup that Christ's near ones must share with Him. This image is meant to echo the cup of poison that kings sent condemned men to drink. The Son of God is depicted in the Gospels as a man condemned, to whom the Father in heaven sends a cup of death (John 18:11). "And be baptized with the baptism that I am baptized with?" This is an expression of the same thought—bearing suffering is imagined as a full immersion in water.

The apostles answered in the affirmative. St John Chrysostom says they spoke in the fire of zeal, not knowing what they said; they said the same thing that all the disciples were saying, when they promised to follow the Lord even unto death. "You will indeed drink the cup that I drink." It is as if the Lord is saying, "Even though you promise without thinking, but truly in the future you will be like Me in bearing your labors patiently. As for the one sitting on My right hand in this kingdom, which you imagine to be earthly, it is not Mine to give, but is prepared by My Father." This means that it is not in Christ's authority to give this to whomsoever desires it, but only to those for whom these places were prepared, who will have deserved them through their labors. The rest of the apostles were angry, evidently envious of the brothers. The Lord then gives them all instruction, telling them not to seek to be first.

In answer to their nascent ambition, the Lord teaches them that the essential rule of the morality of the members of His kingdom, unlike kingdoms of this world, is humility and self-denial. As an example of such humility and self-denial, the Lord gives the apostles Himself. He came not "to be served, but to serve, and to give His life a ransom for many." Here He says "many" instead of "all." All people were in spiritual bondage to the devil and worked for sin. In order to free them, it was necessary to "buy them out," to give ransom (*lytron*, in Greek). The Lord pays this price, this redemption (*apolytrosên*) with the price of His passion and death on the cross.

HEALING THE TWO BLIND MEN IN JERICHO (MATT 20:29–34; MARK 10:46–52; LUKE 18:35–43)

Jericho was a large city during that time, important for its historical memory. Not far from there, the Jews miraculously crossed the Jordan when they came from Egypt (Josh 3:16). This was the first city that the Hebrews took miraculously (Josh 6:20). Here also were situated the schools of the prophets (2 Kgs 2:5), here Elisha performed the miracle of making the bitter waters sweet (2 Kgs 2:21). The surrounding area is remarkable for its greenery and wonderful climate, but closer to Jerusalem there was a forlorn, rocky desert, in which many wild animals and robbers lived. When the Lord was walking out of Jericho along the usual road from Galilee through Perea toward Jerusalem, many people followed Him, many of whom were also going to Jerusalem for the feast of Passover.

There were two blind men by the wayside asking for alms, who began to shout, "Have mercy on us, O Lord, Son of David!" This exclamation was itself a witness of their living faith in Jesus Christ as the Messiah. The people tried to force them to remain silent, not to bother Jesus Christ, probably because Christ was teaching the masses at this moment. The Lord asked what they wanted from Him, and received the answer: "Lord, that our eyes may be opened." He touched their eyes and healed them, after which they followed Him.

The three Synoptics speak of this healing, but only St Matthew speaks of two blind men. St Mark and St Luke mention only one, and St Mark even gives him a name—Bartimaeus, meaning "son of Timeus." It can be assumed that one of these blind men was well known, while the other was an unknown, unnoticed by many, which would explain why two of the Evangelists do not mention him. One more difference between the accounts is that Matthew and Mark have Christ healing the man on the exit from Jericho, while St Luke places it at His entry to Jericho. Bishop Michael interprets this apparent contradiction thus—the word St Luke uses (*engisin*) means not exactly "enters" but "is located near something." Consequently, it would be more correct to translate Luke to say that Jesus healed the man while *near* Jericho, whether at the entrance or exit, it does not matter.

The Lord Jesus Christ Visits Zacchaeus (Luke 19:1–10)

Only St Luke mentions this visit to the chief publican Zacchaeus. Having healed the blind men, the Lord went into Jericho, where a certain very rich man named Zacchaeus wanted to see Him very much. This name is Jewish, meaning "pure" or "righteous." Jericho was wealthy due to its production and sale of balsam, and the collector of Jericho's taxes was an important man who was also very rich. Zacchaeus was not a mere collector of tax, but the chief publican, to whom, most likely, the publicans of an entire district answered. The Gospel underlines that he was a rich man; after all, so few rich men followed the poor Galilean Teacher. Zacchaeus was short of stature, and so he climbed a fig tree in order to better see the Lord, who was surrounded by a crowd of people. Evidently knowing Zacchaeus's good moral disposition, his desire to see the Lord that was more than mere curiosity, the Lord honored his house with a visit.

The great joy that the Lord did not disdain him as a sinner finally awakened Zacchaeus's conscience, effecting a complete moral transformation in his soul. Admitting that his conscience was not clear with respect to the means he used to get rich, he gives a general pronouncement, a triumphant promise to expiate his sin of avarice: "Look, Lord, I give half of my goods to the poor; and if I have taken anything from anyone by false accusation, I restore fourfold" (all of which is the proper restitution, according to the law in Exod 22:1). The Lord answered: "Today salvation has come to this house, because he also is a son of Abraham," not only by descent but according to the spirit. The repentance of Zacchaeus is a model of true repentance that is not limited by a fruitless remorse over sins committed, but strives to expiate the sins through virtues that are the sins' opposites. Therefore, the Gospel reading concerning Zacchaeus is always read the week before the preparatory period for Lent begins, the week before the Sunday of the publican and the Pharisee.

The Parable of the Ten Pounds, or the Talents (Luke 19:11–28; Matt 25:14–30)

While still in Zacchaeus's house, the Lord began to tell the parable of the ten pounds, which has many similarities with St Matthew's parable of the talents. While they have many similarities, there are some essential differences as well; in addition, as we see in the Gospel of Matthew, the parable of the talents was told by the Lord much later, in connection with His conversation regarding the Second Coming, the end of the world, and the Final Judgment. Nevertheless, the main idea of both parables is the same, and so we can discuss them in parallel.

In the parable of the pounds, Christ speaks of a person of noble birth who travels to a distant country in order to come into his inherited kingdom, then returns home. This image is taken from the political reality of Palestine at that time—local kings had to go directly to Rome in order to be confirmed in their royal dignity. Archelaus, son of Herod the Great, as well as Herod Antipas, tetrarch of Galilee, both had to do this. In the parable of the talents, however, the protagonist is merely a man who leaves to a far country. In both parables this person is an image of Christ, who was supposed to (in the Hebrew consciousness) begin an earthly kingdom. In the parable of the pounds, the lord gives ten slaves ten pounds, one pound per slave, ordering them to use the money to make a profit.

In the parable of the talents, the lord gives his slaves *all* his possessions, giving each a portion according to his abilities. A talent was a solid piece of silver, worth a significant amount of money. Of course, in both parables, the slaves are the disciples and followers of Christ, who receive from the Lord various gifts and external good things, which they must multiply for the glory of God, for the benefit of their neighbors and the salvation of their souls. Later in the parable of the pounds, we find a certain circumstance that is not found in the parable of the talents. The citizens came to hate this noble man and sent an embassy after him, saying, "We will not have this man to reign over us." Here is a characteristic that reminds us of an event from the life of Archelaus on his way to Rome. The Jews, who hated him, sent an embassy of fifty people to Rome to beg that he not be confirmed as king of Judea, but their efforts were fruitless. As it refers to the Lord Jesus Christ, this detail reminds us of how the Jewish people rejected Him as their Messiah, but also without purpose because He remained the King and Judge of the whole world, Who will demand an account from His slaves and will punish those who refuse to accept His authority.

In both parables, the return of the Lord is reminiscent of the Second Coming of Christ, when every person will have to give an account at the Dread Judgment of how he used those external good things given him by God. Those who multiply their pounds and talents will be worthy of praise and will receive each according to his zeal. The one who hid his pound or talent will be punished as a "wicked servant," who did not want to labor with those benefits of God's goodness, in whom the grace of God remained without fruit. The accusation of the lazy servant that his master is cruel is merely a typical self-justification of the sinner, who lost his feeling of being a son of God due to his sinfulness. Such a sinner only imagines God to be cruel and unfair. Whoever uses his gifts well will increase them; a slothful and careless person will lose even what he has already. Therefore, "to everyone who has will be given; and from him who does not have, even what he has will be taken away from him." The parable of the pounds finished with the threat of a harsh punishment to the Jewish nation for their not accepting the Lord Jesus Christ as the Messiah. After finishing the parable, the Lord continued on His way to Jerusalem.

THE RAISING OF LAZARUS (JOHN 11:1–46)

Only St John tells of this event. While the Lord was still in Perea, He received news of the illness of His dear friend Lazarus, who lived in Bethany with his sisters Martha and Mary. This family was especially close to the Lord, and He often visited them to rest from the noise of the crowds and the antagonism of His enemies during His pilgrimages to Jerusalem. The sisters sent word to the Lord: "he whom You love is sick," hoping that the Lord Himself would hurry to them in order to heal the sick man. But the Lord not only did not hurry, but even purposely remained in the same place where He was another two days, saying, "This sickness is not unto death, but for the glory of God, that the Son of God may be glorified through it." The Lord knew that Lazarus would die, and if He said that the illness would *not* result in his death, that was because He intended to resurrect him.

Only two days later, when Lazarus was already dead, did the Lord say to His disciples: "Let us go to Judea again." The Lord did not say Bethany, but Judea, because that was the goal of their journey, in order to bring to the fore the hidden thought in their hearts about the danger awaiting Him in Judea. Through this, the Lord wanted to strengthen in the disciples the thought of the necessity and thus the inevitability of the suffering and death of their Teacher. And the disciples did react with fear for Him, reminding Him that just a short time ago the Jews wanted to stone Him in Jerusalem. The Lord answers their fear with an allegory taken from His surroundings. It was most likely early morning as the sun was rising; consequently, they had twelve hours for their journey. During these twelve hours, travel along the roads would be considered safe. It would only become dangerous if they had to travel after the setting of the sun or at night, but there was no need to do this because their travel to Bethany would take less than a day. In the spiritual sense, this means that the time of our earthly life is determined by God's will, and so, while we live, we can go along the path at our feet without fear and do the work to which we are called. We are safe, for God's will protects us from all dangers, as the light of the sun protects those who walk during the day. There would be a danger if, during our work, night would catch us, that is, if we continued to work beyond the time allotted to us, contrary to God's will. Then we would be in danger of stumbling on the road.

In reference to Jesus Christ, this means that the life and work of the Lord Jesus Christ would not finish earlier than its allotted time, and so the disciples should not be afraid of the dangers awaiting Him. By completing His ministry in the light of the will of God, the God-Man could not be subjected to unexpected danger. Having explained this, the Lord indicated the immediate purpose of their going toward

Judea: "Our friend Lazarus sleeps, but I go that I may wake him up." The Lord called Lazarus's death sleep, as He did in certain other situations (see Matt 9:24; Mark 5:29). For Lazarus, death truly was like sleep because it was so short. The disciples did not understand that the Lord was speaking of Lazarus's death, remembering His previous words that his illness was not deadly. They thought that the Lord would come and miraculously heal him. "Lord, if he sleeps he will get well" (see John 1:1–16), they said this, probably, to disabuse Him of His notion to go to Judea: "there is no need to go, since the sickness took a turn for the better."

Then the Lord, putting aside any arguments concerning their journey, desiring to underline the necessity of traveling to Judea, said clearly: "Lazarus is dead." He also added that He was joyful for the disciples that He was not in Bethany when Lazarus was sick, since a simple healing would not strengthen their faith in Him as much as the forthcoming great miracle of raising him from the dead. Cutting off the conversation regarding their fears definitively, the Lord said, "Let us go to him." While their wavering was quashed, their fears did not dissipate, and one of them, Thomas, called Didimus, which means "twin," expressed this fear in a very moving way: "Let us also go, that we may die with Him." In other words, if we cannot dissuade Him from this journey, will we leave Him to it alone? Let us also go to die with Him.

When they approached Bethany, it became clear that Lazarus was already dead for four days. "Bethany was near Jerusalem, about two miles away," about half an hour's walk. This detail is given by St John in order to explain why so many people were in Martha and Mary's house, despite Bethany being a very small village. Martha, the sister with a much livelier character, when she heard of the Lord's coming, hurried to meet Him, without even telling her sister about it, because Mary was at home in great sorrow accepting the condolences of those who came to mourn with her for her brother. With sorrow she said, not rebuking the Lord, only expressing her regret that it happened in this way: "Lord, if You had been here, my brother would not have died."

Her faith in the Lord, however, made her sure that even now not all was lost, and maybe a miracle could be performed, although she does not say this openly, rather saying, "But even now I know that whatever You ask of God, God will give You." To this the Lord gives her a straight answer: "Your brother will rise again." Almost as if to check herself to see if she understood Him correctly, and desiring the Lord to qualify His answer and help her clearly understand which resurrection He referred to, the miracle that He intended to perform now, or the general resurrection of the dead at the end of the world, Martha said, "I know that he will rise again in the resurrection at the last day." Martha thus expressed her faith that God would fulfill any petition of Jesus; consequently, she did not yet have faith in Jesus Himself as the all-powerful Son of God. Therefore, the Lord raises her to this higher faith, concentrating her faith on His own person, saying, "I am the resurrection and the life. He who believes in Me, though he may die, he shall live. And whoever lives and believes in Me shall never die."

The meaning of these words is the following: "In Me is the source of resurrection and eternal life, and so if I want to resurrect your brother now, I can do so, even before the general resurrection. "Do you believe this?" He asks her, and receives an affirmative answer that she believes in Him as the Messiah Christ who came into the world. Then, urged by the Lord, Martha went to call her sister Mary to bring her also to Him. Since she told Mary in secret, and the Jews mourning with her did not know where she was going, they went with her, thinking that she was going to the tomb of Lazarus to mourn there. Mary fell at Jesus's feet with tears, uttering the same words as Martha. The Lord "groaned in the spirit and was troubled" seeing such sorrow at Lazarus's death. Bishop Michael believes that this sorrow and disturbance in Christ's heart was inspired by the presence of the Jews who were ritually mourning without sincerity, and who were all filled with hatred against Him Who was planning to perform this great miracle. He wanted to perform this miracle to give His enemies every chance to repent and believe in Him before His passion. But instead of that, they only increased in their hatred and definitively condemned Him, finally with the death sentence.

Having overcome His inner turmoil, the Lord asked, "Where have you laid him?" The question was directed at the sister. Blessed Augustine says, "The God-Man knew where Lazarus was buried, but, since He was communicating with people, He spoke as a man." The sisters answered, "Lord, come and see."

"Jesus wept." This, of course, is an expression of His human nature. The Evangelist John later writes of the impression that these tears made on those who were there. They were moved, while others said, with anger in their hearts, "Could not this Man, who opened the eyes of the blind, also have kept this man from dying?" Their rationale is this: if He could have prevented Lazarus's death, He would have, since He loved him; but He could not, and therefore He weeps. Again putting down within Himself His sorrow at the hatred of the Jews, the Lord came to the tomb of Lazarus and told them to remove the stone.

Tombs in Palestine are built in the form of a cave whose entrance is blocked with a large stone. Opening such caves is allowed only in extreme cases, and only soon after the burial, not four days afterward, when the body was already rotting. In the warm climate of Palestine, the rotting of bodies after death begins very quickly, which is why the Jews buried their dead on the same day as their death. The rot on the fourth day could be so far advanced that even faithful Martha could not stop herself from contradicting the Lord: "Lord, by this time there is a stench, for he has been dead four days."

Reminding Martha of His previous words, the Lord said, "Did I not say to you that if you would believe, you would see the glory of God?" When the stone was rolled away, the Lord raised His eyes to heaven and prayed: "Father, I thank You that You have heard Me." Knowing that His enemies ascribed His miraculous power to the demons, the Lord wanted to show with this prayer that He performs miracles through power of His oneness with God the Father. The soul of Lazarus returned to his body, and the Lord exclaimed in a loud voice, "Lazarus, come forth!"

The loud voice here is an expression of His strong will, which is sure that its command will be heeded; or it is the voice intended to wake a sleeper. To the miracle of the resurrection another miracle was added: Lazarus, though tied hand and foot in a burial shroud, came out of the cave himself, after which the Lord commanded him to be untied. The fine details given in this account bear witness to the fact that St John the Evangelist was there to see the miracle. As a result of the miracle, the usual division occurred among the Jews—many believed, but others went to the Pharisees, the worst of the Lord's enemies, with evil feelings and intentions, in order to tell them of what had just occurred.

THE DECISION OF THE SANHEDRIN TO KILL THE LORD JESUS CHRIST (JOHN 11:47–57)
News of the miracle had such a disturbing effect on the enemies of the Lord that the high priests and Pharisees immediately called a special session of the Sanhedrin, the Supreme Court of the Jews. In their own company, they were not afraid to speak completely openly, and so immediately they raised the question: what should be done to preserve their power and their influence over the people? They acknowledged the miracles of the Lord as authentic miracles, but they expressed fear that a national uprising might be the result, and the Romans might use that as an excuse to destroy what little independence the Jews still had. The fatality of their reasoning was apparent—they did not accept the Lord as the Messiah since He did not correspond to their twisted ideas about the Messiah, but still expressed fear that He could stand at the head of an insurrection and through this bring an even greater calamity to the whole Jewish nation.

"One of them, Caiaphas, being high priest that year [this does not mean that the high priests were only chosen for a year, but only shows that under Roman rule, high priests were frequently changed by the rulers of Judea] said to them, 'You know nothing at all, nor do you consider that it is expedient for us that one man should die for the people, and not that the whole nation should perish." In other words, they must prevent this dangerous situation of an insurrection against Rome with Jesus at the head by killing Jesus. Here, Caiaphas put on the mask of a zealot for the good of the nation, and at the same time finds a nationalistic-political consideration as an excuse for their conspiring to murder. The Evangelist John indicates that these words were an involuntary prophecy by Caiaphas about the fact that the Lord Jesus Christ had to "die for the people," that is, to suffer for mankind to redeem them.

The high priests, as the messengers of the will of God, were mediators between God and men, and in this capacity they could even prophecy unwillingly, which is exactly what happened even with such a high priest as Caiaphas; except that Caiaphas was only speaking of the Hebrew nation, while Christ died for the salvation and gathering into one Church of both Jews and Gentiles as "children of God" who were scattered abroad. And so they made an official decision to kill Jesus, and gave an order that He be taken.

When Jesus found out about the conviction, He left Bethany to go to Ephraim, near the desert of Jericho, for His hour to suffer had not yet come. As a true Paschal Lamb, He had to die on the Passover, triumphantly, not secretly, as the Sanhedrin evidently hoped to kill Him, fearing the people (Matt 26:4).

THE DINNER IN BETHANY AT THE HOME OF LAZARUS (JOHN 12:1–11)

This dinner was prepared for the Lord six days before the Passover and is not the same dinner as the one described by the first two Evangelists, St Matthew and St Mark, which occurred two days before the Passover in the house of Simon the leper. Of course it was held in the house of Lazarus who was raised from the dead. This is made obvious by the fact that Martha was serving, and Lazarus himself was one of those at the table. At this dinner, Mary anointed the feet of the Lord with precious myrrh, while at the other dinner described by the first two Evangelists, the Lord's head was anointed with myrrh by a certain woman who was a sinner, according to tradition (which is remembered in services of Great and Holy Wednesday, when this anointing is commemorated). According to the Evangelist John, only Judas rebuked Mary regarding the cost of the myrrh, while in Matthew and Mark, all the disciples do. There is nothing strange in the possibility that the Lord was twice anointed. Mary did this from a sense of deep gratitude for the resurrection of her brother, while the sinful woman did this as a sign of her repentance, for which she was promised a great reward. Mary had this myrrh most likely left over from the burial of her brother Lazarus, as if she had known to save some with a prophetic foreknowledge.

 Chapter 6

The Last Days of the Earthly Life of the Lord Jesus Christ

The Entry of the Lord into Jerusalem
(Matt 21:1–11; Mark 11:1–11; Luke 19:29–44; John 12:12–19)

The Lord Jesus Christ now walked to Jerusalem in order to accomplish all that was written of Him, as the Messiah, by the prophets. He went in order to drink the cup of redemptive suffering, to give His soul for the redemption of many, and later to enter into His glory. Therefore, in contrast to how He entered Jerusalem the last time, it behooved Him to make His final entry into Jerusalem in full triumph. The first three Evangelists, St Matthew, St Mark, and St Luke, give us certain details that prefaced the triumphant entry. When the Lord and His disciples, surrounded by many people who accompanied Him from Bethany and whom they met along the way, approached the Mount of Olives, He sent two disciples into the village ahead of them with the instruction to bring back a female donkey and her young colt.

The Mount of Olives was named so because it was covered in olive trees. It is found east of Jerusalem and is separated by a river, which almost completely dried up during the summer. On the western slope of the river, the one facing Jerusalem, there was a garden called Gethsemane. On the eastern slope, there were two villages called Bethphage and Bethany. From the top of the Mount of Olives, one could see all of Jerusalem. From Bethany, two roads led to Jerusalem—one went around the mount on the south, the other went over the summit, this latter of which was shorter, though more difficult and strenuous. In Palestine there were few horses, and those were used exclusively by soldiers for wartime. For household work and travel, donkeys, mules, and camels were used. To sit on a horse was a sign of war; to sit on a mule or a donkey was a symbol of peace. In peaceful times, both kings and national leaders rode around on the more domestic animals.

Thus, the entry of the Lord Jesus Christ into Jerusalem on a donkey was a sign of peace—the King of Peace was coming to His capital on a donkey, the symbol of peace. It is remarkable that the owner of the donkey and her colt, after hearing the request of the Lord, immediately gave Him his animals when the apostles told him for Whom they were taking them. Noting the unusual nature of this fact, St John Chrysostom said, "The Lord wanted to let them know that He could easily overcome the stubborn Jews when they came to seize Him and force them to be silent; however, He did not want to do this."[56]

The Evangelists Matthew and John indicate that this was the fulfillment of the prophecy of Zechariah, which they cite in truncated from, and which in its fullness reads thus: "Rejoice greatly, O daughter of Zion! Shout, O daughter of Jerusalem! Behold, your King is coming to you; He is just and having salvation, Lowly and riding on a donkey, A colt, the foal of a donkey" (Zech 9:9). This prophecy is similar to Isaiah 62, from which Matthew takes the beginning of his rendition of the prophecy: "Say to the daughter of Zion, 'Surely your salvation is coming . . .' "

Understanding the significance of this moment, the apostles themselves tried to decorate this procession with pomp—they covered the donkey and her colt with their outer clothing, which was intended to mimic the gold fabric that would decorate a king's horse. And the Lord sat on the clothing, riding on the colt, as we see in Mark, Luke, and John, with the donkey walking nearby. "And a very great multitude spread their clothes on the road," following the example of the disciples, while others, who did not have outer robes due to their poverty, "cut down branches from the trees and spread them on the road," in order to make the road softer and more comfortable for the colt, giving honor to the one sitting astride it.

By taking all four evangelical accounts together, one can draw the following picture: "Then, as He was now drawing near the descent of the Mount of Olives," when He was coming to the place where Jerusalem would have been most visible, "the whole multitude of the disciples began to rejoice and praise God with a loud voice for all the mighty works they had seen" and the salvation of the world effected by the Christ. St John adds the following words: "A great multitude that had come to the feast, when they heard that Jesus was coming to Jerusalem, took branches of palm trees, and went out to meet Him." Thus, two crowds came together—one was coming from Bethany with Christ, the other was coming from Jerusalem to meet Him. The view of Jerusalem in all its glory inspired joy in this mass of people, which was expressed in their loud exclamations: "Hosanna to the Son of David. Blessed is He who comes in the name of the Lord. Hosanna in the highest!"

"Hosanna" literally means "save" or "grant salvation." This exclamation was used as an expression of joy and piety and glorification. "Hosanna in the highest" is a request that the same joyful expressions be uttered for the sake of the King of Israel in the heavens. "Blessed is He who comes in the name of the Lord" means "worthy of blessing and glory is the one who comes from the Lord with His authority, as the king's representatives come, bearing all the authority and power of the king who sent them" (compare with John 5:43). The Evangelist Mark also adds another exclamation: "Blessed is the kingdom of our father David that comes in the name of the Lord." The kingdom of David was to be restored by the Messiah,

Whose throne would remain for eternity and Whose power would spread over all the nations. In these words, the sons of Israel glorified Christ, Who came to restore this kingdom of David. St Luke adds another one: "Peace in heaven," meaning "let all true spiritual good and eternal salvation come down from heaven."

St John explains that the reason for this great joy in meeting the Lord was the resurrection of Lazarus, while St Luke indicates all the miracles performed by Him. In this event, the Holy Church sees a special providence of God and inspiration of the Holy Spirit. From this point of view, one can understand the Lord's answer given to the hateful council of the Pharisees, "Teacher, rebuke Your disciples": "If these should keep silent, the stones would immediately cry out" (Luke 19:39–40). In other words, this glorification of the Messiah was placed in the hearts and mouths of the people by God Himself, and if someone tried to act against God's will in this, the soulless stones would replace the people in glorifying the Lord. In these words, the Church sees also a metaphorical indication of the pagans, who were at first stone-hearted, but later replaced Israel, who rejected Christ. The same meaning can be applied to the answer the Lord gives the Pharisees in the account given by Matthew when they were angry that the Jews were exclaiming in the Temple, "Hosanna to the Son of David": "Yes. Have you never read, 'Out of the mouth of babes and nursing infants You have perfected praise?'" (Ps 8:3; Matt 21:15–16). In other words, the Lord tells the Pharisees that God Himself prepared the praise to come from the mouths of children and suckling babes.

When the Lord saw the city, as St Luke tells us, He began to weep on its account, knowing of its imminent destruction. It is interesting to note that in A.D. 70, the Romans, when they began the siege of Jerusalem, set up their camp on the same place on the Mount of Olives where Christ was standing at that moment, and the siege began not long before Passover that year. "If you had known [as I do], even you, especially in this your day [or in the 'time of your visitation'], the things that make for your peace [that is, those things that are for your salvation]! But now they are hidden from your eyes [that is, you close your eyes stubbornly to not see that by rejecting Me you are preparing your own destruction].… You did not know the time of your visitation," the time when the Lord was merciful to you and called you to salvation through the Messiah, Whom you rejected instead of following.

St Matthew witnesses that when He went into Jerusalem, "all the city was moved," so great was the impression of this triumphant entry.

CASTING OUT THE MERCHANTS FROM THE TEMPLE
(MATT 21:12–17; MARK 11:15–19; LUKE 19:45–48)

After entering Jerusalem, the Lord immediately went to the temple and once again cast out all the merchants. Only the Synoptics write of this event, and St Mark's account differs from the other two in that Jesus first went to Bethany for the night and cast out the merchants only on the next morning, after He cursed the fig tree. There is no reason to see any great contradiction here—the apostles were not always interested in a strict chronological order in their Gospel accounts. For them, a logical order is more important. Some even say that there were two cleansing of the temples, one on each day. And let us not forget that three years previously, when the Lord came to Jerusalem for the first Passover of His public ministry, He found the courts of the temple transformed into a market-place, and cast out the merchants then as well. In the year after that, He came to Jerusalem again, but apparently the markets had not yet been reinstated. On the third Passover, the Lord did not come to Jerusalem. When the fourth Passover was approaching, the Jews were wondering whether Jesus would come or not. Knowing that the rulers had sentenced Him to death, and thinking that He would not dare come to Jerusalem to His obvious death, the merchants, with the permission of the high priests, once again brought the herds into the courts. They set up their stands with various wares, tables with money-changing stations, cages with doves that the high priests themselves sold, and began to sell. The Lord's coming into the temple was an unexpected event for them. After the people had all greeted Him with cries of "Hosanna," no one dared to contradict Him when He, as in the first Passover of His public ministry, "began to drive out those who bought and sold in the temple, and overturned the tables of the money changers and the seats of those who sold doves." St Mark also adds that the Lord "would not allow anyone to carry wares through the temple," meaning anything that had no relevance to the services being performed in the temple. Apparently, the greatness and power of His divinity were shining from His face at this moment, so that no one even dared to raise their voice against Him, and all involuntarily submitted to Him. The high priests evidently also dared to do nothing against the Lord, seeing how the people "were astonished at His teaching."

GREAT AND HOLY MONDAY: CURSING THE FRUITLESS FIG TREE
(MATT 21:18–19; MARK 11:12–14)

After the triumphant entry into Jerusalem, the Lord spent the night with His disciples in Bethany, while in the morning of the next day, on the way to Jerusalem, He saw a fig tree and wanted to eat its fruit. But He found nothing on it, even though it was covered with leaves, and He said, "Let no one eat fruit from you ever again." And in the morning, as they passed by, they saw the fig tree dried up from the roots, which greatly astonished the disciples. The Evangelists say that the Lord was hungry, and so searched for the fruit. This should not make us wonder, for the Lord Jesus Christ, according to His human nature, was subject to all the weaknesses of human nature and was like us in all things except in sin; for He was not merely God, but the God-Man. It is characteristic that He never uses the power of God to satisfy His human needs, but in such cases only used human means, rejecting once and for all the first demonic temptation to turn the stones into bread.

St Mark also includes the detail that the fig tree had no fruit because it was not yet the right time of the year. But the tree deserved to be cursed because it was fooling the passersby with its appearance and leading them into delusion. On a fig tree, the leaves usually appear only after the fruits have come out, but this fig tree promised to be full of fruit because of its many leaves, while in actual fact it carried nothing but leaves on its branches. According to the teaching of the Church, the fig tree was a symbol of the rulers of the Jewish Old Testament Church—the high priests, scribes, and Pharisees, who had only the external appearance of those who fulfilled the Law of God, but in actual fact brought no fruits of faith. The Lord condemned them to be withered as a punishment for their hypocrisy, and warned, as we see later, that "the kingdom of God will be taken from you, and given to a nation bearing the fruits of it" (Matt 21:43).

THE DESIRE OF THE GREEKS TO SEE JESUS CHRIST AND THE LORD'S WORDS CONCERNING THEM (JOHN 12:20–50)

After the triumphant entry into Jerusalem, probably on the very next day, several Greeks came to the Apostle Philip and asked him: "Sir, we wish to see Jesus." These Greeks were most likely proselytes, that is, Gentiles who converted to Judaism. Philip passed on their request to Andrew. It is appropriate that only Philip and Andrew, of all the apostles, carry Greek names. In Decapolis, there were many Greeks among the settlers, and since Philip was from Bethsaida of Galilee, it is possible that these were Greeks who knew him personally. Their request is not a result of idle curiosity, for every person could see Him when He was walking in the court of the temple and teaching. Apparently, these Greeks were seeking a more intimate conversation with the Lord. Bishop Michael expresses the opinion that they wanted to offer Him the idea to travel to Greece to preach, knowing of the general antagonism of the scribes and Pharisees, similarly to how King Apgar offered Christ to come to visit him, according to ancient tradition. In any case, evident in their request is the striving of the Gentiles to take part in the kingdom of Christ—this was the first hint of the conversion of the entire pagan world to Christ as a result of His death on the cross, His redemptive sacrifice for the sins of all mankind. This is why this request of the Greeks resulted in Christ going deep into thought concerning His imminent sufferings and the profound significance of His cross. This is why their request inspired in Him a long, impassioned speech that only St John relates.

"The hour has come that the Son of Man should be glorified." What is this hour? With respect to Christ Himself, this hour is the time of His suffering and death on the cross, and His resurrection. With respect to the prince of this world, this hour is the time of his being cast out; with respect to humanity; this hour is the time of their approach to Christ who is raised up on the cross. The Lord calls Himself the Son of Man here, indicating that He must suffer and die as a man in order to enter in His glory as the God-Man, thereby bringing to Himself all of mankind. As in visible nature, where death does not always result in destruction but can sometimes be the beginning of new life, like a seed of wheat, which must appear to die in the earth in order to grow, so His death will become the beginning of new life and the multiplication of the followers of His kingdom on this earth.

Therefore, the followers of Christ must not fear death ("love his life"), but on the contrary, should sacrifice this earthly life for the sake of gaining eternal life. The human nature of the Lord, however, was afraid at the thought of the coming sufferings: "Now My soul is troubled." This is the beginning of that battle between the human and divine natures of Christ, which later reached its apogee in the garden of Gethsemane. The human nature wants to pray, "Father, save Me from this hour," but the divine nature immediately conquers this confusion with the prayer, "Father, glorify Your name," that is, "Let that for which I have come be accomplished." In answer, the heavenly Father Himself strengthened His Beloved Son for His forthcoming suffering, thundering from the heavens: "I have both glorified it and will glorify it again." In other words, the Father is saying, "I have already glorified it with many works, signs, and miracles, and once again I will glorify it through Your imminent suffering, death, and resurrection."

The impression of this celestial voice was different among various people, which is explained by the different spiritual states of the people in attendance. The people who did not believe in Christ said that they heard simple thunder, while others said it was the voice of an angel. The Lord, answering these incorrect thoughts, explained that this voice was "for your sake," so that everyone would come to believe in Him, and even in these final hours would come to their senses, for soon would come the hour of judgment over "the ruler of this world," the devil, and the time for him to be cast out of the souls of people.

The devil is called the ruler of this world in many places of Scripture, as one who has power over all people who do not believe in Christ or are even enemies of Christ. "And I, if I am lifted up from the earth, will draw all peoples to Myself." The crucifixion of the Lord, and the subsequent resurrection and ascension to heaven, will be followed by the conversion of all mankind to Christ. The people thought that by saying He was to be "lifted up" Jesus was speaking of His death, and so they expressed their dismay because if He would die, who would then rule on the earth? This had to do with the popular notion that the Messiah would rule on earth for eternity. The Lord answers them that they should use their time wisely, while He ("the light") is still with them, and believe in Him. He then left them, probably going back to the Mount of Olives or to Bethany, where He spent His nights, while during the day He taught in the temple.

Later, John the Evangelist has a personal aside, in which he laments the reasons for the lack of faith among the Jews in the Lord, indicating that this lack of faith was actually predicted by Isaiah (Isa 6:9-10, 53:1), where the Prophet spoke of the hearts of the chosen nation becoming hard as stone. The reason for their antagonism to Christ is the same preference for human glory, rather than the glory of God. In conclusion, St John brings the last words of instruction that the Lord gave to the Jews in the temple. Christ says that He came to save the world, and His word will judge people in the last day, for this word is nothing less than the commandment of the Heavenly Father to all mankind.

GREAT TUESDAY: THE WITHERED FIG TREE AND THE TEACHING ON THE POWER OF FAITH (MATT 21:20–22; MARK 11:20–24)

St Mark gives the more detailed account of this event. He mentions that only on the second day, probably when the Lord was walking from Bethany to Jerusalem on the same road as the previous day, the disciples noticed that the fig tree that had been cursed the day before had withered. In answer to their astonishment, the Lord teaches them the power of faith, saying that if they will have faith in God, which overcomes all doubts, then they will be able to perform even greater miracles. "Whoever says to this mountain, 'Be removed and be cast into the sea,' and does not doubt in his heart, but believes that those things he says will be done, he will have whatever he says." The extravagant image of the mountain is of course only used to illustrate the fact that nothing is impossible for faith that is free from doubt. Therefore, even in prayer we must ask for everything with faith, and only then will we receive. St Mark adds to this that the condition for effective prayer is forgiveness of offenses (Mark 11:25–26). Whoever does not forgive his neighbor insults the love of God, and such a person cannot have truly firm faith; neither, consequently, can he have true prayer.

CONVERSATIONS IN THE TEMPLE: THE LORD ANSWERS THE ELDERS REGARDING HIS AUTHORITY (MATT 21:23–27; MARK 11:27–33; LUKE 20:1–8)

When the Lord once again came to the temple and began to teach, as was His custom, the high priests and elders came to Him with the question: "By what authority are You doing these things? And who gave You this authority?" The question referred to His actions in daring to send away the merchants on the previous days. It is clear that they did not really want to know the truth of the matter; rather, it was malicious disputation. As always, the hate-filled enemies of the Lord wanted to catch Him saying something unlawful. But the Lord, not answering their question, Himself traps them with His own question: "The baptism of John—where was it from? From heaven or from men?"

The question regarding John's baptism was at the same time a question of his prophetic dignity and his being a messenger of the divine will. John witnessed of Jesus as the Messiah, the Son of God Who came into the world to save sinners. To admit that John was sent by God would mean to admit that Jesus is the Messiah, and then their question regarding His authority would automatically be answered by their own words. This irritated the Jews, since they were placed in an evident dilemma—they knew the people honored John as a prophet, and they were afraid to say outright that John was not a prophet. But admitting openly that John was a prophet would mean accepting John's witness to Jesus as the Son of God. Finally, they could not give a concrete answer, and so they said, "We do not know."

Such a Sanhedrin, who could not offer a concrete answer to such an important question, a question that was within their competency to answer, showed himself to be invalid, unworthy of the Lord's direct answer to their query. Therefore, the Lord answered: "Neither will I tell you by what authority I do these things." It was pointless to answer Him because of course they knew perfectly well by what authority He acted, but they consciously fought against this authority. All three Synoptics agree on all major details in their accounts of this conversation.

THE PARABLE OF THE TWO SONS (MATT 21:28–32)

Continuing His conversation with them, the Lord told them a parable, desiring that they should pass sentence on themselves. "A man had two sons." As we see from the rest of the parable, the man is an image of God, the first son is meant to represent the harlots and publicans, meaning all sinful people in general, while the second son is the scribes and Pharisees, and whoever else considers himself to be a righteous man. "Go, work today in my vineyard." The vineyard represents the Church, and the work in it is all pious deeds, the fulfillment of God's commandments. The first son answers his father's command with a firm, "I will not." This, sinners do with their entire lifestyle, but then they repent, as the publicans and harlots repented after the preaching of John the Baptist, and begin to do the will of God. The Pharisees and so-called righteous men tell the Father, "I go, sir." With their lips, they fulfill the will of God, but not with their actions, for they do not accept the Lord's preaching concerning repentance. Not understanding the meaning of the parable, the enemies of Christ answered the Lord when He asked them which son had fulfilled the will of the Father by saying, "The first." Then the Lord revealed to them the meaning of the parable, which was a condemnation of them. He showed them that those people whom they despise as sinners ended up becoming more worthy of entering the kingdom of the Messiah, the Church of Christ.

THE PARABLE OF THE WICKED HUSBANDMEN (MATT 21:33–46; MARK 12:1–12; LUKE 20:9–19)

All three Synoptics give exactly the same account of this parable. A certain master, a symbol for God, planted a vineyard, an image of the Old Testament Church. He surrounded it with a hedge, which is interpreted by exegetes to mean the law of Moses and all laws intended to preserve the chosen nation of God from pagan influence. He dug a winepress in it, and built a tower intended for guards who would protect the vineyard from thieves and animals. The winepress and the tower are interpreted as being symbols of the altar and temple. Having done everything for the proper care of the vineyard, the master gave it to some husbandmen to work it and prepare wine for his table. The husbandmen here are representative of the leaders of the Jewish nation, especially the chief priests and members of the Sanhedrin. Then, the master left. This means that the Lord left them full authority over the Jewish nation in order for them to later show Him the fruit of their husbandry, that is, to show Him that they had prepared the people properly, in the spirit of the Law of God.

After some time had passed, the master sent his servants to collect the fruit of the vineyard, who are meant to represent the prophets. But the evil husbandmen "took his servants, beat one, killed one, and stoned another." This is how the leaders of the Jewish nation dealt with the prophets that God sent them. They ruled the people with no concern for their spiritual perfection, only pursuing personal interests and agendas, and so cruelly persecuted the prophets of God who reminded them of their true responsibilities. All of Jewish sacred history witnesses to this (Jer 44:4–6; 2 Chr 24:20–21, 36:16; Neh 9:26; and others). Finally, the master sent them his son (in Mark, he is his only and "beloved" son), representing of course the coming of the only begotten Son of God, Jesus Christ, to the Jewish people. "This is the heir," said the evil husbandmen. "Come, let us kill him and seize his inheritance." The Lord Jesus Christ is called an heir in the sense that everything is given Him by the Father (Matt 11:27). The chief priests and elders of the Jews decided to kill Him so that they would not lose their authority over the Jewish nation. "So they took him and cast him out of the vineyard and killed him," just as the Jewish leaders killed the Lord Jesus Christ, taking Him out of Jerusalem, the holy center of the Old Testament Church, beyond its walls.

As He finished the parable, the Lord wanted the listeners to condemn themselves out of their own mouths, which is exactly what they did in Matthew's account, while in Mark's the Lord even confirms the correctness of their self-conviction. According to St Luke, the chief priests and elders, understanding that they were forced to speak a condemnation over themselves, said, "Certainly not!" The coming of the master should be here understood not as the Second Coming of Christ, for the parable speaks of the vineyard being given to other husbandmen (meaning that life was to continue after the master punished the evil husbandmen), but rather that Christ is speaking of the destruction of Jerusalem, the end of the Old Testament priesthood, and the power of the Sanhedrin, the end of the importance of the scribes and Pharisees. Then "other vinedressers" (the apostles and their successors) will receive the vineyard and become pastors of the Church of Christ. In conclusion, Christ applies to Himself verses 22 and 23 of Psalm 117 (118), calling Himself the stone that the builders rejected, but which became the head of the corner, the cornerstone, the weight-bearing foundation of the majestic building of the New Testament Church. The coming into the world of the Son of

God Himself was from the Lord, and is marvelous in the eyes of men, from the point of view of mankind. Calling Himself a stone, the Lord indicated two kinds of people—those who will not believe in Him and those who will be punished for this lack of belief. For the first, He will be a stumbling block, while for the others, who remained without repentance and cruelly arose against the Lord and began to fight against the establishment and spread of His kingdom, the stone will grind them to dust. The fault of the latter is greater. He who has stumbled over a rock and fallen can still get up again, while being ground means being destroyed completely, something that will happen to all hardened enemies of Christ. As a result of this lack of submission among the Jews, who were initially the chosen ones of God, "the kingdom of God will be taken from [them] ... and given to a nation bearing the fruits of it," a new chosen people of God, all the future members of the kingdom of God, or the Church of Christ, who are here described as one nation— the new Israel.

Having fully appreciated the meaning of the parable, the chief priests and Pharisees "sought to lay hands on Him, [but] they feared the multitudes," or an uprising in support of the Lord among the people who considered Him a prophet.

THE PARABLE OF THOSE CALLED TO THE WEDDING FEAST OF THE SON OF THE KING (MATT 22:1–14)

In form and content, this parable is similar to the other parable regarding those called to the dinner feast in Luke (14:16–24), but without any doubt, these parables were spoken at different times. The parable in Luke was told by the Lord in the house of a Pharisee on a Sabbath long before His triumphant entry into Jerusalem, while contextually it is obvious that this parable was spoken already after the entry, probably on Tuesday. The main thought of the parable in Luke is that many will find themselves outside the kingdom of God because of various earthly cares. This parable, however, is connected with the parable of the evil husbandmen. Both parables, as well as the ones that come after this one in Matthew's account, speak of various servants who are either persecuted or killed, as well as the terrible punishment awaiting those who persecute the servants. In this parable, as in the first one, those who are called are representative of the entire nation of Israel; the servants of the king are the Old Testament prophets. The destruction of the killers and the burning of their city must be understood as the destruction of Jerusalem and the scattering of the Jewish nation. The call to the wedding feast of all whom the servants meet is the call of all mankind into the kingdom of God, which occurred after the Jews rejected the apostolic preaching (see Acts 13:46). All are called to the bridal feast in the kingdom of God, both good and evil people, for entry into the feast is not limited to those who are holy or full of merits. Not deeds, but the mercy of the One who calls is the only prerequisite for entry. The judgment—the separation of the good and the evil, those who are worthy to remain in the kingdom of

God and those who are not—will be later, at a different time. Therefore, whoever is called once must walk worthily of this calling—in other words, he must put on bridal clothing.

In the ancient time, kings and princes in the East would give guests special festal clothing in which they would be expected to appear at the feast. In the same way, every person who is called into the kingdom of Christ is given (in baptism) bright clothing of spiritual purity. Whoever disdains this clothing and comes to the feast in clothing dirtied by sin is worthy of condemnation and punishment. As St John Chrysostom says: "To enter in dirty clothing means to lose grace due to an impure life. Therefore the parable clearly says: he remained silent. Since he had nothing with which to defend himself, he condemned himself and was subjected to terrible punishment."[57]

Those who chose not to wear the festal clothing would routinely be cast out of the brightly lit chambers of the feast into the dark area outside (the outer darkness), where they would gnash their teeth from the cold. In the same way, on the Dread Judgment, unrepentant sinners will be cast out of the community of those being saved in the Church of Christ, since they soiled their baptismal robes with their sinful impurity.

The concluding thought of this parable is the same as in Luke: "Many are called, but few are chosen." This means that many are invited to the kingdom of Christ, all who will listen to the preaching of the Gospel, but true members of this kingdom are not all who are called, only a chosen few. Thus, all the Jews were called into the kingdom of Christ, but only a few entered into it; it is the same with all other nations. Even though many were called, among them there were, and will be, only a few true Christians.

Having heard all this, the shamed members of the Sanhedrin began to speak among themselves once again about what means could be employed against the Lord, and they thought to send people who could catch Him saying something unlawful in order to make His arrest seem more legitimate.

THE LORD'S ANSWER REGARDING PAYING TAXES TO CAESAR
(MATT 22:15–22; MARK 12:13–17; LUKE 20:20–26)

Among their disciples and the party loyal to Herod (to whom many Jews did not want to pay taxes since he was not a Jew), the Pharisees chose a few cunning people whom they sent to speak to the Lord Jesus Christ with the ill-intentioned question: "Is it lawful to pay taxes to Caesar, or not?"

The crafty question was intended to yield no satisfactory answer. On the one hand, if the Lord said that one had to pay taxes to a pagan emperor so hated by the Jews, He would risk alienating the people; while on the other hand, if He said that one should not pay taxes, then the Pharisees would be able to immediately denounce Him before the Roman authority as an insurrectionist. In the question was hidden a certain way of thinking: the Jewish nation is the chosen people of God, which accepts only God as the legitimate King, and so cannot serve a foreign power, especially if it be pagan, or they risk acting in enmity to God who chose them. Consequently, what must they do? Pay a tax to a pagan Caesar or remain faithful to God?

The Lord answered wisely that one must do both—"Render therefore to Caesar the things that are Caesar's, and to God the things that are God's." In other words, fulfill all your commitments both to God and to the civil authority since the two in no way contradict each other.

SHAMING THE SADDUCEES WITH RESPECT TO THE RESURRECTION OF THE DEAD (MATT 22:23–33; MARK 12:18–27; LUKE 20:27–40)

After putting to shame the Pharisees and the Herodians with His wisdom, immediately He was accosted by the Sadducees, a sect that did not believe in the resurrection from the dead and life after death (see Acts 23:8). They constantly argued with the Pharisees, striving to prove that in the books of Moses not only are there no indications that the soul is immortal, but rather there are some commandments that contradict the teaching on the resurrection of the dead, such as levirate marriage. This is the reasoning with which they approached the Lord, asking Him to answer the question regarding an odd case of seven brothers who all concurrently married the same woman, then died. From the point of view of the Sadducees, this aspect of the law inherently denied the possibility of a future life, for "whose wife of the seven" brothers would the woman be in the next life?

St John Chrysostom appropriately remarks on the absurdity of such a case, for the Jews, so remarkable for their superstitions, would never take a wife whose husbands had the unfortunate habit of dying one after the other. The Lord gave the Sadducees a wise answer, accusing them that they do not understand what the future eternal life would be like because in eternity there is nothing fleshly or carnal, and people will live a different kind of life, a spiritual, angelic one. If people after death would completely be annihilated, then God, when He spoke to Moses from the burning bush, would not have said, "I am the God of Abraham, the God of Isaac, and the God of Jacob" (Exod 3:6), for "God is not the God of the dead, but of the living" (Matt 22:32). In other words, the dead forefathers were alive in God, for God cannot be the God of that which does not exist. St Luke adds that this answer even pleased the scribes, who could not contain themselves and even praised Him for speaking right, while the assembled people, seeing the shame of the Sadducees, were amazed at the wisdom of Jesus.

CONVERSATION REGARDING THE GREATEST COMMANDMENT OF THE LAW AND THE DIVINITY OF THE MESSIAH (MATT 22:34–46; MARK 12:28–37; LUKE 20:40–44)

The Pharisees, having found out that the rival Sadducees were publicly humiliated, assembled in the temple for a council and decided to offer Jesus what they believed to be the most difficult question regarding the most important commandment in the law. The cunning behind the question becomes obvious if we consider that the Jewish scribes distinguished between "greater" and "lesser" commandments and constantly argued about which ones were greater or lesser. Some considered the greatest commandment to be the one regarding sacrifice; others, the Sabbath; and still others, circumcision; but all of them agreed that external, ritual commandments were the most important.

The Lord answered their question with a direct citation from Deuteronomy (6:3): "'You shall love the Lord your God with all your heart, with all your soul, and with all your mind.' This is the first and greatest commandment. And the second is like it: 'You shall love your neighbor as yourself'" (see Lev 19:18). St Mark adds that this answer delighted the lawyer who had asked the question, and he exclaimed, "Well said, Teacher. You have spoken the truth." The lawyer's sincerity touched Jesus, and seeing that this sinner could yet be converted, the Lord said to him, "You are not far from the kingdom of God."

After all these unsuccessful attempts to catch the Lord speaking unlawfully, the Pharisees no longer dared ask Him about anything, but in order to show them how ignorant they were in the true knowledge of the Scriptures, and how ignorant their assumptions were regarding the Messiah, He began to ask them difficult questions: "What do you think about the Christ? Whose Son is He?" Without even thinking about it, they all answered, "The Son of David," of course, because David was promised that the Messiah would come from his line. The Lord answers them that if they think the Christ is only a man, then "how then does David in the Spirit [that is, inspired by the Spirit of God] call Him 'Lord,' saying: 'The Lord said to my Lord, "Sit at my right hand ...."'" If the Messiah-Christ were a mere descendant of David, then how could He already exist when David writes about Him, but if He did exist when David lived, and David called Him his Lord, then, consequently, He is not a mere man, as the Pharisees assumed, but is at the same time God, the God-Man. The Pharisees, blinded by the letter of the law and having lost the key to the correct understanding of the law, could not answer the Lord. In this way, the Lord revealed their ignorance of the law and simultaneously gave another proof of His divinity and pre-eternal existence. Having been so decisively defeated, the Pharisees no longer approached the Lord to ask Him any questions, and the majority of the people heard Him with joy (Mark 12:37).

Accusing the Scribes and Pharisees (Matt 23:1–39; Mark 12:38–40; Luke 20:45–47)

Having shamed the Pharisees and left them speechless, the Lord went on the offensive. In order to warn His disciples and the people against the spirit of pharisaical teaching, the Lord rebuked them fiercely, uncovering their greatest false teachings regarding the faith and the proper way of living. This speech is given in its fullness only by Matthew, while Mark and Luke give shortened versions. The Lord began His speech with the words: "The scribes and the Pharisees sit in Moses' seat," meaning they took Moses's place as leaders of Israel and gave themselves the exclusive right to teach and interpret the law of Moses. "Therefore whatever they tell you to observe, that observe and do, but do not do according to their works; for they say, and do not do." Here, the Pharisees are accused that they, while teaching the law, do not live by it.

"For they bind heavy burdens, hard to bear," like a heavy weight placed on beasts of burden, they put on them various and numerous commandments of the Mosaic law (see Acts 15:10), placing inordinately high expectations on their fulfillment to the last iota, but themselves do not help the people fulfill these difficult requirements. If the Pharisees do any of those things that they demand of others, then they do it not to please God, but so that others would see them and praise them. They "make their phylacteries broad," meaning they make extraordinarily large boxes on their prayer shawls in which to place the scrolls of the law, which were attached to the left hand and the forehead during prayer (see Exod 13:1–17; Deut 6:4–10; 11:13–22). The custom of wearing phylacteries came from a literal understanding of the words in Exodus 13:9: "It shall be as a sign to you on your hand and as a memorial between your eyes, that the Lord's law may be in your mouth; for with a strong hand the Lord has brought you out of Egypt." The Jews believed that these phylacteries were charms against evil spirits.

"And enlarge the borders of their garments." There are four tassels that are sewn to the edges of the outer clothing, and from these tassels were attached ribbons of ruby color. These garments were required by law to distinguish the chosen nation from all others. Pharisees, in vanity, liked to wear especially ostentatious ribbons.

"They love the best places at feasts, and the best seats in the synagogues." In the East, people did not eat sitting at a table, but reclining on special pillows that were laid near a *pi*-shaped, low table. The most important place was in the middle of the table, and the Pharisees always tried to sit there, while in the synagogues they demanded the seats nearest to the central raised platform. "But you, do not be called 'Rabbi,'" meaning do not seek to be praised as teachers, fathers, and rulers because in the proper sense for all people there is only one Father, God, and only one Teacher, Jesus Christ. This prohibition to be called "father" or "teacher" or ruler cannot be understood literally, as Protestants love to do, because there are many examples in the writings of the apostles where such names were used by the genuine followers of Christ (see, for the use of the term "father": 1 John 2:13; Rom 4:16; 1 Cor 4:15; Eph 6:4; Phlm 2:22; 1 Thess 2:11; 1 Tim 5:1; for the use of the term "teacher": Acts 13:1; Jas 3:1; Rom 2:20; 12:7; 1 Cor 12:28–29; 1 Tim 2:7; 2 Tim 4:3; Heb 5:12; for the use of the term "instructor" or "ruler": 1 Cor 4:15; Heb 13:7). It is impossible to concede that the apostles broke a commandment given by the Lord Himself to them. It would be more correct to understand these words to refer to the apostles directly, to warn them against raising themselves to a higher dignity than their right, reminding them that they are all equals, while the one who wants to be greater should be everyone's servant. It is not proper to give the honor appropriate only to God to any person, or to respect teachers and leaders more than is proper, as though teachers were speaking their own wisdom, not God's word.

"Woe to you, scribes and Pharisees, hypocrites! For you shut up the kingdom of heaven against men" in the sense that they themselves did not believe in the Messiah and tried to convince others to do the same. "For you devour widows' houses" by fooling widows with your false piety and taking their money for yourselves. "For you travel land and sea," you go great distances to convert proselytes from among the Gentiles, without worrying about instructing them in the true faith, instead corrupting them even more with the evil example of your hypocritical life.

"Woe to you, blind guides, who say, 'Whoever swears by the temple, it is nothing; but whoever swears by the gold of the temple, he is obliged to perform it.'" The Jewish teachers distinguished between "great" and "small" oaths, teaching that not abiding by a small oath is not a grave sin. Swearing an oath by a gift to the temple or by the gold of the temple was considered to be a great oath, while swearing by the temple or the altar itself was a small oath. The Lord indicates that to swear by any of these things means to swear by God Himself, and so none of these oaths can be broken. "Woe to you ... for you pay tithe of mint and anise and cumin, and have neglected the weightier matters of the law: justice and mercy and faith." The Pharisees, in fulfilling the law of tithes (see Num 18:20–24; Deut 14:22–28), brought in a tenth of herbs, which the law does not even mention because they are so insignificant. The Lord also accuses them of the fact that while they fulfill such trivial details of the law, they do not pay attention to more important matters such as justice in court procedures, mercy to the poor and miserable, and faithfulness to God and His Law.

"Blind guides, who strain out a gnat and swallow a camel!" This is a popular saying in the East. By paying attention to miniscule details while at the same time ignoring weightier matters, the Pharisees are similar to those who take great care to pull a mosquito out of a drink, while they do not even think to swallow a camel whole (of course, this is an intentional hyperbole). In other words, they pay attention to the small sins, while ignoring or even allowing the big ones. "You cleanse the outside of the cup and dish, but inside they are full of extortion and self-indulgence." The outside of the cup, which the Pharisees always carefully washed, is contrasted to that which is inside the cup—food gotten through extortion and unfairness. One must first pay attention to inner purity, to gather one's daily bread in a just manner.

"You are like whitewashed tombs." Every year on the fifteenth of Adar, the caves that were used to house the dead were whitened so that people would not accidentally approach and touch them, since touching a tomb, according to the law, meant that you would be unclean for seven days (Num 19:16). Whitened graves seem to be beautiful from the outside, just like the Pharisees, who put on the appearance of righteousness, while truly they were hypocrites and breakers of the law. Later, the Lord accuses the Pharisees for their building beautiful graves for the prophets and raising monuments to the righteous men who were killed by their fathers. It appears as though they are honoring the killed prophets, but actually they are even worse than their fathers because they are proud of their ancestry, for they are planning on doing even more than they did—killing the Lord Himself. "Fill up, then, the measure of your fathers' guilt," meaning that they will be even worse than their fathers in their killing of the righteous.

"I send you prophets." Here, Christ is speaking of the apostles and their fellow preachers of the Gospel; here, the Lord foretells that they will persecute the apostles like their fathers persecuted the prophets and killed them. "That on you may come all the righteous blood." Being evil, the Pharisees will take on themselves the responsibility for the deaths of all righteous men that were ever killed, by them and their ancestors, beginning with the blood of Abel, killed by his brother Cain, and ending with the blood of Zechariah, son of Berechiah, killed between the altar and the sanctuary. Some consider this Zechariah to be the one killed by Joash, though that Zechariah's father was Jehoiada, but it was not unusual for Jews to have more than one name. The other common interpretation (St Basil the Great, Gregory the Theologian, and others) is that this Zechariah is the father of John the Baptist. For all the crimes committed by the leaders of the Jewish nation, the scribes and Pharisees, the Lord pronounces a harsh condemnation on Jerusalem, "See! Your house is left to you desolate." This occurred only thirty-six years later, in A.D. 70, when Titus Flavius at the head of a Roman army razed Jerusalem to the ground.

The Lord speaks these words with great sorrow, showing His love for this stubborn and cruel nation, like the love of a hen for its chicks. "You shall see Me no more till ye shall say, 'Blessed is He who comes in the name of the Lord!'" Here, the Lord indicates not the triumphant entry, which already occurred, but His Second Coming, when even those who did not believe will, against their will, praise the divinity of Christ.

THE WIDOW'S MITE (MARK 12:41–44; LUKE 21:1–4)

In the so-called woman's court of the temple was the treasury, the very large coin jar into which the people would put their voluntary donations to the temple. Before the feast of Passover, it was customary to give a lot more than usual. Every person who went into the temple would put something into this treasury, depending on the person's zeal and financial status. Many rich people put in a great deal, but the poor old woman put two pennies, the smallest coin possible. The Lord said that this poor wife put in more than all the rest, not, of course, in terms of quantity, but relative to her general financial situation. All others gave money that they could easily do without, but she put in the last money that she had, and in this way she gave God everything that she owned.

THE LORD SPEAKS WITH HIS DISCIPLES ON THE MOUNT OF OLIVES ABOUT THE SECOND COMING AND THE END OF THE WORLD (MATT 24:1–51; MARK 13:1–37; LUKE 21:5–38)
Leaving the temple, the Lord and His disciples went to the Mount of Olives. Along the way, He foretold the destruction of the temple, which occurred in A.D. 70, with the final destruction occurring later, during the reign of Trajan. Titus Flavius wanted to preserve the temple because it was a marvel of architecture, but the providence of God must be fulfilled—a Roman soldier accidentally threw a charred log, which burned the temple to the ground. From the Mount of Olives, one could see a fantastic view of Jerusalem and the temple, and the disciples, alone with the Lord, continued the conversation He had begun about the future. The disciples believed that Jerusalem would stand until the end of the world, and so they asked the Lord a double question: "When will these things be? And what will be the sign of Your coming, and of the end of the age?"

The Lord answered in the same way as they asked, without distinguishing the two events in correspondence with the disciples' limited understanding. From the prophet's point of view, events that are near and far away sometimes show themselves as if on one painting, and in perspective, from a distance, they seem to melt into one event, especially if one event serves as a precursor to a later one. Here, it is doubtless that the destruction of Jerusalem and the horrors that would accompany it are a foretaste of those terrors that will occur at the end of the world before the Second Coming of Christ. And at the same time, the Lord lets them understand clearly that the Second Coming and the end of the world will not occur soon after the destruction of Jerusalem.

The first sign of the coming judgment of God is the appearance of false christs. The historian Josephus writes that before Jerusalem's fall there truly were numerous messiahs. The second sign will be wars, both geographically near and far away. But these wars and natural disasters will only be the beginning of the coming horrors that, in their heaviness, the Lord compared with giving birth. The third sign is the fierce persecution that will occur against the disciples and followers of Christ, which are well documented in the Book of Acts and history itself (see Nero's persecution and others). The mere name "Christian" became hated by the pagans, as a result of which countless numbers of martyrs were killed for Christ.

"And then many will be offended," meaning many will deny their faith and will give up their own brothers to be killed and martyred in order to save themselves. False prophets will arise. During the time of Jerusalem's siege, these false prophets promised the Jews that help would come from heaven. "But he who endures to the end shall be saved." Whoever will not deny Christ, despite the persecutions, and will not listen to the false prophets, will be deserving of eternal salvation. The fourth sign of the coming judgment will be the spread of the Gospel throughout the whole world. The Gospel will be "preached in all the world as a witness to all the nations," meaning Christ will not come a second time until the Gospel will be an accusing witness against those who, having heard it, refused to listen and believe. "Then the end will come."

In the near perspective, this end refers to Jerusalem's destruction, but all these same signs will also indicate the coming of the end of the world and the Final Judgment. In summary: (1) Jerusalem's judgment has already come as a result of its lawlessness and lack of love; in the same way, the end of the world will come about as a result of the increase of lawlessness in the world and the waning of love among people who will forget that they are brothers in Christ. (2) Just as in the last days of Jerusalem, so in the time before the end of the world, a great number of false teachers will appear. (3) Jerusalem fell after the Lord did everything He could to save it. It heard the Gospel preaching directly from His mouth. In the same way, the end of the world will occur only when all the nations of the world will have heard the preaching of the Gospel, so that on the Dread Judgment, they will also, as the Jews, have no justification.

Later, the Lord lists specific signs referring particularly to the fall of Jerusalem. "The abomination of desolation" that was foretold by Daniel the Prophet (Dan 9:27) is the Roman army carrying the graven images of the emperor and the eagles that were worshiped as gods into the temple of the true God. "Let them flee into the mountains, where there are many caves and hiding places in order to avoid the Romans. "Let him who is on the housetop not go down" (Matt 24:17). During times of calamity it was wise not to go down into the house to take something with you first, but immediately come down into the street and flee. In the same way, those who are in the fields should run and not come back home "to get his clothes," because in the field people usually did not wear their outer clothing. The historian Eusebius witnesses that the Christians in Jerusalem, remembering Christ's warning, at the first sight of the Romans truly did flee to Pella and other cities beyond the Jordan, and thanks to this, they were saved from all the horrors of Jerusalem's destruction.

The Lord admonishes them to pray for the calamities not to come in a time when it would be difficult for people to run away far, referring to winter conditions and to the Sabbath rules that one could not travel more than 2000 cubits on a Sabbath. "For then there will be great tribulation," so great, in fact, that all Jews would have been destroyed, if there were not among the Jews some "chosen," that is, faithful to Christ, for whom "those days were shortened." Flavius Josephus writes that truly "all the calamities that mankind has suffered through were nothing compared to what happened to the Jews."[58] During the siege and the war, more than one million Jews were killed. Most of them died of hunger, which was so terrible that there was a case of a mother killing and eating her own child. A huge number of Jews were crucified on crosses, and in this way, the terrible oath that the Jews themselves uttered was fulfilled, when they demanded that Pilate crucify Christ ("His blood be on us and on our children," Matt 27:25). All these calamities were the fulfillment of a prophecy uttered by Moses (Deut 28:49–57). Titus, the war leader who besieged Jerusalem, wanted at first to force the Jews to give up the city by starving them, but the emperor required him to return to Rome more quickly than he expected, and he decided to storm the city, which lessened the time of suffering for the Jews.

After this, the Lord once again began to speak of His Second Coming: "For false christs and false prophets will rise and show great signs and wonders to deceive, if possible, even the elect." These false miracles will even fool some of the righteous. According to the Apostle Paul (2 Thess 2:9–10) and the Apocalypse (chap. 13), these miracles will be performed by the Antichrist and his servants. The appearance of the Son of Man will be like lightning, meaning that it will be immediately apparent to everyone. In contrast to the false messiahs who will hide either in hidden rooms or in the desert, the true Messiah, when He begins His judgment of the world, will make it obvious and terrifying all over the world, where there will be spiritually dead sinners, similarly to how scavengers fly from all over, attracted by the scent of a dead body. "Immediately after the tribulation of those days," as soon as the calamities that will come upon Jerusalem end, the people will give themselves up to loose living (see Matt 24:37–39). St Luke adds to this that Jerusalem will be overcome by the Gentiles until the time of the Gentiles concludes. In other words, there may be a great deal of time between the destruction of Jerusalem and the Second Coming, during which, according to St Paul, all of the nations will enter the Church of Christ and will become the new, spiritual Israel (Rom 11:25).

"After the tribulation of those days, the sun will be darkened, and the moon will not give its light." Although these words are not as specific in indicating a long period of time between the destruction of Jerusalem and the end of the world, they do let the reader understand that after the destruction of Jerusalem, there will be other days that will be incomparably worse than the horrors of the Jewish war. The Greek text of this verse allows the following paraphrasing: "Do not think that after the destruction of Jerusalem, the Second Coming will immediately come. No, it will be otherwise. Other days will come before that event. Then, the sun will darken and the moon will no longer cast its light."

St Matthew uses the word "immediately," but in the Scriptures, the word does not usually mean "occurring without delay after another event," but only "suddenly," which is how it is translated into the Russian. The word "immediately," when used in the ancient prophetic sense, can sometimes encompass entire centuries (Bishop Michael). "The powers of the heavens will be shaken," meaning the entire cosmos will begin to fall apart. Characteristics of this terrible time are given in more detail by St Luke (21:25–26): there will be earthquakes, insurrections, the sea will rise up in fury, and people will be in despair from fear and the expectation of continuing natural disasters that begin to take up a universal character.

"Then the sign of the Son of Man will appear in heaven." St John Chrysostom considers this sign to be the cross, which will appear before the coming of Christ Himself, as the emblem of the conquering king is carried before him in triumph. This will be the sign that will force those who did not believe in Christ, the Jews and all godless people, full of pointless and belated repentance, to cry out, "Blessed is He who comes in the name of the Lord!" All the unfaithful will then begin to weep, seeing how mistaken they were, living in the darkness of lack of faith. "And they will see the Son of Man coming on the clouds of heaven with power and great glory."

At the sound of the mystical trumpet, the dead will be resurrected, and the angels will gather all the people from all ends of the earth. Even in Moses's time, the Jews were called together by silver trumpets—this method of gathering people became a custom and was used by the Jews in the rest of their history (Lev 25:9; Num 10:2; Judg 3:27), which is why the Saviour uses this image now, so familiar to all the Jews, in order to describe a certain action of God, which will summon the angels to gather "His elect from the four winds," from all the ends of the earth. The angels will also gather "all workers of iniquity" (see Luke 13:27), for eternal damnation.

"Now learn this parable from the fig tree." The coming of summer is judged by the leaves on the fig trees that grow in profusion on the Mount of Olives together with the olive trees, and in the same way the coming of the end of the world should be discerned by those signs of the times that the Lord already described. "This generation will by no means pass away till all these things take place." "These things" are put in conscious contrast with "that day and hour" (Matt 24:36). The destruction of Jerusalem did occur within the lifespan of those who followed Christ. But this expression can also be attributed to the end of the world. In that case, according to St John Chrysostom, "this generation," refers to the generation of those who seek the Lord (Ps 23:6), the generation of those who believe in Christ, who, despite all horrors, will remain until the end of the world.

"Heaven and earth will pass away, but My words will by no means pass away." This is a confirmation of the truth of the uttered prophecy. Seeing how exactly the Lord's words were fulfilled in the Jewish wars, no one can doubt that everything He said about His Second Coming will also occur as He described it. "But of that day and hour no one knows." Mark even says that "the Son" does not know about it either, of course as a man, not as God. According to Luke, people will live as they did before the Flood—aimlessly and wantonly—and the day of the

Second Coming will come suddenly, like a net falling on all those living on the face of the earth (Luke 17:26–27; 21:34–35). This comparison of the last days to the days of Noah is also found in Matthew.

"Then two men will be in the field." These words show how quickly and suddenly the division between righteous and sinner will occur, even if they were close to each other in the moment of the Second Coming, doing the same work, or even sleeping in the same bed (Luke 17:34). "Watch therefore, for you do not know what hour your Lord is coming." Here naturally comes the necessity of constant vigilance. The Lord desired that we not sleep, spiritually speaking, not live carelessly, but be attentive to the signs of the times, and always be ready to meet Him by leading a righteous life. The coming of Christ is so sudden and unexpected that it is often compared with the coming of a robber in the night.

The subsequent parable about the good and the faithless stewards of the house has as its purpose the more vivid inculcation of the need for constant spiritual vigilance. This parable has a close connection to spiritual pastors and civil leaders, who must fear laziness in the fulfillment of their responsibilities, remembering that they will have to give an answer for their actions.

THE PARABLE OF THE TEN VIRGINS (MATT 25:1–13)

In this parable, the Second Coming of Christ is imagined as the coming of a bridegroom to the house of his bride. The bridegroom, who arrived with his friends (John 3:29; Matt 9:15), was met with great pomp, all the guests coming out to him with lit oil lamps. Since his coming was not always known in advance, the guests needed to keep some extra oil in reserve so that the lamps would not go out before the coming of the bridegroom. Using this image from the daily life of the East, the Lord compared the expectation of the Second Coming with waiting for the bridegroom, who must be met by ten virgins with oil lamps. Of the ten, five were wise, meaning they were prepared in advance with reserve oil, while five were foolish, meaning they did not bother to bring any oil with them, and their lamps began to go out. While they left to buy extra oil, the bridegroom came, the doors of the bridal chamber were closed, and they were not allowed into the feast by the bridegroom when they finally came back.

The wise virgins are symbols of true Christians who are always ready to meet the Lord; who have good deeds ("oil") in addition to their pure and sincere faith. The foolish virgins are symbols of Christians only in name, who do not take care for their spiritual life, who have no virtues. Such will not enter the bridal feast, meaning the kingdom of heaven, for the Lord said, "Not everyone who says to Me, 'Lord, Lord,' shall enter the kingdom of heaven, but he who does the will of My Father in heaven" (Matt 7:21). The last words of the parable, "Watch therefore," again indicate the necessity for constant spiritual vigilance and expectation to meet the Lord, the hour and day of whose coming is hidden from us.

ON THE DREAD JUDGMENT (MATT 25:31–46)

The full, vivid representation of the Dread Judgment of God over all mankind is given only in St Matthew's Gospel, in direct connection with the Lord's previous words regarding constant spiritual watchfulness and readiness to meet the Second Coming of Christ. The parable of the talents precedes the description of the Final Judgment, which is very similar to the parable of the pounds, which we have already analyzed in detail. The main idea of this parable is that every person must give an answer to God on the Final Judgment regarding the use and development of the gifts given from God, both spiritual and natural.

The description of the actual Judgment is preceded by Christ's comparing His Second Coming to a triumphal procession of a victorious king "in His glory." "He will sit on the throne of His glory," meaning that the Lord will appear as a King and Judge of the universe. "All the holy angels" will accompany Him, while all mankind will meet Him, both those who are still alive when He comes as well as those resurrected from the dead. Before His coming, the universal resurrection will occur, and the resurrected will arise in special, transformed spiritual bodies, while those still alive will also transform in the "twinkling of an eye" (1 Cor 15:25–54; 1 Thess 4:16–17). "And He will separate them one from another, as a shepherd divides his sheep from the goats." Here, the sheep are symbols of the righteous, since they are an image of innocence and simplicity used often in the Scriptures, while the goats are those who are condemned, since traditionally they are associated with all negative moral qualities (see Ezek 34:17). The sheep will be put on the right hand, since the right hand of the king is the place of honor, given to those closest to the king. The goats will go to the left, the side of lesser honor, in this case, the side of the condemned. "Come you blessed of my Father, inherit the kingdom prepared for you from the foundation of the world."

Those Christians who have been found worthy of the blessing of God the Father in the New Testament are often called inheritors of promised blessings, as true children of God, to whom belong all blessings prepared by God for mankind (Rom 8:17; Gal 4:6–7; Heb 1:14). God saw their works from eternity, and so from eternity He determined their rewards—for their virtues, the kingdom of heaven; for evil deeds, suffering. As we see from this picture of the Dread Judgment, the kingdom of heaven will be inherited by the righteous for their good deeds of love and mercy to their neighbors. Faith is not mentioned here because it is assumed already in the actions of love, which are the fruits of faith (John 13:35; 1 Cor 13:1). Equally, prayer and all other labors of faith are not mentioned because without them true love for one's neighbor is impossible, neither are sincere, guileless works of compassion and mercy. Only works of compassion are mentioned here because they prove true faith and Christian piety (Jas 2:14–26; 1 John 4:20–21; 1 John 3:15–18).

The answer of the righteous proves their humility and knowledge of their own unworthiness. This is the law of moral perfection—the more a person perfects himself morally, the more he realizes the worthlessness of his perfections. The Lord calls His followers His brothers, as near ones, as ones related to Him in spirit, in disposition, in sufferings. He calls them "the least of these" because of their humility and poverty. "Depart from Me, you cursed." "Cursed" here means "lacking in the gifts of blessing." They are condemned to "everlasting fire prepared for the devil and his angels." Here, fire represents the worst degree of suffering, since death by burning is the cruelest form of execution. This image is also taken from the valley of Hinnom to the southwest of Jerusalem, where the Jews during their times of unfaithfulness would bring sacrifices to Moloch, and later all forms of uncleanness were dumped, including the bodies of the dead, where a fire always burned to purify the air. This is why this valley was called the valley of fire, Gehenna, and became an image of hellfire.

These eternal sufferings are indicated for those who rose up against God—the evil spirits; but since sinners become participants of their evil, they are condemned to the same punishment. "And these will go away into everlasting punishment." The punishment of sinners, despite some popular false teachings, will never end, because they willingly rejected the Law of God. These tortures, as many believe, will consist of terrible but fruitless accusation by the conscience. Some people already experience this hellish suffering on earth (for example, the feeling of inconsolable sorrow). Equally endless and eternal will be the blessedness of the righteous, and they also foretaste this blessedness in this life.

GREAT AND HOLY WEDNESDAY: THE COUNCIL OF THE CHIEF PRIESTS AND ELDERS REGARDING THE DEATH OF JESUS, JESUS'S ANOINTING BY THE SINFUL WOMAN IN THE HOUSE OF SIMON THE LEPER, AND THE BETRAYAL OF JUDAS (MATT 26:1–16; MARK 14:1–11; LUKE 22:1–6)

Having concluded all the aforementioned conversations with His disciples, the Lord once again foretold the imminent hour of His suffering in words written only in St Matthew's Gospel, "You know that after two days is the Passover, and the Son of Man will be delivered up to be crucified." The Passover begins on 14 Nisan (near the end of March according to our calendar) in the evening, and in that year, it fell on a Friday (John 19:14). Therefore, these words were uttered either on Tuesday evening or Wednesday.

Passover is the most important and triumphant feast for the Jews. It is celebrated in remembrance of the deliverance from Egyptian bondage. The word "Pesach" means "salvation" or "passing," which recalls the moments when the angel that killed all Egyptian firstborns passed by the Jewish houses and spared the Jewish firstborns (Exod 12). Together with the feast of the unleavened bread, which began on the second day of the Passover, the entire feast was celebrated for eight days, from the eve of the fourteenth to the twenty-first Nisan. On the tenth of Nisan, the heads of families had to choose a year-old lamb, without blemish, which would then be sacrificed on the fourteenth after the proper preparation, and then would be baked. In honor of the way the Hebrews sprinkled their doorways with blood to ward off the avenging angel, the altar was also sprinkled with blood, which is why the lamb was sacrificed near the tabernacle, and later in the temple itself. The prepared lamb was then eaten in its entirety, without leaving a bone or any other pieces, with unleavened bread and bitter herbs. This meal began immediately after sunset on the eve of 14 Nisan. First of all, they drank from the common cup filled with wine and water. Having given praise to God, the head of the family drank from it, then all the assembled drank in their turn—this was called the "first cup."

After this, they washed their hands, giving thanks to God. Then they would slowly begin to eat the Paschal lamb with the unleavened bread, the bitter herbs, and a thick sauce made from dates, figs, and vinegar, all the while praising God, after which the platters were taken away and once again a cup of wine and water was passed around. The platters were taken away in order to inspire the curiosity of children, and to take the opportunity to explain the various aspects of the feast to them (Exod 12:26–27).

The head of the family would tell the history of the Hebrews in bondage to the Egyptians, being freed, and the establishment of this feast of Passover. When the platters were once again brought in, he would utter these words: "This is the Passover which we eat in memory of how God had mercy on our homes in Egypt." Raising up the unleavened bread and the bitter herbs, he explains that the bread is a reminder of the speed of the flight from Egypt, while the latter reminds of the bitterness of Egyptian bondage. Then, the first alleluia is sung (Ps 110–14), a short prayer read, and once again wine passed around, called the "second cup." Again they washed their hands and again they ate some of the lamb, the bread, and the herbs. The lamb must be eaten in its entirety by the beginning of the next day. Then, once again, they would wash their hands and drink the "third cup," called the "cup of blessings," since the one drinking it, usually the head of the family, would read a special prayer, blessing God for His special grace. In conclusion, the fourth cup is drunk, called "hillel," since after it the second alleluia is sung (Ps 115–18). This Paschal meal, based on the universal conviction of liturgists, was the foundation for our own Eucharistic service.

The words "will be delivered up to be crucified" show the divine omniscience of God. He knew the day of His death, even though His enemies expressly said, "Not during the feast, lest there be an uproar among the people."

All three Synoptics write of the high council of the Jewish elders when they once again decide to put Jesus to death. Fearing an insurrection, which could have easily begun on account of the people's love for Jesus, they decided to take Him by cunning, quietly away from the people and after the feast had passed. But when they found an appropriate traitor, they decided not to wait for the feast, filled with hatred for Christ. St Matthew writes that this council was held in the house of the high priest Caiaphas, in the courtyard. Courts in the East were found inside the house and were often places of meeting. Caiaphas's proper name was Joseph, while Caiaphas was either his nickname or his last name. He was the son-in-law of the previous high priest Annas, who was removed by the Roman proconsul.

Later, Matthew and Mark speak of the Lord being anointed by a certain woman in the house of Simon the Leper. This anointing is distinguished by tradition from Mary's anointing six days before the Passover, before the entry into Jerusalem. Simon the Leper was called this because he was apparently healed of leprosy by the Lord. Also according to church tradition, which is very beautifully memorialized in the services for Holy Wednesday, the woman who came to the Lord in order to anoint Him with precious myrrh was a repentant prostitute. She brought myrrh in an alabaster vessel. Myrrh is a sweet-smelling oil with various fragrances, usually made out of a base of pure olive oil together with various essences. Alabaster is the kind of marble remarkable for its lightness, translucence, and beauty. It was used to make vases, urns, and vessels for keeping fragrant oils. Being anointed with myrrh in the East was not only used for official purposes such as the consecration of kings and high priests but also in everyday life by rich and noble people for their own pleasure. Usually one anointed the hair, forehead, face, beard, and clothing (see Ps 22:5; 132:2; Eccl 9:8; and others). It was considered a sign of great respect to anoint someone's feet.

"But when His disciples saw it, they were indignant, saying, 'Why this waste?'" Not knowing the profound thoughts and deep repentance of the sinful woman, the disciples condemned her, knowing that their Teacher avoided all kinds of excess and considered works of mercy and compassion to be far more important than luxuries. But in this case, they were mistaken. The Lord justified her action since it came from warm faith and pain in her heart. "You have the poor with you always," meaning you can always do good to them, "but Me you do not have always," another hint about the coming passion. In addition, the Lord gives a special symbolic significance to this action: "For in pouring this fragrant oil on My body, she did it for My burial," for the ancient custom was to wash the bodies of the dead with fragrant oils. As a reward for her good deed, the Lord said that her actions would be forever remembered among Christians, which is true, because not only is this event written in the Gospel but it is included in our hymnography. The hymns of Great and Holy Thursday praise the actions of this woman, contrasting them to the betrayal of Judas, which occurred immediately after this event.

"Then one of the twelve, called Judas Iscariot, went to the chief priests and said, what are you willing to give me if I deliver Him to you?" The word "then" is not put here to strictly establish chronological order, but rather to establish a logical chain. Judas expected the Lord Jesus Christ to give him earthly goods, riches, and power. His avarice was losing patience with the Lord, seeing His complete nonacquisitiveness. He even began to reward himself by dipping into the bag of money that he was in charge of, as St John the Evangelist tells us (John 12:6). This event in the house of Simon the Leper finally convinced him that it was useless to wait for riches from a Teacher who taught willing poverty and self-denial. Disappointment with the Lord, Who, he believed, had fooled him and proven all his hopes to be useless, and a desire to use any possible circumstance for personal profit, made him into a traitor. Already knowing of the decision of the Sanhedrin to seize the Lord, he went to the chief priests to offer them his services (to deliver Christ to them in a secret place, away from the people) for money.

"What are you willing to give me?" These words show his sorrow and even hatred against his Teacher, whom he had already decided to betray, without particularly haggling for a price. Therefore, he agreed to a rather insignificant sum—the price for a good slave, thirty pieces of silver, no more than twenty or thirty dollars. They obviously chose this price in order to show their full disdain for the Lord, and also knowing that Judas was so grasping that he would take any money without arguing much. And truly, Judas agreed immediately without demanding any more, and "from that time he sought opportunity to betray Him," a moment when Jesus would be alone without the usual crowds surrounding Him. This sum of money also had symbolic significance; in it was fulfilled the prophecy of Zechariah, where thirty pieces of silver are all that the ungrateful nation considers the Lord's solicitude to be worth (Zech 11:12–13).

GREAT AND HOLY THURSDAY: THE MYSTICAL SUPPER
(MATT 26:17–29; MARK 14:12–25; LUKE 22:7–30; JOHN 13:1–30)

All four Evangelists tell of the last supper the Lord shared with His disciples before His passion, but not all of them do it with equal fullness. In addition, the timeline used by the Evangelists Matthew, Mark, and Luke regarding the day during which the Mystical Supper was held seems to contradict certain phrases that establish a different timeline in John's account. We know one thing without a doubt—the Mystical Supper occurred on the fifth day of the week, a Thursday by our reckoning; just as obviously, the Lord was condemned and crucified on the sixth day of the week, on a Friday, then was buried on the seventh, a Saturday, and rose from the dead on a Sunday. But there is some confusion and difference of opinion regarding the calendar date of the Mystical Supper—was it held on 14 Nisan, the eve of which marks the beginning of the Passover, or 13 Nisan, the day before the eve of the Passover? This confusion appears as a result of the following indications by the Evangelists themselves regarding the time of the supper: St Matthew—"Now on the first day of the Feast of the Unleavened Bread" (Matt 26:17); St Mark—"On the first day of Unleavened Bread, when they killed the Passover lamb" (Mark 14:12); St Luke—"Then came the Day of Unleavened Bread, when the Passover must be killed" (Luke 22:7); and St John—"Now before the feast of the Passover" (John 13:1).

Passover began on the eve of 13 Nisan, and consequently, if one were to keep to a strict biblical use of the words, "the first day of Unleavened Bread" could only be 15 Nisan, the second day of Passover. Evidently, Matthew, Mark, and Luke did not keep to this strict usage, but rather wrote colloquially. Apparently, colloquially, one could call "the Day of Unleavened Bread" not 15 Nisan, not even 14 Nisan, but 13 Nisan, the day before Passover, which is indicated clearly by the Evangelist John, who insists that the Mystical Supper was "before the feast of the Passover." In addition, St John has other proof that the Jewish Passover that year only began in the evening on Friday, when the Lord was crucified: (1) when those who brought Jesus to Pilate did not enter the Praetorium, lest they defile themselves and not be able to eat the Paschal lamb (John 18:28), and (2) the desire of the Jews to break the knees of the crucified men so that their bodies would not remain on the crosses on the high day of the first day of Passover, meaning they ate the Paschal lamb the night before, after they had crucified the Lord (John 19:31).

This begs the question why Christ decided to perform the Passover meal one day earlier than the accustomed day. (There is no doubt that the Mystical Supper was the traditional Jewish Passover meal, even though the apostles are not described as performing the customary rites, because their attention was entirely taken up by the establishment of the New Testament Passover—the communion of the Body and Blood of Christ.) It is possible that, since Passover in that year (14 Nisan) fell on a Sabbath, the lamb was killed a day earlier not to break the law concerning Sabbath rest. St Mark's account ("when they killed the Passover lamb") as well as St Luke's ("when the Passover must be killed") seem to agree with this supposition. In addition, it is well known that after the Babylonian captivity, the Jews, especially the Galileans, began to celebrate the major feasts a day earlier. There was apparently also a practice to allow the sacrifice of the Paschal lamb a day earlier for the sake of the Galilean pilgrims. This was done also for the sake of the priests, who had to perform 256,000 sacrifices in the course of a few hours on 14 Nisan, which is almost humanly impossible. Finally, there are some opinions that the Lord Himself prepared the meal a day earlier, knowing that He would be arrested and killed on the next day, so that His sacrifice on the cross, whose foreshadowing was the Passover lamb, would occur on the same day and hour when the Paschal lambs were being killed and eaten in Jerusalem. In any case, we know that the purpose of the Gospel of John was to fill any gaps in the accounts of the Synoptics, and so we must accept his direct indication that the Mystical Supper was performed by the Lord before the beginning of the Passover, not on 14 Nisan, but on 13 Nisan.

Even the mere preparation of the meal was miraculous. The Lord sent two disciples from Bethany into the city (Jerusalem), telling them that they would meet a certain person carrying an urn of water. They should follow after him, and say to the master of the house into which the servant carrying the water enters,

"The Teacher says, 'My time is at hand,'" I can no longer delay the celebration of the Passover and today "I will keep the Passover at your house with My disciples." The disciples, who were Peter and John according to St Luke, went and everything happened exactly as the Lord had said. The master of the house took them to an upper room already prepared for the feast, and they prepared the meal there. Of course, this is yet another example of Christ's divine omniscience. At the same time, the words of the Lord indicate a need for haste, considering the fact that all the great and final events of His earthly life were about to occur.

St John movingly relates the beginning of the meal: "Jesus knew that His hour had come that He should depart from this world to the Father, having loved His own who were in the world, He loved them to the end." Here we see the perfect symphony of Christ's divinity and humanity—as God, He knows of the closeness of the hour of His death and Himself walks toward it, while as a man, He sorrows that He will have to be parted from His beloved disciples, and this resulted in an especial expression of His love for them. This love He showed in its completeness during all the events and words spoken during the Mystical Supper.

St Luke said that the Lord began the meal with the words: "With fervent desire I have desired to eat this Passover with you before I suffer; for I say to you, I will no longer eat of it until it is fulfilled in the kingdom of God." This would end up being the last Passover meal that the Lord could share with His disciples in His earthly life, and instead of the Passover according to the law, which was merely a foreshadowing, He intended now to establish the true Pascha, the Mystical Supper of His Body and Blood, the mystery of the Eucharist. This would be the last Old Testament Passover for all of His disciples; after this, they would only commune of His Body and Blood until they would enter into the full communion with Him in the future blessed life, in the "kingdom without evening," as is sung in one of the troparia of the resurrectional canon. In this future life, the intimacy of communion of all true Christians with Christ can be compared to the closeness that the apostles felt to their Teacher at the Mystical Supper. Consequently, the meaning of Christ's opening words can be paraphrased thus:

"This Passover that you see before you is the last you will eat in this form, and it will not be repeated until it be fully completed in the future age, in the Church triumphant." In St Luke's account, the Lord immediately followed these words with the first cup of wine mixed with water, following the Passover ritual, and said: "I will not drink of the fruit of the vine until the kingdom of God comes," or, in St Mark's account, "until that day when I drink it new in the kingdom of God." The Church teaches us about this new wine when we sing the canon for the resurrection: "Come and drink the new wine—let us partake of the divine joy at the coming of the Kingdom of Christ." Therefore, the new wine is the joy of the kingdom of Christ, because wine is a symbol of gladness and joy.

One must assume that after these words of Christ, the Paschal food was eaten with the usual prayers and rites, which all the Evangelists decided to omit since their main purpose was to show the Lord's establishment of a new, Christian Passover—the mystery of the Eucharist. This New Testament meal began with the washing of the feet.

The Washing of the Feet (John 13:2–20)

There was a custom to wash one's feet before the beginning of a meal, a task usually performed by a servant. But this custom was not always followed (see Luke 7:44), and was evidently not usually performed in the small circle of Jesus's acquaintances because the Lord Himself wanted to show them an example of humility and self-denying love. St Luke writes that during the meal, the disciples began to argue among themselves about who was the greatest among them. Apparently, this argument became the reason for Christ to show them a true example of humility and love through washing of their feet.

Only St John speaks of this event, and in great detail, since it was usual for him to complement the other Gospel narratives. "Jesus, knowing that the Father had given all things into His hands, and that He had come from God and was going to God." The meaning of this phrase is the following: God the Father gave the God-Man all possible means to use for the salvation of mankind, whatever He would find useful, and this is the reason why He now prepares to do such an unusual act, so contrary to mere human wisdom. He gets up, and amid the general amazement of the disciples, He takes off his outer clothing so it would not hinder Him, of course, and remains only in a tunic, like a slave. Then He takes a towel, and also like a slave, he girds Himself with it, pours water into a basin, and begins to perform the responsibilities of a servant, washing the feet of His disciples and wiping them with the towel with which He was girded. This was the silent but profound testament of the Teacher to His disciples, the testament of humility and mutual service, without anyone raising himself up over another. What a powerful answer this is to the false Roman Catholic teaching regarding the primacy of the Apostle Peter over all the other apostles, the foundation for their false dogma of papal primacy in the Church!

"Then He came to Simon Peter." Here, we see that Simon was not the first apostle whose feet were washed, and apparently he did not even recline near Christ at the table (see John 13:24). Peter was astonished at the Lord's actions and found them to be inappropriate to His high dignity, which is why he dared, for the second time, to contradict the Lord (see Matt 16:22): "You shall never wash my feet!" For this contradiction, he heard a stern warning that if he would continue to stubbornly resist, putting his own reasoning above the mind of Christ, then he would have no "part" with Christ. In other words, he would be cast out of communion with Christ. Afraid at these words and on fire with love for his divine Teacher, Peter offers Christ to wash "not my feet only, but also my hands and my head." In other words, he tried to express his readiness to submit to his Lord even more than the others, who only had their feet washed.

Bishop Michael has the following to say concerning Peter's words: "How typical is this of Simon Peter's character, who decides to walk to the Lord on the waters and then cries out, 'I perish!'; who strikes the servant of the high priest with a sword, then runs away, who enters the inner court where Christ is being questioned, then denies Him, then walks away weeping bitterly!"[59] In His answer, the Lord indicates the deeper meaning of His actions and at the same time even consoles Peter after His stern rebuke. "Ye are clean, but not all of you." Here, He gives an obvious hint to the traitor Judas. Having finished washing their feet, the Lord explains the intention with which He did this, teaching them that they should serve each other with love, never considering any hard work done for another to be demeaning, and never becoming proud before one's brothers.

THE LORD DECLARES THAT HE WILL BE BETRAYED
(MATT 26:21–25; MARK 14:18–21; LUKE 22:21–23; JOHN 13:21–31)

St John gives the most detailed account of Christ's declaration regarding Judas because he was physically the closest to Christ during the meal, even reclining against His breast, as we see in the Gospel. After washing their feet, the Lord "was troubled in spirit" from the knowledge that even in these triumphant hours when He is establishing the greatest mystery of the communion of His Body and Blood and is preparing to give them their final instructions, the man who will betray Him is sitting among those assembled. Of course, the Lord wanted Judas to repent and not accomplish the terrible deed he intended to do, and so the Lord said, "Most assuredly, I say to you, one of you will betray Me." These words inspired a completely understandable confusion among the disciples; they were immediately upset that their beloved Master would be betrayed by one of their own.

Clearly understanding the profound fall of human nature to sin, none of them were sure if perhaps they would be the one to betray Him, and so asked, "Lord, is it I?" St John adds that they began to look at each other, doubting who would be capable of such an action. According to St Matthew, even Judas asked "Rabbi, is it I?" to which the Lord quietly answered, "You have said it," trying to induce him, one last time, to repent, but without success.

"Now there was leaning on Jesus' bosom one of His disciples, whom Jesus loved." This is how St John refers to himself in his own Gospel, not giving his name for humility's sake. It was usual for the diner to have his face and chest pointed toward the table, his left elbow bearing the weight of the body against a pillow, and the right hand free to reach toward the table, while the feet were stretched out away from the table so that the next person's head was not at the feet but at the chest of his neighbor. This is how John had his head "leaning on Jesus' bosom," meaning he was to Christ's immediate right at the table. Peter took advantage of this situation, and made a sign to John for him to ask the Lord about the traitor. This shows us that Peter was not physically near Christ and did not occupy the first place at Christ's right hand (once again speaking against the papist interpretation of Peter's primacy).

With special daring that was only possible for a dearly beloved apostle, John came very close to Christ's breast and asked "Lord, who is it?" And "Jesus answered, 'It is he to whom I shall give a piece of bread when I have dipped it.' And having dipped the bread, He gave it to Judas Iscariot, the son of Simon." The bread on the Passover meal was dipped in a special vessel that held a sauce of dates and figs. The head of a family would give out such pieces of bread as signs of favor. With this, of course, the Lord once again tried to awaken Judas's conscience. This sign was evident only for John himself. For the other apostles, the words concerning dipping the bread in the vessel had a more general ring to it.

"Woe to that man by whom the Son of Man is betrayed!" The Lord directs everyone's attention not to the wickedness of the traitor but to the unfortunate fate of the traitor, and even expresses sorrow for him. St John Chrysostom writes:

> But another may say that if it is written that Christ must die in this way, then why is Judas condemned? He merely did that which was foretold. But he did not do it with that intention, but rather with hatred in his heart. If you will not look at the goal of an action, you may even come to excuse Satan himself. But no, no! Both the one and the other are worthy of countless tortures, even though the cosmos was saved. For it was not the betrayal of Judas that saved us, but the wisdom of Christ and His great fore-knowledge which transforms the evil actions of others into our favor. What, you may ask, if Judas had not betrayed Him; would someone else have betrayed Him in that case? If all were good, then our salvation would not have been accomplished. God forbid! For the All-Wise Himself knew how to effect our salvation if there would not have been a betrayal. His Wisdom is great and incomprehensible. Therefore, lest someone think that Judas was a servant of Divine economy, Jesus calls him the most miserable of men.[60]

The Lord wanted to awaken his conscience by giving him the bread, a gesture of honor, but the opposite happened with the darkened soul of Iscariot: "after the piece of bread, Satan entered into him." Despite Christ's words of warning and even this magnanimous gesture calling him to repentance, Judas became even more hardened toward the Lord, as often happens with souls that have become mired in evil. The Lord, as the knower of hearts, saw what happened in the soul of Judas, but He did not want to accuse him publicly before the disciples, lest they take up forceful measures against Judas and have the pointless thought to act against divine providence, so He only said, "What you do, do quickly." This is a forceful command of the Lord, who thirsted to quickly fulfill the will of God and complete His redemptive sacrifice for mankind. At the same time, it was a good opportunity to free the community of disciples from Judas's presence and to establish the great mystery of the Eucharist *without* the attendance of Judas.

St John further insists that no one understood these words of the Lord, including John himself, who did not think that the betrayal would happen that very night, and everyone assumed that the Lord was giving Judas one of his usual tasks of purchasing whatever they needed—this time for the Passover meal itself. This is yet another indication that the feast proper had not yet begun; consequently, the Passover meal was prepared the night before the beginning of the Passover—13 Nisan. No buying or selling was allowed on the eve of the feast itself; you could not even find beggars begging, in order to give them alms, for all (both rich and poor) did not leave their homes, solemnly celebrating the feast.

Judas went out when it was night, as St John mentions, and Blessed Theophylact interprets this to mean that Judas the traitor was finally covered in the total darkness of avarice. Immediately, St John begins to describe the final conversation of Jesus Christ with His apostles, beginning with the words, "Now the Son of Man is glorified," which is liturgically read as the first of the twelve Passion Gospels on Holy Friday Matins. It is necessary, however, to assume that immediately after the exit of Judas, the Lord first established the mystery of the Eucharist, which John omits because of the existing detailed accounts in all three Synoptics, and only later addressed the apostles with the words that St John wrote down in such detail as an addition to the accounts given by the Evangelists Matthew, Mark, and Luke.

ESTABLISHING THE MYSTERY OF THE EUCHARIST
(MATT 26:26–29; MARK 14:22–25; LUKE 22:19–20)

The accounts in the Synoptics agree in many respects. The Lord took bread and blessing it, He broke it and gave it to His disciples, saying, "Take, eat; this is My body." The word for bread in the Greek is *artos*, which means "leavened bread" that was baked with yeast, unlike the word *azymos*, which is the usual Greek word denoting unleavened bread, the kind used by the Jews during the Passover meal. It must be assumed that this kind of bread must have been specially prepared by command of the Lord in order to establish a new sacrament. The importance of leavened bread is that it is alive, symbolizes life, while unleavened bread does not rise, and is in this way "dead bread." "Blessing" and "giving thanks" indicate a verbal expression of thanks to God the Father, as Christ did many times, such as in the moment before He raised Lazarus. The petition was, of course, answered in the same moment as it was asked, which is why it simultaneously became a reason to give thanks.

It is especially important to note that the Lord said, "*This* is My body" (emphasis added). He did not say, "This bread is my body," because in that moment the bread was no longer bread, but had become the true Body of Christ, with only the visible appearance of bread. The Lord did not say, "This is an image of My body," but "This is My body," a fact noted by both St John Chrysostom and Blessed Theophylact. As a result of the Lord's prayer, the bread took on the essence of the Body, keeping only the external appearance of bread. Blessed Theophylact further elucidates, saying, "Since we are weak and would not be able to eat flesh, especially human flesh, the Lord gives us bread, which in actual fact is flesh."[61] St John Chrysostom asks: "Why were the disciples not disturbed when they heard these words? Because Christ had spoken a great deal about this mystery, preparing them in advance"[62] (see John 6).

By "Body of Christ," we mean the entire physical substance of the God-Man, united indivisibly with His soul and His divinity. This same substance of the God-Man is given to us in the form of wine, not for the second time, but for the fullness of its visible manifestation, which is why the expression "communion under two species" is an exact expression, meaning "communion of one and the same substance."

But this does not mean that the Body can be replaced by the Blood, and that it is enough merely to partake of the Body alone. If this was the case, then the Lord would not have instituted the mystery under both kinds. And after He communed His disciples with His body, He took the cup, and once again gave thanks, that is, once again through prayer He invoked the Spirit of the Father who changes the wine into the true Blood of Christ, saying, "Drink from it, all of you. For this is My Blood of the new covenant, which is shed for many for the remission of sins." It is not by accident that the Lord said "all of you." Wine could not be divided like the broken bread, which the Lord Himself broke and divided among His disciples. The cup was one, and was given from one disciple to the next. In order not to deprive any one of them of His Blood, Christ tells all of them to drink of the cup.

Here, once again, it is impossible not to consider the incorrectness of the Roman Catholic practice, which deprives the laity of the Blood of Christ. "Since strong food cannot be taken by all," explains Blessed Theophylact, "but only by those who have reached mature age, while anyone can drink at any age, then for this reason the Lord said, 'drink of it *all of you*.'"[63] Again He says, "This is My Blood," not just an image, not a symbol of blood, but genuine and actual blood. What does "of the new covenant" mean? St John Chrysostom explains: "As the Old Testament had its oxen and calves, so the New has the Blood of Christ. By this the Lord also shows that He suffered death, which is why He mentions the covenant and remembers it with the old, because the old was also renewed by blood."[64]

The word "covenant" in its original meaning is synonymous with "testament." The covenant in this sense contains within itself a promise, but with the promise also the conditions for reception of the promised gifts, in this case—following the commandments of God. From this point of view, the word "covenant" can be defined as an agreement between man and God. An agreement is always witnessed and confirmed by something. The Lord wants to say that this new agreement between mankind and God, instead of the old, is confirmed by His Blood, "which is shed for many for the remission of sins." This means that the suffering and death of the only begotten Son of God became the sacrifice of atonement for the sins of the entire human race (but note that He says "many," not "all"), by which are then forgiven all those who believe in Christ and commune of the most pure Body and Blood of Christ.

St Luke and St Paul (1 Cor 11) say that the Lord also said: "Do this in remembrance of me." However, this in no way means that the Eucharist is simply a remembrance of the Mystical Supper, as the Protestants believe. Christ said this because He would no longer be with His disciples and followers in a visible way and, when they enter communion with Him mystically through eating His Body and Blood, they will remember His first communion with them, accomplished in the body. In the Book of Acts, in the Epistles of St Paul, and in many ancient Christian writings, we find a great number of proofs of the fact that every prayerful gathering of Christians in the early times was accompanied by communion of the Body and Blood of Christ in the visible form of bread and wine. In the first centuries of Christianity, all Christians, except those excommunicated for reasons of penance, came to church on Sundays and feast days and communed every time they were in church.

THE DISCIPLES ARGUE ABOUT PRIMACY (LUKE 22:24–30)

St Luke tells that after communion, the disciples immediately began to argue regarding who was the first among them. When the Lord washed their feet, He humbly showed them by example that they must serve each other, but through this He did not completely destroy the ideal of hierarchy, nor did He make His Church an association of total equality, since He never denied His own status as Lord and Master, even while He washed their feet. Once again instructing the disciples, the Lord said that even the greater must serve others. If one were to take the Roman Catholic position that the Apostle Peter was the head of the apostles, then the very presence of this argument would be an absurdity, and the Lord should have ended it by confirming that the first among them was Peter. But the Lord says something completely different—as in other similar circumstances, the Lord only tells the apostles that they should not strive to be first, but only should think of serving each other. He also promises them that for their faithfulness to Him they will inherit the kingdom of heaven and will all equally sit on thrones to judge the twelve tribes of Israel, meaning they will all receive equal honors in the future life.

THE LORD'S PARTING WORDS TO HIS DISCIPLES
(JOHN 13:31–38; 14; MATT 26:30–35; MARK 14:26–31; LUKE 22:31–38)

This remarkable and touching conversation between the Lord and His disciples is given in its fullness by St John; St Luke gives a short version, while the Evangelists

Matthew and Mark only mention the Lord's prophecy regarding Peter's denial and of His meeting with the disciples after the resurrection in Galilee. This speech in its entirety is extremely expansive and takes up several chapters. Together with the "High Priestly Prayer" that immediately follows it in St John, it is read in its entirety as the first of the twelve Passion Gospels at Holy Friday matins.

According to St John, the Lord began this parting discourse immediately after Judas left with the words, "Now the Son of Man is glorified, and God is glorified in Him." However, it would be correct to assume that this conversation was not begun immediately after Judas's departure, but after the institution of the mystery of the Eucharist, which St John omits, since the Synoptics all give a detailed account of it. Having given His disciples His Body and Blood, and seeing the mystery of atonement as though already completed, as though He were already brought as a sacrifice and the victory over all the powers of the enemy were already accomplished, the Lord exclaimed the aforementioned introductory words, which sound quite victorious.

Now, on this terrible and mystical night, the glorification of the Son of Man has come, which is at the same time the glorification of God the Father, who gave His Son as a sacrifice for the salvation of mankind, and this earthly glorification of His Son is the beginning of His future heavenly glorification as the victor over death and hell. Desiring to bring His disciples from their disturbed frame of mind brought about by the thought of the imminent betrayal at the hands of one of their own, the Lord raises their thoughts to His divine power, which will be revealed in His forthcoming sufferings and resurrection and ascension to heaven. "And glorify Him immediately," meaning that Christ's humiliation will not last a long time, and soon His visible glorification will begin.

"Little children, I shall be with you a little while longer." This is an incredibly gentle mode of address that is found in no other place of the Gospel. It seems to have poured out of a deep sense of their impending separation during the heavy sufferings that were to test their faith so sorely. As I said before to the Jews, now I tell you as well, that I am leaving you along a path that you cannot take, leaving you in the world for the continuation of my work, "a new commandment I give to you, that you love one another; as I have loved you, that you also love one another." From My love for mankind I lay down My life for them and you must follow Me in this. The commandment of love for one's neighbor was given in the law of Moses, but Christ gives this commandment a new character, which it did not have in the Old Testament. This kind of love will even give up one's life in Christ's name for *one's enemies*! Such pure, selfless and self-denying love is a sign of true Christianity.

St Peter, full of fear and sorrow, asked, "Lord, where are You going?" The Lord confirms that now he cannot follow Him, but He gives him indications of the way in which he will follow in the future, the path of martyrdom. Then He foretells

Peter's denial, a detail which all four Evangelists include. Warning Peter against being too self-assured, when Peter began to insist that he would die for Him, the Lord said, in Luke's account: "Simon, Simon! Indeed, Satan has asked for you, that he may sift you as wheat." It is interesting to note that here the Lord calls him not Peter, but Simon, for the apostle who would deny Christ cannot be "the rock." This "sifting" refers to the temptation of the devil, which attacked all the apostles during the hours of their Master's suffering, when their faith in Him was almost shattered. With His all-powerful prayer, the Lord protected His disciples, especially Peter, from an irreparable fall; He allowed Peter to fall temporarily, so that he would be that much stronger and more firm in his faith, and able to confirm others in their own faith.

"But I have prayed for you," even though the danger from the devil threatened all the disciples, the Lord prayed especially for Peter, for he was in the worst danger due to his impulsive and fiery nature. "When you have returned to Me, strengthen your brethren." With these words, the Lord lets Peter know that after he repents of his denial, he will become for all a model of true repentance and an example of steadfastness. In answer, in all four evangelical accounts, Peter begins to insist on his total faithfulness and readiness to follow Him both to prison and to death. But the question arises: How could the denial of Peter have occurred if the Lord prayed for Him, to strengthen his faith? But Peter's faith did not waver; he denied Christ in a moment of fear for himself, not lack of faith in Christ, and we see that he immediately regretted his action and walked away weeping in remorse. All four Evangelists have Christ telling Peter that he will deny Christ three times before the cock crows, while in Mark, Christ even says that the cock will crow twice. This detail in Mark is explained by the fact that his account follows Peter's remembrances of Christ. The first crow of the rooster happens around midnight, the second before dawn. Consequently, the meaning of this detail is that Peter would deny Christ three times before the next morning came.

Evidently, Christ foretold this denial to Peter twice—the first time during the meal itself, described by Luke and John, and the second time already on the road to Gethsemane, after the conclusion of the meal, as in Matthew and Mark. Luke also adds another prophecy, that struggle and battle await the disciples: "When I sent you without money bag, knapsack, and sandals, did you lack anything?" While before, the disciples needed to worry about nothing because everywhere they found food and all other necessities while they walked and preached the Gospel in Judea and Samaria, now comes a different time, when the anger of people against their Master would be inflicted on them as well. The rest of the words regarding money bag, knapsack, even swords, of course one must not understand literally, but metaphorically. The Lord is just warning them that a very difficult period in their lives is about to begin, and they must prepare for it themselves. Hunger and thirst and misfortunes, enmity from others—this is what awaits them, and if their Master was considered by these people to be a criminal, then what good can His disciples expect from them? The apostles, in their naiveté, understood Christ's words literally, and said, "Lord, look, here are two swords." Seeing that they did not understand Him, the Lord ended the conversation with the words, "It is enough."

"Let not your heart be troubled"; the thought of Christ's imminent departure should not disturb the disciples because this departure is only a means to bring them into constant, eternal communion with Him. The Lord promises them that when that time should come, He will take them personally into the eternal habitations of His heavenly Father. Still clouded by their incorrect presuppositions regarding the earthly kingdom of the Messiah, the disciples did not understand these words of the Lord, and so Thomas said, "Lord, we do not know where You are going." In answer, the Lord explains that He is Himself the way along which they must travel to reach the Father, to reign in their prepared eternal mansions. "No one comes to the Father, except through Me." Since Christ is the Redeemer, only faith in His work of mankind's redemption can lead to salvation. "If you had known Me, you would have known My Father also," for in Christ is the full revelation of God, as He earlier said to the Jews, "I and My Father are one" (John 10:30). Since the disciples know Christ, they should also know the Father.

Of course, they still know Christ poorly, but were coming closer to true knowledge, that knowledge that the Lord gave to them when He washed their feet, communed them of His Body and Blood, and gave them His parting words. Similar in character with Thomas, and possessed of the same deliberateness, Philip asked the Lord, "Show us the Father, and it is sufficient for us," meaning, of course, a physical vision of the sort that the prophets had, for example. The Lord answered almost with regret at Philip's lack of understanding, and tells him that his request is a pointless one, since in Him, through His works, through His teaching, through His very Person—they should have long ago come to know the Father.

Continuing His instruction, the Lord promises to give them the power to work miracles and to answer all their petitions—the prayer in the name of the Lord Redeemer will work miracles. If the disciples, loving the Lord, will keep His commandments, the Lord promises to send them a Comforter Who will be with them for all time, the Spirit of Truth, Who will be like a replacement for Christ and thanks to Whom they will have constant mystical communion with Christ. "The world," meaning all those who do not believe in Christ and are antagonistic to Him, who in all ways are foreign to the Spirit, the Comforter, cannot accept Him, and He will remain with the apostles thanks to their intimacy with the Lord during His earthly life, and He will be in them, to remain with them for all time, when He descends on them on the day of Pentecost.

"I will not leave you orphans; I will come to you," both in visible form after the resurrection, and mystically through spiritual union in the mystery of the Eucharist, thanks to the mediation of the Holy Spirit. "You will live also," together with

Me, as the source of eternal life, while the world, spiritually dead, will not see the Lord. "At that day [that is, the Pentecost] you will know that I am in My Father, and you in Me, and I in you." You will then understand the essence of spiritual communion with God in Christ. The condition of this intimacy with God is love for the Lord and keeping His commandments. Judas, not Iscariot, called Levi or Thaddeus, who, evidently, still could not part with the favorite thought of the Jews—the earthly kingdom of the Messiah—understood the Lord's words to literally mean that He would appear physically to those who love Him and keep His commandments. He did not understand why the Lord wanted to appear only to them, not to the world as the founder of the great universal kingdom of the Messiah. The Lord explains that He is speaking of His mystical, spiritual appearance to His followers, repeating the previous thought of the necessity to love Him and keep His commandments. The world, which does not love Him and does not keep His commandments, is incapable of this spiritual communion with the Lord. The commandments of the Lord are at the same time the commandments of the Father. All this may yet be abstruse to the disciples, but when the Comforter will come, the Holy Spirit, Whom the Father will send in the name of Christ, He will teach the apostles, instructing them about everything and reminding them of all the teachings of Christ. He will reveal to them the mystery of the spiritual life, the life in Christ.

As the Passover meal is ended, the head of the family says to the whole family: "Peace be to you," and then the meal concludes with the singing of psalms. The Lord, desiring to leave the room where the meal was held, and hinting that the hour was near for His departure, followed the ritual, also offering them peace, but the peace from above, much more exalted than normal earthly peace: "My peace I give to you." This is the peace that completely harmonizes all the powers of the human soul, brings into order all the inner moods of a man, calms all disturbances and fear. This is the peace of which the angels sang on the night Christ was born. Therefore, the apostles should in no way be troubled or afraid.

The meal ended. The time came to leave the upper room on Zion, where the meal was held. Outside was the darkness of indeterminacy, fear of separation from Christ, and helplessness in the antagonistic world. Therefore, the Lord once again comforts the disciples with a promise to come to them, saying they should be glad that He is going to the Father, "for My Father is greater than I." This means, of course, that He is greater only in that He is the source of the Godhead (the Son, being born of the Father, takes His essence from the Father), greater, as God, than the God-Man. All must occur as it was written, as the Lord warned His disciples many times before. When all occurs as written, the disciples will be assured of the truthfulness of all of Christ's words. "I will no longer talk much with you"; there are only a few hours before the time when Judas will come with soldiers to seize the Lord. The Lord already saw with His spiritual vision the coming of His enemy, the "ruler of this world," Satan in the person of Judas with his soldiers, and the coming temptation in Gethsemane, where the devil would attack the Lord, tempting Him with fear of the hour of death, the last attempt to divert the Lord from His redemptive work for the salvation of mankind. The Lord adds that the devil "has nothing in Me," meaning that due to Christ's sinlessness, the devil can find nothing in Christ that he can use against Him. This is proof of the total moral freedom of the Lord, with which He, only by His love, gives away His life for the salvation of the world, in fulfillment of the will of His Father. "Arise, let us go from here," let us go to meet the enemy, the ruler of this world in the person of Judas the traitor.

Many exegetes believe that after these last words, one should read the account in Matthew, which is the same as the passage in Mark that reads, "And when they had sung a hymn, they went out to the Mount of Olives," meaning that they sang the customary "alleluias" (Ps 115–18), and went in the direction of the Mount of Olives; and that the rest of the conversation we have in John was given while walking. However, Bishop Theophan the Recluse believes that the conversation continued in the upper room, and only later did they leave, after the entire conversation and the high priestly prayer of Christ. The first opinion does seem to be more likely, especially since it concerns Christ as the vine, while the road to the Mount of Olives is covered in vineyards, and the Lord could have easily used them as a vivid illustration of His words.

CONTINUING THE PARTING WORDS OF CHRIST (JOHN 15; 16)

Therefore, walking through the vineyards and indicating the vines to the disciples, the Lord used them to illustrate the spiritual relationship between Him and His faithful: "I am the true vine, and My Father is the vinedresser." The Father, as the owner of the vineyard, works it Himself and through others—He sent His Son to earth, arraying Him like a fruitful vine, so that the dried and fruitless branches of humanity, when grafted into this vine, will accept from Him new life and will themselves become fruitful. Those branches that bring no fruit are cut off—whoever does not show his faith with works is cast out of the community of the faithful while still in this life, and finally in the day of dread judgment. Those who believe and bring fruits of faith, however, are purified by the power and action of the Holy Spirit, through various temptations and suffering, so that they would become even more perfect in moral life.

The apostles of Christ had already purified themselves by hearing the teaching of Christ, but in order to uphold and perfect this purity, they had to constantly work on it, to become united finally with Christ. Only he who is in constant spiritual communion with Christ can bring the fruits of Christian perfection: "Without Me you can do nothing." The branches that bring no fruit shall be gathered, "cast ... into the fire, and they are burned." The time of year when the Lord was giving this instruction was the time of cleansing the vineyards of dead branches, and maybe there were even fires before them in which these useless vines were being burned. This was a very effective image for spiritually withered people, for whom the fires of Gehenna are prepared in the future life.

Subsequently, the Lord promises His disciples that if they will remain in constant spiritual communion with Him, every one of their prayers will be answered, as long as they are according to the will of God. But in order for this to happen, they must remain always in the love of Christ and keep His commandments. The expression of their constantly remaining in His love will be their mutual love one for another, which must be strong enough even to willingly sacrifice one's life for another. "You are My friends if you do whatever I command you." Mutual love between the disciples will make them friends one with another, and since this is a union of mutual love in Christ, Who loved them with the same love, then they, by becoming friends with each other, will become friends of Christ as well. In the power of this Love the Lord revealed to them the will of God—this is proof that they are not slaves, but friends of Christ. Having revealed in all fullness His love for the apostles, which was expressed in the fact that He chose them for a great mission, the Lord finished this part of His instruction with a repeated commandment: "These things I command you, that you love one another."

Afterward, the Lord generally warns the disciples of those persecutions that await them from the world that so hates Christ (John 15:18–27; 16:1–3). They should not fear this hatred of the world, knowing that their divine Master was first subject to this hatred. This hatred is understandable because the Lord singled out the disciples from a world that only loves what belongs to it, what corresponds to its spirit of all types of sin, hatred, and evil. When they are persecuted by the world, the disciples should comfort themselves with the thought that they are not greater than their Master and Lord. However, the sin of the world is not forgiven since the very Son of God came into it with the preaching of repentance, but the world, seeing His wondrous works, still did not repent, but rather hated Him. To hate the Son means to hate the Father. Strengthening the disciples in their coming struggles, the Lord once again reminds them of the coming of the Comforter, the Spirit of Truth, Who proceeds from the Father, Who will be a witness of Christ to the world through the apostles. The Lord Jesus Christ Himself will send the Comforter, as part of His redemptive power, but He will send the Spirit not from Himself, but from the Father, for the eternal procession of the Spirit is from the Father ("who proceeds from the Father"), not the Son. This verse by itself completely refutes the Roman Catholic false teaching regarding the dual procession of the Spirit from the Father and the Son. The Lord further foretells that the apostles will witness to Him in the world since they saw His glory and were the first to accept His grace and truth.

"These things I have spoken to you, that you should not be made to stumble," so that your faith will not become shaken during the coming sufferings.

These sufferings will be so extreme that you will be cast out of the synagogues and killing you will be considered a deed pleasing to God. Jewish fanaticism truly did reach such a level of blindness. The Jews were convinced that whoever spills the blood of the unrighteous is doing the same thing as bringing sacrifice. Thus, the first victim of this fanaticism was the protomartyr Stephen. The persecutor Saul, who later became the Apostle Paul, also thought that by killing Christians he was doing the work of God (Acts 8:1; 22:20; 26:9–11; Gal 1:13–14).

Apparently, these words of the Lord so deeply depressed the disciples that the Lord began to console them, explaining how important His departure would be for them and for the entire world, for only in this case would the Comforter come to them, who will "convict the world of sin, and of righteousness, and of judgment." "Convict" is here used in the sense of "will bring out into the open," "will show how offensive and criminal sin is" (see also John 3:20; 8:9, 46; 1 Cor 14:24; Titus 1:9; Matt 18:15; Luke 3:19). This conviction is the same thing as moral judgment over the world. As a consequence of this judgment, only one of two paths are possible—following Christ through repentance or total spiritual blindness and hardening (Acts 24:25; Rom 11:7). This conviction of the world by the Holy Spirit must occur through the preaching of the apostles and their successors and all faithful in general, who have accepted in themselves the Holy Spirit and become His vessels.

The first subject of judgment and conviction is the sin of not believing in the Lord as the Messiah, the heaviest sin, for by it one rejects the Redeemer and Saviour of mankind. The second such subject refers to "righteousness, because I go to My Father," meaning that Christ truly is the Son of God, whose righteousness is completely different from the false righteousness of the Pharisees, and this is proved by God Himself, because He placed Christ on His right hand (Eph 2:6). The third subject is judgment over the ruler of this world, the devil, the same condemnation that awaits all who are unrepentant and hardened as he is. In this way, with the help of the Holy Spirit, the apostles will claim a great moral victory over the world that lies in sin, even though it will persecute them.

This prophecy of the Lord was fulfilled when the formerly terrified and frightened disciples, who ran in different directions as soon as the Lord was taken and then hid in a locked room for fear of the Jews, bravely and fearlessly preached Christ before thousands of people after the descent of the Holy Spirit, witnessing of Him to the whole world without fear, even when they were brought before kings and lords of the world (Matt 10:18).

"I still have many things to say to you, but you cannot bear them now." Here, the Lord tells His disciples that before they are illumined with the grace of the Holy Spirit, they are incapable of fully understanding and apprehending all that He must tell them, but the Holy Spirit, when He comes, "will guide you into all truth," meaning He will guide them in the understanding of the difficult aspects of Christian truth. All these revelations of the Holy Spirit will be taken from the same source of divine wisdom as the teaching of Jesus Christ. He will speak in the same way as Christ, all that which He "heard from the Father" (see John 3:32; 5:30; 12:49–50)," the Source of divine truth. By these actions of the Holy Spirit, Christ will be glorified, because He will teach the same truth that Christ taught, and in this way He will justify the entire work of Christ in the world.

"He will take of mine," because the Son and the Father are one, and all that the Spirit says belongs equally to the Son and Father. "A little while, and you will not see me." The Lord once again turns to the thought about His departure from the disciples, but immediately consoles them with the hope of newly meeting them, both physically after the resurrection and spiritually after the ascension. These words of the Lord appeared to some of the disciples to be incomprehensible, which is yet another example of their spiritual immaturity. The rest of the parting speech is dedicated to explaining these words of the Lord. The source of their lack of understanding was once again their incorrect idea about the earthly kingdom of the Messiah. If the Lord wanted to establish a kingdom on earth, then why is He leaving? If He does not want to establish such a kingdom, then why is He promising to return?

By saying "a little while, and you will not see Me," the Lord means that they will "weep and lament" as the world fulfills its murderous intentions and puts the Lord to death. "And again a little while, and you will see Me," this means that their "sorrow will be turned into joy," like the sorrow of a woman giving birth becomes great joy when a child is born. Here, Christ is speaking of the joy they will feel when they see Him risen from the dead, a joy that never left them for the rest of their lives: "and your joy no one will take from you." "In that day," in the day of the descent of the Holy Spirit, from which day the apostles will enter into constant spiritual communion with Christ, all the divine mysteries will become clear to them, and every prayer will be answered to make their joy grow even more.

"Because I go to the Father" means: "I have come from the Father into the world, and once again I leave the world, and return to the Father." So for Christ to go to the Father means to return to that state in which He was before the Incarnation, as the hypostatic Word. These words astonished the disciples with their clarity, and they mentioned how content they were that the Lord now spoke to them directly, not using any parabolic speech, and they expressed their fiery faith in Him as the true Messiah. This was a genuine and profound faith, but the gaze of the Lord saw the incompleteness of this faith, which was yet to be illumined by the Holy Spirit. "Do you now believe?" He asks. No, your faith is still insufficient, and it will not withstand even the first temptation, when you will all "be scattered, each to his own, and will leave Me alone."

The Lord finished His parting discourse with the disciples with these words: "These things have I spoken to you, that in Me you may have peace," that you may not fall into despair in the hours of the coming temptation, remembering that

I warned you about all of it in advance. In spiritual communion with Me, you will always find the necessary spiritual calm.

"In the world," which is at enmity with Me and My ministry, "you will have tribulation," but do not lose your courage, and remember that "I have overcome the world." Overcome by the great work of mankind's salvation through My death, I have defeated the spirit of pride and anger that reigned in the world through My humility and self-humiliation even to death, and I laid a good foundation for the transformation of this world from the kingdom of Satan to the kingdom of God.

THE HIGH PRIESTLY PRAYER OF THE LORD JESUS CHRIST (JOHN 17)

After these parting words, when, according to some exegetes they had already reached the river of Kedron on the way to the Mount of Olives, before crossing it He uttered aloud His triumphant prayer to God the Father. This prayer is generally called the "high priestly prayer," since in it the Lord prays as the Great High Priest, Who brings Himself as a sacrifice so significant for the world that its full meaning is not attainable.

"Father, the hour has come. Glorify Your Son, that Your Son also may glorify You." With these majestic words, the Lord begins His prayer: "The hour of My suffering is at hand, let Me reveal in this hour all the power of My love for You and the world created by You, so that through this redemptive sacrifice for mankind, Your glory will be revealed."

"As You have given Him authority over all flesh." The Father gave the Son the entire race of man, so that He could work out their salvation and give all men eternal life. The Lord determines eternal life to be the knowledge of God and the Saviour of the world, sent by Him. Before the spiritual gaze of the Lord, His entire work is already completed, and so He says, "I have glorified You on the earth." Now it is time for Him to enter divine glory even as a man, and this is the substance of His prayer: "And now, O Father, glorify Me." This is the first part of the prayer of the Lord, concerning Himself (John 17:1–5)

Having finished prayer for Himself, the Lord prays for His disciples, for those to whom He is giving the responsibility for the spread and foundation of His kingdom on earth (John 17:6–19). It is as though the Lord is giving an account to His Father about what He did—He revealed to His disciples the full and correct understanding of God, and they became special chosen ones of God, having accepted the divine teaching brought to them from the Father by the Son of God, and they understood the mystery of divine economy. Then the Lord prays for His disciples, that the Heavenly Father would take them under His special protection in this antagonistic world in which they will remain alone after His departure. May He preserve them pure and holy in spiritual unity of faith and love among each other, unity like the union of God the Father and God the Son. The Lord adds that He, when He was in the world, guarded them from falls, and "none of them is lost except the son of perdition," meaning Judas the traitor, "that the Scripture might be fulfilled" (see Ps 40:10). While praying to the Father for the preservation of His disciples from all evil in this world that has come to hate them, the Lord asks that they be blessed with the word of divine truth. In other words, He asks the Father to send them special gifts of grace that would help them successfully serve in the spreading of the teaching of truth in the whole world. He further says that He sanctifies Himself for their sakes, that is, He brings Himself as a sacrifice so that they can follow His steps and become witnesses (martyrs) and sacrifices for the truth.

The third part of the prayer is for all the faithful (John 17:20–26). The Lord prays for them, "that they all may be one, as You, Father, are in Me, and I in You; that they also may be one in Us: that the world may believe that You sent Me." The unity of the faithful in Christ must be like the union of God the Father with God the Son— here, of course, the unity presupposed is a moral one. Such a unity of all Christians in faith and love can make it possible for the whole world to come to believe in Christ as the Messiah. This is what we see in the first centuries of Christianity. Seeing the way the first Christians lived, Jews and Gentiles (except for those who had become blind spiritually and had hardened their hearts), were captivated by the exalted beauty of Christ's teaching and themselves became Christians. This oneness of all the faithful the Lord then defines as oneness in the glory of God and Christ.

The Lord already contemplates His Church in heavenly glory in unity with God in the kingdom of the Messiah (John 17:22–24), and says that this glory will force even the world that hates Christ to realize that the Lord Jesus is the true Messiah. The words: "Father, I desire that they also whom You gave Me may be with Me where I am." This is similar to a final will and testament of Christ before His death, which must be fulfilled, especially since the will of the Son of God is indivisible from the will of God the Father. Here, the Son of God Who gives His life for the salvation of the world asks God the Father to grant the faithful those heavenly mansions, which He already promised the apostles in the beginning of His parting discourse (John 14:2).

In the conclusion of this high priestly prayer, the Lord appeals to the Father as to the all-righteous giver of rewards (John 17:25–26). The Lord here shows the supremacy of the faithful over the rest of the world in that they have known God, and so they are capable of accepting the gifts of divine love. The Lord asks that God the Father set them apart before the world with His blessings and make them participants of that love that He has for the Son: "that the love with which You loved Me may be in them." For this, the Lord Jesus Christ Himself promises to "be in them," so that the love of the Father, indivisibly residing in the Son, would spread from the Son and on behalf of the Son onto those in whom the Son resides. And so, all-encompassing, all-restoring love will accomplish all things in the eternal kingdom of the Father, Son, and the Holy Spirit.

THE PRAYER IN THE GARDEN OF GETHSEMANE
(MATT 26:36–46; MARK 14:32–42; LUKE 22:39–46; JOHN 18:1)

As St John writes, when Jesus finished His prayer, "He went out with His disciples over the Brook Kidron, where there was a garden, which He and His disciples entered." Kidron, which means "black," was an insignificant rivulet that would only fill with water after heavy rains, while the rest of the time its bed was either dry or barely muddy. It ran through the valley Jehoshaphat and separated Jerusalem from the Mount of Olives. St John writes that there is a garden beyond the brook where Jesus and the disciples entered, not naming the garden and saying nothing about what occurred there until the coming of Judas with the soldiers. Matthew and Mark call the garden "Gethsemane," while St Luke merely indicates its placement on the Mount of Olives. All three Synoptics write of the Lord's prayer in the garden. "Gethsemane" means "stone press for olives." Evidently, this was an olive garden and a place where olive oil was made. It can also be assumed that this garden belonged to an owner who was friendly to Christ, for, according to John, the Lord Jesus Christ "often met there with His disciples" (John 18:2), which is why Judas knew to lead the soldiers there, sure that he would find the Lord there after the Mystical Supper, in which he was not mistaken.

Having entered the garden, the Lord stopped His disciples, saying, "Sit here while I go and pray over there," and, taking with Him Peter, James, and John, walked away a stone's throw (St Luke) and "began to be sorrowful and deeply distressed. Then He said to them, 'My soul is exceeding sorrowful, even to death. Stay here and watch with me." He walked away from them a little, fell on His face in prostration, and prayed, "O My Father, if it is possible, let this cup pass from me; nevertheless, not as I will, but as You will." The prayer was so intense, St Luke says that the sweat on His brow was like drops of blood. Some say that in rare cases extreme psychological suffering can in actual fact result in sweating blood. St Luke also mentions that "an angel appeared to Him from heaven, strengthening Him." God the Father seemed to have abandoned His Son for a time (see Matt 27:46), and so He is comforted and strengthened by an angel.

Why was the Son of God so sorrowful and in such agony in the garden of Gethsemane?

Who of us sinful people can dare to say that we truly understand what was going on in the pure and holy soul of the God-Man in this moment, when the hour of His betrayal to death on the cross for the salvation of mankind was at hand? However, in times past and even in our day, people try to explain the reasons for the agonies the Lord felt and suffered in these last hours in the garden of Gethsemane. The most natural suggestion is that the suffering was from the fear of death, felt by His human nature. Blessed Theophylact says, "Death entered human nature unnaturally, and so human nature fears death and flees from death."[65] Death is a consequence of sin (Rom 5:12, 15), and so the sinless nature of the God-Man should not have been subjected to death. Death for Him is a phenomenon contrary to nature, and for this reason, the sinless nature of Christ rebels against death, grieves and sorrows at its appearance. These emotional sufferings of Christ are a very good proof of the existence of two natures in Him—divine and human, a fact rejected by the Monophysites, as well as two wills, rejected by the Monothelites.

At the same time, this agony occurred without a doubt also because the Lord took upon Himself all the sins of the world, and took them to the cross. That which the whole world should have been feeling on account of its sinfulness now was concentrated on Him alone! It is also not out of the realm of possibility that the devil, who had left Him after the temptations "until an opportune time" (Luke 4:13), now returned with new temptations, trying to dissuade Him from His coming Passion, although without success. The sorrow of Christ the Saviour was also a result of the knowledge of human cruelty, humanity's lack of gratitude to God.

As described by the first two Evangelists, St Matthew and St Mark, the Lord, when He rose up from prayer, twice came to the three apostles whom He left not far off; but instead of finding them praying together with Him, vigilant and ready to help Him in any way, He finds them sleeping, and meekly rebukes them for this, saying, "Watch and pray, lest you enter into temptation. The spirit indeed is willing, but the flesh is weak." How could the apostles have fallen asleep at such a time? St Luke explains that they fell asleep from sorrow. Life shows us that intense suffering can actually cause the nervous system such stress that the body shuts down and falls asleep. The Lord rebukes Peter before the rest, because only a short while ago he had especially sworn to the Lord that he was loyal until death. The disciples were faced with a terrible temptation, a test of their faith, and so the Lord encourages them in the necessity of being vigilant and praying in order to overcome these temptations. "The spirit indeed is willing, but the flesh is weak"; this means that although their souls are inclined to fight these temptations and are even able to overcome them, nevertheless, human nature is weak in essence, and when vigilance and prayer become weak, the flesh is capable of great falls into sin.

Three times the Lord stands at prayer. The first time, He prays that His sufferings may pass Him by; the second time, He expresses His total submission to the will of God, and an angel was sent to Him to strengthen Him fully in God's will, after which in full conviction He exclaimed, "Your will be done!" After the third prayer, He returns to the disciples with a warning about the imminent coming of the traitor: "Are you still sleeping and resting? Behold, the hour is at hand, and the Son of Man is being betrayed into the hands of sinners." Either He is telling them that He has no need of their help, since the time has come for the betrayal, or He is asking if they are resting in order to shame them, saying something like, "Here comes the traitor. If you would prefer, however, and the time allows it, sleep on!" (Blessed Theophylact). As for the phrase "into the hands of sinners," St John Chrysostom says that Christ with these words is actually encouraging the disciples, "showing them that what will happen to Him is the work of hatred of sinful men, not His fault for some unknown sin."[66] "Rise, let us be going"; in other words, He tells them that they will go to meet the traitor, so that all can be accomplished as it was written in the prophets.

THE BETRAYAL OF JESUS CHRIST AND THE FLIGHT OF THE APOSTLES
(MATT 26:47–56; MARK 14:43–52; LUKE 22:47–53; JOHN 18:2–12)

All four Evangelists give complementary accounts, and each one has unique details that add to the general picture. Most likely, Judas brought a group of soldiers, not Romans, but the small armed band that protected the Sanhedrin. Even though the moon was full, the crowd came with torches, expecting that the Lord might try to hide in the garden. The soldiers were armed with swords, and some of the other servants had cudgels, expecting some armed resistance.

The betrayal by a kiss is worthy of especial notice. The high priests, obviously fearing the reprisals of the people, ordered Judas to take Jesus in secret, carefully. Apparently, the soldiers were not even told whom they were to seize; rather, they were told to take the one whom Judas would indicate. Judas, keeping his quarry secret, only told the soldiers to take the one whom he would kiss. One can even assume that Judas intended to come to Jesus with the usual greeting, to kiss Him as a friend, and then to join his friends, as though he were not the traitor at all, as though the soldiers had come on their own. But he was not able to do this.

When he came to Jesus and said, "Rabbi..." in confusion, the Lord meekly asked him, "Friend, why have you come?" Not knowing how to answer this question, Judas answered in confusion, "Greetings, Rabbi," and kissed Him. In order to show Judas that he could not hide his treachery, the Lord said to him, "Judas, are you betraying the Son of Man with a kiss?" In the meantime, the soldiers had arrived, and in St John's account the Lord asked them directly, "Whom are you seeking?" Together with the soldiers were some of the Jewish elders, of course, and they answered, "'Jesus of Nazareth.' Jesus said to them, 'I am He.'" The soldiers had been told that they must take Jesus secretly, by cunning if possible, since He had many followers who could fight for Him. And suddenly He openly, as if not fearing anything, admits to being Jesus of Nazareth! These words of Christ had a mystical power in them. Both the unexpectedness of the answer and the power of His spirit had an unexpected effect on the enemies of Christ: "They drew back and fell to the ground." When they had somewhat come to themselves from the shock, the Lord asked them a second time, "'Whom are you seeking?' And they said, 'Jesus of Nazareth.'" The Lord answered them, "I have told you that I am He. Therefore, if you seek Me, let these go their way." How moving is this care of the disciples on the part of our Lord!

St John explains that the words of His high priestly prayer had to come to pass, when He prayed that no harm would come to any of His disciples. And truly, the soldiers let the apostles go and approached Jesus to take Him. But here the apostles finally decided to intervene and, without waiting for an answer to the question one of them raised—"Lord, shall we strike with the sword?"—irascible Peter himself attacked with a sword and cut off the ear of a certain Malchus, a servant of the high priest. But the Lord healed the man with a touch (Luke 22:51), saying to Peter, "Put your sword in its place, for all who take the sword will perish by the sword." Of course this is not strictly speaking a prophecy, but only an expression of certain undeniable spiritual laws—whoever attacks another with the intention of killing or maiming him is worthy of the same treatment from another. This same thought is included in the commandment given by God after the Flood: "Whoever sheds man's blood, By man his blood shall be shed" (Gen 9:6).

"Do you think that I cannot now pray to my Father, and He will provide Me with more than twelve legions of angels?" A legion was a Roman company of soldiers numbering nearly ten thousand foot soldiers. The entire angelic world would come out to defend the Son of God if He did not go to His death willingly. The twelve legions are like a contrast to the twelve apostles. "How then could the Scriptures be fulfilled, that it must happen thus?" This means that all is occurring in fulfillment of the Old Testament prophecies. Among those who came for Jesus, as St Luke witnesses, were some of the chief priests and leaders of the temple. It was to them that the Lord spoke in rebuke: "Have you come out, as against a robber, with swords and clubs to take Me?" He accuses them of acting unrighteously, because if they wanted to accuse the Lord, they should have done so openly before all and taken Him as a breaker of the law in the middle of the day, in the presence of the people; while they instead used the darkness and cover of night. "But this is your hour, and the power of darkness."

"Then all the disciples forsook Him and fled," and therefore Christ's prophecy, uttered just a bit earlier (Matt 26:31) was fulfilled. Only Mark adds a detail about a certain young man, wrapped in a linen sheet, who walked behind the soldiers taking Jesus. Considering this to be suspicious, the soldiers took this youth, but he managed to get away naked, leaving only the sheet in their hands. It is probable that the young man lived somewhere nearby, woke up from the commotion, and walked out of his house to see what was happening. Ancient tradition says that the youth was the Evangelist Mark himself. It was common for Evangelists to leave out their own names from their accounts of the Gospel.

But not all the disciples left Christ for good. Two of them—Peter and John—followed at a safe distance and came to Jerusalem, seeing that their Master was brought to the house of the high priest Annas. Where the rest of the disciples went is not clear, but apparently they were so frightened and shocked by all that occurred, they locked themselves up somewhere and hid behind closed doors (see John 20:19).

JUDGMENT OVER THE LORD BY THE HIGH PRIESTS ANNAS AND CAIAPHAS
(JOHN 18:12–23; MATT 26:57–68; MARK 14:53–65; LUKE 22:54, 63–65)

Having taken the Lord Jesus, His enemies tied Him up (a detail only included in John) and took Him to the house where the high priests lived. While filling out the accounts of the Synoptics, St John is the only one to mention that Jesus was initially brought to Annas, who questioned Him first, then to Caiaphas. St John also explains why the Lord was brought first to Annas and not to Caiaphas, who was the ruling high priest at the time—he was Caiaphas's father-in-law. Those who took Jesus thought that they would show special honor and attention to the famous relative of the actual high priest, and in addition, the old fox Annas still commanded a great deal of respect and authority. Apparently, despite being removed from the position of acting high priest, Annas still lived in the house of the high priest, and as Caiaphas was his relative, the houses of the two shared a courtyard, though they lived in two separate wings of the large house set aside for the high priest.

St John also says that not only Peter followed after Jesus, but "another disciple," doubtless John himself. St John was a personal acquaintance of the high priest, although the exact nature of their relationship is not clear. There is a tradition that the Zebedees provided fish directly to the house of the high priest. This is why he was able to enter the inner courtyard unopposed, and then even convince the door warden to allow Peter in as well. Here, Peter denied Christ the first time, according to St John's account, when during the questioning of the Lord by Annas, Peter stood at the fire pit in the courtyard and warmed himself.

Cunning Annas, at first not accusing the Lord of anything, began to ask Him only about His teachings, and asked Him to name His disciples. Thus, he set a tone of danger for the rest of the questioning, by insinuating that Jesus was the leader of some sort of secret insurrection with a secret, esoteric teaching and unknown goals. But the Lord refused to play his game, answering, "I spoke openly to the world. I always taught in synagogues and in the temple, where the Jews always meet, and in secret I have said nothing." As proof of His words, the Lord offered the high priest to ask the assembled people, all of whom heard His teaching. Despite the fact that there was nothing shameful or rude in His answer to the high priest, one of the servants, probably trying to gain the goodwill of the high priest, struck the Lord in the face, saying, "Do You answer the high priest like that?"

If the Lord had quietly borne this attack, the assembly might have thought that He was silently admitting the blow to be a fair one, while the servant might become puffed up with pride at Christ's silence, which he would interpret as agreement with his accusation. Therefore, in order to cut off the evil in the very beginning and to make the servant realize his sin, the Lord remonstrated: "If I have spoken evil, bear witness of the evil; but if well, why do you strike Me?"

Annas then sent Jesus, still tied up, to Caiaphas. It is likely that the Lord was just led across the same inner court where Peter stood and warmed himself, after having once already denied Him. Caiaphas's questioning is given in detail by Matthew and Mark. Almost the entire Sanhedrin was assembled. Despite it being late at night, they all tried to quickly find appropriate witnesses against Jesus so that in the morning, at the official session of the Sanhedrin, they would be able to officially condemn Him to death. But they could not find any appropriate witnesses. Finally, two witnesses came (as required by the law, see Num 35:30; Deut 17:6) and told of the words spoken by the Lord when He first cast out the sellers from the temple; but they gave them a negative connotation, interpreting them to mean something that Christ never intended. The Lord had said, "Destroy this temple, and in three days I will raise it up" (John 2:19), but He certainly did not say, "I can destroy this temple," as they implied. Nor did He say that He could "build it in three days," instead saying that He could "restore" it (*egero*, in Greek, not *ikodimiso*). He was then speaking of the temple of His Body, while the false witnesses interpreted His words as an idle boast (in which, it happens, there was nothing remotely unlawful), which is why St Mark adds that this witness was still not enough to convict Christ.

Jesus remained silent throughout this entire farce because there was nothing to say to such idiotic and convoluted accusations (St Mark even mentions that some of the witnesses contradicted each other). This annoyed Caiaphas, and he decided to force the Lord to condemn Himself out of His own mouth, so that the Sanhedrin would be able to convict Him to death as a blasphemer. As was proper for the court customs of the Jews, he addressed the Lord with these words: "I put You under oath by the living God: Tell us if You are the Christ, the Son of God!" This was the usual formula when the accused had to answer under oath. The Lord could not avoid answering such a direct question, especially since there was no longer any need to hide His Messianic dignity; rather, the time had come to triumphantly witness to His own divinity. Therefore, He answered, "It is as you said," an affirmative, but also adds, "Hereafter you will see the Son of Man sitting at the right hand of the Power, and coming on the clouds of heaven."

These words were a citation of Ps 109:1, in which the Messiah is described as sitting on the right hand of God, as well as the prophecy of Daniel 7:13–14 regarding the Messiah as the Son of Man who comes on the clouds of heaven. Through this, the Lord wanted to say that all these unjust judges will see Him reveal His divine power as the Son of God in many signs and miracles. "Then the high priest tore his clothes, saying, 'He has spoken blasphemy!'" Tearing one's clothes was a customary expression of sorrow or distress. The high priest was expressly forbidden to tear his clothes (Lev 10:6; 21:10), and by doing so, Caiaphas wanted to express his especial distress that even forced him to commit an act contrary to the law. Of course, this was nothing more than hypocrisy in order to show that he considered Christ's confession of divinity to be blasphemy.

"What do you think?" asked Caiaphas of all the assembled, and of course receives the desired answer: "He is deserving of death." Now, since He was a convicted criminal, they began to ridicule and mock Him, spitting in His face as a sign of their extreme disdain and His humiliation, struck Him on the ears, the head, the face, and laughed at Him as they asked Him, "Prophesy to us, Christ! Who is the one who struck You?" In other words, if You are who You claim to be, name the man who is striking You, though You do not know him by name. This treatment vividly shows that the trial was little more than a sham, which only barely hid a bloodthirsty hatred for Jesus. These were not judges but beasts, who now could no longer hide their ferocity.

PETER'S DENIAL (MATT 26:69–75; MARK 14:66–72; LUKE 22:55–62; JOHN 18:16–18, 25–27)

There are some interesting differences between the four accounts of Peter's denial, even though they are not differences in essence, only in detail, so by reading all four accounts, one can have a complete picture.

Peter was in the same place during both phases of the trial before the two high priests, warming himself in the inner courtyard. If we consider that there was only one courtyard between the two wings of the same house where both Caiaphas and Annas lived, a seeming contradiction between John and the Synoptics is easily resolved. St John clearly states that the denial occurred in *Annas's* courtyard, while the Synoptics, who say nothing of Annas, describe the three denials as though they were occurring in *Caiaphas's* courtyard. Obviously, this was the same courtyard that was used by both the high priests. When Peter was led into the court at the behest of John, who was known to the high priests, the woman at the gate (according to John's Gospel) said to him, "You are not also one of this Man's disciples, are you?" Peter answered, "I am not," and stood at the fire. However, the servant girl did not leave him alone, and (according to Mark 14:67) continued insisting, "You also were with Jesus of Nazareth." She even told others that he was one of them (Luke 22:56). Peter continued to deny Christ, saying, "Woman, I do not know Him." This was the first denial, beginning at the gates and continuing at the fire.

As St Mark witnesses, Peter, evidently desiring to rid himself of the persistent servant, walked away from the fire into the first part of the court, near the gates, ready to flee at a moment's notice. There he stood for some time. Seeing him once again, the same persistent servant woman began to tell everyone that Peter was "one of them." Another servant joined voices with her, saying that he was truly with Jesus of Nazareth. And yet another person spoke directly to Peter, accusing him of being a disciple of Jesus of Nazareth (Luke 22:58). Peter once again returned to the fire to avoid them, but here some of those warming themselves "said to him, 'You are not also one of his disciples, are you?' He denied it and said, 'I am not!'" (John 18:25). This was the second denial, occurring at the same time that Jesus was being led from Annas to Caiaphas (based on John 18:24–25).

The dawn was not far coming, and with it the usual call of the rooster (Mark 13:35). The trial by Caiaphas was nearing its end. Then, one of the servants, a relative of Malchus, whose ear Peter cut off, said to Peter, "Did I not see you in the garden with Him?" (John 18:26), then others began to add that truly this man was a Galilean, and therefore must be a disciple of Jesus (Luke 22:59; Mark 13:70; Matt 26:73). Peter was suddenly afraid, and he began to "curse and swear, saying, 'I do not know the Man!'" And the cock crowed, a second time, according to St Mark, doubtless from the words of Peter himself (Mark 14:71–72). The first time, the rooster crowed after the first denial (Mark 14:68). "And Peter remembered the word of Jesus who had said to him, 'Before the rooster crows, you will deny Me three times.' So he went out and wept bitterly." This was the third denial, which, evidently, corresponded to the moment when the Lord, already convicted and subjected to mockery and beatings, was led out of the house of Caiaphas into the court, where He was to await the morning, when the Sanhedrin was to officially decide His fate. Peter, struck by the gaze of Christ, was immediately smitten by remorse. He ran away from that place and began to weep bitterly.

GREAT AND HOLY FRIDAY: THE JUDGMENT OF THE SANHEDRIN
(MATT 27:1; MARK 15:1; LUKE 22:66–71)

This second official meeting of the Sanhedrin, only briefly mentioned by Matthew and Mark in a passing verse, is given a fuller account by St Luke. The meeting was called only as a formality, to follow the law concerning the death penalty. In the Talmud, which preserves all the old Jewish laws, it is written that in criminal matters, the death sentence could be pronounced no earlier than the day after the beginning of the trial. But neither Caiaphas nor the rest of the Sanhedrin, of course, wanted to leave the final conviction to the time after the feast of the Passover. Therefore, they hurried to have at least a perfunctory second session. This time, the Sanhedrin gathered at dawn, with even more members, including the scribes (see Luke 22:66), no longer in Caiaphas's house but in the official chambers of the Sanhedrin. Once again, they told Jesus: "If You are the Christ, tell us." This was done partly for the sake of the new members, who were not present at the trial the previous night, and partly in the hope of hearing some more damning words from Jesus's mouth.

Before answering the question directly, the Lord tells them that as the Knower of hearts, He already knows that they will convict Him regardless of His answer. The trial was convened purely pro forma, His fate was already decided in advance, no matter what He might say. But He still tells them that after everything occurs as it must, because of their hatred, they will see Him in the glory of His Father: "'Hereafter the Son of Man will sit on the right hand of the power of God.' Then they all said, 'Are You then the Son of God?' So He said to them, 'You rightly say that I am,'" almost unwillingly. Content with this, the members of the Sanhedrin announced that there was no more need to deliberate further, and they convicted Christ to the judgment of the Roman authority, Pontius Pilate, so that the Romans could pronounce the death penalty over Him.

THE DEATH OF JUDAS, THE TRAITOR (MATT 27:3–10)

Only Matthew speaks of the fate of Judas: "Then Judas, His betrayer, seeing that He had been condemned, was remorseful and brought back the thirty pieces of silver to the chief priests and elders." It is possible, of course, that Judas did not expect Jesus to be condemned to death or, blinded by his avarice, did not stop to consider the consequences of his betrayal. When his Master was convicted, his conscience woke up, and he saw the full horror of his insane betrayal. He had remorse, but, unfortunately for him, his remorse was followed by despair, not hope in the mercy of God that forgives all sins. This "repentance" is nothing more than unbearable pain in the conscience, without any hope for the lessening of the pain, which makes it pointless, fruitless, and led Judas to the horrible act of suicide. He returned the thirty pieces of silver; that which had seemed so desirable to him now appeared disgusting. This is how sin acts in all cases. He should not have thrown the money at the feet of the high priests, but rather thrown himself at the feet of the Lord Jesus Christ, begging His forgiveness, and then he would have been forgiven, of course. But he thought to correct his deed by himself, not calling for help from above. He returns the money, saying, "I have sinned by betraying innocent blood."

According to St John Chrysostom, these words of Judas only increase his fault, as well as the fault of the chief priests, "his—because he did not repent, or if he did, then he did so too late, and from his own mouth he condemns himself, for he confessed that he betrayed Christ in vain; their fault is the greater, because they, when given this chance to repent of their sin, did no such thing."[67] Instead, with coldness and mockery they said to Judas, "What is that to us? You see to it!" This shows their extreme moral desensitization. "Then he threw down the pieces of silver in the temple and departed, and went and hanged himself." That money that the chief priests refused to take back he then cast on the floor of the temple, thinking perhaps to calm the tortures of his conscience, but in vain. These tortures led him to such a state of hopelessness that he hanged himself, after which he apparently fell down from the high place in which he hanged himself, as the Apostle Peter says: "and falling headlong, he burst open in the middle and all his entrails gushed out" (Acts 1:18).

Despite their complete depravity, the chief priests still considered the money impossible to be spent on the temple because it was the "price of blood." Probably they remembered Deuteronomy 23:18, and in this case, they once again showed their extreme hatred to the Lord Jesus Christ, as they showed before when they considered His betrayal to be worth no more than thirty pieces of silver. It is amazing how typical it is of the Pharisees to strive to fulfill the lesser law after having broken the greater—not to condemn an innocent man.

"They ... bought with them the potter's field," land that was useless for crops since it was already all dug up for potter's clay, "to bury strangers in," the strangers being the many Jews and proselytes who may have died in Jerusalem during their pilgrimages for one of the major feasts. "Then was fulfilled what was spoken by Jeremiah the prophet, saying, 'And they took the thirty pieces of silver, the value of Him who was priced, whom they of the children of Israel priced; and gave them for the potter's field.'" There is nothing like this prophecy in the book of Jeremiah; there is only one place that so much as speaks of the purchase of a field. Possibly, Matthew references an addition of a later scribe. There is only one similar place in the prophets, Zechariah 11:12–13. Jeremiah also speaks of a potter's field in chapters 18 and 19, and it is possible that Zechariah took his image from there. Also, in ancient times, proper names in written form were contracted, and the contracted forms of Zechariah (*zriou*) and Jeremiah (*iriou*) are not that different, and could have been confused by a scribe. The meaning of this prophecy in Zechariah is the following: The prophet was given the sheep of the house of Israel into his care as a pastor, the representative of the Great Shepherd, God. The Jews did not listen to the prophet, meaning they refused to listen to God Himself. In order to show the Jews how little worth they place on the prophet's care for them, God commands the prophet to ask them how much they would pay him for his pastoral duties. They gave him the price of a slave—thirty pieces of silver, meaning they considered the care of the prophet (that is, God Himself) to be worthless, like the work of a slave.

Then God told the prophet to give this "high price" by which He was valued (ironically, of course) to the potter (Zech 11:1–12). This prophecy was fulfilled in the betrayal of the Lord Jesus Christ. The Good Shepherd was valued by the Jews at thirty pieces of silver, the price of a slave, and for this money they then bought a field from the potter.

The Lord Jesus Christ Is Brought to Pilate
(Matt 27:2, 11–30; Mark 15:1–19; Luke 23:1–25; John 18:28–40; 19:16)
"And when they had bound Him, they led Him away and delivered Him to Pontius Pilate the governor." From the time of the Roman conquest, the Sanhedrin no longer had the authority to put criminals to death (which is seen in John 18:31). The exception to this, the stoning of Stephen in the Book of Acts, was a willful act of passion, and against Roman law. According to the Jewish law, blasphemers were punished by stoning, but the Jews, unwillingly fulfilling the will of God, wanted Jesus to die a more shameful death—crucifixion—and so led Him to Pilate so that the Romans could put Him to death.

Pontius Pilate was the fifth procurator, or ruler, of Judea. Tiberius assigned him this responsibility in A.D. 26. Pilate was a proud and cruel man, but at the same time, he was weak-willed and a coward. He hated all Jews, and was in return hated by them. Soon after the crucifixion of Christ, he was called back to Rome to give account, imprisoned in Vienne (southern Gaul) and there took his own life. Procurators usually lived in Caesaria, but on Passover, in order to watch over the order of the city, they moved to Jerusalem.

St John gives the most detailed account of the trial with Pilate. He says that the Jews led Jesus into the hall of judgment probably located in or near the fortress of Antony in the northwest direction from the temple, in which the Roman garrison was quartered. Even touching something pagan was considered unclean, so the Jewish leaders did not walk in, so as not to defile themselves and miss the Passover meal (this is yet another clear indication that the Passover was only beginning that evening, and that Christ's Passover meal was a day early, so that He could bring Himself as the true Paschal Lamb on the actual day of the Old Testament Passover, which was a foreshadowing of His passion).

Pilate, in this case pandering to Jewish custom (it is well known that the Romans were careful about keeping to the customs of the peoples they defeated, in order not to give them too many excuses to rebel), came out to them to a place called the Pavement, an open, raised platform before his house, and asked them: "What accusation do you bring against this Man?" The first two Evangelists begin the description of the trial with Pilate's questioning of the Lord, Luke with the accusations from the leaders, while only St John begins with Pilate's preliminary question. Therefore, St John starts from the very beginning, and in general he gives the most detailed account of the sequence of events of the trial, filling in the gaps of the Synoptics.

"If He were not an evildoer, we would not have delivered Him up to you"; the Jews did not want to start the trial process with Jesus from the beginning. They were hoping that Pilate would be willing only to carry out the death sentence that they had already decided on. But Pilate knew what kind of people he was dealing with, and so immediately put them in a position of petitioner, since he was the only legitimate authority in the area, telling them that he could not pass judgment without knowing the facts. Therefore, he told them: "You take Him and judge Him according to your law." The Sanhedrin did have the right to judge and punish criminals according to their own law, but they could not execute anyone.

Immediately changing their proud tone to a submissive one, the Jews admitted that their own rights were limited, and they could not execute this prisoner, whom they considered to be worthy of death. "It is not lawful for us to put anyone to death, that the saying of Jesus might be fulfilled which He spoke, signifying by what death He would die." Christ did predict, and not only once, that He would be given over to the Gentiles (Matt 20:19), and that He would be raised up from the earth, that is, crucified (Matt 26:2; John 12:32). The enemies of Christ, after this, had no choice but to lay out their accusations against Jesus, which we see in St Luke: "We found this fellow perverting the nation, and forbidding to pay taxes to Caesar, saying that He Himself is Christ, a King." These hypocrites, who themselves hated the Romans, used an accusation of a purely political character in order to more easily get their desired death penalty for Jesus. After this accusation, Pilate takes Jesus into the hall of judgment and asks Him alone: "'Are You the King of the Jews?' Jesus answered him, 'Are you speaking for yourself about this, or did others tell you this concerning Me?'" The source of the question was important—if Pilate had himself asked this question, then Christ's answer would be "no," because Christ was not a king in the sense that Pilate would have given the word. But if the question of Pilate was a mere repetition of the question of the Jewish elders, then He would have to give an affirmative answer, since Christ truly was the King of Truth.

Christ was not the political king of Israel, but the theocratic king of the universe. The Lord also wanted to force Pilate to speak, to say in what way he meant the word "king." Was Pilate accusing Christ of usurping this title, or was he merely parroting the Jewish elders? Pilate's answer is full of disdain for Jews in general: "Am I a Jew? Your own nation and the chief priests have delivered You to me. What have You done?" This meant that Pilate did not recognize Christ's claim to kingship, and just wanted to know for what reason the chief priests had betrayed Him, accusing Him of assuming the title "king."

"Jesus answered, 'My kingdom is not of this world.'" The Lord insists that He is truly a king, not in a political sense, but in a spiritual one, not the kind of a king that Pilate imagines. "Are You a king then?" was Pilate's question. Having understood that Christ did not have any political aspirations, Pilate expresses his doubts that some kind of spiritual kingdom can even exist. Then the Lord confirms that He is truly a king, the King of the spiritual kingdom of truth and that He came to the earth to witness to the truth, meaning by "truth," of course, the religious truth of His divine teaching. Pilate, of course, as a crude pagan, could not understand these words of the Lord and said with disdain, "What is truth?" But he still understood that this kingdom of Jesus was not a political one and in no way threatened Roman rule.

By this historical time period, the classical world had become so morally corrupt that the possibility of objective truth was simply dismissed. This question of Pilate, "What is truth?" is an expression of this desperate lack of faith in truth, so much so that Pilate was not interested in hearing the answer; all he could do was go to the Jews and announce that he had found no fault in Jesus.

This announcement wounded the pride of the members of the Sanhedrin, and they, as the Synoptics relate, began to accuse Jesus of many different crimes, desiring to obtain a conviction at any cost. The Lord kept silent the entire time, so that Pilate was greatly astonished (Matt 27:12). Here they said too much: when waxing eloquent about how He was stirring up the people starting in Galilee and ending in Judea, Pilate, when He found out Christ was from Galilee, sent Him to Herod, who was in Jerusalem at that time on pilgrimage for the feast (Luke 23:5). Only Luke mentions this second trial before Herod (Luke 23:7–12). Evidently, Pilate hoped to receive from Herod more reliable information concerning the accused and His crimes because he still did not understand why the Jews wanted Him dead. From the testimony of St Luke, who mentions that they were enemies at the time, Pilate may have sent Jesus to Herod as a gesture of friendship, hoping by this to end their long-standing enmity. Perhaps he was also hoping to hear something positive from Herod regarding Jesus, so he could deliver the Lord from the hands of His accusers.

Herod was very happy when he saw Jesus. This was the same Herod Antipas who killed John the Baptist, and, having heard of Jesus's miracles, thought that He was John who rose from the dead. Herod hoped to see some kind of miracle, not to believe in Christ, but just to have a good show, like the people who watch illusionists swallow snakes and swords, and are amazed (Blessed Theophylact). Herod apparently considered Christ to be some kind of magician. He also asked Him many questions, hoping to hear something interesting and unusual, but the Lord answered all his questions with total silence. The chief priests and scribes continued to accuse the Lord without stopping, probably trying to prove that His preaching was just as dangerous for Herod as it was to Caesar. After he had mocked Jesus, Herod put white clothing on Him and sent Him back to Pilate. White clothing was a mark of candidacy for a political position in Rome (the word "candidate" comes from the Latin *candidus*, which means white or bright). By dressing Jesus in this way, Herod wanted to show that he also saw Jesus as an amusing pretender to the Jewish kingship, but not a serious political threat. Pilate understood the gesture in the same way.

Citing the fact that Herod found nothing in Jesus that was worthy of execution, Pilate offered the chief priests, scribes, and people to scourge Him and let Him go. Pilate was hoping to satisfy them with the lesser punishment. He also remembered that the Jews had a custom every Passover to petition the Roman governor to pardon one criminal sentenced to death. Pilate offered them Jesus: "'Whom do you want me to release to you? Barabbas, or Jesus who is called Christ?' For he knew that they had handed Him over because of envy." Pilate was apparently hoping that among the common people he would find a different attitude toward Christ, and so he directed his request at the large crowd that had gathered before his house: "Which of the two do you want me to release to you?"

At this moment, another event occurred that further inclined Pilate to exonerate Jesus. When he was sitting in his judgment seat on the open, raised platform called the Pavement (*Gabbatha*, in Hebrew), a servant approached him, sent by his wife, who told him to do nothing to this righteous man, "for I have suffered many things this day in a dream because of Him." Some ancient Christian writers even give her a name—Claudia Procula. They believed that she may have been converted to Judaism, or at least was sympathetic to it, while tradition tells us that later she became a Christian. Probably, she had heard a lot about the Lord Jesus Christ and was afraid that her husband could be punished by God for condemning Him. It is not known what kind of a dream she saw, but we can assume that Jesus Himself appeared to her, as the innocent sufferer, and she was tortured in the dream by her conscience, ashamed that her husband was the torturer.

But while Pilate listened to the message from his wife, the Jewish elders began to incite the people to ask Pilate to release Barabbas, and the people listened to their evil words. When Pilate asked for the second time, "'Which of the two do you want me to release to you?' They said, 'Barabbas.'" Pilate asked what he should do with Jesus, called Christ. They answered, "Let Him be crucified." St Luke has them saying, "Let Him be put to death." Then Pilate, still desiring to release Christ, raised his voice and asked, "'Why? What evil has He done?' But they cried out all the more, saying, "Let Him be crucified!"

Euthymius Zigabenos has the following interpretation: "They do not limit themselves by saying, 'let Him die,' but specifically call for His crucifixion, so that the very manner of His death would show Him to be a criminal."[68] This is how the prophecies had to be fulfilled concerning Christ's manner of death for our sakes. The people, twisted and corrupted by their leaders, preferred Barabbas to the Lord Jesus Christ; Barabbas who was, according to the Evangelists, a famous thief who, together with a group of robbers, raised an insurrection in the city only in order to pillage and murder (Matt 27:16; John 18:40; Luke 23:19; Mark 15:7).

Hearing this cry of the people, which he obviously did not expect, Pilate was left in a difficult position. He was afraid that his continued protection of the Righteous Man might result in serious unrest among the people, which would then have to be put down by force, and that the hate-filled chief priests might accuse him before Caesar, saying that he was responsible for the unrest by protecting a well-known political criminal. Under the influence of these feelings, Pilate decided to try to satisfy their bloodlust by scourging the Innocent One. Evidently, he hoped to be able to secure Jesus's release, after letting the people have their fill of blood.

"So then Pilate took Jesus and scourged Him" (John 19:1). All four Evangelists write about the scourging. According to Matthew and Mark, the soldiers took Jesus into the "common hall," away from the increasing crowd in the streets, and all of them assembled to take part in the beating. They undressed Jesus and began to beat Him. Such scourging was reserved only for serious criminals, and in general was limited to slaves. The whips were made from ropes or leather thongs, and sharp sticks, either of bone or metal, were attached to the ends. These scourgings were so severe that many died in the process. The one scourged was usually tied to a post in a reclining position, and the soldiers scourged his uncovered back. The body began to rip apart even from the first blows, and the blood flowed freely. Pilate subjected One Whom he believed to be innocent to such a cruel punishment, but still it must be underlined that he did it not out of any hatred for Christ personally, but in order to ultimately have Him released.

After they finished scourging Him, the hard-hearted soldiers began to mock the Sufferer—they dressed Him in a "scarlet robe," a soldier's cloak intended to mimic royal vesture. These cloaks were without sleeves and were put on the shoulder in such a way that the right hand remained free. On the head of the Lord, they put a crown woven from a thornbush, and into His hand they put a stick, which was supposed to mimic a royal scepter. After they did all this to mock the divine Sufferer, the soldiers began to bow before Him and greet Him as a king, as though they were doing Him honor. All this time, they beat Him on the face, spit on Him, took the "scepter" and beat His head with it, so that the thorns would go deeper into His scalp.

All this is described in Matthew and Mark as occurring already after Jesus was condemned to death by Pilate; but St John, whose main purpose in writing the Gospel was to add and explain certain passages left incomplete by the Synoptics, indicates that this scourging and mocking occurred earlier, and were ordered by Pilate with the sole purpose of delivering Jesus from the death penalty. Tortured and exhausted by the scourging, the Lord was led out by Pilate in His humiliation into the Pavement, so that the people, seeing Him so humiliated, would have pity on Him. He was sure that their hearts would be moved by this terrible sight, and they would no longer insist on Jesus being crucified. This was the thought process of a pagan who did not even know the true God and His commandments about love for one's neighbor, but, alas, the spiritual leaders of the chosen nation of God did not have that kind of a thought process since they were already rabid in their insatiable hatred.

When the Lord was brought out to the Pavement, Pilate said, "Behold the man! I am bringing Him out to you, that you may know that I find no fault in Him." Pilate was speaking to their consciences, saying, "Look! Here is a lonely, humiliated, beaten man. Does He look like a dangerous insurrectionist? Does He not inspire pity by His look, not fear?" At the same time, Pilate, not thinking about it, ended up saying the whole truth—the Lord, in His humiliation much more than in earthly power and glory, truly revealed the spiritual greatness and moral beauty of the true Man, Man as he should be according to God's intention. For a Christian, the words of Pilate sound thus: "Behold the model Man, toward Whom all Christians must strive."

But the chief priests and their servants were unmoved. Hardly had they seen the tortured and beaten Christ that they began once more to cry out, "Crucify Him, crucify Him!" Such insistence shocked Pilate and forced him to answer sharply, "You take Him and crucify Him, for I find no fault in Him." If you are so insistent, he was saying, then you should be responsible for His crucifixion, but I will not take part in such an unworthy act as condemning to death a man completely innocent of any wrongdoing. But these words expressed nothing more than his extreme irritation and impatience, and so the enemies of Christ continued to insist on Pilate's official sentence, bringing yet another accusation: "We have a law, and according to our law He ought to die, because He made Himself the Son of God." When Pilate heard this, "he was the more afraid." Of course, the expression "Son of God" would have been understood by him in a pagan sense, in the sense of "demigod," or "hero," those half-divine creatures who populate Greek and Roman mythology, but even this was enough to disturb him, especially when he considered his wife's warning after she saw a dream of this mysterious Person. And so Pilate once again took Jesus to the judgment hall away from the people and asked Him when they were alone: "Where are You from?" The question he intended to ask was: "Where do You come from? Heaven or earth? Are You truly a Son of God?"

"Jesus gave him no answer." It was pointless to ask such a question. The Lord had already explained His provenance to Pilate, but Pilate refused to hear it, dismissing it with a skeptical, "What is truth?" Could this crude pagan-skeptic understand the teaching of the true Son of God? Defeating his inner fear, Pilate decided on a show of power, at the same time trying to get Jesus to speak, "Are You not speaking to me?" The Lord answered these proud words with divine wisdom: "You could have no power at all against Me, unless it had been given you from above." The fact that Jesus was in Pilate's hands is actually due to the providence of God. By giving His people to slavery to the pagan Roman authority, God gave Pilate the power over Jesus. But Pilate would still be responsible for the condemnation of Jesus, even if the greater sin was on those who brought Him willingly to the Roman authority, that is, the Sanhedrin, Caiaphas as their tool, and Judas the traitor. These wise words were apparently pleasing to Pilate, and he once again tried to release Him.

Then, the accusers of Christ decided to go to extremes—they accused Pilate, the representative of Roman power, of betraying the power of the Roman Caesar: "If you let this Man go, you are not Caesar's friend." This frightened Pilate, because the Emperor Tiberius was a suspicious and very cruel despot who listened when an official of his was denounced or accused of wrongdoing. This threat finally convinced Pilate. Officially sitting in the judgment seat in the Pavement, Pilate formally and triumphantly ended the proceedings. John the Evangelist mentions the day and hour of the Lord's formal condemnation: "Now it was the Preparation Day of the Passover, and about the sixth hour," meaning it was the Friday before the Passover and near noon, by our reckoning. It seems that this detail is in contradiction with some of the other Evangelists—Mark says that it was the third hour (Mark 15:25), while from the sixth to the ninth hours there was darkness over all the earth (Matt 27:45; Mark 15:33; Luke 23:44). But the point is that the day, as the night, was divided into four "watches," each of which lasted three hours, and in the New Testament, only the first, third, sixth, and ninth hours are ever mentioned. St John does not say that it was the sixth hour exactly, but "about the sixth hour," meaning it could be any time between nine in the morning and noon.

"And he said to the Jews, Behold your King!" It is hard to understand what Pilate was trying to express with these words, but one must not discount the possibility that this was one last effort to save Jesus from death. Probably irritated that he was being forced to condemn a man to death against his own conscience, he once again hurls an accusation at the Sanhedrin. It is as if he is saying, "You think that you will regain independence someday, you think you have some sort of great calling among all the nations of the world? No one could have accomplished that better than this Man, who calls Himself the spiritual King of Israel. How is it that you, instead of falling on your feet before Him, demand His death? Do you want me, the hated Roman governor, to take away your King from you, Who can truly accomplish all of your most cherished dreams?"

Evidently, the accusers understood the subtext because they angrily answered, "Away with Him, away with Him! Crucify Him!" According to Bishop Michael,

> [This] is a cry of pain after being wounded in the most sensitive place, but Pilate, before finally bowing to their wishes, turns the knife in the wound one more time with the words, "Shall I crucify your king?" If Jesus is calling Himself your king, He is by definition promising you to be freed from the authority of the Romans. How can you then require that I, a representative of that Roman authority, condemn Him to death? Think about what you are asking![69]

To these words, the chief priests, in their mad blindness of hatred toward Jesus, uttered the horrible, fateful words that became the doom of the Jewish nation for the rest of its history: "We have no king but Caesar!"

Before, the high priests would say, "We have no king but God." Now, only in order to get Jesus executed, they give up everything that they have ever believed in, saying that they do not have, and do not wish to have, any other king except the pagan Roman Caesar. Only now did Pilate agree to satisfy their demand, and "delivered Him to them to be crucified."

St Matthew writes that before the formal condemnation, Pilate washed his hands (Matt 27:24). The Jews had a custom to wash their hands to prove that they had no part in the killing of a person found murdered (Deut 21:6–8). Pilate took advantage of this custom as a sign that he was denying responsibility for Christ's execution, Whom he still considered an innocent, righteous man. "You see to it," meaning "you will answer for the consequences of this unjust execution." In order to receive the official sanction, the Jews were willing to say and do anything, without thinking of the consequences: "His blood be on us, and on our children," meaning that if this was a crime, then let God's just wrath fall on us and on our descendants.

St John Chrysostom says, "What insane anger, what an evil passion! It would have been enough had they cursed themselves with God's wrath. Why did they include their children in the curse?"[70] This curse, which the Jews brought on themselves, soon came to pass—in A.D. 70, during the siege and destruction of Jerusalem, a huge number of Jews were crucified. This curse continued to haunt the Jews in their history, as they were dispersed throughout the whole world and subject to periodic persecutions, as a fulfillment of Moses's prophecy (Deut 28:49–57, 64–67).

"Then he released Barabbas to them; and when he had scourged Jesus, he delivered Him to be crucified." In other words, having confirmed the Sanhedrin's conviction of Jesus, he gave them soldiers to crucify the Lord Jesus Christ.

Even though he washed his hands, Pilate, of course, could not thereby wash away his responsibility as he would have liked. "To wash one's hands" has since become axiomatic. God punished Pilate for his lack of will and his unjust condemnation of the One Whom he himself called righteous. He was exiled to Gaul and there, after two miserable years, haunted by his conscience and despair, he committed suicide.

THE LORD'S PATH TO THE CROSS, THE WAY TO GOLGOTHA
(MATT 27:31–32; MARK 15:20–21; LUKE 23:26–32; JOHN 19:16–17)

Matthew and Mark describe this event in exactly the same words: "And when they had mocked Him, they took the robe off Him, put His own clothes on Him, and led Him away to be crucified. Now as they came out, they found a man of Cyrene, Simon by name. Him they compelled to bear His cross." St John says nothing about Simon of Cyrene. St Luke gives the most detailed account. As St John says, and as was generally accepted for those condemned to crucifixion, the Lord carried His own cross to the place of execution. But He was so exhausted by the prayer in Gethsemane, the previous sleepless night, and the terrible scourging, that He was unable to carry the cross to Golgotha. Not out of any sense of pity, naturally, but desiring to conclude the execution quickly, the enemies of the Lord forced a certain Simon from Cyrene, a city in Libya in North Africa (east of Egypt, where many Jews lived), to carry the cross of the Lord, as he was returning home from working the fields. St Mark also adds that Simon was the father of Alexander and Rufus, who were later members of the early Church, mentioned also by St Paul in his letter to the Romans (Rom 16:13).

St Luke also added that "a great multitude of the people followed Him, and women who also mourned and lamented Him." Not only Christ's enemies, but some who were sympathetic to Him, followed Him as well. Despite the customary prohibition for any people to express their sympathy with a condemned criminal, some women in the crowd loudly lamented Christ's unjust condemnation. Their sympathy was so profound and sincere that the Lord found it necessary to speak to them, probably in the moment when the procession stopped, as the cross was being laid on the shoulders of Simon of Cyrene. "Daughters of Jerusalem, do not weep for Me, but weep for yourselves and for your children." "Daughters of Jerusalem" is an affectionate name, showing the Lord's love for these women who were so moved seeing His suffering. The Lord almost seems to forget about His forthcoming suffering and death and looks with His spiritual eyes to the future suffering of the chosen nation, to the terrible punishment it would receive for rejecting the Messiah.

"Weep for yourselves and for your children," in these words the Lord warns them of the coming calamities. Here, He seems to be referring to the terrible curse that the Jews frivolously brought on themselves when they cried, "His blood be on us and on our children." Christ continues to tell them, "For indeed the days are coming," terrible calamites are imminent, when even the great blessing of bearing children will become a curse and those who used to be considered punished by God (the barren) will now be considered blessed. "Then they will begin to say to the mountains, 'Fall on us!'" This is how horrible the coming calamities will be. Doubtless, Christ is again speaking of the destruction of Jerusalem.

"For if they do these things in the green wood, what will be done in the dry?" Evidently, this is a local saying. Christ is referring to Himself as the "green wood," while the "dry wood" is the Jewish nation. If He, an innocent man, is not given any quarter, then how will it be with the guilty nation? "Fire will descend on Judea (compare Ezek 20:47), and if a green tree burns, how much more will the dry trees be annihilated?" (Bishop Michael).[71]

The Crucifixion (Matt 27:33–44; Mark 15:22–32; Luke 23:33–38; John 19:18–24)

The Lord was brought to Golgotha, meaning "the place of the skull," and there He was crucified between two criminals, who were also to be put to death, as St Luke tells us. Golgotha was a small hill, at that time outside the walls of Jerusalem, to the northwest of the city. It either had the appearance of a skull, or the land was full of the skulls of people executed there. According to ancient tradition, this was the place where Adam was buried. The Apostle Paul considers it significant that Christ died outside the gates of Jerusalem (Heb 13:11–12). When Jesus was brought to Golgotha, according to Mark, He was given wine mixed with myrrh, according to Matthew, vinegar mixed with gall (Mark 15:23; Matt 27:34). This was a drink intended to dull one's sensations, given to those condemned to be crucified in order to somewhat lessen the intensity of their sufferings. The Romans called it a "sleeping draught." According to the writings of the Jewish rabbis, this was wine mixed with some tar, thanks to which the condemned man's conscious mind was dulled, lessening his pain. The "myrrh" mentioned by Mark is a kind of tar, most likely. This drink had a very bitter, unpleasant taste, which is why Matthew calls it "gall," while the wine was evidently already sour, therefore called "vinegar." The Lord tasted it, but He desired to drink the full cup of suffering, fully conscious, and so He refused to drink it.

"Then they crucified Him." Crosses were built in different forms, and people were crucified in different ways. Sometimes the criminal was nailed to the cross while the cross was still on the ground, after which the cross was raised and placed in the earth vertically. Sometimes the cross was put up first, then the criminal was nailed to it. Sometimes the criminal was crucified upside down (St Peter was so crucified, according to his own desire). The hands and feet were sometimes nailed to the wood, sometimes only tied. The body of the crucified hung helplessly, twisted in terrible convulsions; all the muscles were constantly cramping, the wounds from the nails would rip apart from the weight of the body hanging down. The condemned also suffered from thirst, a result of the fever due to the infected wounds. The sufferings of a crucified man were so terrible, as well as long (sometimes death came in three days, sometimes even later), that it was reserved only for the worst criminals, and was considered the worst and most shameful of all forms of execution. In order to prevent the hands from being ripped apart by the weight of the body, sometimes a crossbar was added, intended as a kind of stand to support the body. At the top of the cross, above the head of the condemned man, was often a board listing the man's crimes.

Amid the terrible suffering, the Lord did not remain completely silent. He spoke seven times from the cross. His first words were a prayer for those crucifying Him, the second words were directed at the repentant thief, giving him entry into paradise, the third words were to His Mother, as He gave Her care over to St John, the fourth was His exclamation: "My God, My God, why have You forsaken me?" The fifth word was "I thirst." The sixth—"It is finished." The seventh—"Father, into Your hands I commit My spirit."

St Luke gives us His prayer for his tormentors—"Father, forgive them, for they do not know what they do." None of those who crucified Christ knew that He was the Son of God—"had they known, they would not have crucified the Lord of glory" (1 Cor 2:8). Even to the Jews, St Peter speaks thus in his second sermon after healing the lame man: "I know that you did it in ignorance" (Acts 3:17). The Roman soldiers of course did not know that they were crucifying the Son of God, while the Jews who condemned Christ were so blinded by their hatred that truly they did not think they were crucifying their own Messiah. However, such ignorance does not justify their crime, for they had the opportunity and the means to know. The prayer of the Lord shows His greatness of Spirit and gives us a vivid example of how we also must not seek revenge on our enemies, but rather pray to God for them.

"Now Pilate wrote a title"; St John writes that Pilate ordered that a sign be attached to the cross with the Lord's "crime," as was the usual custom (John 19:19–22). Desiring to wound the members of the Sanhedrin one last time, Pilate ordered that His crime be written thus: "Jesus of Nazareth, the King of the Jews." Since the Jews accused Jesus of appropriating the royal dignity to Himself, Pilate ordered that to be the crime, as a way of disgracing the Sanhedrin. The king of the Jews, killed by the order of the leaders of the Jews. Contrary to the usual custom, the "crime" was written in three languages—Hebrew, Greek (the universal cultural language), and Latin (the language of the conquerors). The purpose of this was for as many people as possible to understand the sign. Without realizing it, Pilate was actually an instrument of divine providence—in the minutes of His worst humiliation, the Lord Jesus Christ was universally proclaimed king. The accusers of the Lord understood this to be a cruel joke, and insisted that Pilate take it down, but the proud Roman curtly refused, allowing them to feel his power.

"Then they crucified Him, and divided His garments, casting lots." Roman law gave the clothes of the crucified man as property to the soldiers who performed the crucifixion. There were four soldiers who would usually be present, according to Philo. St John, speaking in more detail about the division of the Lord's garments, says that the outer clothing was torn apart into four pieces, while the lower garment was a whole woven garment with only an opening for the head—meaning that if it were divided into four pieces, it would be useless. Therefore, they cast lots for it. According to tradition, this garment was woven by the Theotokos. While doing this, the soldiers were unwittingly fulfilling an ancient prophecy regarding the Messiah, which St John cites directly, saying, "They parted my garments among them, and cast lots upon my vesture" (Ps 21:19).

Subsequently, the Synoptics write about the mocking and blasphemy directed at the Lord by the soldiers as well as His enemies among the assembled people, and especially, of course, by the scribes, elders, and Pharisees. These jeers were all intended to compare His present situation with the past, to wound Him even more. Remembering all that He had said and done before, they pointed at His helplessness and offered, mockingly, for Him to perform an obvious miracle that would convince everybody—to come down from the cross, promising (hypocritically, of course) in this case to believe in Him. Participating in these blasphemies, according to St Matthew, were both thieves, crucified to the right and left of the Lord.

THE REPENTANCE OF THE GOOD THIEF (LUKE 23:39–43)

Adding to the accounts of the first two Evangelists, St Matthew and St Mark, St Luke writes about the repentance and conversion of one of the two crucified thieves. One of them, getting ever angrier as a result of his sufferings and searching for a subject on whom he could cast his anger, began to blaspheme the Lord, following the example of His enemies. The other thief, apparently not as morally corrupt, preserving a sense of religiosity, began to rebuke his fellow criminal. "Do you not even fear God, seeing you are under the same condemnation? And we indeed justly, for we receive the due reward of our deeds; but this Man has done nothing wrong." Evidently, he saw the tears and sufferings of the Jewish women who accompanied the Lord to Golgotha; even more astonishing was the sign above Christ's head, which made him think about the words of Christ's enemies: "You have saved others." But perhaps most important of all for his conversion was the moving prayer of the Lord for His enemies who crucified Him. In any case, his conscience began to awaken, and he was not afraid, amid the general jeering and mockery, to openly speak in support of the Lord. Not only that, but there was such a monumental shift in his soul that he, loudly expressing his faith in the crucified Lord as the Messiah, spoke to Him with the penitent words: "Lord, remember me when You come into Your kingdom."

He does not ask for glories or blessedness, but asks for the smallest thing, like the Canaanite woman, who desired to receive only one crumb from the table of the Lord. From that moment, the words of the wise thief became an example for all of us of sincere, profound repentance, and even came into regular liturgical use. This amazing confession proves the power of the faith of this repentant thief. He recognized this man who was suffering, in pain, dying, as a king who will come into His kingdom, as the Lord yet to establish His kingdom. This confession was too difficult even for the disciples to utter, who could not comprehend a suffering Messiah. Doubtless this was also a special act of God's grace, which illumined the thief, helping him become an example and lesson for all generations and nations. This confession deserved the highest reward that can be imagined. "Today you will be with Me in paradise," said the Lord to him, meaning that he will be among the first to enter heaven, which once again will be opened for people through the redemptive death of Christ.

The Theotokos at the Cross (John 19:25–27)

Only St John, as an eyewitness and participant, tells of how the Lord Jesus Christ gave the care of the Mother of God into his hands from the cross. When the bestial enemies of Christ had satiated their bloodlust and began to slowly leave the place of execution, some of Christ's followers approached the cross—His Mother, her sister Mary the wife of Cleopas, Mary Magdalene, and "the disciple whom He loved," as John usually calls himself in his own Gospel. With the Lord's departure from this world imminent, His all-pure Mother was all alone in the world, with no one to take care of Her, and so with the words, "Woman, behold your son!" and "Behold thy Mother!" to the disciple, He gave Her care to His beloved disciple. "And from that hour that disciple took Her to his own home." She remained with him until Her death, as tradition tells us, and John cared for Her as though he were Her own son. This is especially important and worthy of comment for the following reason: Protestants and other sectarians never miss an opportunity to degrade the most holy Mother of God, rejecting Her ever-virginity and saying that after Jesus She had other children born in the natural way from Joseph, and that these were the "brothers of the Lord" mentioned in the Gospel. But here arises the question: if the Theotokos had natural children, who would have had to take care of Her according to all laws of custom and love, then why did Christ give Her care to St John? One must assume that both the Theotokos and St John remained at the cross until Christ's death, for St John says in his gospel that he was an eyewitness of the Lord's death and of all that happened afterward (John 19:35).

THE DEATH OF CHRIST (MATT 27:45–56; MARK 15:33–41; LUKE 23:44–49; JOHN 19:28–37)

According to the first three Gospels, before the Lord died, darkness covered the world from the sixth to the ninth hour (from noon to three in the afternoon by our reckoning). St Luke adds that "the sun was darkened." This could not have been a normal solar eclipse, since the Passover always happens on 14 Nisan, the night of the full moon, while a full solar eclipse always happens during a new moon, and never during a full moon. This was a miraculous sign that witnessed to the awful and incredible event of the death of the beloved Son of God. This unusual eclipse, during which the stars were visible, is described even by the Roman astronomer Phlegon, as well as the Greek historian Thallus. St Dionysius the Areopagite, in his letters, also remembers this event, occurring while he was yet a pagan, and mentions another pagan philosopher Apollophanes as a witness.[72] But most amazing was that this darkness was over the whole world, not just over a small geographical area, as would have been with a normal solar eclipse, a fact stressed by St John Chrysostom and Blessed Theophylact. Apparently, this darkness occurred after all the mocking and blasphemy against the crucified Lord; perhaps it was the reason they stopped jeering, instead inspiring the mood so vividly described by St Luke: "And the whole crowd who came together to that sight, seeing what had been done, beat their breasts and returned" (Luke 23:48).

"And about the ninth hour Jesus cried out with a loud voice, saying, 'Eli, Eli, lama sabachthani?'" The word St Mark uses is "Eloi" instead of "Eli." This naturally could not have been a cry of despair, but only an expression of the deepest sorrow in the soul of the God-Man. In order that the redemptive sacrifice be accomplished, it was necessary that the God-Man drink the cup of human suffering all the way to the dregs. For this it was necessary that the crucified Jesus not feel the joy of His oneness with God the Father. The entire anger of God, which, in light of divine justice should have been poured out on sinful mankind, was now, so to speak, concentrated on Christ alone, and it was as though God had left Him. Among all the worst suffering of body and soul that one can possibly imagine, this sense of being forsaken was far more painful, which is why such an exclamation of agony came out of Jesus's mouth.

The word "Eli" is similar in sound to the Hebrew name for Elijah. Therefore, the cry of the Lord became a new source of taunting: "He is calling for Elijah!" This taunt was even more hurtful because before the coming of the Messiah, the Jews awaited the return of Elijah. Laughing at the Lord, it was as if they were saying: "Look at Him now, crucified and humiliated, and He still thinks He is the Messiah, and is calling Elijah to Himself for help." The first two Evangelists, St Matthew and St Mark, write that immediately one of the soldiers ran, took a sponge, filled it with vinegar and, putting it on a stick ("hyssop" in St John, meaning a branch from the hyssop tree), raised it to Jesus's mouth so He could drink. Evidently, this was sour wine, the usual drink of a Roman soldier, especially in hot weather. One of the effects of crucifixion was a terrible, torturous thirst in the sufferers, and St John therefore adds the detail that Christ said, "I thirst," which was the reason the soldier offered Him drink. In addition, in John's account, Christ says this as a fulfillment of Scripture (Ps 68:22), where the psalmist describes the suffering of the Messiah, foretelling that "they gave me also gall to eat, and when I was thirsty they gave me vinegar to drink." Having tasted this vinegar, St John writes that the Lord said, "It is finished," meaning the work of the Messiah, predetermined in the council of God. The redemption of mankind and the reconciliation of God and Man was accomplished through the death of the Messiah (John 19:30). According to St Luke, after this, the Lord said, "Father, into Your hands I commit My spirit" (Luke 23:46), "and bowed His head, and gave up the spirit."

All three Synoptics write that in this moment of the death of Christ, the veil that separated the temple from the holy of holies ripped in two pieces of its own accord. Since this was the time of the evening sacrifice (nearly three in the afternoon by our reckoning), evidently the priest on duty was a witness to this miraculous ripping apart of the veil. This symbolized the end of the Old Testament and the beginning of the New Testament, which would open to people the entry into the kingdom of heaven, until now closed to mankind. "And the earth quaked," a sign of God's wrath over those who committed His beloved Son to death. From this earthquake, "the rocks were split," meaning the cliffs opened up and the graves inside them were revealed to the open air. As a sign of the Lord's victory over death, "many bodies of the saints who had fallen asleep were raised." The bodies of the dead buried in these caves arose on the third day with the Lord and appeared in Jerusalem to those who knew them. All three Synoptics say that these miraculous signs, which accompanied the death of the Lord, made such a powerful, earth-shattering impression on the Roman centurion, that he said, "Truly this was the Son of God!" (Matthew and Mark) or "Certainly this was a righteous Man!" Tradition tells us that this man, named Longinus, became a Christian and a martyr for the sake of Christ (commemorated on October 16).

According to St Luke, all the people on Golgotha were shaken, and "beat their breasts." Such sharp changes in mood are normal in a crowd setting. All three Synoptics also write that among the witnesses of the Lord's death and all that happened afterward were "women who followed Him from Galilee." Among these women were Mary Magdalene, Mary the mother of James and Joses, and the mother of the sons of Zebedee, Salome.

Everything else that occurred after the Lord's death was added by St John, as usual giving a fuller account in some respects than the Synoptics, especially considering that he was an eyewitness to these events. It was Friday (*paraskevi*, in Greek, meaning "preparation"), the day before the "high day" which was the Sabbath, and the first day of the Passover. In order not to leave the bodies of the criminals on the cross for the "high day," the Jews, meaning the enemies of Christ or the members of the Sanhedrin, asked Pilate "that their legs might be broken." This would kill them, and then they could be removed and buried before the evening came, when the Passover meal had to start. According to the cruel Roman custom, in order to hasten the death on the cross, soldiers broke the legs of the crucified. Having received Pilate's permission, the soldiers broke the legs of both thieves crucified with Christ, who were still alive.

"But when they came to Jesus, and saw that He was already dead, they did not break His legs. But one of the soldiers pierced His side with a spear, and immediately blood and water came out." The negative biblical critics spent a great deal of time debating the question of whether or not blood and water could come out at the same time from the dead body of Jesus, deciding that this was physically impossible, since blood cannot pour out of a dead body, remaining liquid only for about an hour after the moment of death; while watery discharge only begins when the body begins to decompose, or in certain cases of specific diseases such as typhus or other fever-related diseases. All these educated guesses are irrelevant. After all, we do not know all the minute details of the crucifixion and death of the Lord, so making such deductions without the necessary information is pointless. However, it is a generally accepted fact that crucified men suffered symptoms of fever, and the piercing of the Lord's side would have happened very soon after the death of Jesus, or in any case not longer than an hour after His death, since it was already evening and people were hurrying to the Passover meal. Also, there is no reason to look at the flow of blood and water as a natural occurrence. St John himself, underlining this event in his Gospel, emphasizes it as a miraculous event: "And he who has seen has testified, and his testimony is true" (John 19:35).

The all-pure body of the God-Man was not subject to the normal physical laws of decomposition; in fact, from the moment of death, the body probably began to enter into that state that ended with the resurrection in a new, transformed, spiritual body. Symbolically, the Holy Fathers explain this event as a mystical means of union of the faithful with Christ in the mystery of baptism and the Eucharist: "with water are we born, while with body and blood are we fed" (St John Chrysostom).[73] St John, standing near the cross and seeing all this, bears witness that he speaks the truth and that he is not being deceived by others, saying, "and he knows that he is telling the truth, so that you may believe." The pouring of blood and water from the pierced rib of Christ is a sign that Christ became our Redeemer, having cleansed us with water in the mystery of baptism and by His Blood, which nourishes us in the mystery of communion. This is why the Apostle John, in his First General Epistle, says, "This is He who came by water and blood—Jesus Christ; not only by water, but by water and blood ... there are three that bear witness on earth: the Spirit, the water, and the blood, and these three agree as one" (1 John 5:6–8).

"For these things were done," that is, not only the piercing of His side but also the fact that His legs were not broken, "that the Scripture should be fulfilled,

'Not one of His bones shall be broken.'" This was foretold in Exodus 12:46—the Paschal lamb, the prototype of the Lord Jesus Christ, had to be eaten whole, without any broken bones, and the rest of the body had to be burnt. "And again another Scripture says, 'They shall look on Him whom they pierced'" (taken from Zech 12:10). In this passage, the Lord in the person of the Messiah is imagined as one pierced by His own nation, and this same nation, when looking at the pierced one, is imagined as falling down before Him in repentance with tears and weeping. These words are gradually being fulfilled among the Jews, by whom the Lord was committed to execution, and will continue being fulfilled until the end of the world, when there will be a general conversion among the Jews to Christ, as foretold by St Paul (Rom 11:25–26).

THE BURIAL OF THE LORD JESUS CHRIST
(MATT 27:57–66; MARK 15:42–47;16:1; LUKE 23:50–56; JOHN 19:38–42)

All four Evangelists are in total agreement in their accounts of the burial, with each giving his own details. The burial occurred as evening was beginning, but the Sabbath had not yet started, though it was near. This means that it was probably an hour or two before sunset, which would announce the beginning of the Sabbath. This is clearly shown by all four (Matt 27:57; Mark 15:42; Luke 23:54; John 19:42), and is especially noted by Mark and Luke. A certain Joseph from Arimathea (a Jewish city near Jerusalem), a member of the Sanhedrin, a secret disciple of Christ (according to St John) who took no part in the condemnation of Christ (Luke 23:51), came to Pilate and asked for Jesus's body for burial. It was Roman custom to leave the bodies on the crosses for the birds to eat, but special petitions were heard for the proper burial of such criminals. Pilate expressed his amazement that Jesus was already dead, since death by crucifixion usually took several days, but after checking with the centurion, who confirmed Jesus's death, he ordered the body to be given to Joseph.

In St John's account, Nicodemus also came, the same man who had come to Jesus in the night (John 3), and brought 100 liters of fragrant oils for the burial (made from myrrh and aloe). Joseph also bought a burial shroud, a long and whole piece of linen. They took down the body, washed it in the fragrant oils according to custom, wrapped it in the sheet, and put it in a new burial cave in the garden of Joseph, located not far from Golgotha. Since the sun was already near setting, everything was done assiduously but also with some haste. Having placed a heavy stone at the mouth of the tomb, they left.

The women who had been at Golgotha saw all that had happened. St John Chrysostom, and Blessed Theophylact after him, consider that "Mary, the mother of James and Joses" mentioned by the Evangelists is the Mother of God, "since James and Joses were the sons of Joseph from his first wife. And since the Theotokos was known as the wife of Joseph, then she was lawfully called their mother, meaning their step-mother."[74] However, others are of the opinion that this was Mary, the wife of Cleopas, a sister of the Theotokos. All of them sat across from the entrance to the tomb, as St Matthew writes (Matt 27:61), and then, according to St Luke, they returned home to prepare more ointments with which to anoint His body after the end of the Sabbath's rest, according to the Jewish custom (Luke 23:56). According to St Mark's account, these women, called "myrrh-bearers," bought the ointments not on the same day as the burial, but after the Sabbath had finished, on Saturday evening. This is not a contradiction. Apparently, there was very little time left before the beginning of the Sabbath day. Whatever they could, they prepared on Friday night, and what they could not finish, they prepared on Saturday evening.

St Matthew also relates an important event that occurred on the next day after the burial, "which followed the Day of the Preparation," on Saturday. The chief priests and Pharisees gathered before Pilate, not even thinking about the fact that they were breaking the Sabbath, and asked him to order a guard to be placed in front of the tomb until the third day. Their request was motivated thus: "Sir, we remember, while He was still alive, how that deceiver said, 'After three days I will rise.' Therefore command that the tomb be made secure until the third day, lest His disciples come by night and steal Him away, and say to the people, 'He has risen from the dead.' So the last deception will be worse than the first." By the first error (falsehood), they mean the fact that Jesus taught that He was the Son of God, the Messiah, while the last lie would be the disciples' preaching of Him as the One risen from the dead, having defeated hell and death. They were afraid of this even more than Christ's public teaching, and in this they were correct, which was only proven by the entire subsequent history of the spread of Christianity.

Pilate answered, "You have a guard," "go your way, make it as secure as you know how." During the feast, the governor gave the members of the Sanhedrin some Roman soldiers to help keep the peace, in consideration of the huge masses of people coming to Jerusalem from all countries. Pilate offered them to use these soldiers and to arrange everything as they would wish, so that later they could not blame anyone for anything. "So they went and made the tomb secure, sealing the stone and setting the guard." They took all possible measures to make the tomb safe; they sealed the tomb with ropes and a seal, in the presence of the soldiers, who then remained near the tomb to guard it.

In this manner, without even realizing it, the evil enemies of the Lord prepared an indisputable proof of His resurrection from the dead.

 CHAPTER 7

The Resurrection of Our Lord Jesus Christ

While recounting the great event of the resurrection of Christ, all four Evangelists say nothing of the mysterious and inconceivable side of this event, not describing exactly how it occurred, how the risen Lord came out of the tomb without breaking the seal. They speak only of the earthquake, the consequence of the arrival of the angel of the Lord to throw down the stone from the entrance of the tomb (already after the resurrection, which is underlined in our hymnography, and not, as is usually imagined, as though the angel opened the tomb to allow the Lord to leave). They also recount the speech of the angel to the myrrh-bearing women, then the entire series of appearances of the risen Lord to the women and His disciples.

THE MYRRH-BEARING WOMEN COME TO THE TOMB; THE ANGEL APPEARS TO THEM (MATT 28:1–8; MARK 16:1–8; LUKE 24:1–12; JOHN 20:1–10)

It seemed to the women who had been at Golgotha and then watched the burial that the priceless Body of the Lord was too quickly prepared for burial, and they were sad that they did not take part in the customary anointing of the body. Therefore, after spending the whole of the Sabbath in rest according to the law, and waiting for the sunrise of the first day of the week, they hurried to the tomb in order to perform their pious rites and their last debt of love to their beloved Master. At the head of this choir of deeply devoted women, who entered history under the name "myrrh-bearers," as all four Evangelists write, was Mary Magdalene. With her went "another Mary," probably Mary the mother of James, Salome, and other women who followed the Lord from Galilee (Luke 23:55). This was a large group of women, some of whom walked fast, almost running, perhaps, while others walked more slowly, not hurrying quite so much. There is nothing strange that the time of their arrival at the tomb is indicated differently by the different Evangelists, even though at first glance it would seem that there is a contradiction in the accounts.

First of all, who is this "other Mary," who is twice mentioned by St Matthew, when he speaks first of the burial, then of the resurrection

(Matt 27:61; 28:1). Ancient tradition, written down in the Synaxarion for the feast of Pascha, says that she was the Mother of God. Why is this not said openly by the Evangelists? As the Synaxarion explains, "so that the resurrection would not appear to be suspicious, due to the biased witness of a mother, the evangelists first mention Mary Magdalene (Mark 16:9), who saw the angel on the stone ... then generally mention many women, among whom was the Theotokos, the same one that the gospel calls the mother of Joses, because Joses was the son of Joseph."[75]

Salome was the mother of the sons of Zebedee—the apostles James and John. Joanna, mentioned by St Luke, was the wife of Chuza, a steward of Herod. The rest of the myrrh-bearing women are not mentioned by name, but St Luke clearly says that there were others with them (Luke 24:10). Among these "others," Church tradition also includes: Martha and Mary, the sisters of Lazarus, Mary the wife of Cleopas, and Susanna, as well as many others, "as the saintly Luke wrote, calling them those who served Christ and His disciples from their wealth."[76]

The myrrh-bearing women waited for the end of the Sabbath rest, and some of them had already bought ointments on Friday afternoon (Luke 23:56), while others waited until after the Sabbath (Mark 16:1).

The account of St John's Gospel differs the most from all the rest, which is understandable, since he often omits those things already said by the first three and adds details to their accounts that they missed. In this particular account, he adds some details regarding Mary Magdalene and two of the disciples. When put together, the four Gospels give a complete picture. Of course, the event described only in Matthew—the earthquake that occurred as a result of the descent of the angel who removed the stone from the mouth of the tomb—occured before the coming of the myrrh bearers. Its purpose was to make the guards flee and show the tomb to be empty, but Christ had already risen before then, which is stressed in our hymnography: "When the tomb was sealed, Thou, the Life, O Christ our God, didst rise up from the grave."[77] "Lord, though the grave was sealed by lawless men, You came from the tomb as You had been born from the Mother of God; Your bodiless Angels did not know how You had become incarnate, the soldiers guarding You did not know when You arose; for both are sealed for those who inquire, but the wonders have been revealed to those who with faith worship the mystery which we hymn; give us joy and great mercy."[78]

Therefore, the images that have become popular in recent years (due to Western influence) of Christ coming out of the tomb, the stone rolled to its side, and the soldiers on their faces in fear, in no way correspond to reality. The angel came from heaven and pulled away the stone after Christ already had risen from the dead, to show that He was no longer in the tomb. This caused great fear in the guards, and they ran away to Jerusalem.

Combining all four evangelical accounts, a vivid picture begins to reveal itself. The first one to come to the tomb, while it was still dark in the morning of Sunday, was Mary Magdalene. But she walked with other women who also came to anoint Jesus. Only she, due to her fiery temperament and special love for Christ, walked ahead of the other women and arrived when it was still dark, while the others came up when the sun was already about to rise. The fact that she went not alone is seen in John's account, for when she returned to the apostles Peter and John, she spoke in the plural: "*We* do not know where they have laid him" (John 20:2, emphasis added).

When she saw that the stone was rolled from the tomb (she did not see the angel who appeared to the women later), she thought that the body of the Lord was carried away, and she immediately ran to tell Peter and John. On the way back she, of course, met the rest of the women, who were discussing the problem of who would remove the stone from the tomb (Mark 16:13), and she told them of her worries. While she went to the apostles, the rest of the women approached the tomb and saw the angel, heard from him the good news of the resurrection of Christ, and quickly went to the apostles to share their joy with them. All this is told in detail by the Synoptics (Matt 28:5–8; Mark 15:4–8; Luke 24:3–8).

In the meantime, Peter and John hurried to the tomb after hearing Mary Magdalene's account and not yet having heard of the resurrection (or maybe they did hear it from the other women, but did not believe them; see Luke 24:11). John, who was much younger than Peter, ran ahead and came to the tomb earlier, when the rest of the women had already left, but he did not enter the tomb. Perhaps he was afraid to enter the tomb alone. However, he did lean in to look at the opening, and he saw the linen sheet lying there. Afterward, Simon Peter came, and owing to his brave and impulsive character, he did not think twice before entering. Inside, he saw only the sheets, including the towel used to wrap the head, "not lying with the linen cloths, but folded together in a place by itself" (John 20:7). Then he entered and "the other disciple, who came to the tomb first [meaning John], went in also; and he saw and believed." He believed in the truth of the resurrection because if someone had stolen the body, there would have been no point in unwrapping the body, taking off the linen sheet, and neatly laying them next to each other on the ground. "For as yet they did not know the Scripture, that He must rise again from the dead."

Until the moment that the Lord "opened their understanding, that they might comprehend the Scriptures" (Luke 24:45), they did not understand the Lord's words concerning His suffering and resurrection (as we see repeatedly, for example, Luke 18:34; Mark 9:10), and so needed physical proof. For John, that proof was the fact that the linen napkin and sheet were carefully folded next to each other; however, only St John was convinced by this. St Luke says that Peter walked away wondering what it all meant (Luke 24:12). The state of his soul, after he had denied Christ three times, was likely very heavy and not inclined to living faith. And so, probably, after his return from the tomb, the merciful Lord appeared to him personally and consoled him, giving peace to his heart, as St Luke briefly mentions, as well as the Apostle Paul (Luke 24:34; 1 Cor 15:5). As we see in these passages, the Lord appeared to Peter alone, before the rest of the apostles.

THE RISEN LORD APPEARS TO MARY MAGDALENE AND THE OTHER MARY
(JOHN 20:11–18; MARK 16:9–1; MATT 28:9–10)

After the apostles Peter and John left the tomb, only Mary Magdalene remained. Her soul was in confusion, and she wept, thinking the body of the Lord was stolen. While she cried, she leaned over to the entrance of the tomb and saw two angels sitting on the slab where the body had been laid. Her sorrow was so great, that all other emotions were muted, and so Mary was apparently not very amazed by the appearance of these angels, and when they asked her, trying to console her, "Woman, why are you weeping?" As though she were conversing with normal people, she simply and movingly related her sorrow in the same words that she spoke to the apostles: "Because they have taken my Lord, and I do not know where they have laid Him." Saying this, she (perhaps accidentally, in a confusion of feelings, or perhaps she had an inner spiritual instinct) turned around and saw Jesus, but did not recognize Him. She did not recognize Him because He appeared different than He had in life, as later He did to the travelers to Emmaus, in a "humble and not remarkable form" (St John Chrysostom),[79] which is why she thought He was a gardener. Or perhaps she did not recognize Him because her eyes were full of tears, she was bowed down by grief, and never expected to see the Lord alive. She did not even recognize His voice at first, when He asked her, "Woman, why are you weeping? Whom are you seeking?" Thinking Him the gardener, which was natural, since no one but a gardener would be in a garden early in the morning, she said, "Sir, if you have carried Him away, tell me where you have laid Him, and I will take Him away," without even thinking how she, a weak woman, would be able to pick Him up. Then the Lord revealed Himself to her, uttering her name in an intonation that she had long ago become accustomed to: "Mary."

"She turned," which means that after speaking to the "gardener" she had turned back to the tomb, "and said to Him, 'Rabboni!' (which is to say, Teacher)." And at this moment, apparently in indescribable joy, she fell to His feet, desiring to touch Him, perhaps to become sure that it was truly a living Jesus, not a spirit. The Lord, however, forbid her, saying, "Do not cling to Me, for I have not yet ascended to My Father; but go to my brethren and say to them, 'I am ascending to My Father and your Father, and to My God and your God." It was as if He was meekly rebuking her: "Believe not your senses, but my Word." The meaning of this prohibition is also that the Lord wanted to tell Mary: "Leave Me, because you cannot remain with Me indefinitely, you cannot keep Me with you, but rather go and preach My resurrection. For Me it remains to leave you soon, and not remain with you any more, but ascend to My Father in heaven." A good explanation of the meaning of this prohibition to touch the Lord can be seen in the resurrectional sticheron for the eighth tone: "The woman is still thinking in an earthly fashion, therefore the Lord sends her away without touching Him."[80]

"Mary Magdalene came and told the disciples that she had seen the Lord, and that He had spoken these things to her." If we put these words together with Matthew's account, we must assume that along the way, Mary Magdalene met the "other Mary," and to both of them the Lord appeared (a second time) and said, "Rejoice!" They then fell at His feet, and He once again repeated His command to go to the disciples, calling them "my brethren," and to tell them of His resurrection, having repeated that which the angel had said to them previously: "Go to Galilee." How moving is this name—"brethren," with which the risen Lord names His disciples, now that He is the glorified Messiah, ready to go to His Father. He is not ashamed to call them brothers, as especially underlined by St Paul (Heb 2:11–12).

St Mark then says that the myrrh-bearing women were so afraid (of course, in a reverent fear) that they "said nothing to anyone." This must be understood in the sense that they, along the way, told no one of what they saw and heard. But when they came into the house, they told all the apostles, which St Mark himself also includes in his account, as well as the other Evangelists (Mark 16:8, 10; Luke 24:9).

Thus, following the four evangelical accounts, the first appearance of the Lord after His resurrection would seem to be to Mary Magdalene (Mark 16:9–10). But the Holy Church from ancient times keeps a special tradition that the risen Lord first appeared to His all-pure Mother, which is of course natural and understandable. In Jerusalem, in the Church of the Holy Sepulcher, to this day there is a place indicated where the Saviour appeared to His Mother after His resurrection, not far from the tomb. Such an ancient tradition, sanctified by the centuries, cannot but be established in fact. While the Gospels say nothing about this, this is because there are a great many things not written in the Gospels that nonetheless happened, as St John himself says (John 20:30–31; 21:25). It is also probable that the Theotokos's own humility did not allow the Evangelists to openly speak about the cherished secrets of Her life, and this is why there is very little written about Her in the Gospels, except for the absolutely necessary facts, which were connected directly with the life of the Lord Jesus Christ Himself. And in general, the Evangelists tried to avoid openly mentioning Her in the Gospels, because the witness of a Mother does little to convince skeptics (see the Synaxarion for the feast of Pascha). The Evangelists say that the words of the myrrhbearers regarding the resurrection were not believed by the apostles (Luke 24:11). If even the apostles did not believe the myrrhbearers, would strangers believe the witness of a Mother?

THE LIE OF THE JEWS AND BRIBING THE GUARDS OF THE TOMB (MATT 28:11–15)

"Some of the guards" who had watched the tomb and then run away, probably the ones in charge, as responsible for leaving the place of their designation, told everything to the chief priests. Note that they went first to the Jews, not Pilate, since Pilate had given them to the Jews' charge. The chief priests called a session of the Sanhedrin and decided to bribe the soldiers, telling them to hide the truth of the resurrection and announce a lie in its stead. St John Chrysostom says, "They bought His blood when He was yet alive, and after His crucifixion and resurrection again with money they try to sabotage the truth of the resurrection."[81]

"Tell them, His disciples came at night and stole Him away while we slept.'" This is what they told the soldiers to say. Chrysostom continues,

> Their words are completely improbable and have no basis in truth. How could the disciples steal Him, these poor and simple people who did not even dare show their faces (after He was arrested). ... Was not the tomb sealed? Was not the entire area surrounded not only by soldiers, but by simple Jews? Were the guards not expecting exactly that to happen, is not that why they were placed there? Would they not have taken special care not to fall asleep on the watch? And what would be the point of stealing His body? In order to make up a story about His Resurrection? How could people who preferred to live in seclusion make up such a story? How would they have removed the heavy stone? How would they have remained hidden in such a populous place?[82]

All the interpreters of the Gospels agree that all the efforts of the Sanhedrin to guard the body as fully as possible in the tomb ended up being the best possible proof for the truth of the resurrection, despite their opposite intentions. After all, grave robbery was a completely unknown phenomenon among the Jews, who were afraid of defiling themselves by touching a dead body (Num 19:11–22). And how could it be that professional soldiers all fell asleep in such an amazingly deep sleep on the *third day—the exact day they expected the disciples to come!* And their sleep needed to be extraordinarily deep if they did not even hear how a huge stone was being rolled away from the tomb. Even if they all had decided to sleep, which is completely improbable for a Roman soldier, they would of course have fallen asleep in front of the entrance to the tomb, to make it impossible to roll away the stone without crushing their sleeping bodies. But the most improbable part of the story is how the frightened disciples, who all fled when Christ was taken, could suddenly decide to attempt such a pointless theft, which would give them absolutely no benefit, with immense dangers outweighing any possible good. It is also strange that Roman soldiers could have allowed such a falsehood to be spread and not expect to be punished for such dereliction of duty. This was the invention of the hateful Jews, who stubbornly refused to believe in the truth of Christ's resurrection, even though it was evident, and yet they only managed to confirm the great truth of Christianity.

The Appearance of the Risen Lord to the Disciples on the Road to Emmaus (Luke 24:13–35; Mark 16:12)

Only St Luke gives a detailed account of this event, and according to tradition, he was one of the two disciples who witnessed this event. The other was Cleopas, probably the husband of the Theotokos's sister. They were both numbered among the seventy apostles. St Mark gives a short reference to this appearance (Mark 16:12). Even the unusually vivid nature of the description of this event and the fullness of its expression, complete with the emotions of those involved, shows that one of the two was Luke himself, though he did not name himself, as was the custom for Church writers. The disciples were traveling to the village of Emmaus, which was sixty furlongs from Jerusalem (1.2 kilometers), on the way to Joppa. On foot, walking slowly, the journey could take as long as three hours, but half as long if walking quickly.

This occurred on the "same day," meaning the day of the resurrection. They were walking slowly, talking about all the sorrowful events connected with the last days of the earthly life of the Lord, everything that lay as a heavy weight on their hearts. They also spoke of the events of the day, not knowing what to think about the reports of the resurrection, and apparently not yet believing in it themselves, for they still walked sorrowing (Luke 24:17). Along the way, the Lord Himself joined them in the form of a traveler walking the same road. "But their eyes were restrained, so that they did not know Him." St Mark explains that the Lord appeared to them "in another form," and so they did not recognize Him. The Lord did this on purpose, for He did not want them to know Him immediately, in order to give them the necessary instruction for their spiritual state. According to Blessed Theophylact, He wanted them to "open up all their doubts, to reveal their wounds and only then to accept the medicine, to appear the more pleasant to them after the long delay, to teach them from Moses and the prophets, and only then to be recognized, so that they could better believe that His body, although the same body as the one that had suffered and died, is visible now only to those whom He allows to see."[83]

The One Who knows all wants to hear from them personally what was the source of their sorrow: "What kind of conversation is this that you have with one another as you walk and are sad?" With this question, the Lord tells His disciples to reveal all their feelings to Him. Cleopas believed the Lord to be a Jew who had come to Jerusalem for the feast from some other country, for he could not understand how a resident of Palestine would not know of all that occurred in Jerusalem the last few days. Then the disciples confessed all their sorrow to the Lord. It is still characteristic, however, that they call Jesus only a "prophet," expressing at the same time that their hope that He would be the Messiah had not been actualized. "But we were hoping that it was He who was going to redeem Israel." In general, they themselves seem not to know what to think of all that occurred, since some women, who this morning were at the tomb, told incredible tales of the absence of His body and the appearance of angels that told them that He lived. Evidently, Luke and Cleopas left Jerusalem before they had heard that the Lord appeared to Mary Magdalene and the other myrrh bearers. "And certain of those who were with us went to the tomb," meaning, apparently, Peter and John, "but Him they did not see." This is what confuses them, and they do not know what to think about all this.

Then the Lord, still not revealing Himself to them, begins His instruction, letting them understand that the reason for their unsettled spiritual state is their own foolishness and hard-heartedness. "Ought not the Christ to have suffered these things and to enter into His glory?" He calls Himself the Christ openly, and explains that everything had happened in accordance with the Old Testament prophecies of Christ, that through His sufferings, the Messiah entered "into His glory," not an earthly glory, but His spiritual glory.

With increasing attention and inner warming of the heart, the disciples listened to their mysterious fellow traveler and were so internally inclined to Him with their hearts, they began to ask Him to remain with them to stay the night in Emmaus, citing that the day was already close to its end, while walking alone in the dark was not without its dangers. The Lord stayed with them, and when it came time for the evening meal, He, as the eldest, "took bread, blessed and broke it, and gave it to them." Apparently, this gesture, characteristic of their Master, was the final impetus that opened their eyes, and "they knew Him; and He vanished from their sight." As we see from the evangelical accounts, the glorified body of the Lord was already transformed, not the same as a natural, mortal human body. For Him, normal physical boundaries no longer applied, and He could suddenly appear and disappear as suited Him.

Why did the Lord only let them know it was He so late in the day? The purpose of His appearance was to explain to the disciples how all the Old Testament prophecies had been accomplished in Him. The impulsive joy that they would have felt if they had immediately recognized Him would only have hampered their calm contemplation of the truth of His resurrection and possibly have hindered their belief in it. But since the Lord led them to a profound appreciation of that truth slowly, forcing, as they themselves admitted, their hearts to "burn within" them, He only strengthened their faith when He suddenly revealed Himself at the end, and then no doubt or temptation could sway them.

Despite the fact that it was already night, they immediately hurried back to Jerusalem to share their joy with the rest of the disciples. The disciples in their turn told them that "the Lord is risen indeed, and has appeared to Simon!" But St Mark says that the rest of the disciples did not believe Luke and Cleopas's account. One must assume that they were confused by the sudden appearances of the Lord in various places, which is impossible for a mere man, and also by the fact that

He appeared to them in a "different form." Their faith was not yet firm, since they did not yet understand the new, transformed life of the Lord after the resurrection, nor did they appreciate the transformed aspects of His glorified body. This is why, when He appeared to them all together, when the doors were shut, they thought He was a ghost.

THE APPEARANCE OF THE RISEN LORD TO THE TEN DISCIPLES ON THE DAY OF THE RESURRECTION (MARK 16:14; LUKE 24:36–45; JOHN 20:19–23)

St Mark briefly mentions this event, while St Luke and St John give more expansive accounts, mutually adding to each other's stories. According to St Luke, the Lord appeared to the ten disciples gathered together (Thomas was not there, according to St John), at the same time as Luke and Cleopas were telling them all how they saw the Lord, as if to dispel any doubts that the disciples might have and heal their remaining lack of faith. According to St John, this was late on the first day of the week. Here St John departs from the usual Jewish manner of telling time, which would have called the evening already the beginning of the next day. The doors of the house were locked for fear of the Jews. Apparently, the disciples heard the rumors that they had stolen the Lord's body, and so they were afraid of reprisals from the antagonistic Jews. And so, "when the doors were shut … Jesus came and stood in the midst, and said to them, 'Peace be with you.'"

Here we see one of the aspects of Christ's risen body—physical barriers did not present a hindrance to Him, and He could walk through them. This miraculous walking through walls "terrified and frightened" the disciples since they "supposed they had seen a spirit." They thought this was the Lord's ghost that appeared to them out of Sheol, meaning this was an appearance of a dead man, not a living one. In order to convince them that it was He, the Lord showed them His hands and feet, and the wounds from the nails helped convince them that this was the same body that was crucified on the cross. He even offered them to touch Him to make sure that it was He, not His ghost. Desiring to remove the last traces of their doubt, the Lord even ate with them, probably a piece of fish and some honeycomb left over from their evening meal.

"Then the disciples were glad when they saw the Lord." Their doubts were dispelled, and they were filled with the same joy that the Lord had foretold at the Mystical Supper (John 16:22). According to St Mark, the Lord then rebuked them for their lack of faith and hard-heartedness, that they did not believe those who had seen Him risen from the dead, meaning the myrrh bearers, Luke, and Cleopas (Mark 16:14).

"These are the words which I spoke to you." All that had happened was a fulfillment of that which He had told them before time and time again, when He spoke of the need for the sufferings and the resurrection. All this was foretold in the Old Testament writings—the "Law of Moses and the Prophets and the Psalms," and therefore it all had to happen. Here the Lord indicates the tripartite division of the Hebrew Scriptures that is still followed by the Jews today. They divide their Scriptures into three parts: (1) the Law, meaning the Pentateuch or Torah; (2) the prophets, which included the historical prophetical books; and (3) the psalms, which include the books of instruction and some of the smaller historical books. In this way, as the Lord Himself indicated, the entire Old Testament is filled with prophecies concerning Him. Previously, the apostles did not understand these prophecies correctly, but now, after the special illumination of grace given by the Lord, He "opened their understanding, that they might comprehend the Scriptures." St John adds that He said a second time, "Peace to you!" and then gave them a visible sign—He breathed on them, giving them, before Pentecost, an initial gift of the grace of the Holy Spirit, saying, "Receive the Holy Spirit. If you forgive the sins of any, they are forgiven them; if you retain the sins of any, they are retained." The full outpouring of the Holy Spirit on the apostles would occur on the day of Pentecost; but evidently before that day, the apostles needed some of the power of the Holy Spirit to strengthen them in firm and unshakable faith in the resurrection of Christ, to help them correctly understand the Scriptures, to awake in them the faith in their divine mission, faith in the knowledge that they were not merely fellow travelers and listeners of the Lord Jesus Christ, but apostles, His messengers, sent by Him to the great service of spreading the Good News through all the world. "As the Father has sent me, I also send you." This is a "hint" of the Spirit, who is necessary for the strengthening of the apostolic community. At the same time, with this inbreathing of the Spirit, the apostles were given the authority to remit sins, which was earlier only promised to Peter and some of the other apostles (Matt 16:19; 18:18).

THE APPEARANCE OF THE RISEN LORD TO THE ELEVEN APOSTLES ON THE EIGHTH DAY AFTER THE RESURRECTION, AND THE DOUBT OF THOMAS (JOHN 20:24–31)

St John writes that during the Lord's first appearance to all His assembled disciples, the Apostle Thomas, also known as the Twin (Didimus, in Greek) was not in attendance. As we see in other places of the Gospel, the character of this apostle is given as rather narrow-minded, even bordering on stubborn, which is typical for people of a simple but firmly established worldview. When the Lord was planning to go to Judea to resurrect Lazarus, Thomas then expressed his conviction that nothing good can come of this journey—"Let us also go, that we may die with Him" (John 11:16). When the Lord, in His parting conversation told the disciples, "And where I go you know, and the way you know," Thomas immediately contradicted Him, "Lord, we do not know where You are going, and how can we know the way?" (John 14:4–5).

The passion and death of Christ was particularly difficult and dispiriting to Thomas. He became fixed in the idea that Christ was lost forever. His spiritual depression was so great that he was not with the other disciples on the day of the resurrection. Apparently, he decided that there was no more point in gathering together, since all had fallen apart, and now every disciple must somehow continue to lead his separate, individual life. And so, having met the other disciples, he suddenly hears from them: "We have seen the Lord." Completely corresponding to his character, he immediately, decisively refused to believe their words. Considering the resurrection of their Master to be impossible, he announced that he would only believe it if he would not only see Jesus but also would touch with his hands the wounds from the nails on the Lord's hands and feet, and touch His pierced side. "Put my hand into His side"; these words vividly show how deep the wound was inflicted on the Lord by the soldier.

Eight days after the first appearance of the Lord to the ten apostles, the Lord once again appeared, "the doors being shut," apparently in the same house as before. This time, Thomas was with them. Perhaps, under the influence of the other apostles, his stubborn lack of faith began to recede, and his soul little by little was becoming increasingly more capable of faith. The Lord appeared exactly for that—to inspire his faith. As the first time, He appeared suddenly among the assembled disciples and having bestowed peace upon them, the Lord spoke to Thomas: "Reach your finger here, and look at My hands." In answer to Thomas's doubt, the Lord answered Him using Thomas's own words, with which he had conditioned his belief in the resurrection. It is understood that merely this fore-knowledge of the Lord should be enough to convince Thomas. But the Lord added these words, "Do not be unbelieving, but believing." In other words, Christ offers Thomas a choice—two paths lie before him, one is the road of faith, the other is of final spiritual death. In the Gospel, it is not indicated whether or not Thomas touched the wounds of Jesus, but in any case, his faith grew bright as a flame in his heart, and he exclaimed, "My Lord and my God!" With these words, Thomas confessed not only faith in the resurrection of Christ, but faith in His divinity.

However, this faith was still based on physical proof, and so the Lord, to teach Thomas, the other disciples, and all people for all future times, reveals a higher path to faith, blessing those who reach faith not using the path of physical proof, as did Thomas—"Blessed are those who have not seen and yet have believed." Even before, the Lord had not once given preference to such faith, which is based not on miracles, but on the word. The spread of the faith of Christ on earth would have been impossible if every person required the same kind of proof for his faith as Thomas did, such as never-ending miracles. Therefore, the Lord blesses those who reach faith with only trust in the witness of the Word, trust in the teaching of Christ. This is the best path to faith.

This account actually was the end of St John's Gospel. The twenty-first chapter was written by him later, after some time, it is thought because of a rumor that spread about him, that he was going to live without dying until the Second Coming of Christ. He ends this chapter with the words: "And truly Jesus did many other signs in the presence of His disciples, which are not written in this book." Even though St John gave himself the goal to complete the missing parts of the Synoptic Gospels, he did not write everything, by far. However, he considers that what he wrote is more than enough, "that you may believe that Jesus is the Christ, the Son of God, and that believing you may have life in His name." The little that he wrote is enough to confirm one's faith in the divinity of Christ and for salvation through this faith.

THE APPEARANCE OF THE RISEN LORD TO THE DISCIPLES AT THE SEA OF GALILEE (JOHN 21:1–24)

Even before His sufferings, the Lord announced to His disciples that He would appear to them after His resurrection in Galilee. The same was said to the myrrh bearers by the angels who were sitting at the tomb (Matt 26:32; 28:7). Remaining in Jerusalem the full eight days of the Passover, the apostles returned to Galilee, where quite naturally they continued to practice their profession—catching fish on the Sea of Galilee.

Here, "Jesus showed Himself again to the disciples at the Sea of Tiberias." This was, in St John's count, the third appearance of the Lord to His assembled disciples. This time, there were seven of them—Simon Peter, Thomas, Nathaniel, the sons of Zebedee (James and John), and two more who are not named. In his humility, St John places himself, along with his brother, in the last place of the list of disciples, not even naming himself and his brother. Usually, in his Gospel, he puts himself and his brother after Peter and Andrew in the list of the apostles. The whole night they labored, but caught no fish. This doubtless was intended to remind them of that night three years before, when the Lord called them to apostolic service (Luke 5:5). This time, something similar occurred.

"But when the morning had now come, Jesus stood on the shore; yet the disciples did not know that it was Jesus." Once again, it seems the Lord appeared suddenly. The disciples did not recognize Him, perhaps because this time He also appeared "in another form," as He did to Luke and Cleopas, or merely because it was dark or there was a morning fog. "Children, have you any food?" asked the Lord, meaning fish, of course. When they answered in the negative, He told them to throw the nets "on the right side of the boat," and once again the same miracle occurred that they had experienced three years before. They were unable, again, to lift the nets because of the number of fish they caught. This miracle, as the first, was doubtless a foreshadowing of their future apostolic work in catching men, which they had to accomplish with their own labors, but always guided by the Lord.

"That disciple whom Jesus loved" (St John himself, as he called himself many times before), amazed at this miraculous catch, immediately knew in his heart that it was the Lord standing on the shore, and he shared his guess with Peter: "It is the

Lord!" Not daring to appear before the Lord in his nakedness, Peter tied an "outer garment" around himself in order to put it on when he arrived onshore, and threw himself in the sea to reach the shore, where the Lord stood. From this episode, we see the unique character traits of both Peter and John. John is more exalted; Peter is more fiery. John is more capable of contemplation; Peter is more quick to act. Blessed Theophylact writes, "John is more able to get at the heart of the matter, while Peter is more on fire with emotion. John was the first to recognize the Lord, Peter the first to hurry to His side."[84] The other apostles, by this time, managed to bring the boat to shore, "dragging the net with fish." There were so many fish that they did not want to pull them onto the boat, lest the boat sink, and so they dragged the net to the shore, where it would be easier to pull it out without risking the boat.

"As soon as they had come to land, they saw a fire of coals there, and fish laid on it, and bread." The Lord once again prepared food for them in a miraculous fashion, but desiring that they would at the same time eat from the labor of their own hands, said, "Bring some of the fish which you have just caught." Simon Peter returned to the boat and together with the other disciples, pulled out the net, in which they found 153 fish. It was evidently another miracle that despite the huge amount of fish, the nets did not break. In any case, one must assume that this miraculous catch had a very strong effect on St John, since he even remembered the exact number of fish caught. Probably due to their awed reverence at all that occurred, the apostles stood at a slight distance from their Lord, for which reason He invited them to come closer and to eat, saying, "Come and dine." It seems that Christ Himself was at some distance from them, because John then says, "Jesus then came." As a Master, He began to treat the apostles as a host would, giving them the bread and fish He prepared. "Yet none of the disciples dared ask Him, 'Who are You?'—knowing that it was the Lord." There was something extraordinary in the Lord's appearance. He did not appear the way they normally saw Him, since His body after the resurrection was glorified, filled with special magnificence and divinity, but they knew it was He.

REINSTATING PETER INTO HIS APOSTOLIC DIGNITY AND A PROPHECY CONCERNING HIS MARTYR'S DEATH (JOHN 21:15–25)

"So when they had eaten, Jesus said to Simon Peter, 'Simon, son of Jonah, do you love Me more than these?'" Simon had promised before the passion, more than all the rest, that He would remain faithful to the Lord (see Matt 26:33; John 13:37; Mark 14:31; Luke 22:33). But despite all his fiery words, Peter denied the Lord three times, and through this, of course, he was deprived of his apostolic standing and ceased to be one of the twelve apostles. This fact is directly indicated in the Gospel of Mark, doubtless from the very words of Peter, "His disciples and Peter." Peter is separated from the rest because he fell away from the ranks of the apostles due to his denial, and is now placed in the last place, after all the rest of the apostles.

For his sincere and profound repentance, the Lord mercifully restored Peter into his apostolic dignity. Peter denied Christ three times, and now the Lord asks him the question three times: "Do you love Me?" and forces him to answer, "Yes, Lord; You know that I love You." After each of these expressions of love, Christ gives him, as to an apostle, the care of the flock (lambs and sheep). The doxasticon for the Feast of the Apostles Peter and Paul has the following phrase: "By asking you three times if you love Him, the Lord blotted out your triple denial."[85]

The Roman Catholics are completely incorrect if they see some special kind of gift or preference given to Peter over the other apostles by Christ in this passage. The "lambs" that the Lord tells Peter to care for are the youngest, "newborn" members of Christ's Church, who need the special care of the pastor, while the "sheep" are the already spiritually mature members of the Church who do not require such close supervision and care. It is quite characteristic that the first time the Lord asks Peter, "Do you love Me *more than these*," as if reminding him that Peter promised the Lord greater loyalty and faithfulness than all the others. Also interesting is the fact that Jesus calls him by his first name, Simon, not Peter, for by denying Christ, he showed a lack of firmness of spirit characteristic of a stone ("Petros"). Humbly confessing the depth of his fall, Peter no longer compares his love with the other disciples, but merely cites the Lord's omniscience—"You know that I love You."

Not only that, but in his humility, Peter does not use "*agapan,*" the word Christ himself used to indicate complete and perfect love, but instead "*philin,*" meaning a personal attachment and love. When Christ asks Peter the third time, He used the word "*philin.*" This is what upset Peter, because it seemed that the Lord was doubting Peter's personal attachment to Him, and so the third time he is most adamant about his love for Christ, again citing His omniscience. Just as Peter had denied Christ most vehemently the third time, even swearing to it, so the Lord inspired him to confess his love for Him with great force the third time.

Along with his restoration to the ranks of the apostles, Jesus adds a prophecy of Peter's future martyrdom, to which the love he just confessed for the Lord will bring him. "When you were younger, you girded yourself and walked where you wished; but when you are old, you will stretch out your hands, and another will gird you and carry you where you do not wish." Peter's martyr's death is here likened to the way an old man cannot walk where he wants, but is easily led by others wherever they want. St Peter truly was crucified in Rome by the emperor Nero in A.D. 68. "Follow Me," are the last words in the restoration of fallen Peter to the rank of the apostles. After these words, Jesus walked away, and the disciples apparently followed after Him. Seeing the beloved Apostle John, Peter was filled with a desire to know if John's fate would also be martyrdom for Christ's sake. But it was not pleasing to the Lord to reveal the manner of death of the beloved apostle. He answered Peter that to know this was not his business—"What is that to you? You follow Me."

Here once again is another repudiation of the Roman Catholic false teaching that the rest of the apostles were subject to Peter's authority, that he was placed as a "prince" over them. If the Lord had assigned Peter as His immediate successor and had given him all the other disciples under his authority, then Peter would have been within his rights to ask about John's fate, and the Lord would not have answered him in the way that He did. As for John, the Lord uttered words that gave some reason to think that John would remain alive until the Second Coming of Christ: "If I will that he remain till I come, what is that to you?" But the Evangelist himself rejects such a reading of Christ's words, underlining that the Lord spoke conditionally: "*If* I will ..."

John ends this episode and the whole of his Gospel with a witness: "This is the disciple who testifies of these things, and wrote these things; and we know that his testimony is true." These words prove the authenticity of this Gospel and the truth of all that he wrote in the Gospel. In conclusion, St John again repeats that there was much not written in his Gospel, for if he were to write about everything in detail, "I suppose that even the world itself could not contain the books that would be written." This might seem to be an exaggeration, a hyperbolic expression, but St John is speaking of the immensity of Christ's works, the meaning of which this limited world is not capable of conceiving. Some believe that these last two verses (John 21:24–25) were added to the Gospel by some of his earliest readers, who desire for all time to confirm the authenticity of the Gospel of John.

THE LORD'S APPEARANCE TO THE DISCIPLES ON THE HILL IN GALILEE
(MATT 28:16–20; MARK 16:15–18; LUKE 24:46–49)

"Then the eleven disciples went away into Galilee, to the mountain which Jesus had appointed for them. When they saw Him, they worshipped Him; but some doubted." Since the angels told the myrrh bearers that the Lord would wait for them in Galilee, then it must be assumed that not only the apostles hurried to Galilee to see the Lord there. Many consider that this appearance of the Lord on the hill is the same one that is mentioned by the Apostle Paul, where he says that the Lord appeared to more than five hundred of the brethren at the same time (1 Cor 15:6). It is not clear which hill this was, but it is very probable that it was Tabor, where three apostles had seen the foretaste of that blessed state of the Lord in which He appeared after His resurrection. Some of the assembled "doubted," which shows that this could not have been a mass hallucination, as many unbelievers like to say.

"And Jesus came," meaning came closer, in order to dissipate any doubts that it was truly Him, "and spoke to them, saying, 'All authority has been given to Me in heaven and on earth.'" As the only begotten Son of God, He had such authority from the beginning, but now, as the Victor over hell and death, He acquired the same authority over all these things as a man as well, as the Redeemer of the world. Having appeared in the world as a man, the Son of God limited Himself in the use of His divine power, for He did not want to complete the work of the salvation of mankind only with His omnipotence. Through the resurrection, He took up His full divine power already as the God-Man, and now the completion of the work of salvation remained—sending the Holy Spirit to establish His Church and sending the apostles to preach throughout the whole world. "Go therefore and make disciples of all the nations," as St Matthew writes. According to St Luke, "Thus it is written, and thus it was necessary for the Christ to suffer and to rise from the dead the third day, and that repentance and remission of sins should be preached in His name to all nations, beginning at Jerusalem. And you are witnesses of these things." Now the Lord is already not limiting His preaching to the Jews as before (Matt 10:5–6; 15:24), but sends the disciples to teach all nations, for the entire world is redeemed by the passion of Christ and must be called into the kingdom of heaven.

"Baptizing them in the name of the Father and of the Son and of the Holy Spirit." The God-Man gives His disciples the right and responsibility to baptize all people in the name of the Holy Trinity. This means that those who baptize do not do this of their own authority, but by the power given them by the tri-hypostatic God, while the ones baptized take upon themselves the responsibility to believe in the Holy Trinity and to dedicate their lives to the One Who called them, Who redeemed them, and gave them a second birth—one God in three hypostases. This baptism is a sign of the remission of sins of mankind by the invisible action of the Holy Spirit and a sign of a man's entrance into the Church of Christ for new life in God. Baptism must be accompanied by teaching the catechumen everything that the Lord Saviour commanded: "teaching them to observe all things that I have commanded you."

St Mark adds that many miraculous signs will appear as consequences of faith for those who will believe: "In My name they will cast out demons; they will speak with new tongues; they will take up serpents; and if they drink anything deadly, it will by no means hurt them; they will lay hands on the sick, and they will recover." Because of mankind's sin, the whole world fell into disorder, and evil began to rule in the world. But those who believe in Christ the Redeemer will receive power and strength to defeat this evil and to restore the lost harmony of the world. These miracles, as the entire history of the Church shows, were actually performed by the apostles and many true Christians.

"And lo, I am with you always, even to the end of the age." While He lays on the apostles such a heavy labor of spreading the evangelical good news to the world, the Lord encourages them, promising them that He will be mystically, invisibly present with them until the end of the world. But since the apostles did not live until the "end of the age," the promise given to them automatically comes down to us, who are their successors. This does not mean that after the end of the world the Lord will cease to be with His apostles. "No, He will be with them even more so then," says Blessed Theophylact.[86] It only means that until the end of the world, He will doubtless be Himself invisibly among the true believers, at the head of the Church He established and continues to guide for the salvation of all men.

THE ASCENSION OF THE LORD (LUKE 24:50–53; MARK 16:19–20)

The last appearance of the risen Christ, which ended with His ascension into heaven, is described with the greatest detail by St Luke. St Mark speaks of it very briefly, as well. This appearance was in Jerusalem, where the apostles traveled again from Galilee, after forty days during which the Lord appeared to them many times, teaching them of the kingdom of God, as St Luke tells us (Acts 1). The Lord gave them a command to remain in Jerusalem until they would be endued with power from on high, promising to send them the promise of His Father, by which we understand He meant the descent of the Holy Spirit to help them in the world with their worldwide mission. The Holy Spirit had to give them the necessary strength to complete this great work: preaching the Gospel to the whole world. Then the Lord led His disciples out of Jerusalem to Bethany, which was on the eastern slope of the Mount of Olives, "and He lifted up His hands and blessed them," uttering the evidently obvious words as was customary in the Old Testament, which are not here written. The symbolic action of raising one's hands during blessing was known in the Old Testament (Lev 9:22). "Now it came to pass, while He blessed them, that He was parted from them and carried up into heaven."

"What a wonderful image," says Metropolitan Philaret of Moscow, and continues:

> The Lord blesses and does not finish His blessing, but in the process ascends into heaven. What does this mean? It means that He does not want to stop blessing us, and does continue blessing His Church and all who believe in Him without stopping. Let us think, brothers, that even now His hands are extended over us, as well as His gaze and His blessing. What a shame and fear for those who in the cares of the world forget Him. What joy for those who love Him.[87]

The disciples bowed before the ascending God-Man and "returned to Jerusalem with great joy." This joy was a result of seeing the glory of their Lord and Master with their own eyes, and in anticipation of receiving the promised Gift of the Holy Spirit. They were like men reborn, doubtless because of the forty days spent with the risen Lord, who taught them the mysteries of the kingdom of God. In this prayerful state of spiritual exaltation, they "were continually in the temple praising and blessing God" for everything that they had experienced, seen, and heard, as well as for the forthcoming great work of preaching the Gospel. St Mark adds that the Lord, having ascended, "sat down at the right hand of God." This is a metaphorical phrase based on some visions (Acts 7:36), which means that the Lord in His humanity took up divine authority over the whole world together with God the Father, since sitting "at the right hand" in the language of the Bible means sharing the authority of the One at Whose right one sits. St Mark ends his Gospel with a testimony of what occurred after the descent of the Holy Spirit: that the Apostles "went out" from Jerusalem, "and preached everywhere, the Lord working with them and confirming the word through the accompanying signs," meaning that they testified to the truth of their words by performing miracles, which is recounted in detail in the Book of Acts. The entire Gospel ends with the word "Amen," which means, "truly this all happened as it has been written in the Gospel."

 Sources

This present work, titled *Commentary on the Holy Scriptures of the New Testament*, consists of two parts: *Part I: The Four Gospels* and *Part II: The Epistles*. It in no way pretends to be an original work. This work merely provides a synthesis of various prerevolutionary works and textbooks on the Holy Scriptures of the New Testament, which were published in Russia and used both as a means for self-education and as part of the curricula of our various theological academies and seminaries. In its present form, this *Commentary* is a summary of the course I taught at Holy Trinity Seminary from 1951 until 1953.

I used the following works when writing this synthesis:

1. Bishop Michael, *The Annotated Gospels*, in three volumes.
2. Bishop Michael, *The Annotated Epistles*, including the Acts and the General Epistles.
3. Bishop Theophan, *The Evangelical History of God the Word*.
4. Bishop Theophan, *Exegesis of the Epistles of the Holy Apostle Paul*.
5. M. Barsov, *A Collection of Articles on Exegetical and Instructive Reading of the Acts of the Apostles*.
6. M. Barsov, *A Collection of Articles on Exegetical and Instructive Reading of the Book of Revelations*.
7. M. Barsov, *A Collection of Articles on Exegetical and Instructive Reading of the Four Gospels*, in two volumes.
8. Fr Paul Matveevskii, *The Evangelical History of the God the Word, the Son of God, Our Lord Jesus Christ, Who Was Incarnate and Became Man for Our Salvation*.
9. B. I. Gladkov, *Exegesis of the Gospels*.
10. Fr T. Butkevich, *The Life of Our Lord Jesus Christ: A Historical-Critical Summary of the Evangelical History*.
11. F. V. Farrar, *The Life of Jesus Christ*. Translated by A. P. Lopukhine.
12. S. V. Kokhomskii, *An Explanation of the Most Important Passages from the Four Gospels*.
13. Fr Michael Kheraskov, *An Exegetical Summary of the Holy Books of the New Testament*.

14. I. V. Ivanov, *A Handbook for Studying the Holy Books of the New Testament.*

15. Fr N. Alexandrov, *A Manual for Studying the Holy Books of the New Testament.*

16. Prof. N. N. Glubokovskii, *The Gospels and Their Good News About Christ the Savior and His Redemption.*

17. Prof. N. N. Glubokovskii, *The Good News of Christian Freedom in the Epistles of the Holy Apostle Paul to the Galatians.*

18. Bishop Cassian, *Christ and the First Generation of Christianity.*

 Notes

Introduction

1. This distinction is present in the Russian language, but lacks the same connotation in English.

2. See Matthew D'Ancona and Carston Thiede, *Eyewitness to Jesus* (New York: Doubleday, 1996).

3. St Irenaeus of Lyons, *Against Heresies* 3.2.1.

4. *Homilies on the Gospel of St Matthew* 1.2.

5. Ibid.

6. *Commentary on the Gospel according to Matthew*, Preface; *Patrologia Graeca* (further–PG) 123.148B.

7. Eusebius of Caesarea, *Ecclesiastical History* 3.39.

8. See Matthew 5:17; also see the Prayer before the Consuming of the Gifts, Divine Liturgy of St John Chrysostom.

9. *Against Heresies* 3.1.1.

10. *Dialogue with Trypho* 106.3.

Chapter 1

11. *Commentary on the Gospel according to John* 1; PG 123:1137C.

12. Blessed Theophylact of Ochrid.

13. *Homilies on the Gospel of St Matthew* 6.3.

14. *Homilies on the Gospel of St Matthew* 8.3.

Chapter 2

15. Bethabara is replaced by Bethany in some early manuscripts

16. Flavius Josephus refers to the activity of St John the Baptist in his *Jewish Antiquities* 18.5.2.

17. *Homilies on the Gospel of St John*, 22.2.

Chapter 3

18. *Homilies on the Gospel of St Matthew* 29.1.

19. Ibid., 29.2.

20. Ibid., 30.2.

Chapter 4

21. *Homilies on the Gospel of St John* 38.4.

22. *Commentary on the Gospel according to Matthew* 5; PG 123.192C.

23. Athanasius of Alexandria, *Fragments from Sermons and Commentaries on the Gospel of St Matthew*; PG 28:1369A.

24. *Homilies on the Gospel of St Matthew* 19.3.

25. *Homilies on the Gospel of St Matthew* 23.2.

26. See, for example, heirmos of the third ode of the Great Canon of St Andrew of Crete.

27. *Commentary on the Gospel according to Matthew* 11; PG 123.253B.

28. *Homilies on the Gospel of St Matthew* 44.2.

29. *Homilies on the Gospel of St Matthew* 45.1.

30. *Commentary on the Gospel according to Matthew* 11; PG 123.283B.

31. *Homilies on the Gospel of St Matthew* 46.2.

32. Ibid. 46.2.

33. St Jerome, *Commentary on Matthew* 1, 10.11.

34. *Homilies on the Gospel of St Matthew* 32.2.

35. *Commentary on the Gospel according to St John* 6; PG 123.1305A.

Chapter 5

36. *Homilies on the Gospel of St Matthew* 51.1.

37. *Homilies on the Gospel of St Matthew* 54.1.

38. *Exposition of the Gospel according to Matthew* 16; PG 129.472D.

39. St Theophan the Recluse, *Thoughts For Each Day of the Year* (Platina: St Herman of Alaska Brotherhood, 2010), Day 206 (emphasis added).

40. Bishop Michael (Luzin), *The Annotated Gospels* [in Russian] (Minsk: Harvest, 2000), 1.349.

41. *Ecclesiastical History* 2.35.

42. *Commentary on the Gospel according to Matthew* 18; PG 123.341BC.

43. Bishop Michael (Luzin), *The Annotated Gospels* [in Russian], 3.272.

44. St Theophylact of Ochrid, *Commentary on the Gospel according to John* 7; PG 123.1328A, see also St John Chrysostom, *Homilies on the Gospel of St John* 57.2.

45. St Theophylact of Ochrid, *Commentary on the Gospel according to John* 7; PG 123.1333A.

46. Bishop Michael (Luzin), *The Annotated Gospels* [in Russian], 3.282.

47. See *Homilies on the Gospel of St John* 52.2.

48. The unworthy shepherds "pasturing themselves" is a phrase that does not occur in the English Bible due to different source material for the translation, the Slavonic using primarily the Septuagint and the English the Hebrew text, for the Old Testament.

49. *Commentary on the Gospel according to Matthew* 11; PG 123.256D.

50. *Homilies on the Gospel of St Matthew* 74.3.

51. *Commentary on the Gospel according to Luke* 14; PG 123.933A.

52. Ibid.; PG 123.941A.

53. Ibid. 16; PG 123.964BC.

54. *Homilies on the Gospel of St Matthew* 62.3.

55. Ibid. 63.2.

Chapter 6

56. *Homilies on the Gospel of St Matthew* 66.2.

57. *Homilies on the Gospel of St Matthew* 69.2.

58. Josephus, *The Jewish War* 1.12.

59. Bishop Michael (Luzin), *The Annotated Gospels* [in Russian], 3.467.

60. *Homilies on the Gospel of St Matthew* 81.2.

61. *Commentary on the Gospel according to Matthew* 26; PG 123.444D.

62. *Homilies on the Gospel of St Matthew* 82.1.

63. *Commentary on the Gospel according to Matthew* 26; PG 123.445A.

64. *Homilies on the Gospel of St Matthew* 82.1.

65. *Commentary on the Gospel according to Matthew* 26; PG 123.448CD; see also St John of Damascus, *An Exact Exposition of the Orthodox Faith* 3.23-24 (67–68).

66. *Homilies on the Gospel of St Matthew* 83.2.

67. *Homilies on the Gospel of St Matthew* 85.2.

68. *Exposition of the Gospel according to Matthew* 27; PG 129.716B.

69. Bishop Michael (Luzin), *The Annotated Gospels* [in Russian] 3.598.

70. *Homilies on the Gospel of St Matthew* 86.2.

71. Bishop Michael (Luzin), *The Annotated Gospels* [in Russian], 2.592.

72. *Letter* 7.2.

73. *Homilies on the Gospel of St John* 85.2.

74. Blessed Theophylact, *Commentary on the Gospel according to John* 19; PG 124.279A.

Chapter 7

75. *Pentecostarion*, Pascha Matins, Synaxarion after the Sixth Ode of the Canon.

76. *Pentecostarion*, Sunday of the Myrrh-Bearing Women, Matins, Synaxarion after the Sixth Ode of the Canon.

77. *Pentecostarion*, Sunday of Antipascha (Thomas Sunday), Troparion.

78. *Octoechos*, Tone 5, Sunday Matins, Sticheron on Praises.

79. *Homilies on the Gospel of St John* 86.1.

80. *Octoechos*, Sunday Matins, 8th Matins sticheron, tone 8.

81. *Homilies on the Gospel of St Matthew* 90.1.

82. Ibid.

83. *Commentary on the Gospel according to Luke* 24; PG 123.1113C.

84. *Commentary on the Gospel according to John* 21; PG 124.305B.

85. *Menaion*, June 29, Vespers.

86. *Commentary on the Gospel according to Matthew* 28; PG 123.485D.

87. St Philaret (Drozdov), Metropolitan of Moscow, "Homily on the Feast of Ascension of the Lord and the Translation of the Relics of Holy Hierarch Alexis of Moscow (1854)," in *Collected Works, Letters, Memoirs* [in Russian] (Moscow: St Tikhon's Orthodox Institute, 2003), 476–81.

Scripture Index